The Realities of Domestic Violence.
Volume 2
John W Elmy
2015

Author. John W Elmy
Title, The Realities of Domestic Violence
Volume 2
© 2015, John W Elmy

(pickmenow50@yahoo.com)

Acknowledgements

NATIONAL COALITION ON DOMESTIC VIOLENCE
AGAINST MEN

Ed Bartlet, Mark D. Rosenthal,

R.A.D.A.R: Respecting Accuracy In
Domestic Abuse Reporting. ®

My best friend Dan Byers.

My mother, Nancy L Brown.

Equal Justice for All

Dr. Charles E. Cory

Contents

CHAPTER 1
Myths of the ABA Commission on Domestic Violence

EXECUTIVE SUMMARY

Programs designed to curb domestic violence rely on valid research and an accurate understanding of that research by legal practitioners and policy makers. This Special Report analyzes the American Bar Association's flyer, 10 Myths about Custody and Domestic Violence and How to Counter Them. Developed by the ABA's Commission on Domestic Violence, the flyer highlights a series of 10 purported myths, their associated claims, and supporting research.
The present analyses shown are in two documents:

1. Myths of the ABA Commission on Domestic Violence: Summary Report

2. Myths of the ABA Commission on Domestic Violence: Detailed Findings Only 3 of the 10 purported myths is found to be indeed being myths, and of the 19 claims, only two are correct.

The quality of many of the cited documents is poor or very poor.

Overall, the great majority of assertions and conclusions in the CODV flyer found to be unsupported, misleading, or wrong. In its quest to expose custody and domestic violence misconceptions, the American Bar Association has ironically ended up misleading legal practitioners.

In the end, children will be harmed.

Myths of the ABA Commission on Domestic Violence: Summary Report

Intimate partner violence is a continuing problem in American society. Unfortunately, a number of myths, half-truths, and false statistics pertaining to family violence have turned out to be embedded in the fabric of American consciousness. These misrepresentations frustrate good policymaking, undermine the even-handed administration of justice, and handcuff efforts to develop effective programs. Professor Richard Gelles, who has devoted his career to the study of family violence, has warned Policy and practice based on these factoids and theory might actually be harmful to women, men, children, and the institution of the family.

In 2006, the American Bar Association (ABA) Commission on Domestic Violence published a two-page flyer titled, 10 Myths about Custody and Domestic Violence and How to Counter Them. The flyer has been has been widely distributed, can be downloaded from the ABA website, and is available for purchase. the flyer's introduction explains its purpose: Attorneys who represent victims of domestic violence in custody matters often en-counter the following false claims. To assist in overcoming these myths, the ABA Commission on Domestic Violence provides these facts and statistics for use in litigation.

The handout lists 10 purported myths, along with their 19 associated claims and studies designed to counter the myths. The House of Delegates of the ABA Board of Governors has not approved the flyer.

The purpose of this Special Report is to analyze each of the myths, claims, and supporting documents. In-depth documentation can be found in the accompanying Special Report, Myths of the ABA Commission on Domestic Violence: Detailed Findings. To facilitate the analysis, each claim is numbered according to its corresponding myth. For example, the second claim under Myth 4 is Claim 4.2.

What Does the Research Say?

In order to analyze these myths, it is helpful to understand key research findings:

1. Women are at least as likely as men to engage in partner aggression. A recent Centers for Disease Control survey of young adults found that in cases of one-way partner aggression, women were the instigators in 71% of cases (see Figure 1 on the next page). The woman acting in self-defense explains less than one in five cases of female violence.

2. In at least half of all cases, partner violence is mutual. Several studies, including large and nationally representative samples, have found that the most prevalent pat-tern is mutual violence, explains family researcher Murray Straus.

3. In most cases, partner aggression does not escalate. If the conflict does turn into a full-scale altercation, the woman is more likely to be injured.
Nonetheless, males represent 38% of persons who suffer physical injury from partner aggression.

4. Domestic violence rates vary depending on the couple's marital status. Among intact married couples, partner violence rates are quite low—only 0.9/1,000.16 but among separated couples, partner violence rates rise sharply to 49.0/1,000—a 50-fold increase.

5. Child abuse is also cause for concern. According to the Department of Health and Human Services, mothers acting alone are responsible for 40% of child maltreatment, compared to fathers acting alone, who account for 18% of cases17 (see Figure 2). Likewise, child homicides are twice as likely to be perpetrated by mothers as by fathers.

6. Compared to their peers in two-parent homes, children who grow up in single-parent households are at far greater risk of experiencing social pathologies such as child abuse, school disciplinary problems, drop-outs, sexual promiscuity, juvenile delinquency, homicide, injuries, suicide, and poverty.

A Note on Terminology

The National Academy of Sciences report: Advancing the Federal Research Agenda on Violence Against Women has noted the confusion that arises from vague use of terms. For purposes of this Special Report, we employ the following definitions:

A. Abuse: Any form of psychological, sexual, or physical mistreatment

B. Intimate partner violence: A physical assault against a spouse, ex-spouse, boyfriend, or girlfriend

C. Battering: Repeated, severe, and usually unilateral physical violence Abuse is the broadest term that encompasses intimate partner violence. Because battering is a pejorative term, this report generally avoids the use of that word.

WHAT THE ANALYSIS REVEALS

A summary of the Findings and Assessments of the CODV Myths and Claims can be seen in the Appendix of this report. The detailed analysis is found in the accompanying Special Report, Myths of the ABA Commission on Domestic Violence: Detailed Findings. The analysis reveals widespread flaws in 10 Myths about Custody and Domestic Violence and How to counter them, specifically flaws in how the myths are framed, the claims that are made, and the quality of the documents cited in the CODV flyer.

Myths Of the 10 purported myths, the following 3 are indeed confirmed as myths:

Myth 1: Domestic violence is rare among custody litigants.

Myth 2: Any ill effects of domestic violence on children are minimal and short-term.

Myth 4: Domestic violence has nothing to do with child abuse.
The following 4 myths frame the issue in a misleading manner:

Myth 3: Mothers frequently invent allegations of child sexual abuse to win custody.

Myth 7: Parental Alienation Syndrome (PAS') is a scientifically sound phenomenon.

Myth 8: Children are in less danger from a batterer/parent once the parents separate.

Myth 10: If a child demonstrates no fear or aversion to a parent, then there is no reason not to award unsupervised contact or custody.

The following myths are, in fact, not myths but true statements:

Myth 5: Abusive fathers don't get custody.

Myth 6: Fit mothers don't lose custody.

Myth 9: Parents who batter are mentally ill, OR Parents with no evidence of mental illness cannot be batterers.

Claims

Of the 19 claims delineated by the American Bar Association, only 2 are correct:

Claim 2.2: Adverse effects to children who witness DV are well-documented, including aggressive behavior, depression, and/or cognitive deficiencies.

Claim 10.1: Children can experience traumatic bonding _with a parent who abuses the child or their other parent, forming unusually strong but unhealthy ties to a batterer as a survival technique (often referred to as Stockholm Syndrome).
The following 3 claims are unsupported by the available research:

Claim 4.1: A wide array of studies reveals a significant overlap between domestic violence and child abuse, with most finding that both forms of abuse occur in 30–60% of violent families.

Claim 6.1: Mothers who are victims of DV are often depressed and suffering from posttraumatic stress disorder, and as a result, can present poorly in court and to best-interest attorneys and/or custody evaluators.

Claim 8.1: Many batterers 'motivation to intimidate and control their victims through the children increases after separation, due to the loss of other methods of exerting control.

The following 3 claims are misleading:

Claim 2.1: Children who are exposed to domestic violence may show comparable levels of emotional and behavioral problems to children who were the direct victims of physical or sexual abuse.

Claim 7.1: The American Psychological Association has noted the lack of data to support so-called parental alienation syndrome,' and raised concern about the term's use.

Claim 9.2: Psychological testing is not a good predictor of parenting capacity.

The following 11 claims are found to be false:

Claim 1.1: Studies show that 25–50% of disputed custody cases involve domestic violence.

Claim 2.3: A continuing study by the CDC has shown a significant relationship between exposure to adverse childhood experiences' (including witnessing domestic violence) and development of adult health problems, including pulmonary disease, heart disease, hepatitis, fractures, obesity, and diabetes (not to mention IV drug use, alcoholism, sexually transmitted diseases, and depression).

Claim 3.1: Child sexual abuse allegations in custody cases are rare (about 6%), and the majority of allegations are substantiated (2/3).

Claim 3.2: False allegations are no more common in divorce or custody disputes than at any other time.

Claim 3.3: Among false allegations, fathers are far more likely than mothers to make intentionally false accusations (21% compared to 1.3%).

Claim 4.2: Other studies have shown intimate partner violence (IPV.) to be a strong predictor of child abuse, increasing the risk from 5% after one act of IPV to 100% after 50 acts of IPV.

Claim 5.1: Abusive parents are more likely to seek sole custody than nonviolent ones

Claim 5.2: and they are successful about 70% of the time.

Claim 5.3: Allegations of domestic violence have no demonstrated effect on the rate at which parents are awarded custody of their children, nor do such allegations affect the rate 4 at which parents are ordered into supervised visitation.
(I.e. abusers win unsupervised custody and visitation at the same rate as non-abusers)

Claim 9.1: Mental illness is found only in a minority of batterers.

Claim 9.3: Mental health testing cannot distinguish a batterer from a non-batterer.

Cited Documents

The CODV flyer cites 20 research studies, literature reviews, or reports in support of its claims. The quality of the documents was evaluated using six criteria: methodological rigor, generalization, appropriate citation of prior research, recency of publication (i.e., published in 2000 or later), gender inclusiveness of subjects, and absence of ideological bias.

The quality was found to range from Good to Very Poor: 1, Excellent: 0, Good: 9, Acceptable: 3, Poor: 4, Very Poor: 4

1 Documents determined to be Good: Johnston, Edleson, Dube, Thoennes, Appel, Gondolph, Gelles, Brodzinsky, and O'Leary; Acceptable: Morrill, Ross, and Golding; Poor: Keilitz, Brown, Bala, and Kernic; and Very poor: Jaffe, American Psychological Association, American Judges Foundation, and Bancroft.

ANATOMY OF MISREPRESENTATION

Numerous myths exist in the area of domestic violence, and the persistence of such myths is cause for concern. In that sense, the attempt of the Commission on Domestic Violence to discredit such myths is commendable. In the final analysis, however, the 10 Myths about Custody and Domestic Violence and How to Counter them is inadequate, confusing, and suggests policy directions contraindicated by science. As explained above, 7 of the purported 10 myths are either misleading or found not to be myths.

Eleven of the 19 claims are actually false. And the quality of 9 of the 20 cited documents is poor or very poor. In its quest to debunk a series of custody and domestic violence misconceptions, the ABA Com-mission on Domestic Violence ironically has ended up reinforcing old misconceptions.

What went wrong?

Was it the unfortunate confluence of a series of honest mistakes, minor oversights, and impossible deadlines? Perhaps, or was it an attempt to misrepresent a contentious field of knowledge and sow confusion in the minds of legal practitioners?

Indeed, the nature and extent of the flaws is troubling:

1. Not citing recent relevant research
(e.g., Claims 1.1, 2.1, 3.1, 3.2, 9.1)

2. Citing a press release instead of the actual research report
(e.g., Claim 2.3)

3. Misquoting a key number from a research study
(e.g., Claim 3.1)

4. Citing empirical research that is poor in quality
(e.g., Claim 3.2)

5. Citing a review article that is unreliable as a basis for practice
(e.g., Claim 4.1)

6. Not citing the original source of a key statistic, thus disseminating unverifiable factoids (e.g., Claim 4.1)

7. Accepting the statements of cited documents at face value without assessing their scientific value
(e.g., Claims 5.1 and 7.1)

8. Presenting a claim that does not directly address its associated myth
(e.g., Claim 8.1 and Myth 8)

9. Using pejorative terminology such as batterer
(e.g., Myths 8 and 9)

Many of the errors can be considered egregious:

1. Citing documents that do not distinguish between the legal precepts of allegation vs. judicial finding (e.g., Claims 1.1 and 5.3)

2. Sidestepping the problem of false allegations of domestic violence during custody disputes
(e.g., Myth 3)

3. Framing statements in a way that portrays fathers in a negative light
(e.g., Claim 3.3, Myth 5)

4. Making shocking claims without providing any research to support these assertions
(e.g., Claims 5.2 and 8.1)

5. Citing studies that downplay or ignore the problem of female-initiated abuse
(e.g., Claims 5.3, 6.1, 8.1, and 10.1)

6. Framing statements in a way that implies mothers are treated unfairly by the courts
(e.g., Myth 6, Claim 6.1)

7. Asserting the exact opposite of the finding from the cited research
(e.g., Claim 9.3)

Overall, the CODV flyer conveys the belief that mothers are often mistreated by family courts (Myth 6).
The flyer suggests that only fathers engage in child abuse and domestic violence (Claims 2.3 and 5.3), that such fathers are more likely to seek child custody (Claim 5.1) and to falsely accuse mothers of child sexual abuse (Claim 3.3), and that they succeed in 70% of cases (Claim 5.2). Suffice it to say, these statements represent a profound distortion of the truth.

CONCLUSIONS

The Commission on Domestic Violence website features this disclaimer: The ABA Commission on Domestic Violence does not engage in research, and cannot vouch for the quality or accuracy of any of the data excerpted here. Users are advised to independently confirm data with source documents cited. This analysis reveals that 10 Myths about Custody and Domestic Violence and How to counter them does not meet minimum standards of quality and accuracy. Under the guise of exposing myths, the American Bar Association has lent the imprimatur of legitimacy to numerous falsehoods about domestic violence, child abuse, and custody.

A recent review of 24 longitudinal studies concluded that a father's active and regular engagement with the child predicts a range of positive outcomes, including less juvenile delinquency and economic disadvantage in low income families, as well as fewer behavioral problems in boys and psychological problems in girls.34 But the numerous misrepresentations in the CODV flyer may serve to preclude fathers from active and regular engagement with their children. To the extent that they influence legal practice, judicial decisions, and government policymaking, the CODV distortions could have a deleterious impact on children.

10 Myths about Custody and Domestic Violence and How to counter them is profoundly and systematically biased. It is unworthy to be used as a foundation for legal practice or public policy.

Appendix

FINDINGS AND ASSESSMENTS
Following is a listing of each of the CODV Myths and Claims, along with their respective Findings and Assessments. An in-depth analysis, including citations of the scientific literature, is found in RADAR's companion Special Report, Myths of the ABA Commission on Domestic Violence: Detailed Findings.

Myth 1: "Domestic violence is rare among custody litigants."
Claim 1.1 Studies show that 25–50% of disputed custody cases involve domestic violence. Finding Claim 1.1 is false. It would be correct to state, Studies show that one-quarter to three quarters of disputed custody cases involve an allegation of domestic violence.
Assessment of Myth 1 The statement Domestic violence is rare among custody litigants is indeed a myth.

Myth 2: "Any ill effects of domestic violence on children are minimal and short-term."

Claim 2.1 Children who are exposed to domestic violence may show comparable levels of emotional and behavioral problems to children who were the direct victims of physical or sexual abuse.
Finding Claim 2.1 is misleading with regard to sexual abuse. It would be more accurate to state, some children who are exposed to domestic violence show levels of emotional and behavioral problems comparable to those in children who were the direct victims of physical abuse.

Claim 2.2 Adverse effects to children who witness DV are well documented, including aggressive behavior, depression, and/or cognitive deficiencies.
Finding Claim 2.2 is mostly correct. A fully correct summary of the research would state, adverse effects to children who witness DV are well documented, including aggressive behavior, depression, and/or academic problems.

Claim 2.3 A continuing study by the CDC has shown a significant relationship between exposure to adverse childhood experiences' (including witnessing domestic violence) and development of adult health problems, including pulmonary disease, heart disease, hepatitis, fractures, obesity, and diabetes

(Not to mention IV drug use, alcohol-ism, sexually transmitted diseases, and depression).
Finding Claim 2.3 misrepresents the findings of the Adverse Childhood Experiences Study.

Claim 2.3 is mostly false.

Assessment of Myth 2 The statement any ill effects of domestic violence on children are minimal and short term is indeed a myth.

Myth 3: "Mothers frequently invent allegations of child sexual abuse to win custody."

Claim 3.1 Child sexual abuse allegations in custody cases are rare (about 6%), and the majority of allegations are substantiated (2/3).
Finding Claim 3.1 carelessly misreports the findings of the Thoennes and Tjaden study; the reported occurrence of sexual abuse allegations was 2%, not 6%.

Claim 3.1 also ignores other pertinent research.

Claim 3.1 is false.

Claim 3.2 False allegations are no more common in divorce or custody disputes than at any other time.
Finding Claim 3.2 is false.

Claim 3.3 among false allegations, fathers are far more likely than mothers to make intentionally false accusations (21% compared to 1.3%).

Finding Claim 3.3 is false.
Assessment of Myth 3 The statement Mothers frequently invent allegations of child sexual abuse to win custody is misleading because it ignores the widespread problem of false allegations of domestic violence.

Myth 4: —Domestic violence has nothing to do with child abuse.

Claim 4.1 a wide array of studies reveals a significant overlap of domestic violence and child abuse, with most finding that both forms of abuse occur in 30–60% of violent families.
Finding a literature search reveals the probable source of the 30%–60% statistic is a 2003 book by Peter Jaffe. Jaffe in turn cites research by Edleson. A review of the Edleson paper was unable to identify the research that forms the basis of the 30%–60% figure. This is an example of how an unverifiable factoid is disseminated.

Claim 4.1 is unsupported.

Claim 4.2 Other studies have shown intimate partner violence (IPV') to be a strong predictor of child abuse, increasing the risk from 5% after one act of IPV to 100% after 50 acts of IPV.
Finding, given the serious methodological problems with the cited study and the fact that its findings have never been replicated,

Claim 4.2 is false.

Assessment of Myth 4
The statement Domestic violence has nothing to do with child abuse is indeed a myth.

Myth 5: "Abusive fathers don't get custody."

Claim 5.1 Abusive parents are more likely to seek sole custody than nonviolent ones
Finding Claim 5.1 is an implausible statement derived from an unspecified statement in an unavailable publication that lacks a scientific basis.

Claim 5.1 is false.

Claim 5.2 and they are successful about 70% of the time.

Finding Claim 5.2 represents a bald misrepresentation of the truth. Claim 5.2 is false.

Claim 5.3 Allegations of domestic violence have no demonstrated effect on the rate at which fathers are awarded custody of their children, nor do such allegations affect the rate at which fathers are ordered into supervised visitation. (I.e. abusers win unsupervised custody and visitation at the same rate as non-abusers)

Finding Claim 5.3 is false. It should also be noted that the wording of Claim 5.3 inappropriately equates an allegation of domestic violence with being an actual abuser.

Assessment of Myth 5
The purported myth Abusive fathers don't get custody is false.

Myth 6: "Fit mothers don't lose custody."

Claim 6.1 Mothers who are victims of DV are often depressed and suffering from post-traumatic stress disorder, and as a result, can present poorly in court and to best-interest attorneys and/or custody evaluators. Finding although the first part of Claim 6.1 is correct

(Mothers who are victims of DV are often depressed and suffering from post-traumatic stress disorder), there is no known research that addresses the effects of these mental health disorders on custody evaluations.

Claim 6.1 is not supported by the existing research.
Assessment of Myth 6 the purported myth Fit mothers don't lose custody is false. Even though most fathers are parentally fit, in 85% of cases child custody is awarded to the mother.

Myth 7: "Parental Alienation Syndrome („PAS") is a scientifically sound phenomenon."

Claim 7.1 The American Psychological Association has noted the lack of data to support so-called parental alienation syndrome, _and raised concern about the term's use.
Finding Claim 7.1 is, at best, misleading.
Assessment of Myth 7

Asserting that the statement Parental Alienation Syndrome (PAS') is a scientifically sound phenomenon is a myth is misleading. Parental alienation is a scientifically recognized condition, even though debate continues as to whether the condition meets all the criteria for being a syndrome. It would be correct to state, Parental alienation is a problem that has been widely observed and scientifically validated.

Myth 8: "Children are in less danger from a batterer/parent once the parents separate."

Claim 8.1 many batterers 'motivation to intimidate and control their victims through the children increases after separation, due to the loss of other methods of exerting control.
Finding Claim 8.1 is unsupported.

Assessment of Myth 8 There is no systematic evidence that shows that children are at greater risk of harm by the abuser parent if the non-abusing parent has physical custody of the children—indeed common sense argues for the opposite conclusion. Research does show, however, that when a couple separates, the risk of child abuse by the custodial parent increases dramatically.

Myth 8, Children are in less danger from a batterer/parent once the parents separate, is misleading. A true statement would read, Children are at far greater risk of abuse and harm once the parents separate.

Myth 9: "Parents who batter are mentally ill, OR Parents with no evidence of mental illness cannot be batterers."

Claim 9.1 Mental illness is found only in a minority of batterers.
Finding since Claim 9.1 pertains to batterers, who by definition are at the far end of the abuse continuum, this claim is false.

Claim 9.2 Psychological testing is not a good predictor of parenting capacity.
Finding Claim 9.2 is misleading because it implies that psychological testing has little or no value. An accurate statement would read, Used alone, psychologist testing is not a good predictor of parenting capacity.

Claim 9.3 Mental health testing cannot distinguish a batterer from a non-batterer.
Finding Claim 9.3 states the opposite conclusion from the study that it cites, an assessment with which researcher Daniel O'Leary concurs.36 The CODV claim is inconsistent with other research. Claim 9.3 is false.

Assessment of Myth 9

Myth 9, Parents who batter is mentally ill, OR Parents with no evidence of mental illness cannot be batterers is in fact not a myth. In addition, Myth 9 is ambiguous because mental illness is a vague term and there is controversy as to whether a personality disorder

(Axis 2 in the American Psychiatric Association Diagnostic and Statistical Manual) constitutes a mental illness.

A true statement would read, Parents who engage in severe and frequent physical abuse usually have diagnosable psychopathology.

Myth 10: "If a child demonstrates no fear or aversion to a parent, then there is no reason not to award unsupervised contact or custody."

Claim 10.1 Children can experience traumatic bonding 'with a parent who abuses the child or their other parent, forming unusually strong but unhealthy ties to a batterer as a survival technique (Often referred to as Stockholm syndrome').

Finding Claim 10.1 can sometimes be true. However, traumatic bonding between an abusive parent and child is unusual, and should be regarded as such.

Assessment of Myth 10, Myth 10, if a child demonstrates no fear or aversion to a parent, then there is any reason not to award unsupervised contact or custody, is misleading.

The statement contains a potentially harmful implication:
(If a child demonstrates affection to a parent, this should be taken as evidence of Stockholm syndrome).
A true statement would read, Attachment between a parent and child should be presumed to be evidence of a healthy and loving parent-child relationship, unless there is good evidence of severe child abuse.

CHAPTER 2
Myths of the ABA Commission on Domestic Violence, Detailed Findings

INTRODUCTION

The Commission on Domestic Violence (CODV) of the American Bar Association (ABA) has developed a two-page flyer: 10 Myths about Custody and Domestic Violence and How to Counter Them. In an effort to validate the CODV flyer, Respecting Accuracy in Domestic Abuse Reporting (RADAR) undertook a detailed review of the statements featured in the flyer.

RADAR's analysis of these statements is shown in two companion documents. A summary of the analysis is contained in the Special Report Myths of the ABA Commission on Domestic Violence: Summary Report.1 This Special Report Myths of the ABA Commission on Domestic Violence: Detailed Findings presents an in-depth review of each of the 10 myths, 19 claims, and 20 cited documents.

These are the findings about the 10 purported myths:

Myths confirmed to be myths: 3
Myths presented in a misleading manner: 4
Myths that are, in fact, not myths but true statements: 3
These are the findings about the 19 CODV claims:
Correct claims: 2
Claims unsupported by the available research: 3
Claims that are misleading: 3
Claims that are false: 11

These are the findings about the quality of the 20 cited documents:

Excellent: 0
Good: 9
Acceptable: 3
Poor: 4
Very poor: 4

Seven of the 10 purported myths turned out to be either misleading or not myths after all.
Seventeen of the 19 claims are unsupported, misleading, or false. Many of the cited documents are outdated, contain serious research flaws, or do not consist of research and thus cannot substantiate the CODV claim.

Myth 1: —Domestic violence is rare among custody litigants.
The ABA Commission on Domestic Violence seeks to refute this myth on the basis of
One claim:

Claim 1.1: —Studies show that 25–50% of disputed custody cases involve domestic violence.

Citations: Keilitz S, Davis C, Flango C, et al. Domestic Violence and Child Custody Disputes: A Resource Handbook for Judges and Court Managers. Williamsburg, VA: National Center for State Courts, 1997.

Johnston JR. High-conflict divorce. Future of Children, Vol. 4, No. 1, 1994.

Summary of Keilitz Report Developed by the National Center for State Courts (NCSC),

This report summarizes the results of a study of 150 courts across the country that examined how courts identify, process, and resolve disputed child custody cases. The report considers evidence of domestic violence to include civil protection orders, self-reports in questionnaires and interviews, allegations in the pleadings, and other evidence in the case record.

In Baltimore and Louisville, the percentage of cases with allegations of partner violence was found to be about 25%, compared to Las Vegas, which had more than twice this number. Overall, the estimated pro-portion of custody and visitation disputes

That involves domestic violence is:

57% of courts — less than one-quarter of the caseload
37% of courts — one-quarter to one-half of the caseload
6% of courts — more than one-half of the caseload

Summary of Johnston Article

The Johnston article is a summary of the research on high-conflict divorce and its effects on children.3 she concludes that children of high-conflict divorce, especially boys, are two to four times more likely to be clinically disturbed in terms of their emotions and behaviors.

Analysis

Figure 1 in the NCSC report is titled Percentage of Courts Reporting a Given Incidence of Domestic Violence in Custody Cases, but in truth the figure is based on soft evidence such as allegations, civil protection orders (often issued with no objective evidence of violence), and self-reports, not judicial findings. Hence, the NCSC report blurs a fundamental distinction in the law: an allegation versus a judicial finding.

This conflation surfaces repeatedly in the report. The report is further biased by its claim on page 3 that extensive research shows that in the vast majority of partner abuse cases, men perpetrate violence against women. The report does not cite any research to support that claim. That misrepresentation is found throughout the report. The report by the National Center for State Courts is legally and scientifically flawed.

In contrast, the research by Janet Johnston was well conducted and her conclusions are based on sound evidence. The research she cites indicates that 65% to 75% of high-conflict divorces involve allegations of domestic violence.

What Other Research Shows

Only one statewide study was located probing the occurrence of domestic violence allegations during divorce proceedings. The analysis was based on a large (n = 3,806) representative sample of all divorces in Oregon from 1995 to 2002. Overall, 24% of divorces had allegations of partner aggression. Passage of shared parenting legislation in 1997 was found to increase the number of allegations.

Similarly, Chandler found that among couples who sought mediation on a voluntary basis, 23% of cases involved reported domestic violence, based on pre-mediation screening questionnaires. In disputed divorces, however, allegations of abuse in-crease substantially.

Four studies have examined the extent of allegations of violence made by couples participating in mediation: Depner and colleagues studied 1,699 divorce mediation sessions and found that domestic violence was alleged by one or both parents in 65% of families. Mathis and Tanner found that among 131 couples, 60% reported some level of violence. Saccuzzo and colleagues reported that among 193 California couples, 84% involved an allegation or restraining orders relating to domestic violence.

Two studies surveyed divorcing couples in California for whom mediation had failed or disputes continued even after a legal settlement had been reached:

Johnston and Campbell reported allegations of physical aggression in 75% of couples separated an average of 30 months. Johnston reported a 70% aggression rate among couples separated an average of 42 months.

Finally, one study reveals the importance of distinguishing between allegations of abuse versus actual abuse:

In a study of couples involved in custody disputes, DV allegations were made in 55% of the cases. Of those allegations, 59% could not be substantiated as true.

Finding Claim 1.1

Is false. It would be correct to state, Studies show that one-quarter to three quarters of disputed custody cases involve an allegation of domestic violence.

Assessment of Myth 1

Based on the finding of about half of DV allegations cannot be substantiated as true, it appears that ⅛ to 3/8 of cases of litigated custody cases involve substantiated partner violence.
The statement Domestic violence is rare among custody litigants is indeed a myth.

Myth 2: "Any ill effects of domestic violence on children are minimal and short-term."

The ABA Commission on Domestic Violence seeks to refute this myth on the basis of three claims:

Claim 2.1: —Children who are exposed to domestic violence may show comparable levels of emotional and behavioral problems to children who were the direct victims of physical or sexual abuse.

Citation:

Jaffe P, Wolfe D, Wilson S. Children of Battered Women. Newbury Park, CA: Sage Publications, 1990.

Summary

This book provides an overview of the problem of domestic violence; describes its cognitive, emotional, and behavioral effects on children; discusses assessment and intervention strategies; and reviews implications for related children's services. The book cites research and highlights numerous case studies.

At one point, the book acknowledges the high incidence of wives 'abuse of their husbands but dismisses that concern with the assertion that much of this behavior is in self-defense.

Analysis

The book's one-sided depiction of domestic violence is evident from its title. The book is characterized by ideologically rooted claims that family violence is considered acceptable behavior within a patriarchal society (a false statement, research shows) and is interwoven with the very fabric of society's attitudes and values (a meaningless assertion). Its claim that much of women's violent behavior is done in self-defense is factually incorrect —the actual figure is less than 20%.Its portrayal of fathers is negative. The tome makes frequent claims about research findings without commenting on the study's limitations. Its alarmist tone and frequent reliance on anecdotes detracts from the book's ability to objectively present the impact of partner violence on children.

Contrary to the impression left by Children of Battered Women, mothers are as likely as fathers to engage in partner violence, even for severe, unilateral violence sometimes referred to as battering.

What Other Research Shows

More recent and rigorous reviews of the literature have been published by Wolfe and Kitzmann. Wolfe concluded, Forty of these studies indicated that children's exposure to domestic violence was related to emotional and behavioral problems, translating to a small overall effect. Kitzmann similarly concluded that her analysis indicates that about 63% of child witnesses were faring more poorly than the average child who had not been exposed to interparental violence. Notably, however, this result also means that about 37% of the child witnesses showed outcomes that were similar to, or better than, those of nonwitnesses.

So while it is true that some children from homes characterized by domestic violence are more likely to have emotional and behavioral problems, other children from such homes do not experience clinically significant levels of psychopathology. However, research does not support the notion that witnessing adult partner aggression can be compared to being a direct victim of sexual abuse.

Finding Claim 2.1 is misleading with regard to sexual abuse. It would be more accurate for it to state, some children who are exposed to domestic violence show comparable levels of emotional and behavioral problems to children who were the direct victims of physical abuse.

Claim 2.2: —Adverse effects to children who witness DV are well-documented, including aggressive behavior, depression, and/or cognitive deficiencies.

Citations: Morrill A, Dai J, Dunn S, Sung I, Smith K. Child custody and visitation decisions when the father has perpetrated violence against the mother. Violence against Women, Vol. 11, No. 8, 2005, pp. 1076–1107.

Edleson J. Children's witnessing of adult domestic violence. Journal of Interpersonal Violence, Vol. 14, No. 8, 1999.

Summary of Morrill Article

This study evaluated the impact of state statutes that mandate a presumption against custody by a person who has perpetrated partner violence. The authors examined 393 custody and/or visitation orders entered by 60 judges in six states. They found that in states with a presumption against custody awards to abusers, judges were more likely to award sole legal and physical custody to mothers. However, the Morrill study analyzed child custody awards, not the effects of witnessing DV on children. This study should have been cited under Claim 5.3.

Summary of the Edleson Paper

This paper reviews 31 rigorous studies that examined the effects of a child witnessing domestic violence. These studies evaluated the childhood problems associated with witnessing partner violence, the factors that moderate the impact of these experiences, and the rigor of the research methods used in these studies.

The ABA flyer uses this citation: Edleson J. Problems associated with children's witnessing of domestic violence. 1999. However, this is an incomplete version of the journal article that is referred to above.

Analysis

The Edleson review provides a useful but now outdated summary of the research. Its main deficiency is that it ignores the problem of female-initiated partner aggression.

What Other Research Shows Claim 2.2 states that witnessing abuse worsens cognitive deficiencies. Although the Kitzmann review concluded that child witnesses were more likely to have academic problems, cognitive deficiencies were not assessed. See also previous discussion under Claim 2.1,

Finding Except for the statement about cognitive deficiencies, Claim 2.2 is correct. A fully correct summary of the research would state, adverse effects to children who witness DV are well documented, including aggressive behavior, depression, and/or academic problems.

Claim 2.3: —A continuing study by the CDC has shown a significant relationship between exposure to „adverse childhood experiences" (including witnessing domestic violence) and development of adult health problems, including pulmonary disease, heart disease, hepatitis, fractures, obesity, and diabetes
(Not to mention IV drug use, alcoholism, sexually transmitted diseases and depression).‖

Citation: The CODV claim does not cite a specific study. Instead it references a 1998 press release and the website of the Adverse Childhood Experiences Study (ACES). That website lists the following article:

Felitti V, Anda R, Nordenberg D, Williamson D, Spitz A, Edwards V, Koss M, Marks J. Relationship of childhood abuse and household dysfunction to many of the leading causes of death in adults. American Journal of Preventive Medicine, Vol. 14, No. 4, 1998.

But that article does not address the specific statement of Claim 2.3. Further extensive searches identified a single article from the Adverse Childhood Experiences Study that addresses the impact of witnessing partner abuse:

Dube S, Anda R, Felitti V, Edwards V, Williamson D. Exposure to abuse, neglect, and household dysfunction among adults who witnessed intimate partner violence as children:
Implications for health and social services. Violence and Victims, Vol. 17, No. 1, 2002.

Summary The Adverse Childhood Experiences Study was a retrospective survey of adults who were members of an HMO in southern California. Persons were asked about a variety of childhood risk factors they had experienced, including violence against the mother.

Experiences of witnessing violence against the father were not assessed. The researchers analyzed the association of those factors with subsequent health behaviors and disease conditions. The researchers conclude in their 2002 article, there was a positive graded risk for self-reported alcoholism, illicit drug use, and depressed affect as the frequency of witnessing IPV [interpersonal violence] increased.

Analysis Retrospective surveys have well-known weaknesses, including selection bias, faulty recall of previous events, and inability to demonstrate causation. The failure of the survey to assess violence against fathers does not require further comment. The Adverse Childhood Experiences Study identified a link from childhood exposure to partner violence and alcoholism, illicit drug use, and depressed affect, but not a link to pulmonary disease, heart disease, hepatitis, fractures, obesity, diabetes, or sexually transmitted diseases.

What Other Research Shows No other studies could be found that link childhood witnessing of partner violence to its long effects on physical health, such as pulmonary disease, heart disease, hepatitis, fractures, obesity, diabetes, or sexually transmitted diseases.

Finding Claim 2.3 misrepresents the findings of the Adverse Childhood Experiences Study.

Claim 2.3 is false.

Assessment of Myth 2

The statement any ill effects of domestic violence on children are minimal and short-term is indeed a myth.

Myth 3: —Mothers frequently invent allegations of child sexual abuse to win custody.

The ABA Commission on Domestic Violence seeks to refute this myth on the basis of three claims:

Claim 3.1: —Child sexual abuse allegations in custody cases are rare (about 6%), and the majority of allegations are substantiated (2/3).

Citation: Theonnes N, Tjaden PG. The extent, nature, and validity of sexual abuse allegations in custody and visitation disputes. Child Abuse and Neglect, Vol. 14, 1990.

Summary Thoennes and Tjaden obtained information from over 200 court administrators, judges, custody mediators, and child protection workers throughout the United States, including

Note: In the interest of impartial inquiry, this analysis examines whether mothers and fathers frequently invent allegations of child sexual abuse to win custody.

70 in-depth interviews at five sites. According to records kept by family court workers, less than 2% of disputed child custody or visitation cases involved any allegation of sexual abuse. The authors conclude, In the 129 cases for which a determination of the validity of the allegation was available, 50% were found to involve abuse, 33% were found to involve no abuse, and 17% resulted in an indeterminate ruling.

Analysis The authors 'reliance on data collected in 1986 from a small convenience sample in only 12 venues limits the generalization of their findings.

What Other Research Shows One study analyzed data from 7,672 child maltreatment investigations reported in the Canadian Incidence Study of Reported Child Abuse and Neglect. Among the 798 cases of alleged sexual abuse, only 38% were substantiated. Likewise, Wakefield and Underwager reported that out of approximately 200 divorces and custody cases in which they provided expert consultation, in three-fourths of cases there was no determination of sexual abuse by the legal system. Allegations of child sexual abuse are indeed rare in divorce actions, but appear to be more likely in the context of custody disputes.

Finding Claim 3.1 carelessly misreports the findings of the Thoennes and Tjaden study the frequency of sexual abuse allegations was 2%, not 6%. Claim 3.1 also ignores the findings from two other larger studies.

Claim 3.1 is false.

Claim 3.1 should state, Allegations of child sexual abuse appear to be rare in divorce actions (about 2%), and only in about one-third of cases are allegations of child sexual abuse substantiated.

Claim 3.2: False allegations are no more common in divorce or custody disputes than at any other time.

Citation: Brown T, Frederico M, Hewitt L, and Sheehan R. Revealing the existence of child abuse in the context of marital breakdown and custody and access disputes.
Child Abuse and Neglect, Vol. 24, No. 6, 2000.

Summary The study by Thea Brown and colleagues analyzed 357 allegations of child abuse made by parents involved in custody and access disputes in Melbourne and Canberra, Australia. Of the 357 claims, 19.6% involved an allegation of solely child sexual abuse.26 However, Brown does not compare the rate of false allegations of child sexual abuse during divorce and custody disputes to the rate at other times.

Analysis The Brown article consists of a confusing, poorly described study conducted in Australia in the 1990s. It does not provide data that addresses the focus of Claim 3.2, the rate of false allegations of child sexual abuse during divorce and custody disputes compared to other situations. The relevance of data collected in Australia to the United States is unknown.

What Other Research Shows It is generally believed that allegations of abuse, as well as false allegations of abuse, are more common during divorce and custody disputes. One study analyzed data from the Canadian Incidence Study of Reported Child Abuse and Neglect. Ten percent of these cases involved allegations of sexual abuse. The authors conclude Rates of false allegations were significantly higher in these cases: 12% of cases involving custody or access disputes compared to only 3% in other cases.

Finding The best available research indicates that rates of false allegations increase fourfold during custody and access disputes.

Claim 3.2 is false.

Claim 3.3: —Among false allegations, fathers are far more likely than mothers to make intentionally false accusations (21% compared to 1.3%).

Citation:
Bala N and Schuman J. Allegations of sexual abuse when parents have separated.
Canadian Family Law Quarterly, Vol. 17, 2000.

Summary The Bala and Schuman study consists of a compilation of 196 judicial opinions rendered from 1990 to 1998 in Canada on alleged sexual and physical abuse occurring in the context of parental separation. The authors note these judicial opinions are unlikely to be representative of all allegations of child abuse, because in cases with strong evidence of abuse, the perpetrator is likely not to contest the issue of abuse in family law proceedings, as they explain.

Analysis The Bala and Schuman article is not the original source of the 21% and 1.3% statistics. The source of those numbers is the 1993 Ontario Incidence Study of Child Abuse.

What Other Research Shows The Ontario Incidence Study of Child Abuse relied on the opinions of child protection workers, not judicial findings, to evaluate whether the allegations were intentionally false.

Such assessments are notoriously unreliable. Studies have documented evaluator bias that imputes negative motivations to men, especially in the context of child custody disputes.

Several researchers have reached similar conclusions:

A false allegation is in the eye of the beholder, Mark Everson and Barbara Boat explains.
University of Michigan researcher Kathleen Faller has highlighted the difficulty of determining whether a false allegation is intentional.

One Canadian blue ribbon panel concluded, we do not know the actual incidence of abuse allegations in cases in which parents have separated, or the proportion of cases in which the allegations are intentionally false.

Finding Claim 3.3 ignores the expert panel that concluded, we do not know the proportion of cases in which the allegations are intentionally false.

Claim 3.3 is false.

Assessment of Myth 3

Myth 3 sidesteps the issue of false allegations of domestic violence, which are often used to gain an unfair advantage in a divorce action. Various studies of divorcing couples with custody disputes have found that allegations of partner violence are made in 55% to 68% of cases.
Attorneys have likewise expressed concerns about the problem.

Overall, about 85% of claims of domestic violence are filed by women.

In the context of a divorce action, mothers are seven times more likely than fathers to file false or exaggerated claims.

Considering the fact that less than half of all restraining orders are based on an allegation of physical violence, and judging by the fraction of temporary restraining orders that are approved by a judge at a final hearing, many such claims can be considered false or unnecessary.

The purported Myth 3, Mothers frequently invent al-legations of child sexual abuse to win custody is misleading because it ignores the widespread problem of false allegations of domestic violence.

Myth 4: —Domestic violence has nothing to do with child abuse.

The ABA Commission on Domestic Violence seeks to refute this myth on the basis of two claims:

Claim 4.1: —A wide array of studies reveals a significant overlap between domestic violence and child abuse, with most finding that both forms of abuse occur in 30–60% of violent families.

Citation: Appel A, Holden G. The co-occurrence of spouse and physical child abuse:
A review and appraisal. Journal of Family Psychology, Vol. 12, No. 4, 1998.

Summary The Appel and Holden article consists of a review of 31 studies that evaluate the co-occurrence of spousal and physical child abuse.
The studies are categorized by the method used to assess rates of abuse co-occurrence:

Representative surveys of community residents, with a co-occurrence rate of 6% to 21% (Table 1)

Reports from female victims of violence, who reported co-occurrence rates of 4% to 100%, depending on the persons involved, referent period, and assessment tool used (Table 2)

Reports from child abuse victims, showing co-occurrence rates of 26% to 59% (Table 3)

Analysis Appel and Holden note that any conclusions from their study are severely handicapped as a result of competing and sometimes unspecified or idiosyncratic determinations of physical child abuse. The wide range of values they report from the various studies—4% to 100%—shows that no firm conclusions can be reached. In-deed, the authors state, The clearest conclusion from this review is that there is an inadequate database with which to evaluate the extent of co-occurrence.

What Other Research Shows The methodological limitations identified by Appel and Holden remain unresolved to this day. A recent community-based study reported a 7% co-occurrence figure.

Finding Given that Appel and Holden do not highlight the 30%–60% figure, one wonders where the CODV obtained this number. A literature search reveals that the probable source is a book by Peter Jaffe that states, 30–60% of children whose mothers had experienced abuse were them-selves likely to be Abused. Jaffe in turn cites research by Edleson, which was dis-cussed previously under Claim 2.2.

A review of the Edleson paper was unable to identify the research that forms the basis of the 30%–60% figure.

This is an example of how an unverifiable factoid comes into existence, and it reflects the slipshod methods used to develop the CODV flyer.

Claim 4.1 is unsupported.

Claim 4.2: —Other studies have shown intimate partner violence („IPV") to be a strong predictor of child abuse, increasing the risk from 5% after one act of IPV to 100% after 50 acts of IPV.

Citation:
Ross SM. Risk of physical abuse to children of spouse abusing parents. Child Abuse and Neglect, Vol. 20, No. 7, 1996.

Summary Susan Ross re-analyzed data from interviews of 3,363 parents who participated in the 1985 National Family Violence Survey. The centerpiece of her analysis is a logistic regression graph shown in Figure 1 of the article. The author acknowledges that the skewed distributions of the varia-bles make for difficult statistical analysis and she had to perform several different combinations of marital violence and child abuse to replicate the findings.

Based on Figure 1, Ross concludes, the probability of child abuse by a violent husband increases from 5% with one act of marital violence to near certainty with 50 or more acts of marital violence. The predicted probability of child abuse by a violent wife increases from 5% with one act of marital vio-lence to 30% with 50 or more acts of marital violence.

Analysis The Ross study contains a number of serious flaws:

A close examination of the title of Figure 1 reveals that the graph only applies to male children. Ross does not present a graph for the whole data set, which casts doubt on her conclusions.

The skewed distribution of the data violates the requirements of regression analysis.

The pseudo-R2 of only 5%–6% is considered very weak.

The conclusion presented in the Abstract gives no hint of the highly selected sample used to calculate Figure 1. 51

What Other Research Shows Several other studies have found mothers who hit their partners have similar levels of increased risk of child abuse as partner-aggressive fathers.

Finding Given the serious problems with the Ross study and the fact that her findings have not been Replicated, we conclude that

Claim 4.2 is false.

Assessment of Myth 4

The statement Domestic violence has nothing to do with child abuse is indeed a myth.

Myth 5: "**Abusive fathers** don't get custody.

The ABA Commission on Domestic Violence seeks to refute this myth on the basis of three claims:

Claim 5.1: "Abusive parents are more likely to seek sole custody than nonviolent ones …"

Citation: American Psychological Association. Violence and the Family: Report of the American Psychological Association Presidential Task Force on Violence and the Family. Washington, DC. 1996.

Summary This 141-page document consists of a compilation of broad assertions about family violence.

None of the claims or conclusions in the APA paper is supported by citations from the scientific research.

This report is no longer available from the American Psychological Association. The APA removed the report in 2006 because, according to the APA representative, it is a very old document and several statements in the report need to have a better research analysis.

Analysis By the admission of the American Psychological Association, the cited report is out-dated and many of its claims are questionable. The absence of a scientific citation renders it virtually impossible to verify the claim. A previous analysis concluded flatly, this monograph is not a scholarly publication.

What the Research Shows There is no known research that shows abusers are more likely to seek child custody than non-abusers.

Finding Claim 5.1 is derived from an unspecified statement in an unavailable publication with admittedly questionable claims that lack a scientific basis. Claim 5.1 consists of an unverifiable factoid.

Claim 5.1 is false.

Claim 5.2: "… and they are successful about 70% of the time."

Citation: American Judges Foundation. Forms of emotional battering. In Domestic Violence and the Court House: Understanding the Problem … Knowing the Victim. Undated.
Note: In the interest of impartial inquiry, this analysis examines whether abusive fathers and mothers don't get custody.

Summary The American Judges Foundation publication asserts, Studies show that batterers have been able to convince authorities that the victim is unfit or undeserving of sole custody in approximately 70% of challenged cases. The publication does not include any citations to support this or any of its other claims. The lead author of the referenced publication is Lenore Walker, EdD, a psychologist who works with the Florida-based Domestic Violence Institute. She is well known for her advocacy work in the area of Battered Women's Syndrome, a condition that is not recognized in the Diagnostic and Statistical Manual and has been described as having a low level of scientific support.

Analysis The apparent source of the 70% figure is a 1989 report by the Gender Bias Committee of the Massachusetts Supreme Judicial Court, which concluded, Refuting com-plaints that the bias in favor of mothers was pervasive, we found that fathers who actively seek custody obtain either primary or joint physical custody over 70% of the time.58 But that 70% figure is implausible in the light of the fact that in 85% of cases custody is awarded to the mother, according to the Bureau of the Census.

Indeed a subsequent review found the Gender Bias Committee's conclusion was flawed. A reanalysis of the raw data showed that when mothers sought sole custody, the court granted the request at a rate 65% higher than it did when fathers made the same request.

The SJC's claim regarding court bias in custody cases appears less like objective research than like an exercise in manipulating numbers and there is more to the factual contortions.

The American Judges Foundation document refers to batterers who seek custody only in challenged cases. But the CODV claim refers to abusers who seek custody in all cases. The majority of abusers, however, are not batterers. Thus, the CODV claim pertains to a much broader segment of the population.

What Other Research Shows No known research assesses how often abusive parents who seek custody succeed in their efforts.

Finding Claim 5.2: represents an egregious misrepresentation of the truth.

Claim 5.2 is false.

Claim 5.3: —Allegations of domestic violence have no demonstrated effect on the rate at which fathers are awarded custody of their children, nor do such allegations affect the rate at which fathers are ordered into supervised visitation. (i.e., abusers win unsupervised custody and visitation at the same rate as non-abusers)

Citation Kernic M, Monary-Ernsdorff D, Koepsell J, Holt V. Children in the crossfire: Child custody determinations among couples with a history of intimate partner violence. Violence against Women, Vol. 11, No. 8, 2005.

Summary The study by Kernic and colleagues identified 324 cases that were positive for intimate partner violence (IPV), defined as cases in which one or more of the following applied:

A restraining order had been filed.

A police report had been made.

Court dissolution records indicated unsubstantiated allegations of IPV.

Court dissolution records indicated substantiated allegations of IPV by the husband against the wife. Then the authors excluded IPV cases in which the husband was the victim, except for cases in which additional documentation confirmed the male partner of the couple as the primary aggressor. The authors did not justify this exclusion or state what documentation they used to determine primary aggressor.

The authors concluded, we found that mothers with a history of IPV victimization were no more likely than comparison group mothers to be awarded child custody.

Analysis Credible evidence of domestic violence includes eyewitness accounts, police reports of probable cause, confirmatory medical records, and judicial findings. But Kernic used none of these. The evidence that she did rely on is known to be flawed:

1. Restraining orders are often issued with no hard evidence of abuse.

2. Police reports often state that no violence likely occurred.

3. Court records which indicate unsubstantiated allegations of IPV are exactly that unsubstantiated.

Kernic then excluded cases of female-on-male violence, further biasing her results. This study is an example of advocacy research in which the investigator reworks the definitions and cherry-picks the results in order to arrive at a predetermined conclusion.

Note: In the interest of impartial inquiry, this analysis examines the broader question of the rate at which fathers and mothers are awarded child custody or ordered into supervised visitation.

What Other Research Shows According to an analysis by the American Bar Association, divorce courts in 26 states are required to consider domestic violence as a best interest of the child criterion. In 23 states, a finding of domestic violence is considered a rebuttable presumption against shared custody. And in five states, a domestic violence finding prohibits joint custody.

One study analyzed 393 child custody/visitation orders in six states. In states with a legal presumption against awarding custody to domestic violence perpetrators, judges were more likely to award sole legal and physical custody to the non-perpetrator.

Finding Claim 5.3 is false. It should also be noted that the wording of Claim 5.3 appears to equate an allegation of domestic violence with being an actual abuser. A fundamental precept of jurisprudence is that an allegation is not synonymous with the occurrence of an offense or a judicial finding.

Assessment of Myth 5

All three claims listed under Myth 5 are false. Therefore the purported myth Abusive fathers don't get custody is also false.

Myth 6: —Fit mothers don't lose custody.

The ABA Commission on Domestic Violence seeks to refute this myth on the basis of one claim:

Claim 6.1: —Mothers who are victims of DV are often depressed and suffering from posttraumatic stress disorder, and as a result, can present poorly in court and to best-interest attorneys and/or custody evaluators.

Citations: Golding J. Intimate partner violence as a risk factor for mental disorders: A meta-analysis. Journal of Family Violence, Vol. 14, 1999.

Kernic M, Monary-Ernsdorff D, Koepsell J, Holt V. Children in the crossfire:
Child custody determinations among couples with a history of intimate partner violence.
Violence against Women, Vol. 11, No. 8, 2005.

Summary of the Golding Article This meta-analysis of research examined the effects of domestic violence on victims' depression, suicidality, post-traumatic stress disorder, alcohol abuse, and drug abuse.

Female victims of violence had an odds ratio ranging from 3.55 to 5.62, indicating a substantially higher risk of mental disorders.

Note: In the interest of impartial inquiry, this analysis examines whether fit mothers and fathers don't lose child custody.

Summary of the Kernic Article The article by Kernic and colleagues is discussed under Claim 5.3. That study analyzed the impact of substantiated cases of marital interpersonal violence on subsequent child custody and visitation outcomes. For reasons described previously, the Kernic study is flawed.

Analysis Overall, the Golding article is thorough and methodologically robust. The major shortcoming of the article is that it does not report the effects of domestic violence on men's mental health status, based on the author's spurious claim that surveys which show gender symmetry in abuse rates are thought to be methodologically flawed.

What Other Research Shows Both male and female victims of domestic violence suffer from a variety of mental health disorders, although it is generally believed that women suffer more ill effects.

Finding Although the first part of Claim 6.1 is correct (Mothers who are victims of DV are often depressed and suffering from post-traumatic stress disorder), there is no known research that addresses the effects of these mental health disorders on custody evaluations.
Claim 6.1 is not supported by the existing research.

Assessment of Myth 6

The one claim listed under Myth 6 is unsupported by the research. Therefore, the purported myth Fit mothers don't lose custody is false. It should also be noted that even though most fathers are parentally fit, in 85% of cases custody of the child is awarded to the mother.

Myth 7: —Parental Alienation Syndrome („PAS") is a scientifically sound phenomenon.

The ABA Commission on Domestic Violence seeks to refute this myth on the basis of one claim:

Claim 7.1: —The American Psychological Association has noted the lack of data to support so-called „parental alienation syndrome," and raised concern about the term's use.

Citation: American Psychological Association. Violence and the Family: Report of the American Psychological Association Presidential Task Force on Violence and the Family. Washington, DC. 1996.

Summary This document consists of a series of broad assertions about family violence. None of the claims or conclusions in the paper is supported by citations from the scientific research. The APA removed the report in 2006 because, according to the APA representative, it is a very old document and several statements in the report need to have a better research analysis.

Analysis As discussed under Claim 5.1, the American Psychological Association document cited in the CODV flyer consists of an array of unsubstantiated claims. The scientific validity of its conclusions is doubtful.

What Other Research Shows One of the earliest and most influential studies in this area was a 12-year study of 700 divorce families commissioned by the American Bar Association, which detailed numerous?

Instances of children who had been intentionally alienated from one parent.

Numerous research studies and clinical reports reveal that children can become hostile to a parent a result of relational aggression by the other parent. In his authoritative review, psychologist Richard A. Warshak concludes, there is consider-able scientific research which…validates key facets of PAS. Although 56 experts debate whether parental alienation meets all the criteria of being a syndrome, there is no controversy that the problem does occur.

Anyone who works in the field of forensic psychology in the context of divorce will say, yes, it's possible for a child to be turned away from a loving parent, explains noted custody consultant Michael Bone.

Even though the American Psychological Association has not taken an official position on whether parental alienation is actually a syndrome, a search of the APA PsycINFO database yields 265 hits on parental alienation and 244 hits on parental alienation syndrome.

The APA's Guidelines for Child Custody Evaluations in Divorce Proceedings favorably cites an authoritative reference book on this topic. At least 355 books have been published on parental alienation.

Finding Claim 7.1 is at best misleading.

Assessment of Myth 7

Asserting that the statement Parental Alienation Syndrome (PAS') is a scientifically sound phenomenon is a myth is misleading. Parental alienation is a scientifically recognized condition, even though debate continues as to whether the condition is actually a syndrome. It would be correct to state, Parental alienation is a problem that has been widely observed and scientifically validated.

Myth 8: —Children are in less danger from a batterer/parent once the parent's separate.

The ABA Commission on Domestic Violence seeks to refute this myth on the basis of one claim:

Claim 8.1: —Many batterers'' motivation to intimidate and control their victims through the children increases after separation, due to the loss of other methods of exerting control.

Citations: Bancroft L, Silverman J. The Batterer as Parent: Addressing the Impact of Domestic Violence on Family Dynamics. Thousand Oaks, CA: Sage Publications, 2002.

Langford L, Isaac N, Kabat S. Homicides related to intimate partner violence in Massachusetts 1991–1995. Boston, MA: Peace at Home, 1999. It should be noted that Myth 8 and Claim 8.1 address two very different issues—the physical risks to children versus an abuser's use of children to control his or her victim. The following discussion addresses both issues.

Summary of the Bancroft and Silverman Book

Based largely on the authors' clinical experience and amplified by selected research findings, this book analyzes the personality profile and behavior of parents who severely assault their partners and the effects this behavior has on children. The authors also explore the dynamics of custody and visitation disputes. The book cites the research of leading family researcher Murray Straus and colleagues, but fails to mention their most important findings:

Women are as likely as men to engage in severe partner violence.

Partner abuse is often mutual.

Bancroft and Silverman acknowledge the problem of lesbian battering, stating that the behavioral profile of lesbian and gay male batterers appears to correspond closely to that of heterosexual abusers. But then they ignore female battering in the context of heterosexual relationships.

Summary of the Langford Article

The report by Langford and colleagues consists of an anecdotal collection of 194 DV related homicides that occurred in Massachusetts over a 5-year period.

The study did not compare rates of child abuse or partner violence before and after separation. It did not systematically report on perpetrators 'motivations such as a desire to intimidate or control.
The project did not undertake detailed analyses of the data or test for statistical significance.
The document spotlights the occurrence of male-perpetrated violence against their partners, but does not mention the fact that mothers are more likely than fathers to commit child homicides.
The 18-page document reads like a police investigation, not a research report in the usual sense.
Analysis

Lundy Bancroft views domestic violence from a decidedly ideological perspective, and his commitment to objectivity and balance has been questioned. In an early article, he drew a parallel between partner abuse and militaristic imperialism:

Male battering and U.S. intervention are often viewed, even by political [sic] conscious people, as irrational or as aberations [sic] from the norm. ... Battering and war play a critical role in keeping sexism and imperialism alive.77 Bancroft played a lead role in the ill-fated Public Broadcasting Service program,

Breaking the Silence: Children's Voices.

This controversial show was repudiated by PBS ombudsman Michael Getler because the totality of the presentation came across as quite tilted. Likewise, Ken Bode, ombudsman at the Corporation for Public

Broadcasting, found the film so totally unbalanced as to fall outside the boundaries of PBS editorial standards. And Bancroft, who once worked as a domestic violence educator for the Massachusetts family courts, boasted that he was fired for his excessive zeal hardly a qualification that a credible researcher would be proud of.

This book has been criticized for presenting one-sided analyses of domestic violence based on self-selected and non-representative samples.

The highlighting of lesbian battering while denying heterosexual female battering seems illogical. Bancroft and Silverman's book deftly ignores the research on female-initiated violence, plies emotion-laden terms like batterer, and readily embraces false gender stereotypes. Overall, the book reads more like an ideological manifesto than an even-handed commentary.

What Other Research Shows There is no good research that sheds light on a perpetrator's motivations to control his or her victim during separation? Nonetheless, clinical reports reveal that in the course of marital dissolution, both parties may attempt to draw their children into the conflict see discussion of Claim 7.1 above.

Finding Claim 8.1 is unsupported by the research.

Assessment of Myth 8

Myth 8, Children are in less danger from a batterer/parent once the parents separate, is misleading.

A true statement would read, Children are at far greater risk of abuse and harm once the parents separate. There is no systematic evidence which shows that children are at greater risk of harm by the abuser-parent if the non-abusing parent has physical custody of the children; indeed, common sense argues for the opposite conclusion. Research does show, however, that when a couple separates, the risk of child abuse by the custodial parent increases dramatically:

The National Incidence Study (NIS) of Child Abuse and Neglect found that, compared to children living with both parents, children living with a single parent face a 77% greater risk of being harmed by physical abuse and about an 80% greater risk of suffering serious injury or harm. Of children who were maltreated by their birth parents, mothers were the perpetrators in 75% of cases, compared to fathers 46% of the time (some children were maltreated by both parents).

A British study that found that, compared to children residing with married biological parents, those residing with single mothers have a 14-fold higher risk of experiencing serious child abuse and a 7-fold higher risk of suffering fatal child abuse.

Myth 9: —Parents who batter are mentally ill, OR Parents with no evidence of mental illness cannot be batterers.

The ABA Commission on Domestic Violence seeks to refute this myth on the basis of three claims:

Claim 9.1: —Mental illness is found only in a minority of batterers.

Citations: Gelles R, Straus M. Intimate Violence. New York: Simon and Schuster, 1988. (Reporting that mental illness accounts for only 10% of abusive incidents)

Gondolf EW. MCMI-III results for batterer program participants in four cities: Less pathological than expected. Journal of Family Violence, Vol. 14, No. 1, 1999.

Summary The Gelles and Straus research was conducted on a nationally representative sample of persons who had engaged in any form of physical partner aggression. They found that mental illness accounts for only a small fraction of abuse incidents.

The Gondolf study tested 840 men attending batterer intervention programs in Pitts-burgh, Houston, Dallas, and Denver in 1995. He found that 90% of the participants had scores on at least one of the MCMI subscales that were suggestive of a clinical personality pattern and 25% of men had evidence of severe mental disorder.

Analysis It is generally recognized that as the severity and frequency of partner violence in-creases, so does the level of mental illness. Thus, it is not surprising that in a nationally representative sample in which minor violence predominates; mental illness is present in only 10% of incidents of physical abuse. In contrast, the Gondolf study examined a sub-set of abusers who were participants in batterer intervention programs and were likely to have engaged in severe partner abuse hence the higher rates of mental disturbance.

What Other Research Shows In his review, psychologist Donald Dutton concludes, Studies have found incidence rates of personality disorders to be 80–90 percent in both court-referred and self-referred wife assaulters. … As the violence becomes more severe and chronic, the likelihood of psy-chopathology in these men approaches 100 percent.[83] Likewise, elevations in personality disorders have also been documented among women convicted of spousal assault.

Finding since Claim 9.1 pertains to batterers, who are, by definition, at the high end of the abuse con-tinuum, this claim is false.

Claim 9.2: —Psychological testing is not a good predictor of parenting capacity.

Citation: Brodzinsky D. On the use and misuse of psychological testing in child custody evaluations. Professional Psychology: Research and Practice, Vol. 24, No. 2, 1994.

Summary The Brodzinsky article reviews a variety of psychological measures of intelligence, aca-demic functioning, and personality used to predict parenting capacity for child custody assessments. He concludes that psychological testing has a very legitimate place in child custody evaluations, but cautions that such tests should only be used in conjunction with other standard data-gathering tech-niques, such as interviews and observations.

Analysis Although now somewhat outdated, the Brodzinsky article represents a thorough and objec-tive summary of the research.

What Other Research Shows Carr and colleagues have reached a conclusion similar to Brodzinsky's that psychological tests alone are not valid predictors of parenting capacity.

Finding Although technically correct, Claim 9.2 is misleading because it implies that psychological testing has little or no value. An accurate statement would read, Used alone, psychologist testing is not a good predictor of parenting capacity.

Claim 9.3: —Mental health testing cannot distinguish a batterer from a non-batterer.

Citation:
O'Leary D. Through a psychological lens: Personality traits, personality disorders, and levels of violence. In Gelles R and Loseke D, Eds. Current Controversies on Family Violence. Newbury Park, CA: Sage, 1994.

Summary The O'Leary chapter reports that mildly abusive men score high on personality tests for impulsiveness, aggression, and suspicion of others. In contrast, extremely abusive men found in DV treatment programs usually have been diagnosed with severe psychological problems such as schizoid/borderline, possessive/dependent/compulsive, and narcissistic/antisocial personality traits.

Analysis While Claim 9.3 states that mental health testing cannot identify a severe abuser, the O'Leary chapter cited by the CODV reached the exact opposite conclusion. As Dr. O'Leary explained, Batterers consistently score higher on a broad range of psychological measures.

What Other Research Shows The research indicates that persons who are engaged in severe, frequent physical violence can usually be diagnosed with severe psychological disorders in both male[88,89] and female batterers.

Finding Claim 9.3 misrepresents the study that it cites and is inconsistent with other research. Claim 9.3 is false.

Assessment of Myth 9

Purported Myth 9, Parents who batter is mentally ill, OR Parents with no evidence of mental illness cannot be batterers is in fact not a myth. In addition, Myth 9 is ambiguous because mental illness is a vague term and there is controversy as to whether a personality disorder (Axis 2 in the American Psychiatric Association Diagnostic and Statistical Manual) constitutes a mental illness.

A true statement would read,
Parents who engage in severe and frequent physical abuse usually have diagnosable psychopathology.

Myth 10: —If a child demonstrates no fear or aversion to a parent, and then there is no reason not to award unsupervised contact or custody.

Claim 10.1 Children can experience traumatic bonding'with a parent who abuses the child or their other parent, forming unusually strong but unhealthy ties to a batterer as a survival technique
(*Often referred to as Stockholm syndrome'*).

Finding Claim 10.1 can sometimes be true. However, traumatic bonding between an abusive parent and child is unusual, and should be regarded as such.

Assessment of Myth 10

Myth 10, if a child demonstrates no fear or aversion to a parent, then there is any reason not to award unsupervised contact or custody, is misleading. The statement contains a potentially harmful implication: if a child demonstrates affection to a parent, this should be taken as evidence of Stockholm syndrome.

A true statement would read, Attachment between a parent and child should be presumed to be evidence of a healthy and loving parent-child relationship, unless there is good evidence of severe child abuse.

CHAPTER 3
Effects of VAWA, Are Abuse Shelters Helping the True? Victims of Domestic Violence?

Victims of battering are among the most vulnerable in our society. Thanks to the courageous efforts of tenacious volunteers, an estimated 1,200 domestic violence shelters are now located throughout the United States.

1. These shelters are considered the mainstay of treatment services for many victims of domestic violence. These shelters have done much good. But three decades after the establishment of the first shelters we need to ask: Are these programs reaching the persons who are most in need? Are they providing the necessary services? Most importantly, are they helping victims break the cycle of violence? In far too many cases, former residents say they suffered more mistreatment in the facility than they had experienced out-side, in one case triggering a suicide attempt:

Women violating women…It was repulsive.

2. Eventually, the feeling of constant siege by shelter staff and all the crazy making‘ interactions pushed me over the edge, and I cut myself with a knife.

3. One former shelter worker confessed: It wasn‘t the horrific stories that the women had to tell me that did me in. It was the horrific treatment I was supposed to dole out to these vulnerable women and their children, and the fact that I was to do it in the guise of care.

4. Even more tragic was this incident:
On October 21, 2007, Milaus Almore was admitted to the SafeSpace abuse shelter. Ten days later, the 26-year-old woman lay dead, victimized by an attack that left a gaping knife wound in her neck. The perpetrator was Marilyn Hooks, another resident at the Stuart, Florida, facility.

5.Insider reports suggest that these are not isolated accounts: Many safe houses now seemed more like prisons or social‘ bed and breakfasts

Shelter programs were no longer a safe place for all battered women.

6. Some of the stories I hear today break my heart…Programs have a Do Not Re Admit‘list longer than my arm. And just to be completely sure this woman can‘t use‘the system, these names get shared with every program within a 50-mile radius.

7. This Special Report probes the question, Are abuse shelters helping the true victims of domestic violence?

In assembling this report, we did an exhaustive search of research articles and reports, reviewed the websites of over 75 abuse shelters, analyzed tax records, and interviewed numerous former employees and residents of abuse shelters.

Background

What is the historical origin of abuse shelters, and what services do they provide?

Historical Background

The first abuse shelters were established in the United States in the 1970s. These programs were created in pursuit of a praiseworthy goal: to provide succor and safety to the victims of intimate partner violence. But over time, shelters began to shift their focus. Psychologist David Fontes recounts the experience of a woman who founded a well-known domestic violence shelter in California in the mid-1970s. She told me that about two years after she started the shelter, she had to leave this place that she herself had founded, Fontes explains.

Why?

Because radical feminists got on their board of directors and replaced her family system approach of treatment with a gender-feminist model. One advocate explained it differently We knew that foundations were not going to fund a house for a bunch of homeless bar dykes. We realized the language that would be understood was the language of battered women. Feminist ideology views domestic violence as a consequence of sexism in patriarchal society. Research, of course, portrays a very different reality.

Nonetheless, that ideology now pervades many abuse shelters and shapes the services they provide. One national survey found that only 25% of shelters focused on providing treatment and support for victims of abuse, while 45% viewed their main role as promoting feminist political activism. One state's certification program theorizes that abuse occurs when there is an imbalance of power and this situation is maintained and reinforced by our culture. And the Marin (California) Abused Women's Services states that its mission is to create innovative and dynamic solutions to end the violence, abuse, oppression, and intimidation of women—but says nothing about counseling, anger management, parenting skills, or job training.

Shelter Services

Shelters provide a broad range of services, including emergency housing, counseling, childcare, hotline, public outreach, and legal advocacy. Shelters are staffed by both paid employees and volunteers.

Upon arriving at the shelter, the client under-goes an intake assessment. Normally the intake worker does not verify the allegations of abuse. The client is required to sign a form to abide by shelter rules and not disclose what transpires inside the shelter. If a woman deviates from shelter policies, she may be involuntarily exited from the facility.

Daily routines are flexible. The woman may go to her place of employment, arrange for job interviews, or apply for welfare services. Or she may stay in the shelter, watching TV and socializing with other residents. Residents are allowed to come and go as they wish, although most shelters have curfew requirements.

Abuse shelters set a time limit for the stay typically 1 to 2 months. After that time, the resident may qualify for transitional housing.

Economics of Abuse Shelters

Abuse shelters no longer operate on the shoestring budgets they once had to contend with. The average shelter income and salary of executive directors at 115 shelters in five states is shown in the table:17

Region Midwest /State Indiana/Number of Shelters 24/ Average Total Income1 $741,125/ Average Salary of Executive Director2$43,958

Region Northeast /State Connecticut/ Number of Shelters 14/ Average Total Income1$1,619,714/ Average Salary of Executive Director2$80,846

Northwest /Oregon 25 $597,640 $42,880

Southeast /Florida 32 $1,965,109 $65,063
Southwest /Colorado 20 $811,950 $50,263

Average $1,169,796 $55,000

The bottom row shows shelter's average annual income nears $1.2 million. Extrapolating to all 1,200 shelters around the country, we estimate $1.4 billion is allocated to abuse shelters each year. These monies come from awards by federal and state governments, as well as charitable organizations and private contributions.

While the average salary of shelter directors is $55,000, some directors enjoy substantially higher compensation and benefits packages:

Paige Flink, Family Place, Dallas, Texas: $163,176

Kristine Hazzard, Center for Women and Families, Bridgeport, Connecticut: $102,604

Christel Nichols, House of Ruth, Washington, DC: $157,743

Shelters are paid on a fixed rate or cost reimbursement basis. Each month staff tallies up the services pro-vided including the number of shelter admissions, case management, counseling, safety plans, and so forth, and then submits a form for payment.

In addition, shelters provide legal and educational services.

These are the amounts that Florida shelters are paid:

1 IRS Form 990, Line L

2 IRS Form 990, Part V-A, Column C

3 $1,169,796 x 1,200 shelters = $1,403,755,200

Restraining order: $39020

Regional Youth Leadership Training: $75021

Statewide Primary Prevention Institute: $750

Curriculum Draft: $2,000

Curriculum Final: $1,000

Primary Prevention Programming with Youth: $5,000

Additional agreements and reporting forms are available. Notable is the fact that none of the forms require attestation of the severity of domestic violence or even that domestic violence occurred. The basic problem with fixed rate or cost reimbursement contracts is that financial incentives and violence-education objectives are not properly aligned. Shelters are not rewarded to reduce actual violence, but rather to increase the volume of services regardless of benefit or need.

How Many Persons in Abuse Shelters are truly "Battered"?

Abuse shelters declare their mission is to heal abused women and help them break the cycle of violence. But how many shelter residents are true victims of battering?

One way to answer that question is to assess their need for medical treatment:

1. In the San Diego area, a survey of 599 women and counselors from six abuse shelters identified client needs at the time of intake. Only 10% of persons identified a need for medical services, ranking it as the lowest priority.

2. In Florida, a series of focus groups assessed the needs of persons residing at abuse shelters around the state. Medical/health needs were mentioned only 9% of the time, with lack of low-cost dental care being the most salient medical need.

3. In Hawaii, only 8% of persons seen by shelter service providers required emergency medical attention and emergency care often includes non-abuse related problems.

Accounts from individual shelters portray a similar picture:

At the First Step shelter in Harrisonburg, Virginia, a former resident revealed, I soon discovered that I was the only woman there for protection purposes.

The former director of a mid-Atlantic shelter explained, Only about 1 in 10 women had experienced any kind of physical injury.

A former worker at an Oklahoma facility noted, In all the time that I volunteered there, I saw only one woman who showed signs of physical abuse.

Truth is told here, the shelter does not really serve primarily victims of domestic violence.

These are drug addicted and alcoholic women that use the cover of domestic violence for free services, according to a Clerk of Courts employee in reference to the Naples (Fla.) Shelter for Abused Women and Children. These surveys and reports consistently reveal that medical care is an issue for, at most, 1 in 10 shelter residents, and these medical care needs may have nothing to do with partner violence.

Why are shelters filled with persons who have suffered no physical injury?

The reason is evident intake workers seldom require proof of violence:

Shelters have few criteria that prohibit a client from being admitted, according to a California survey.

We don't really refuse anyone service, says the client services director of St. Jude House in Indiana.

At SafeSpace in Florida, We don't put up any more barriers for victims wanting to enter the shelter.

The YWCA Crisis Center in Enid, Oklahoma reassures potential residents, we do NOT require proof of abuse.

What are Residents" Needs?

If violence-related injuries are rare, then what are the needs of persons who reside in shelters? The answer to this question can be adduced from surveys of shelter residents, behavior assessments, and administrative records.

Housing

According to several surveys, housing is the most pressing need of shelter residents. Residential needs were cited by 84% of service providers in Hawaii, 48% of respondents in San Diego, and 17% of shelter residents in Florida. Not surprisingly, demand for shelter housing soars during times of economic distress. In Kansas, many of the same programs cited in a statewide listing of homeless shelters and services are the abuse shelters funded by the state's domestic violence coalition.

Substance Abuse

Alcohol and drug abuse is a problem for many shelter residents. In California, drugs and alcohol are involved in at least 50 to 60 percent of their domestic violence cases, according to a survey of shelter staff. In Hawaii, one in four shelter residents is referred for substance abuse services.

Among women admitted to La Casa in Las Cruces, New Mexico: 39% admitted to engaging in illegal activities to get drugs during the previous year. 85% were using alcohol during the incident that triggered the woman's shelter admission.

14% had injured themselves or others as a result of drinking. At the First Step shelter in Harrisonburg, Virginia, Most of the other women were using the shelter as a halfway house, according to one resident.

Interpersonal Aggression

Women are as likely as men to initiate partner violence. In one study, CDC researchers found that half of all cases of domestic violence are mutual, and of the non-mutual cases, 70% are female-perpetrated.44 In some cases, the female aggressor ends up in a shelter:

Erin Pizzey, founder of the first abuse shelter in the world,

reports that among the first 100 women who came to her program, were at least as violent as the partners that they were leaving.

A recent survey found 67% of women in shelters had committed one or more acts of severe partner violence in the previous year.

At one Alabama shelter, one-fourth of the residents were currently engaged in stalking their partners. Given these findings, it's not surprising that physical altercations sometimes erupt. One woman revealed, one night, a drug-addicted woman came into my room while I slept…She held a pocketknife to my throat and told me that if I didn't give her my phone card she'd slit my throat. Childcare and Parenting Skills Many women bring their children to the shelter—74% of residents according to one survey. These women often face challenges in providing appropriate childcare.

A recent study found 35% of shelter residents had committed one or more acts of severe aggression against their children in the previous year.

In California, 17% of residents had a case open with Child and Protective Services.

In Florida, 15% of shelter residents cited needs with childcare, making it the second leading priority. Poor parenting skills are also a concern. One former shelter worker laments the problem of mothers who return to the shelter so intoxicated and drugged up that they can't properly care for their own children.

In addition, some shelters fail to provide adequate supervision and protection for children:

Toddler Myliak Dale was run over while playing in the parking lot at SafeSpace in Florida.
At the Penelope House in Alabama, the night counselor discovered two women engaged in sexual activities while two children were in the room. Report of the incident left the shelter supervisor unfazed.

A misbehaving 8-year-old boy was confined to a closed van in the middle of summer—even though the manager at Another Way in Lake City, Florida knew of the action.

The Mismatch between Resident Needs and Shelter Services

The previous discussion reveals that shelter residents 'greatest needs are for housing, substance abuse treatment, violence counseling, and childcare/parenting skills. So how well do shelters meet these needs?

Housing

Housing needs are commonly addressed by shelter staff, and appear to be adequately met within existing resource constraints.

Substance Abuse

Abuse shelters do a generally inadequate job of treating alcohol and drug abuse, as revealed by these facts:

Shelters are not staffed by an appropriately qualified mental health professional.

Shelters may not enforce bans on illegal drug use, and even dissuade workers from reporting such incidents to the police.

Some shelters do not run background checks on job applicants, allowing persons with drug histories to become shelter employees.

Violence Counseling

Abuse shelters seldom provide counseling to address female-initiated aggression, because shelters do not acknowledge that the problem exists. One researcher reported receiving letters from violent women who were turned away or being offered no help when they called a crisis line or shelter. Or if shelters do offer services for women, they may portray female offenders as the victims. In researching this Special Report, the websites of over 75 shelters were reviewed. None stated it had a Certified Addictions Counselor or Licensed Alcohol and Drug Abuse Counselor on staff.

Childcare

No systematic survey of the adequacy of childcare arrangements at abuse shelters has been undertaken, although numerous instances of problems have been identified. An internet search of the terms abuse shelter and parenting skills reveals only a small fraction of shelters list this service on their websites. In conclusion, shelters appear to do an acceptable job in addressing the housing needs of residents.

In contrast, they perform poorly in providing counseling for sub-stance abuse and violent behavior to their partners. How well shelters respond to residents 'childcare needs is not known.

Harmful, Unethical, and Illegal Practices

Many shelters have engaged in a variety of activities that range from the harmful to the overtly unethical and even the patently illegal. Ten such activities are described here:

1. Endorsing a Victim Mindset

Abuse shelters aim to promote female empowerment, so it's remarkable that shelter workers would discourage women from moving on with their lives:

A former support group member found that the real message was to accept the indoctrination and embrace my victimhood…I realized that I never heard a facilitator encourage a woman to heal and move on with her life.

At Bethany House in Virginia, staff would infuriate the woman with propaganda, and then exploit the wife's frustration and anger as retaliation against the husband.

In Kentucky, certified Domestic Violence Advocates are required to reassure the client that she/he is not responsible for the abuse that she/he has suffered.

This statement is of course true, but in practice it is used to gloss over the problem of female-initiated abuse.

2. Harming Families

According to the belief that pervades most shelters, marriage is an inherently baleful institution. Consistent with that concept, shelters often require clients to terminate all contact with their spouses or partners:

At Safe horizon in New York City, clients may be forced to sever relationships with family and friends.

The only solution championed by the shelter was to get free from that big, malicious male, reveals a judge who served on the advisory committee of a Seattle-area shelter.

And Erin Pizzey, founder of the international shelter movement, worries that many shelters now foster a women-versus-men mentality. But many who are in an abusive relationship wish to continue the relationship at some level. Demanding that a woman stop seeing her partner is not only unrealistic, it runs afoul of the ethical principle that counselors must respect the rights of clients to make decisions.

3. Reliance on Coercive and Punitive Tactics

Shelters sometimes resort to extreme measures. In Massachusetts, one mother charged that clients in shelter-run groups were coerced by use of threats, intimidation, and fear of losing their children. In the end, she filed a lawsuit alleging a variety of civil rights violations. Shelter staff may be ill-disposed to residents who file a complaint:

Christina Wilson made a complaint about the Cherokee (Georgia) Family Violence Center. As a consequence, she was discharged from the facility.

At Women care in Bellingham, Washington, shelter staff exposed a resident's newly changed name in retaliation for a complaint she filed with the state human rights council.

4. Lack of Accountability

Abuse survivor Emi Koyama has recounted numerous problems with abuse shelters, attributing the deficiencies to the fact that there are little or no institutional mechanisms to hold service providers accountable to the actual needs and perspectives of people receiving services.

Obtaining even basic information about shelters often presents a challenge. Many shelters have no website, and even when they do, staff listings, financial data, and utilization reports are seldom posted. Some don't list a mailing address.

Performance objectives may consist of vague measures such as 65% of survivors of domestic violence that are provided services will have knowledge of community services.

Some shelter workers do not believe that they are accountable to their own board of directors.
At the Crossroads Safe house in Colorado, shelter employees abruptly resigned because they didn't want to acknowledge, frankly, the necessity of being governed by a board, revealed the board's president.

Many states have no regulations governing shelter operations. Or if they do, the standards may be optional, as in Arkansas, or administered by the state domestic violence council, which amounts to little more than self-regulation.

Following the stabbing death of Millie Almore at the SafeSpace shelter, an investigation found basic management tools such as an organizational chart were absent. The group concluded that Almore's untimely death was caused by the egregious failure of the entire agency to satisfactorily assure the health, safety, and welfare of both its clientele and staff.

5. Misuse of Confidentiality Protections

Abuse shelters sometimes thwart law enforcement efforts by citing confidentiality protections. In one case, a 12-year-old boy was raped by a shelter resident at a Tucson, Arizona, center. But staff barred police from interviewing the suspected perpetrator under the pretext that doing so would violate the center's confidentiality agreement with its residents.

In another case, a woman kidnapped a two-month old baby in Illinois and fled to the Hubbard House in Florida. Three weeks later the police discovered the woman out-side the shelter and arrested her. Some police departments release a jailed woman to a local shelter with the understanding that she is to be placed under house arrest. But shelter staffs have allowed the offender to come and go as she wishes, even ignoring curfew requirements:

Women on house arrest were breaking their 5:00 p.m. curfews by leaving at 5:30 p.m. and not returning until 6:00 a.m. But shush'—you can't tell their probation officers because that would breach their confidentiality, 'reveals one former worker.

Ironically, shelters may demand confidentiality for their own operations while at the same time riding roughshod over the protections that their clients are entitled to:

One African-American wrote, I was targeted because I was black … Nothing was confidential and what I discussed with staff was being discussed with clients.

One woman attending support meetings at Independence House in Massachusetts discovered that statements she had made to the group were being forwarded, verbatim, to a shelter supervisor and to the child protective services agency.

6. Inadequately Trained Staff

True victims of domestic violence face serious medical, psychological, and other problems. Some may be suicidal. These persons require the help of a trained professional. But shelter staff often lacks requisite qualifications. Shelter needs assessments from 13 states all revealed the need for well-trained staff.

A recent job announcement from the Dunn House in Oregon illustrates the concern. The advertisement states staff must be able to provide crisis intervention and lists the following qualifications:

The applicant must have a good driving record, pass a criminal check, and possess an understanding of domestic violence, oppression, and related issues —prior experience with persons in crisis would also be helpful.

But the position does not require the person to possess any academic degrees, relevant training, or proven expertise. Poorly trained staff may fail to recognize a problem that requires medical attention.

One nurse who volunteered at a shelter re-counted, I saw one woman who showed signs of physical abuse and shouldn't have been there; in fact I called an ambulance and had her sent to the hospital.

The problem is not limited to unqualified staff. In five states, no staff is assigned to work on shelter premises during night hours. And reflecting a lack of high ethical standards, staffs reportedly have subjected residents or employees to sexual harassment: At Bethany House in Virginia, Ms. Veronica and Ms. Liang were let go as house managers because of misconduct, misappropriation of Bethany House funds, and complaints of inappropriate sexual advances against the shelter residents.

At the Committee against Domestic Abuse in Mankato, Minnesota, nine employees alleged that they had been subjected to lewd proposals and inappropriately touched by senior staffers. As a consequence, the nine complainants (not the harassers) were relieved of their jobs.

7. Failure to Document or Report Incidents

Shelter policies require that incidents be documented in residents'files. But at Safe-Space in Florida, a post-homicide investigation revealed there had been no documentation of the offender's repeated death threats.

By law, shelter staff are required to report child abuse.

At Another Way in Florida, a 5-year-old was sexually assaulted by an older girl. Shelter staff failed to promptly report the incident to law enforcement, despite requests by the mother.

Why do such incidents often go unreported? According to a former employee, the staff is instructed to not document such incidents in order to forestall any consequences in case the Department of Children and Families (DCF) or a father wants to have the records subpoenaed.

8. Encouraging Residents to Make False Claims

Convincing a person to make a false allegation—known as suborning perjury is against the law. But that doesn't stop shelters from engaging in the practice. At SafeNet in Claremore, Oklahoma, employees induced a psychiatrically ill woman to file domestic violence charges against her husband. The judge later ruled, the claims of Crystal Hall as to abuse appear to the Court to have been manufactured or fabricated.

At Bethany House in Virginia, Women with almost no marital problems are declared abused and are coached by the staff to go to court and get a protective order against their husbands, reveal a former shelter volunteer. The Shield Foundation in Phoenix, Arizona, gives a whole new meaning to the word *Shakedown*.

The foundation first encourages women to file an order of protection and then tricks the men into breaking the Orders, getting them arrested. While a man languishes in jail; his house is ransacked for jewelry, electronic equipment, and other goods to be sold on the black market.

9. Financial Malfeasance

Shelters often lure donors with the promise that their contributions will be used to assist battered women. As explained previously in this Special Report, the majority of shelter residents are there for reasons other than domestic violence.

Fund-raising solicitations may contain falsehoods.

At Bethany House in Virginia, in their United Way of the National Capitol Area CVC Code 8046 Charity Application form 2002, which I was involved in; other volunteers and I were told to lie out-right, according to one woman. In California, the Community Fellowship for Battered Women opened a shelter subsidized by the proceeds from donated, used cars.

In 2002, the Fellow-ship took in $186,000, but only 5% of that amount was used to actually help victims of domestic violence.96 The IRS later revoked the group's tax-exempt status.

Embezzlement of funds has been a vexing problem, as well:

Denorvas Stevenson, former director of Project Safe in Shawnee, Oklahoma, was charged with eight counts of embezzlement after an audit revealed more than $56,000 in undocumented and unauthorized expenses.

Paulette Vang, former treasurer of Asian Women United of Minnesota, admitted to stealing $200,000 from the group to use for gambling.

Cindy Lou Shores, former head of the South Central Region Tribal Nations and Friends Domestic Violence Coalition in Oklahoma, was sentenced to 17 months in federal prison and ordered to pay $170,000 in restitution.

In 2008, the director of Domestic Violence Emergency Services in Roanoke, Virginia, was sentenced to a year in jail for stealing shelter funds. Some shelters spend funds for questionable purposes. In Florida, the Shelter for Abused Women and Children offers a beauty salon, promising women will now be pampered in a safe and convenient location.

One former resident at a San Francisco-area shelter complained that residents were often taken on shopping trips to the local mall where a wealth of unaffordable merchandise stared them in the face. One shelter visitor was shocked to see the shelter was full of unopened toys, bikes, and expensive furniture donations. Some shelters even tout their pet-care facilities.

10. Discriminatory Practices

By law, persons cannot be excluded from participation in or be denied the benefits of any program receiving federal assistance.106,107 Provisions in the Violence Against Women Act likewise state that male victims qualify for VAWA-funded services.108 But sex discrimination is not only common-place in the domestic violence industry it appears to represent the norm.109 Mission statements openly proclaim their intention to help women and children, with no mention of assisting men. Judy King Smith, director of the Rape and Domestic Violence Information Center in Morgantown, West Virginia, once admitted, *we do not shelter men in the shelter even if it's empty.*

Why?

For the simple reason that we were founded for the purpose of providing shelter to battered women and their children.

Even more shameful, most shelters refuse to admit male adolescent children. Only recently have a few shelters begun to rescind this ban.

In 2005, a lawsuit was filed against the state of California for unlawful denial of services against male victims. The Third District Court of Appeal in Sacramento later ruled that such practices violate constitutional equal protection guarantees.

Victims Betrayed, a Promise Unmet

This Special Report reaches four conclusions:

1. At most, 1 in 10 residents are in the shelter because of physical violence.

2. The most common needs of shelter residents are housing, misuse of alcohol and drugs, aggressive behavior, and childcare.

3. Abuse shelters do a poor job helping residents overcome substance abuse and partner relationship problems.

4. Many shelters engage in practices that are illegal, unethical, or harmful. Battering is a problem in our society and its victims desperately need our help. Each year the federal government allocates $1 billion to address this problem.

What this report reveals

This Special Report reveals victims of violence must overcome numerous barriers to get the assistance they need:

When a battered woman approaches a shelter for help, she may find it filled with persons who have suffered no physical violence; when a battered man comes for help, he is often turned away.

The victim is required to agree a series of intrusive rules, especially the demand that all contact with the partner be terminated.

Shelter employees lack expertise in crisis intervention and substance abuse counseling, and shelter volunteers may be working to resolve their own personal problems and thus unable to provide help to residents.

The number of residents with interpersonal aggression and substance abuse problems fosters an environment that is hostile and non-therapeutic.

Some shelters engage in practices that are unethical, harmful, or illegal. Fortunately there are a number of model abuse shelters in existence. These include the Antelope Valley (California) Domestic Violence Council that established the first co-ed shelter in the country.

Shelter director Carol Crabson explains, nobody deserves to get hit, whether they are 2 months old or 80 years old, whether they are a man or woman, child or teen. To my knowledge the female residents never had a problem with this practice, reveals the former shelter director.

Other praiseworthy programs are the South Lake Tahoe Women's Center that serves both male and female victims; the Bridge in Fostoria, Ohio providing a critical service for male victims; the Caring Place in Indiana which emphasizes the availability of services for all persons in need, and the Domestic Abuse Shelter Homes in Florida that offers a Women Who Batter Intervention Program.

But other shelters face an identity crisis:

Are they sanctuaries for victims struggling to break the cycle of violence?

Are they childcare facilities?

Way-stations for the homeless?

Refuges for persons in trouble with the law?

Or halfway houses for the addicted?

Abuse shelters are an indispensable resource to our communities and victims desperately need our help. But shelters have strayed from their intended purpose. We must now help shelters refocus on the singular challenge of helping the true victims of domestic violence overcome the cycle of abuse.

CHAPTER 4
VAWA-Funded Immigration Fraud Costs American Taxpayers $170 Million a Year

America prides itself on being a refuge for persons who immigrated to this country in search of a better life. Indeed, the story of immigration is the story of America. The United States currently has an estimated 38 million foreign-born residents, representing 13% of the total U.S. population. About one-third of these persons are in this country illegally, either by entering with no documentation at all or by providing false information on a visa application.

Visa fraud is a widespread problem. A Department of Labor study concluded that 54% of foreign visa applications contain false and possibly fraudulent information. Each year, the United States Citizenship and Immigration Service (CIS) disapproves some 20,000 applications for fraud. According to a Government Accountability Office report, immigration fraud may also involve criminal activity such as money laundering schemes, income tax evasion, or terrorist activity. Many of these cases involve marriage fraud.

According to Tom Depenbrock, special agent at the U.S. Department of State:
Marriage and visa fraud potentially threaten the national security of the United States ...
The U.S. visa is one of the most coveted items in the world...These foreign nationals who enter the country illegally via marriage fraud or any other type of fraud are defrauding the United States of immigration benefits to which they are not en-titled. Marriage scams traditionally involved American citizens who were enticed to marry foreign nationals. In a California case, U.S. citizens were paid to enter into sham marriages with Chinese citizens and were encouraged to fabricate love letters, pose for wedding pictures, and even file joint tax returns.

In recent years, a new form of immigration fraud has emerged that is subsidized by funds from the Violence against Women Act. This Special Report discusses how the immigration process is supposed to work, details the ways in which VAWA encourages immigration fraud, cites other VAWA-related problems, and calculates the tax-payer burden caused by immigration fraud.

How the Immigration Process is supposed to Work

The Citizenship and Immigration Service (CIS) is the federal agency that processes applications for visas, work permits, and citizenship. Immigration law allows an American citizen or permanent legal resident to sponsor a fiancé or spouse to obtain a Green Card (work authorization), permanent residency, and eventual citizenship.

The alien goes through the following steps:

VAWA LEGALIZES IMMIGRATION FRAUD

1. The person obtains a fiancé visa (K-1) or spouse visa (K-3) that allows the person to enter the United States.

2. Once the couple is married and residing in the U.S., the American citizen can sponsor the spouse to obtain temporary residency, based on the stability of the marriage.

3. After two years, the American citizen petitions the Citizenship and Immigration Service (CIS1) for permanent residency and eventual citizenship.

Persons who are approved under this process become eligible for a Green Card, permanent residency, and eventual citizenship. These entitle a person to receive the many government services and benefits that American citizens take for granted. To counter immigration fraud, the CIS has established policies and procedures to check illegal immigration. For example, Fraud Detection Units seek to identify false statements in immigration application forms. Persons who have engaged in immigration fraud are referred to Immigration and Customs Enforcement. The ICE ensures the departure from the United States of all removable aliens through the enforcement of the nation's immigration laws.

How VAWA Encourages Immigration Fraud

Immigration law has long included humanitarian provisions that allow foreign nationals subjected to persecution or extreme cruelty to seek refuge in the U.S. As the discussion below explains, this is the loophole that the Violence against Women Act has steadily expanded.

The original 1994 VAWA allowed immigrants who could demonstrate extreme hardship to bypass usual sponsorship requirements and self-petition. Self-petitioning means that the immigrant applies on his or her own behalf rather than being required to be sponsored by his or her spouse.

The 2000 renewal of VAWA expanded this concept and incorporated several new provisions:

Eliminated the extreme hardship requirement

Removed the U.S. residency requirement

Strengthened confidentiality provisions

Guaranteed legal representation

Eliminated deportation hearings (referred to as cancellation of removal)

From that point on, the Citizenship and Immigration Service has waged an increasingly difficult battle to maintain the integrity of the immigration and naturalization process.

1 After the 9/11 attacks, the Immigration and Naturalization Service (INS) were transferred to the Department of Homeland Security and renamed the Citizenship and Immigration Service.

The Violence against Women Act facilitates immigration fraud in eight ways:

1. Provides Free Legal Services to Those who Claim to be Victims

The Violence against Women Act authorizes up to $65 million per year for legal assistance under civil and criminal law. In addition, VAWA guarantees immigrants access to legal services by authorizing the Legal Services Corporation to represent a person who claims to be an abuse victim.

VAWA monies can be used to assist persons who claim to be victims of abuse, but not those accused of domestic violence an imbalance that undermines the even-handed administration of justice.

2. Broadens the Definition of Extreme Cruelty

For years, immigration groups and attorneys have sought to expand the definition of domestic violence to include actions that do not involve actual violence. Five examples are given below:

A. Legal Momentum (formerly National Organization for Women Legal Defense Fund) cites the following as examples of extreme cruelty:

Emotional abuse

Possessiveness Minimizing, denying, and blaming

B. A Catholic Legal Immigration Network manual states that extreme cruelty and battery include psychological abuse, accusations of infidelity, and acts that may not appear violent but are part of an overall pattern of violence. The publication does not explain what is meant by an act that may not appear violent.

C. Attorney Sally Kinoshita is a staff member of the VAWA-funded ASISTA project. In one article, Kinoshita provides examples of what she considers to be extreme cruelty: a need for apologies, possessiveness, and even what tone of voice was used.

D. The Legal Assistance Foundation of Chicago goes even further, claiming that indicators of extreme cruelty include:

Trying to get legal custody of children

Using gestures that create fear

Needing to walk on eggshells

Being possessive or jealous

E. The Immigrant Legal Resource Center in San Francisco publishes a Spanish-language flyer that cites emotional abuse as a form of domestic violence and openly promotes the benefits that await persons who make such allegations:

If you answered yes 'to any of these questions, you and your children could qualify for:

Work authorization, permission to live in the United States while your application is being processed, obtaining permanent residence without help from your husband medical care and government benefits such as money and food stamps.

These groups seem to agree that possessiveness however one might define the word is proof of extreme cruelty.

3. Eliminates the Need for Hard Evidence

Citizenship and Immigration Service examiners are instructed to evaluate VAWA petitions on what is referred to as the generous any credible evidence standard. According to an internal CIS memo, any credible evidence includes court documents, medical reports, police reports, or sworn statements (affidavits).

The instructions for Form I-360, the application form used by persons who file VAWA self-petitions, further explains that evidence of abuse includes reports and affidavits from police, judges and other court officials, medical personnel, school officials, clergy, social workers, or even an order of protection.

It is well known that civil definitions of domestic violence are broad, and that orders of protection are routinely issued with no hard evidence of abuse. Such orders are available even to persons who entered the country illegally. As the Arizona Domestic Violence Benchbook states, a denial of a protective order would be considered discrimination based on national origin which is specifically prohibited by law.

Sally Kinoshita of the ASISTA project takes the case even further. Arguing for what she calls the subjective test, she implies that not even a restraining order should be necessary:

A finding of extreme cruelty involves the examination of the dynamics of the relationship, the victim's sense of well-being before the abuse, the specific acts during the period of abuse, and the victim's quality of life and ability to function after the abuse.

The self-petitioner's own declaration should cover these factors.

By definition, a test is an objectively determined legal criterion. So a subjective test must be considered an oxymoron.

Immigration and Naturalization Act, Section 240(A)(b)(2)(D)

4. Removes the Substantial Connection Requirement

In CIS parlance, a person who enters the country without permission is referred to as an undocumented immigrant. By law, such persons cannot later apply for legal immigration status, because that would be an obvious incentive for persons to at-tempt to enter the country illegally. In the past, an exception to this rule was allowed if a person could demonstrate a substantial connection showing that extreme cruelty had forced the victim to escape to the United States.17 But under VAWA, the substantial connection requirement has been eliminated.18 The CIS recently revised its Adjudicator's Field Manual to read, The VAWA self-petitioner is not required to show a substantial connection between the qualifying battery or extreme cruelty and the VAWA self-petitioner's unlawful entry. This means that anyone who enters the country illegally and can produce a restraining order or affidavit, even with no hard evidence of abuse, is likely to be approved for a work permit and permanent residency.

5. Bans Evidence by the Alleged Abuser Showing that the Petitioner is Illegal

By law, the CIS classifies a person accused of being an abuser as a prohibited source. This means that the CIS is not allowed to accept any evidence from that person, even if it shows that the petitioner has engaged in illegal behavior. The alleged abuser is often the person who is most knowledgeable about the petitioner's actions. As a result, the CIS will not deport a VAWA petitioner, even if presented with credible evidence that the petitioner is illegal. As one CIS employee admitted, If an abuser reports that the victim is undocumented, they will not pursue the person.

6. Educates Persons on How to Work the System

The Violence against Women Act funds efforts to educate attorneys and other legal personnel on how to take full advantage of VAWA's immigration provisions. In 2006, the Department Of Justice Office on Violence against Women awarded $363,160 to the Legal Assistance Foundation of Chicago. The group provides the following advice to attorneys on how to prepare a client for an interview with the CIS adjudicator:

Some officers may try to trick your client into admitting information that could make her inadmissible and ineligible to adjust, e.g., when was the last time you? Immigration and Naturalization Act, Section 1367(a) voted in the U.S.?

This is relevant because only U.S. citizens can vote; voting illegally is a ground of inadmissibility. 'Such questions are not tricks.

They are legitimate tools to determine whether a potential American citizen is of good moral character.

The following year, the Office on Violence Against Women (OFFICE ON VIOLENCE AGAINST WOMEN) awarded a $1.35 million grant to the ASISTA project, which maintains an immigration Information Clearinghouse and publishes the ASISTA News.

The Fall 2006 issue of the newsletter features an article that encourages women to file a VAWA self-petition if they are in a relationship marked by possessiveness or even a need for apologies. Ironically, the very next article in the newsletter discusses the ABA ethical requirements to bring only meritorious claims and contentions and to disclose misrepresentations or falsehoods.

7. Affords a Loophole for Persons Undergoing Deportation Hearings

If an immigrant is discovered without proper documentation, the CIS refers the per-son to Immigration and Customs Enforcement (ICE) to initiate removal proceedings. But under VAWA, a mere claim of abuse can cancel the deportation proceedings. At a conference session, a CIS official was asked how many VAWA cases have been referred to ICE for removal.

The categorical answer was: Currently, cases are not being specifically referred for removal. Even if the immigrant had been previously ordered to leave the country and re-entered illegally, the CIS official explained, No, VSC is not passing them on to ICE.423 Again, the abuse excuse affords the person a virtually free pass.

8. Eliminates Penalties for Illegal Aliens Who Fail to Leave

The Immigration and Naturalization Act allows for a variety of financial and administration sanctions to be imposed on illegal aliens who are ordered to leave the country but fail doing so. The Government Accountability Office has criticized the CIS for its leniency in applying these sanctions. According to the Violence against Women Act, such sanctions cannot be applied if the extreme cruelty or battery was at least one central reason for the illegal aliens overstaying the grant of voluntary departure. And since extreme cruelty is viewed so broadly, almost any illegal alien who claims abuse can escape punishment.

VSC refers to the Vermont Service Center, the CIS facility where all VAWA self-petitions are processed. VAWA Title VIII, Section 812.

In sum, VAWA condones and promotes immigration fraud through a variety of legal and administrative strategies, even for persons who entered the country illegally.

Elizabeth Howard of Arizona reveals how her father's wife had threatened to kill him. When he called for help, the police arrested both of them. As soon as she got out of jail, she went to the local domestic violence shelter to have him removed from his home.

Then she held yard sales to rid herself of his personal possessions. A friend at work whose family migrated here from Mexico told me it's common knowledge that if a woman marries a U.S. citizen and it doesn't work out, she can claim abuse and get the resources she needs, Howard sadly notes.

Other VAWA-Related Problems

The Violence against Women Act gives rise to other serious problems, including extortion, sex discrimination, and the inability of those falsely accused to prove their innocence.

Those Falsely Accused are Unable to establish their Innocence

The most fundamental principle of a criminal justice system is that the accused must be given the opportunity to refute an allegation of wrongdoing. But under VAWA immigration provisions, a person accused of partner abuse has no legal standing to refute the claim. Indeed, as a result of VAWA confidentiality provisions, the alleged abuser often is not informed that the allegations were made.

There are many reported examples of persons falsely accused. In one case, Dr. Michael Wnuk, professor at the University of Wisconsin-Milwaukee, became romantically involved with a Polish woman, Lidiia Kolisnichenko. Wnuk had been diagnosed with cancer. While on a trip to Poland, he met Kolisnichenko, who promised that she could cure his disease if he would agree to marry her. A month later they returned to the United States and married. While he was away on another business trip, Kolisnichenko filed a self-petition with the immigration service claiming mental abuse. Three days later, she staged a confrontation in which she ran from the house, claiming that she was being chased by Wnuk. The police report stated that there were no injuries in the spot where she reported she was hit.

Later she would claim she had been frequently raped.

On the basis of these unproven allegations, Kolisnichenko was able to obtain assistance from three attorneys from federally-funded legal aid programs. She eventually procured her Green Card. Wnuk sadly wrote, Lidiia followed the script shown on the Internet site Green Card Girls – A Dangerous Breed. 'VAWA Title VIII, Section 817. Michael Wnuk was victimized twice, first by the person who filed the false allegation, and then by a series of legal maneuvers that made it impossible for him to prove his innocence.

Extortion

Under Indian law, dowry payments are banned, and the mere allegation of dowry demands is viewed with the presumption of guilt. So what happens if a legal immigrant from India later marries an Indian woman and then declines to file an immigration petition on her behalf? Under Indian law she has a legal recourse to allege that her husband and his family are demanding a dowry payment. The implausible nature of some of these claims is revealed in this case:

In 2002, an engineer living in California traveled to his native India to marry. Following the ceremony, the couple returned to the United States. But she did not like California and began to drink heavily. After she bit him during an argument, they decided to divorce. But that was likely to complicate her Green Card application. In early 2004, she returned to India, where she was soon served with divorce papers.

In retaliation, she filed a claim against the man's parents, brothers, sister, and sister-in-law, who were living in India, alleging that they had demanded a wedding dowry payment, even though two years had now passed since the wedding. The police inspector eventually concluded, On investigation it is found that there is absolutely no truth regarding the facts mentioned in this complaint, and the woman was later found guilty of immigration fraud. Nonetheless, the innocent man was still forced to pay more than $60,000 plus attorney fees, which depleted his 401K plan and savings.

In response to numerous complaints, the U.S. State Department issued a travel advisory. Many of the charges stem from the U.S. citizen's inability to provide an immigrant visa for his prospective spouse to travel immediately to the United States, the advisory warns. John Peters, the State Department's Citizen Services Specialist for India, cautions, the fact that we issued a warning should be an indication of how widespread the problem is.

Sex Discrimination is fostered

Women are at least as likely as men to engage in partner violence.

A recent 32-nation survey of dating couples found that among severely violent couples, in 55% of cases the violence was mutual, in 16% of cases the violence was male-only, and 29% of the time it was female-only.

In Mexico, partner violence follows a similar picture: 65% mutual, 16% male only, and 19% female-only. Similar patterns could be expected among Mexican immigrants as well.

But organizations that advise immigrants on VAWA procedures routinely fail to acknowledge the existence of male victims and make little attempt to be gender inclusive in their terminology abusers are routinely referred to as he and victims are depicted in the female gender. Thus, male victims of domestic violence may find their allegations ridiculed and their needs dismissed.

The following account reveals the psychological, physical, and financial toll of a false allegation:

Avi Charnis emigrated from Israel to the United States filled with the hope of living the American dream. He eventually became an American citizen. Later, he met a woman named Elena Mamedova, who he sponsored to come to the U.S. on a fiancée visa. Within a few months after their marriage, she made the claim that Sharnis had battered her—with no evidence or proof. Charnis was handcuffed and taken to jail. Devastated by the turn of events, Charnis could not eat or sleep. He lost weight and his hands began to shake. Soon he lost his job.

Tragedy followed tragedy as he lost his health insurance and was then diagnosed with cancer. During all of this, he had to defend himself against the baseless charges of battery and abuse. As soon as Mamedova received her Green Card, she dropped her abuse complaint. With his legal ordeal now over, Charnis left the country where he had worked for more than 20 years. America turned out to be a wicked stepmother for me, he lamented.

Voices of American Immigration Fraud Victims, a victim advocacy group, notes that such stories are not uncommon. Innocent citizens find themselves devastated by the double betrayal of a false charge of abuse, followed by the ex's Green Card Award Ceremony that the American learns about from the confines of his jail cell.

VAWA: The Low-Cost, Sure-Fire Way to Achieve Legal Status

The 2000 renewal of the Violence Against Women Act openly stated that its goal was to remove immigration laws as a barrier that kept battered immigrant women and children locked in abusive relationships [emphasis added].39 Several years later, it appears that this objective has been largely achieved. The immigration provisions of VAWA, along with their broad interpretation by the Citizenship and Immigration Service and lax implementation by VAWA grantees:

Provide free legal services to persons who merely claim abuse

Broaden the definition of extreme cruelty to the point of near meaninglessness

Weaken or eliminate traditional standards of proof

Remove the substantial connection standard

Ban credible evidence of illegal behavior

Educate persons on how to take advantage of these provisions

Override deportation hearings

Provide a loophole for persons in the midst of deportation

VAWA provides incentives for the filing of false claims, removes many of the traditional barriers designed to control illegal immigration, and weakens the traditional sanctions that can be applied against an illegal.

This creates a Sword of Damocles that hangs over the head of every American citizen who develops a romantic relationship with an immigrant. Thus, a VAWA self-petition has become the cheapest and fastest way for a foreigner to achieve legal status.

The Violence against Women Act affords generous services, benefits, and legal rights to illegal immigrants who allege abuse, while overriding the civil rights of law-abiding American citizens.

CHAPTER 5
False Allegations of Domestic Violence Cost Taxpayers $20 Billion a Year

false allegations of domestic violence have become so commonplace that they now threaten the integrity of the American legal system.

As a former domestic violence prosecutor in Georgia revealed:

As politically incorrect as it is to say, many women file charges against boy-friends/spouses on a routine basis, and then recant the charges when the cases come to trial. Some of the alleged perpetrators are really guilty, and [a] very large percentages (though not majority) are not guilty of anything except making the woman in their life angry. Indeed, legal observers note that in four out of five cases, the person who calls for police assistance later recants or drops the charges.

In addition, 2–3 million restraining orders for partner abuse are issued each year in the United States, many of which are false or unnecessary. One study conducted by the Massachusetts Trial Court found that less than half of restraining orders involved even an allegation of violence.

Legal experts now acknowledge that non-meritorious claims are often made during a divorce proceeding to gain a legal edge:

In California, the State Bar admits that protective orders are almost routinely issued by the court in family law proceedings, even when there is relatively meager evidence and usually without notice to the restrained person…it is troubling that they appear to be sought more and more frequently for retaliation and litigation purposes.

An article in the Illinois Bar Journal notes that allegations of abuse and restraining orders are often used as part of the gamesmanship of divorce.

Elaine Epstein, former president of the Massachusetts Bar Association, revealed, everyone knows that restraining orders and orders to vacate are granted to virtually all who apply….In many cases, allegations of abuse are now used for tactical advantage. This report considers a claim or statement that is untrue or unnecessary to be a false allegation. Persons who knowingly make such accusations are almost never subject to legal sanctions.

Casey Gwinn, a San Diego prosecutor and national authority on domestic violence, admits, If we prosecuted everybody for perjury that gets on a witness stand and changes their story, everybody would go to jail, adding that he never had any desire to have false accusers prosecuted.

A previous RADAR report, A Culture of False Allegations: How VAWA Harms Families and Children, documents how a nexus of broad legal definitions, undue incentives, get-tough law enforcement and prosecution programs, child custody practices, and biased judicial education programs have created a climate that is ripe for legal abuse. The report concludes, there can be little doubt that VAWA has contributed to our culture of false allegations.

Even though false allegations are common, to date the financial impact was been unknown. This Special Report outlines the human impact and estimates the public costs associated with such accusations.

How Does Domestic Violence Programs Encourage False Allegations?

1. State domestic violence coalitions lobby for broader definitions of domestic violence, weaker evidentiary requirements, and less attention to due process.

2. Domestic violence coalitions push for generous benefits to persons awarded restraining orders based on scant standards of proof.

3. Abuse shelters, sometimes referred to as one-stop divorce shops, dispense free legal advice.

4. Legal aid clinics script clients' court testimony, which amounts to a form of suborning perjury.

5. Hotlines and websites encourage persons to seek restraining orders for abuse that is one-time, minor, or only emotional in nature.

6. Prosecutors refuse to sanction false allegations of abuse.

7. Judicial education seminars advise judges to play it safe by issuing the restraining order.

8. Checklists instruct judges to hold batterers accountable and increase safety for victims, but say nothing about assuring due process or safeguarding the principle of innocent until proven guilty.

Not surprisingly, VAWA-funded domestic violence programs are largely silent on the matter of false allegations. The term doesn't even appear on the website of the ABA Commission on Domestic Violence.

Sally of Vallejo, California, had been ordered by the court to vacate the family home. But the day she was supposed to move out, she accused her husband, Joe, of pushing her. Joe spent the night in jail. The judge later dismissed the charges. Even the cop was apologetic, said Joe. She told me she didn't believe [my wife], but that she had to arrest me because the accusation had been made.

So whatever came of the notion of probable cause as a requirement for arrest?

The Human Cost of False Allegations

Consider this scenario:

You and your spouse are having marital problems and one night you get into an argument. Your spouse gets angry and calls the police. The police arrive with a restraining order. They force you to vacate the house and refrain from any contact with your partner for two weeks. You feel devastated, since there had been no physical violence. At the hearing, the judge asks, Can you prove that your spouse was not fearful during the argument? How would you demonstrate your innocence?

It is difficult to overestimate the impact of a false accusation of partner violence.

A false claim stigmatizes and humiliates the person and may require him to spend substantial sums to clear his good name. He may lose his security clearance and his job. Even if he is found innocent of the charges, a record of the incident may remain on the books, harming his reputation and career.

And the children may become caught up in a series of claims, counter-claims, and eventual parental alienation. The tragic case of Emily Hindle illustrates the complex dynamics of these cases: 14 Karl Hindle and Sheila Fuith had a baby girl while the two were living in England. Born in early 2002, Emily was diagnosed with lazy eye (amblyopia), which required that she wear an eye patch several hours each day to save her eyesight.

Less than a year after Emily's birth, Fuith tired of the relationship and decided to re-turn to the United States. In order to bolster her custody claim, she accused Hindle of domestic violence. With no evidence or due process, the U.S. State Department granted a visa and authorized Emily's removal. Back in the United States, without warning, Fuith terminated Emily's eye patch therapy and then attempted to place her with a family that included a convicted pedophile.

When the father learned of these developments, he resorted to every available channel to reinstitate his daughter's therapy and have her returned to his care. Fuith moved from state to state, continuing to accuse Hindle of stalking, harassment, and domestic violence. But police investigations and court findings repeatedly found Hindle innocent of the allegations.

As of 2008, Hindle had not seen his daughter for two years. Emily is now blind in one eye. Emily has paid a terrible price and continues to do so—as do we all, laments the heartbroken dad. False allegations take a financial toll, as well. To estimate the financial cost of false allegations of abuse, we must calculate:

1. The total sum spent on domestic violence programs in the United States

2. The frequency of false allegations and their impact on family fragmentation.

These questions are addressed in the following two sections.

What Does the Nation Spend for Domestic Violence Programs?

A previous RADAR report concluded that the federal government spends $1 billion annually for domestic violence programs. This is a conservative estimate, because it does not include the millions of dollars spent on VAWA-mandated housing and immigration programs, including public benefit programs for persons who engage in immigration fraud by falsely claiming to be a domestic violence victim. That $1 billion estimate does not include financial support by state and local governments, by charities, or by individual donors. The amounts from those sources can be estimated by examining the public costs in one state—West Virginia—and then extrapolating to the national level.

Projected Expenses

A. According to a recent analysis by Dr. Benjamin Foster, state and local governments in West Virginia pay for these DV-related programs:
Law enforcement: $11.0 million
Family and magistrate courts: $4.4 million
Public defender: $0.5 million
West Virginia Coalition Against Domestic Violence: $6.9 million
These four cost categories total $22.7 million annually.1

B. Other DV-related expenses include the following:
Costs to hire 10 additional family court judges: $2.7 million

The Realities of Domestic Violence.

Costs for incarceration in state prisons: $4.8 million. (see Appendix, Calculation #1)
1 Figures do not add to $22.7 million due to rounding error.
Costs for supervision of parolees and probationers: $1.8 million.
(see Appendix, Calculation #2)
These three cost categories total $9.3 million annually.

C. Additional costs associated with domestic violence programs, based on conservative estimates:

Buildings, vehicles, and other capital expenses for criminal and civil justice courts and law enforcement departments: Estimated expense: $1 million

Costs for incarceration in local jails: Estimated expense: $4 million

Personnel involved in prosecuting criminal DV cases, including prosecutors, judges, bailiffs, and their assistants: Estimated expense: $3 million

Circuit Court and higher courts involved in processing domestic violence cases: Estimated expense: $1 million

Non-personnel operations for family and magistrates courts: Estimated expense: $0.5 million
Other expenses associated with criminal DV cases such as building maintenance: Estimated expense: $0.5 million

Offender treatment programs: Estimated expense: $0.5 million

These seven cost categories total $10.5 million annually.

Adding the amounts from A, B, and C, the annual public expense associated with domestic violence in West Virginia is an estimated $42.5 million.

Projected Income

The federal government pays these amounts for domestic violence programs in West Virginia:
Violence Against Women Act:21 $8.9 million
Victims of Crime Act: $1.8 million (see Appendix, Calculation #3)
Family Violence Prevention and Services Act:22 $0.2 million
These federal funds total $10.9 million annually.

1.Assuming that these programs are not operating at a deficit, the difference between $42.5 million and $10.9 million—$31.6 million—must come from non-federal sources, including state and local governments and private and charitable contributions.

2. In 2005, Cook County, Ill. renovated its Domestic Violence Courthouse at a cost of $51 million. Cook County Information Center. Press Release, 2005. http://www.friendsofdowntown.org/events.html

3. The Administrative Office of the United States Courts estimates that in FY2004, the following annual costs per inmate: Imprisonment: $23,206; Community correction centers: $20,103.

http://www.uscourts.gov/ttb/may05ttb/incarceration-costs/index.html
Thus, non-federal sources represent about three-quarters (see Appendix, Calculation #4) of the total costs for domestic violence programs in West Virginia.

These figures are summarized in the table below (numbers are in millions of dollars):
Projected Expenses Projected Income
Foster analysis: $22.7 VAWA: $ 8.9
Other expenses: 9.3 VOCA: 1.8
Estimated costs: 10.5 FVPSA: 0.2
Non-federal: 31.6
Totals $42.5

Estimated National Expenditure for Domestic Violence

We know that the federal government spends about $1 billion a year for domestic violence programs. If we extrapolate the three-quarters fraction calculated from West Virginia to the national level, we conclude that each year approximately $4 billion is spent for domestic violence programs. Because of the exclusion of VAWA-mandated costs related to housing and immigration, the $4 billion is a conservative estimate.

False Allegations and Their Impact on Family Fragmentation

One of the most important consequences of an allegation of domestic violence is the award of child custody to the accusing parent. One-third of American children grow up in single-parent households, placing these children at far higher risk of poverty, child abuse, and a broad range of social pathologies. So how many children are involved in false allegations of abuse, and what is the financial impact on society?

These calculations answer that question:

1. Each year more than one million American children experience the divorce of their parents.

2. About one-fourth of divorces involve an allegation of intimate partner violence.

Many children in single-parent households have parents who did not marry. There is no known data available on the rate of allegations of domestic violence or the percentage of false allegations among such couples. Therefore, this analysis extrapolates data from divorcing couples to all separated couples.

It is unknown what percentages of separations by cohabiting, unmarried adults involve an allegation of DV. For purposes of this analysis, we assume the same percentage among married and unmarried couples who separate.

3. In 60%–80% of cases the allegation is deemed to be unnecessary or false.

4. Each year, about 175,000 children are involved in a divorce with a false allegation of domestic violence. (See Appendix, Calculation #5)

5. In all but two states, divorce judges are required to consider allegations or findings of intimate partner violence in the award of child custody. These children grow up in single parent households with restricted or no contact with the other parent, usually the father.

6. The annual taxpayer costs for federal poverty programs arising from fatherlessness and family fragmentation are conservatively estimated at $100 billion28 to $112 billion.29 Thus by conservative estimates, the U.S. taxpayer pays $20 billion annually to support single-parent families that have been harmed by a false allegation of domestic violence. (See Appendix, Calculation #6)

The $20 billion figure excludes other significant costs associated with false allegations, including:

1. The direct personal costs of divorce and lost productivity, estimated to be $14,364 per couple.

2. The legal costs of defending oneself from a false allegation, a process that can be financially and emotionally devastating.

3. The non-monetary costs arising from loss of a normal parent-child bond and its psychological impact on children.

4. The additional taxpayer burden arising from VAWA-supported immigration fraud, estimated at $170 million a year.31

False Allegations: A National Crisis

Our nation's legal system was founded on a series of protections, enumerated in the Bill of Rights, that assure due process for any citizen accused of an offense. But in the past 20 years, those protections have been whittled away in the name of holding batterers accountable and assuring the safety of victims. It is no surprise, then, that false allegations have become commonplace.

It is recognized that allegations of domestic violence may be more common in divorces involving children. However, no data is available on this point. Therefore we make the assumption that the rate of false allegations is the same in divorces with and without children.

This Special Report makes three key findings:

1. Each year our nation spends $4 billion for domestic violence programs.

2. Each year, about 175,000 children are involved in a divorce with a false allegation of domestic violence.

3. These claims, in turn, contribute to $20 billion in public costs and taxpayer burden associated with fragmented families.

We have reached the point where false allegations represent a personal, family, financial, and legal crisis in our society. In the long term, false claims harm the true victims of violence:

Judge Rucker Smith of Georgia was assaulted by his ex-girlfriend. Even though she had instigated the incident and he did not retaliate, he was charged with battery. A jury later acquitted Smith of all charges. The judge subsequently opined, For some-one to falsely accuse another out of anger and vengeance silences the voices of the many real victims.

Legal reforms must be instituted so that the real victims of violence can get the help they need, so persons are no longer falsely accused, so families are safeguarded, and so our children are protected.

Appendix Calculations

Calculation #1:
1. In 2005, the West Virginia correctional population was 5,312, of whom 56% (2,975 inmates) were incarcerated for a violent crime.33
2. Of these 2,975 inmates, an estimated 7% (208 persons) were imprisoned for a crime against an intimate partner.34
3. The annual cost for imprisonment is $23,206 per inmate.35
4. Calculation: 208 inmates x $23,206 = $4,826,848

Calculation #2:
1. In 2003, there were 6,430 probationers and 999 parolees in West Virginia, of whom an estimated 7% (520 persons) had been imprisoned for domestic violence.36
2. The annual costs for supervision by probation officers are $3,453 per person.37
3. Calculation: 520 persons x $3,453 = $1,795,560

Calculation #3:
1. Number of DV victims served in 2002: 16,293
2. Number of victims of adult sexual assault (SA) served: 1,406
3. Total victims served: 33,899
4. Percentage DV and SA: (16,293 + 1,406) ÷ 33,899 = 52.2%38
5. Total VOCA expenditures for domestic violence and sexual assault: $1.8 million39

Calculation #4:
$31.6 million ÷ $42.5 million = 74.4%

Calculation #5:
1,000,000 children x 0.25 DV allegation rate x 0.70 rate of false allegations = 175,000 children

Calculation #6:
$112 billion x 0.25 DV allegation rate x 0.70 false allegation rate = $19.6 billion

CHAPTER 6
$1 Billion for DV Programs That Misuse Taxpayer Money and Place Victims at Risk

Each year the federal government spends $1 billion on the national effort to combat domestic violence. Most persons assume such programs are indeed effective and succeeding in curbing partner violence. But a growing body of research casts doubt on that assumption. A recent incident in a Florida abuse shelter illustrates the concern:

Marilyn Hooks, 25, and Milaus Almore, 8 weeks pregnant, were residents in the SafeSpace shelter in Stuart, Florida. On October 31, 2007, the women fell into an argument. Hooks pulled out a knife and fatally stabbed Almore. Hooks was later charged with second-degree murder. Before the incident, Hooks had made death threats to a staff member and resident, but the shelter manager ignored staff recommendations to evict the woman.

Afterwards the manager was terminated from her position. Over the years, the U.S. Congress has enacted three major laws to fund domestic violence programs and services:

Victims of Crime Act – 19841
Family Violence Prevention and Services Act – 19842
Violence against Women Act – 19943

These laws fund a variety of initiatives administered by the DHHS (DEPARTMENT OF HEALTH AND HUMAN SERVICES) and DOJ (Department Of Justice). The Department of Defense Family Advocacy Program4 and the federally-funded Legal Services Corporation also have major domestic violence components. The total cost of these three laws and two programs is estimated at $915 million annually.

1.In FY2005 the cap on VOCA monies was set by Congress at $620 million: http://www.ojp.usDepartment Of Justice.gov/ovc/publications/factshts/vocacvf/fs000310.pdf , page 2.

According to the National Alliance to End Sexual Violence, Domestic violence and sexual assault victims make up half of those receiving services under VOCA: http://www.naesv.org/ResourcesVOCA.pdf .

This statement is corroborated by a report from the Idaho State Wide Assistance Report that notes 52.4% of the 7,909 persons who received VOCA monies in 2002 were victims of domestic violence or adult sexual assault: http://www.ojp.usDepartment Of Justice.gov/ovc/fund/sbsmap/ovcpfid1.htm .

Therefore, it is estimated that VOCA provides $310 million (620 x .5 = 310) each year for domestic violence and sexual assault services.

2. Funded at $125 million in FY2008: http://www.whitehouse.gov/omb/expectmore/detail/10002150.2004.html

3. In FY2005 the Department of Justice was authorized $391.8 million under the Violence Against Women Act: http://www.ilw.com/immigdaily/news/2005,0802-crs.pdf ,Table 3.

4.The Department of Defense Family Advocacy Program – http://www.defenselink.mil/fapmip/ was funded $22 million in 2003: http://www.ojp.usDepartment Of Justice.gov/ovc/ncvrw/2005/pg4b.html

5. The Legal Services Corporation was appropriated $348 million in FY2007: http://www.lsc.gov/about/FY07app.php .

According to the LSC Fact Sheet, 38% of its caseload involves family matters, specifically domestic violence and child custody: http://www.lsc.gov/about/factsheet_whatislsc.php .

Assuming half of the 38% pertains to domestic violence, it is estimated that the LSC devotes $66 million for domestic violence services: $348 million x 19% = $66 million.

Three other federal programs exist for which the costs are unknown, but are believed to represent a substantial amount:

Citizenship and Immigration Service

Department of State Office of International Women's Issues

Housing and Urban Development Emergency Shelter Grants Program and Community Development

Block Grants

Thus the total federal outlay for domestic violence is conservatively estimated at $1 billion dollars a year. Revenues from state governments and private and charitable contributions amount to an additional $3 billion per year allocated to the domestic violence industry.8 several bodies have been established to provide oversight to federally funded programs:

1. Government Accountability Office, arm of the U.S. Congress that investigates how taxpayer dollars are spent

2. Office of Management and Budget, White House office that oversees the conduct of federal agencies

3. Office of the Inspector General, conducts audits and investigations to deter waste, fraud, abuse, and misconduct This Special Report identifies three major problems in the way domestic violence programs are being administered at the Department of Justice and the Department of Health and Human Services:

1. Lack of Accountability

2. Federal Mismanagement of Grant Monies

3. Grantee Misconduct and Fraud

These problems compromise the availability and effectiveness of programs and services designed to curb intimate partner aggression.

1. Lack of Accountability

In order for a program to be accountable, it must have clearly-defined outcome goals. In turn the achievement of these goals is monitored via management information systems that collect data in a timely manner on appropriate process and outcome measures. But as the following sections reveal, outcome goals and viable in-formation systems have long been elusive for domestic violence programs at the Department of Justice and Department of Health and Human Services.

Victims of Crime Act: $310 million.
Family Violence and Prevention Services Act: $125 million.
VAWA: $392 million. Department of Defense: $22 million.
Legal Services Corporation: $66 million.

Department of Justice

Over the years the accountability measures at the DEPARTMENT OF JUSTICE Office on Violence Against Women (OFFICE ON VIOLENCE AGAINST WOMEN) have come under scrutiny. As early as 2002, the Government Accountability Office testified to Congress about Office on Violence against Women -administered programs. The GAO chided the OFFICE ON VIOLENCE AGAINST WOMEN that information systems are only as good as the management that wields them. In response, OFFICE ON VIOLENCE AGAINST WOMEN officials acknowledged that they were not satisfied with the performance measures they used to gauge their performance.9 In 2006, the Office of Management and Budget raised a similar concern, directing the

Office on Violence against Women to:

Set more ambitious goals for program performance to ensure continuous improvement in program results and Develop a comprehensive evaluation plan for the Violence against Women Programs to obtain better information on the program's impacts. Two years later, the OFFICE ON VIOLENCE AGAINST WOMEN had not established any new goals or drafted an evaluation plan.10

Department of Health and Human Services

The Administration for Children and Families at Department of Health and Human Services is responsible for administering grants authorized by the Family Violence Prevention and Services Act.

DEPARTMENT OF HEALTH AND HUMAN SERVICES enumerates its grant requirements in the Grants Policy Statement, including the requirement that grantees comply with the Education Amendments of 1972 which prohibit discrimination on the basis of sex.11
So how well is the DEPARTMENT OF HEALTH AND HUMAN SERVICES accountability systems operating?

In 2005 the Office of Management and Budget performed an audit of the DEPARTMENT OF HEALTH AND HUMAN SERVICES domestic violence program. On the Program Results/Accountability measure, the DEPARTMENT OF HEALTH AND HUMAN SERVICES scored only 7% out of a possible 100%. To remedy the deficiency, the OMB directed DEPARTMENT OF HEALTH AND HUMAN SERVICES to develop appropriate national grantee-supported performance outcome measures to demonstrate improved efficiencies or cost effectiveness.

Appropriate outcome measures would include measures of intimate partner violence that are found in government-funded surveys such as the National Youth Risk Behavior Study12 and the National Longitudinal Study of Adolescent Health.13 But by early 2008, the DEPARTMENT OF HEALTH AND HUMAN SERVICES had not developed even draft outcome indicators.

In 2007, the Government Accountability Office audited the DEPARTMENT OF HEALTH AND HUMAN SERVICES domestic violence grant records. To its surprise, they learned that the DEPARTMENT OF HEALTH AND HUMAN SERVICES had not established standardized reporting methods, time periods, or forms for grant recipients. The data quality was so poor that the GAO concluded, we could not be assured that any survey data we obtained would be consistent and reliable enough for analysis of the specific information required.

Yet the DEPARTMENT OF HEALTH AND HUMAN SERVICES officials defended the sub-standard information, claiming that grant recipients do not have the resources to devote to these data collection efforts and asserting that collecting demographic data would overburden grantees.

Apparently DEPARTMENT OF HEALTH AND HUMAN SERVICES officials believe that report-ing basic utilization information is merely a paper-work exercise.

2. Mismanagement of Grant Monies

When accountability systems are weak, financial mismanagement becomes a greater concern. Such is the case at the Department Of Justice Office on Violence against Women. The Department Of Justice policies are outlined in its OJP Financial Guide16 and other documents.17, 18 Administering about 1,500 grants annually, the OFFICE ON VIOLENCE AGAINST WOMEN has been the focus of five investigations since 2001:

In response to a request from the Senate Judiciary Committee, the Government Accountability Office performed an audit of 84 grants administered by the OFFICE ON VIOLENCE AGAINST WOMEN.

The probe identified numerous shortcomings, including:
66% of files did not have progress reports for the complete grant period.
85% of progress reports were late.
90% of files did not contain documentation that all planned site visits had occurred.

The GAO concluded that inconsistent documentation and the lack of systematic data could hinder VAWO's ability to measure whether it is achieving its goals.19

2. In 2002, the GAO evaluated the quality of five multi-million dollar program evaluations of OF-FICE ON VIOLENCE AGAINST WOMEN grants. The investigation identified serious data collec-tion and analytical problems that raise concerns about whether the evaluations will produce definitive results. The GAO pointedly asked whether the OFFICE ON VIOLENCE AGAINST WOMEN was making sound in-vestments, given the millions of dollars spent on these evaluations.20

3. In its 2005 Semi-annual Report to Congress, the Office of the Inspector General analyzed OFFICE ON VIOLENCE AGAINST WOMEN grants to Native American and Alaska Native tribes. Accord-ing to its report, OFFICE ON VIOLENCE AGAINST WOMEN did not ensure that funds were made available in a timely manner. Even when required reports were not received from grantees, the OF-FICE ON VIOLENCE AGAINST WOMEN continued to authorize payments. When the grant ended, OFFICE ON VIOLENCE AGAINST WOMEN was not closing out expired grants in a timely 7 At that time the OFFICE ON VIOLENCE AGAINST WOMEN was known as the Violence Against Women Office Violence Against Women's Office. The report concluded the OFFICE ON VIO-LENCE AGAINST WOMEN was not effectively monitoring tribal grant programs.21

4. In 2006, the OIG examined the grant closeout process at the Department of Justice. That investiga-tion identified numerous instances of financial mismanagement by the OFFICE ON VIOLENCE AGAINST WOMEN, including:

54% of OFFICE ON VIOLENCE AGAINST WOMEN grants closed in 2005 did not meet the 6-month grant closeout requirement.

Delays in making debt payments unnecessarily tied up $14.3 million of federal money. Of greater concern, the OIG noted that OFFICE ON VIOLENCE AGAINST WOMEN grant officers had illegally instructed grantees to draw down any remaining funds, even though the 90-day liquidation period has passed. The report reached the worrisome conclusion that the Office on Violence against Women did not conform to federal regulations and their own policies.

5. More recently, the Inspector General probed Department of Justice grant pro-grams and concluded; too often the OIG has observed a misplaced emphasis on expeditiously awarding grants and a lack of commensurate emphasis on monitoring the grants awarded.
Highlighting a long-standing problem, the OIG commented the OFFICE ON VIOLENCE AGAINST WOMEN has failed to ensure that grants were closed in a timely manner.

Grantee Misconduct and Fraud

Given the shortcomings in grant administration procedures described above, it is not surprising that numerous recipients of federal monies have been found to engage in financial misconduct and fraud.

Misconduct

Probes by the Department Of Justice Office of the Inspector General have turned up numerous instances of grant expenditures that were unsupported, questionable, excessive, or non-allowable:

1. A 2003 audit of a grant to Dane County, Wisconsin, to encourage arrest policies identified widespread problems, including the commingling of grant funds and inability to account for expenditures. The report concluded, we question $1,766,964 in grant funds received which amounts to 99% of the total grant expenditures.

2. An audit of a STOP formula grant to the Texas Office of the Governor stated, we question $106,452 in grant fund expenditures. In addition, $348,384 in excess funds drawn down and $852,650 in program matching costs were identified as unsupported. These questionable, excess, and unsupported expenses represented 19% of the total award.

3. A 2005 audit of Legal Aid of Nebraska identified $1.3 million (64.5% of the total grant funds awarded) in non-allowable and questionable expenses. The investigation concluded that Legal Aid:

(1) Did not maintain adequate accounting records of costs charged to the grant;

(2) Did not adequately monitor its contractors; and

(3) Was reimbursed for costs charged to the grant that were not supported by adequate documentation or were not allowable according to the approved grant budget. 18 months later, the OFFICE ON VIOLENCE AGAINST WOMEN had implemented only three of the eleven recommendations arising from the audit, leading the Department of Justice to classify the OFFICE ON VIOLENCE AGAINST WOMEN response as delinquent.

4. Audits revealed the following Indian tribes routinely failed to submit accurate and timely grant reports and often charged for unallowable costs:

Inter-Tribal Council of Nevada
Lac Courte Oreilles Tribal Government
South Puget Intertribal Planning Agency
Yavapai-Apache Indian Nation
Osage Tribal Council
Southern Ute Indian Tribe
Confederated Tribes of the Chugachmiut Indian Reservation
Confederated Tribes of the Umatilla Indian Reservation

Fraud

Reports have revealed several cases of embezzlement by service providers:

1. In 1999, Denorvas Stevenson, former director of a woman's shelter in Shawnee, Oklahoma, was charged with eight counts of embezzlement after an audit revealed more than $56,000 in undocumented and unauthorized expenses. Stevenson was fired after Project Safe board members discovered the agency was $40,000 in debt and owed $12,000 in back payroll taxes.

2. In 2006, Paulette Wang, former treasurer of Asian Women United in Minnesota, pleaded guilty to embezzling $265,000 from her domestic violence organization.

3. In 2007, the Department of Justice reported to Congress about a $299,815 grant to the South Central Region Tribal Nations and Friends Domestic Violence Coalition:

Our investigation determined that the executive director of the Coalition stole over $100,000 in grant funds, and two board members of the Coalition stole approximately $25,000 and $37,000, respectively.

Cindy Lou Shores, Wenona Barnett, and Angela Camp of Ponca City, Okla., were charged with conspiracy and theft of federal funds. Shores was later sentenced to 17 months in federal prison and ordered to pay $170,000 in restitution.

4. In 2008, John Scott, former executive director of Domestic Violence Emergency Services (DOVES) in Roanoke, Va., was sentenced to serve one year in prison and ordered to pay $48,000 in restitution, arising from embezzlement of shelter funds.

A Michigan case involves falsification of financial records:

In June 2006, SafeHouse of Michigan was ordered to repay $483,000 in federal funds because services it had billed for could not be verified. The order followed the resignation of executive director Susan McGee, who admitted that she had falsified federal financial reports to cover up delinquent tax payments.

Federal Foot-Dragging

The previous sections of this report document how domestic violence programs lack accountability and are plagued by financial mismanagement, which in turn creates the shadowy environment in which fraud can arise. Yet federal officials have been notoriously slow to remedy the problem. Four examples illustrate the pattern:

1. As early as 1998, serious problems have been documented with Indian tribe grants. Seven years later, the Office of the Inspector General concluded that the Office of Violence Against Women still was not effectively monitoring tribal grant programs.

2. In 2001, the OMB identified widespread problems with grant management at the OFFICE ON VIOLENCE AGAINST WOMEN . Six years later, a probe similarly concluded that the OFFICE ON VIOLENCE AGAINST WOMEN has failed to ensure that grants were closed in a timely manner.

3. In 2002, OFFICE ON VIOLENCE AGAINST WOMEN officials testified to Congress that they were not satisfied with the performance measures they used to gauge their performance. Four years later; the OMB echoed exactly the same problem. And six years after OFFICE ON VIOLENCE AGAINST WOMEN's admission to Congress, performance measures still had not been operational.

4. In 2005, the OMB directed the Administration for Children and Families to develop appropriate national grantee-supported performance outcome measures. Apparently believing that sound reporting policies would be burdensome to grantees, three years later no new measures had been implemented.48 Why aren't federal employees doing more to assure that taxpayer-funded programs are accountable and effective?

Pitting Effectiveness vs. Ideology

This Special Report portrays a free-wheeling industry in which lack of outcome measures, mismanagement of grant monies, and fraud has become widespread. But misuse of federal money is not the only concern. Scores of research studies show that domestic violence programs are ineffective at best and harmful at worst.

Examples of programs that have been shown to be ineffective are batterer intervention programs and restraining orders.

Mandatory arrest policies for partner assault offer an object lesson of a well-intentioned but harmful violence prevention strategy. Several early evaluations showed that mandatory arrest can harm victims. A recent Harvard University study revealed a 54% increase in partner homicides following enactment of such laws.

Mandatory arrest for restraining order violations may place victims at risk, as well. One evaluation concluded, Increases in the willingness of prosecutors'offices to take cases of protection order violation were associated with increases in the homicide of white married intimates, black unmarried intimates, and white unmarried females.

Despite these findings, $65 million of VAWA monies were authorized in FY2005 to encourage such policies. Even though the 2005 renewal of VAWA shifted from a must arrest to pro-arrest stance, to date none of the 22 states has repealed its mandatory arrest policies. And persons continue to die, needlessly.

Not only are domes-tic violence programs ineffective and harmful, previous reports have 131 documented how domestic violence programs bias the judiciary, violate civil liberties, engage in sex-based discrimination, and weaken families and harm children. So why does the domestic violence industry continue to advocate for dysfunctional policies and programs? The answer, according to the National Academy of Sciences, is that intimate partner violence programs are driven by ideology and stakeholder interests rather than by plausible theories and scientific evidence of cause.

CHAPTER 7
Why Have Domestic Violence Programs Failed to Stop Partner Abuse?

We have no evidence to date that VAWA has led to a decrease in the overall levels of violence against women. — Angela Moore Parmley, PhD, U.S. Department of Justice1 Domestic violence is an important social problem in our country. A major milestone in our efforts to combat intimate partner assault was the enactment of the Violence Against Women Act in 1994. But more than a decade later, persons are beginning to ask, Is VAWA having the intended effect?

Since the early 1980s, all types of violent crime—robberies, simple assaults, and aggravated assaults have been on the decline. That long-term trend can also be seen for crimes against intimate partners. From 1976 to 1994, the number of partner homicides fell 29%.

Number of Victims

A review of non-fatal victimization paints a similar picture. Since VAWA targets aggression by intimate partners, one would expect victimization rates for that type of abuse to drop more rapidly after VAWA's adoption than violence perpetrated by a stranger, acquaintance, or friend. But Department of Justice statistics for the period from 1995 to 2004 show that victimization of women fell across the board, regardless of the perpetrator of the crime:

These percentages reveal that over a 10-year period, violent crime against women fell at almost identical rates, regardless of the offender:

Stranger – 52%
Intimate partner – 55%
Friend or acquaintance – 63%

This Special Report probes why domestic violence programs have apparently failed to reduce partner aggression. The Report analyzes the effectiveness of four key violence reduction strategies currently employed by VAWA-funded programs around the country:

1. Treatment Services
2. Restraining Orders
3. Mandatory Arrest
4. No-Drop Prosecution

Treatment Services

The dynamics of domestic violence are varied and complex. Partner aggression is influenced by factors such as marital status, age, socio-economic level, drug and alcohol use, psychological disorders, childhood abuse experiences, and conflict resolution skills. Effective treatment should be based on a careful clinical assessment and tailored to the psychological and social needs of both the abuser and the partner. Above all, treatment services should be based on sound scientific research and the best practices of the counseling profession.

Couples Counseling

A key factor in the treatment of partner abuse is whether the physical aggression is mutual. Studies typically reveal that at least half of all abuse is reciprocal and is initiated by males and females at similar rates. For example, one Centers for Disease Control survey of adults 18–28 years old found that half of all partner violence was reciprocal.6 Another survey of dating couples reported that 70% of all physical abuse was mutual.7 Logic dictates that counseling for both partners is essential for a successful resolution.

Source: http://www.ojp.usDepartmentOfJustice.gov/bjs/intimate/table/vomen.htm

But under current domestic violence programs, couples'counseling rarely happens.

Why?

Because many of those in the domestic violence industry adhere to the belief that only men are capable of perpetrating domestic violence and those women are only victims a view wholly unsupported by scientific research?

As a result of this belief, treatment standards actually discourage family therapy. One analysis of 30 states implementing standards for offender treatment programs found that 42% of those states prohibit couples counseling.

These restrictions on couples therapy have become a point of contention between VAWA funded batterer intervention providers and mental health providers. As a result, one is pressed to find anywhere in the family violence literature treatment approaches that are both systemic and take seriously violence perpetrated by women. Couples therapy has been shown to be effective in treating violent partners.

But by policy or by law, VAWA-funded programs often prohibit use of such services.

Services for Female Victims: Women's Shelters

The more than 1,200 abuse shelters currently in operation in the United States are considered the mainstay of treatment services for female abuse victims. But what happens inside the protective walls of these shelters? Feminist therapists advocate that women in shelters should be counseled to view their predicament as a consequence of patriarchy, despite a distinct lack of evidence to support that ideological stance.

One national survey found that 45% of shelters viewed their main role as promoting feminist political activism, while only 25% focused on providing treatment and support for abused women. An over-reliance on untrained volunteers is worrisome.

One early report admitted, it is the policy of many shelters to have the majority of their staffs comprised of such [abused] women because they can offer invaluable empathy to victims.

One former shelter director noted that the volunteers were sometimes more of a problem than they were worth because they were still dealing with their own personal issues.

Two anecdotal reports raise concerns about the services that shelters provide:

A former participant in a support group found the real message of the group was to accept the indoctrination and embrace my victimhood. I realized that I never heard a facilitator encourage a woman to heal and move on with her life. They encouraged women to stay stuck in the victim mentality, she noted.

A woman who attended group sessions later admitted that the groups made her feel worse because everyone was supposed to hate the men and want to leave them. Although researchers have been studying women's shelters for more than 20 years, the quality of the studies has been poor and the findings inconclusive.

Such analyses typically lack pre-intervention data or comparison groups and fail to take into ac-count critical variables. One early study suggested that shelter residence could trigger new incidents of abuse. But overall, we simply do not know whether shelter services are effective, benign, or make the situation worse.

Services for Female Abusers

Women are at least as likely as men to engage in partner aggression, according to extensive research. Fewer than one in five cases of female violence are justified by the need for women to act in self-defense.

Female-initiated violence is a cause for concern not only because of the physical and psychological effects on her partner, but also because it raises the concern of retaliatory aggression.

So when abusive women request help from VAWA-funded agencies, they discover, much to their surprise, that requests for treatment are dismissed (often with a comment such as He must have done something to provoke you) or that female-specific services are simply non-existent.

For example, a recent evaluation revealed that among the intervention programs in New York City, there are very few that accept female batterers. As attorney Linda Kelly explains, Today's treatment denies the possibility that women can be violent.

Persons have decried the lack of services for women:

Researcher Susan Steinmetz tells of receiving letters from violent women who recognized that they needed help, but were turned away or offered no help when they called a crisis line or shelter.

Ellen Pence, founder of the Duluth Domestic Abuse Intervention Project, has highlighted the neglect of female abusers: In many ways, we turned a blind eye to many women's use of violence, their drug use and alcoholism, and their often harsh and violent treatment of their own children.

Darlene Hilker of Florida assaulted her husband. I grabbed my husband's genital that's what I was arrested for, she later admitted. In 2006, the judge ordered her to attend the Women Who Batter pro-gram, one of the first such programs ever established in the United States.

Services for Male Victims

The lack of services for male victims of domestic violence is well documented. One survey of 26 do-mestic violence shelters in California acknowledged, *most shelters do not admit males*.

The former director of a shelter in the mid-Atlantic region likewise revealed, the shelter did not pro-vide services to male victims of domestic violence, even when they had suffered physical abuse simi-lar to that experienced by women.

In 2002, abuse victim Ray Blumhorst contacted 10 shelters in southern California to request help. All 10 shelters turned him down.

When the shelters were later sued for discrimination, they chose to ignore the stated intent of Congress that Men who have suffered these types of violent attacks are eligible … for services and benefits that are funded under … the Violence against Women Act.

The shelters believed that discrimination was their right, and went to court to defend that right.

Psychologist David Fontes has observed that if a male victim happens to show up at a domestic violence center, they may try to help him, but are unlikely to have an active outreach program or services specifically set up with his needs in mind.

I am a male survivor and former victim of relationship abuse. I was mentally hi-jacked, emotionally destroyed, and physically beaten by my girlfriend for almost 3 years. … I remember being huddled on the floor … as I watched, not felt, her beat me until she couldn't lift her arms anymore. … After a year of therapy, I still haven't found a support group for abused men.

I am the founder of the national coalition on domestic violence against men, I am also a survivor of domestic violence my son was stolen and I have had the back of my head slammed into a plaster wall, the only place I really had any real help, was the Mormon family services in Idaho Falls, Idaho. I have not found any support groups anywhere either. I have also found that if a male calls a domestic violence shelter he is given the runaround.

Services for Male Abusers

Male offenders are often ordered to attend a Batterer Intervention Program (BIP) as an alternative to incarceration. These group programs are typically based on the Duluth Model devised by the Duluth Domestic Abuse Intervention Project.

The Duluth approach does not resemble psychological counseling in the usual sense of the word. Duluth interventionists do not try to develop a therapeutic relationship with the clients, even though that relationship is the single most important predictor of psychological improvement. Interventionists do not even make a clinical diagnosis because that could provide a rationalization for behavior that may not be accurate.

Rather, *the Duluth model is better viewed as a penal intervention that emphasizes monitoring and group shaming over treatment and rehabilitation.* Psychologist James Kline believes its interventionists act as quasi-probation officers, noting that such individuals have such narrow training and such indoctrination into the batterer model of inter-partner violence, which it leaves them inadequate as diagnosticians and counselors.

The decidedly ideological flavor of such efforts is revealed by one program in New York state: The Domestic Violence Program for Men provides important, serious analysis and topics that explore the roots of sexism, racism and the other oppressions which contribute to the systemic problems leading too much of the violence men commit against their intimate partners. No surprise that such programs often have high drop-out rates. And no wonder the National Research Council deplored the fact that these programs are driven by ideology and stakeholder interests rather than by plausible theories and scientific evidence of cause.

Thus, evaluations have consistently shown the Duluth model to have no positive impact. As psychologist Donald Dutton notes, Research shows that Duluth-oriented treatments are absolutely ineffective, and have no discernible impact on rates of recidivism. Even the sponsor of one such program says they don't work. The New York Model for Batterer Programs admits that Decades of anecdotal reports from partners of men in programs and millions of dollars of research provide the answer: inconclusive, insignificant results.

Summary

This review of research and policy reveals an ironic pattern of available services that are ineffective, along with a general unavailability of services that are effective:

For partners engaged in mutual violence, couples counseling is usually discouraged and often prohibited.

For female victims, no good evidence supports the effectiveness of abuse shelters.

For female abusers, VAWA services are generally unavailable.

Victims, VAWA-funded programs are virtually non-existent.

For male abusers, Duluth model treatment programs are flatly ineffective. With regard to treatment of male abusers, psychologist Julia Babcock once asked, Is the Duluth model set up to fail? In light of these research findings, one might conclude that the entire spectrum of VAWA-funded treatment programs has been set up for failure.

Restraining Orders

Restraining orders are a widely employed strategy used to combat domestic violence. Sometimes known as orders for protection, restraining orders are a legal directive that orders an individual to avoid contact and communication with his partner for a specified period of time. It has been estimated that 2-3 million domestic restraining orders are issued each year in the United States.

Only half of all restraining orders involve any allegation of physical violence-the reason being that most state statutes now employ a broad definition of domestic violence, relying on ill-defined criteria such as fear, apprehension, emotional distress, and harassment. In theory, restraining orders appear to be the easy solution to a difficult problem. The parties can be separated and the violence prevented with a minimum of legal intervention.

But experience suggests otherwise. One early report stated flatly, All observers agree that - at least until they are violated—a civil protection order is useless with the hard core' batterer ... Any abuser who is determined to batter—or kill—his [or her] partner will not be deterred by a piece of paper. Front-line prosecutors have reached a similar conclusion:

Many stakeholders do not believe that orders of protection are an effective means of securing the safety of the complainant.

What light does research cast on this thorny question? Four studies address this issue:

1. One early study interviewed recipients of restraining orders in Pennsylvania. Although the orders appeared to be helpful in reducing the abuse of some women with less serious histories of family violence, the authors concluded that the restraining orders were generally ineffective in stopping physical violence.

2. A project interviewed 212 women with permanent restraining orders and compared the results of the interviews with those for 143 women not having such orders. Although having an order reduced psychological abuse, it was found to have no impact on threats of property damage, severe violence, or other forms of physical violence.

3. A third study followed 150 women in Houston, Texas, who met initial screening criteria for a permanent restraining order. Of these women, 81 were actually granted the order and 69 were not. The two groups of women were interviewed five times during an 18-month period. The women reported the same levels of threats, physical abuse, and stalking, regardless of whether they had received a restraining order or not.

4. An analysis of the availability of domestic violence resources in 48 major cities and the impact of those resources on partner violence concluded, the adoption of certain types of protection order statutes is associated with both decreases in black married female victimization and increases in the number of black women killed by their unmarried partners.

The research can be summarized as follows:

Restraining orders may reduce psychological abuse. Restraining orders are generally ineffective in preventing future physical violence. Among unmarried partners, such orders may actually increase future violence. It is now clear that restraining orders are hardly the panacea that its advocates once envisioned, and may work only for couples at low risk of abuse. As the Independent Women's Forum has concluded, restraining orders seem to only lull women into a false sense of security.

Mandatory Arrest for Assault

Mandatory arrest for partner assault has been a hotly debated topic over the past 25 years, and the focus of a number of evaluation studies as well. The first study, the Minneapolis Domestic Violence Experiment, found that arrest led to substantial reductions in subsequent violence. But the Minneapolis study was hampered by a short follow-up period and small sample size. Follow-up studies have failed to confirm the Minneapolis results.

In Colorado Springs, researchers concluded, an arrest can sometimes make things worse. And in Milwaukee, arrests were found to cause an overall increase in partner violence among Black women, 147 noting that an across-the-board policy of mandatory arrest prevents 2,504 acts of violence against primarily white women, at the price of 5,409 acts of violence against primarily Black women.

Furthermore, these studies did not account for the fact that mandatory arrest might discourage victims from seeking police assistance in the event of future abuse. Recently Harvard economist Radha Iyengar analyzed the impact of the passage of mandatory arrest laws in 15 states. Her surprising conclusion: Intimate partner homicides increased by about 60% in states with mandatory arrest laws.

Clearly, mandatory arrest policies, with their one-size-fits-all approach, cause more harm than good. Furthermore, if a state has mandatory arrest, the likelihood of subsequent conviction drops by more than half. Lawrence Sherman, director of the Milwaukee study, has termed mandatory arrest policies a failure and recommended that such policies be repealed.

Mandatory Arrest for Restraining Order Violations

In 33 states, violation of a restraining order is cause for mandatory arrest. Breaches of such orders appear to be fairly common. Studies have reported violation rates ranging from 35% over a 12-month period to 44% over an 18-month period. Violations of orders occur for a variety of reasons. In some cases the offender continues to harass the victim. Sometimes the couple decides to re-unite but forgets to have the order rescinded.

There is no evidence that prosecution of restraining order violations reduces subsequent abuse, and one Department of Justice-funded study found that such policies actually place victims at greater risk. Increases in the willingness of prosecutors'offices to take cases of protection order violation were associated with increases in the homicide of White married intimates, Black unmarried intimates, and White unmarried females, the study concluded.

Summary

In our determined effort to get tough on domestic violence, the majority of states have enacted laws that mandate or promote arrest for assault. These efforts are promoted by the Violence against Women Act, which authorizes $75 million each year for grants to encourage arrests and enforce protection orders.

These intrusive laws have given rise to a broad range of civil rights abuses, including the undermining of probable cause, disregard of the innocent-until-proven-guilty principle, gender-profiling in the name of primary aggressor assessment, and police reluctance to arrest female batterers. In addition, women who summon the police often just want the situation to be stabilized, they don't want their partner to be arrested.

Victims whose partners are subject to mandatory arrest are less likely to request police assistance in the future. Mandatory arrest policies may be an effective sound-bite for persons running for political office. But as a law enforcement tool, they have proven to be a failure.

No-Drop Prosecution

The majority of abuse cases involve disputes in which the conflict is a minor, mutual, and/or one-time occurrence. The victim often believes that these situations can be better handled through counseling or a brief cooling-off period rather than legal intervention. So, in about 80% of cases, the person who requests police assistance later recants or drops the charges.

But many jurisdictions have come to believe that persons charged with abuse should be prosecuted regardless of the claimant's request, so they have instituted so-called —no-drop policies, which require continued prosecution of the case. One survey revealed that 66% of prosecutors' offices have implemented such policies.

But no-drop policies do a disservice to both alleged abusers and victims. They eliminate prosecutorial discretion, thus increasing the likelihood of frivolous legal action. If the defendant is poor, he or she will have to rely on the counsel of an already over-burdened public defender. In many cases, the accused is eventually compelled to accept a plea bargain arrangement that requires admitting to having committed a lesser crime, even if no violence had occurred.

If the alleged victim refuses to testify, the prosecutor may charge obstruction of justice and threaten to take away the children. In one California case, a county prosecutor put a woman in jail for 8 days after she refused to testify against her boyfriend. She later won a $125,000 settlement for false imprisonment. Overly aggressive prosecution policies dissuade women from seeking future police assistance as well.

One survey of female victims in Quincy, Massachusetts, found that among women who did not report a subsequent incident of abuse, 56% believed that the victim has no say or rights in the criminal justice system. In contrast, among women who did report such incidents, only 12% shared that belief.

Echoing these findings, law professor Kimberle Crenshaw has argued that many women of color are reluctant to seek intervention from the police, fearing that contact with law enforcement will exacerbate the system's assault on their public and personal lives. As the Ms. Foundation for Women notes, victims want their voices to be heard, not silenced. Only one randomized study has evaluated the effectiveness of varying levels of prosecution on subsequent aggression. The research found that only one factor reduced abuser recidivism allowing the victim to select whether and how aggressively the prosecutor would pursue the case. obviously a no-drop prosecution policy eliminates the chance for the victim to make that choice. One analysis reached this sobering conclusion: We do not know whether no-drop increases victim safety or places the victims in greater jeopardy.

Summary

The Violence against Women Act authorizes $225 million for STOP (Services, Training, Officers, and Prosecutors) grants, of which at least 25%—about $56 million-is allocated to prosecutorial activities. In two-thirds of jurisdictions, prosecutors are bound by domestic violence no-drop policies. But we do not know whether such policies are helpful, harmful, or have no effect at all.

Symbols over Substance

Declines in intimate partner homicides began in the mid-1970s, and trend lines continued on the same course following passage of VAWA in 1994. For non-fatal abuse of women, trend lines over the past decade have followed a similar trajectory, regardless of whether the perpetrator was a friend, stranger, or intimate. Hence, there is no evidence that the Violence against Women Act has reduced partner violence.

This report examined the reasons for that failure by analyzing four widely used violence reduction strategies: abuser treatment, restraining orders, mandatory arrest, and no-drop prosecution. Scientific studies reveal that:

Abuser treatment services are either ineffective, or those known to be effective are generally unavailable.
Restraining orders generally have no impact on subsequent physical abuse.

Mandatory arrest laws substantially increase homicides, discourage future requests for police assistance, and reduce conviction rates.

We do not know whether no-drop prosecution increases, reduces, or has no impact on future violence. In sum, we conclude that VAWA-funded programs are generally ineffective and sometimes harmful. Whether viewed at the level of aggregate crime statistics or specific abuse reduction strategies, our nation's approach to curbing partner violence has been a failure.

Others have reached a similar conclusion:

Noted family violence researcher Richard Gelles stated, Policy and practice based on these factoids and theory might actually be harmful to women, men, children, and the institution of the family.

New York University vice provost Linda Mills concluded: At worst, the criminal justice system increases violence against women. At best, it has little or no effect.

Researcher John Hamel wrote, Current policy toward domestic violence, including criminal justice and mental health responses … has proven to be shortsighted and limited in its effectiveness.

So why have ineffective, and possibly harmful, policies been allowed to persist? University of Hawaii law professor Virginia Hench has noted that these policies are a classic example of a get tough'policy that has symbolic value with the electorate, but which can lead to a host of problems. Hench concludes that if we choose symbols over substance, which is a true failure to support those victims of violence.

It is time that we implement effective solutions to partner abuse—solutions based on the sound foundation of valid science and well-tested professional practice.

CHAPTER 8
VAWA Programs Discriminate Against Male Victims

According to the National Violence Against Women Survey, 835,000 men are assaulted each year by their intimate partners.1 About one-third of those assaults are severe, meaning that the men were kicked, bit, hit with a fist, threatened or at-tacked with a gun or knife, or beat up.2 Assume that a victim of severe partner as-sault can be considered in need of assistance, it is estimated that each year about 275,000 abused men need VAWA treatment or rehabilitation services. More recent research shows that women are more likely than men to engage in partner aggression. The U.S. Centers for Disease Control reported that in the 18-28 year-old group, 71% of the instigators of nonreciprocal partner violence are female.3 Renee McDonald likewise revealed that in dual-parent households, women are twice as likely as men to engage in severe partner violence.4 Some women openly admit to being perpetrators. Singer Amy Winehouse has said about her husband, I'll beat up Blake when I'm drunk … If he says one thing I don't like then I'll chin him. *Other women make light of their violence:*

I bounced an alarm clock off my husband's head from across the room once.

I've had many satisfying dreams where I beat up my ex. If I saw him again, I don't thinks me'd is able to restrain myself.

Yeah, I've punched the shit out of a guy. But I don't like to brag.

Despite a pressing need to help male victims of partner assault, gender bias pervades the domestic violence industry. This Special Report describes how men who seek services are ignored, ridiculed, and even accused of the crime to which they have become unwitting victims.

Early Evidence of Concern

From the earliest days in American history, men have been subjected to assaults by their domestic partners. In 1641, the Massachusetts Bay colonists adopted the Body of Liberties, which stated, Every married woman shall be free from bodily correction or stripes by her husband, unless it be in his own defense upon her assault.

Well-known political figures have been victims of domestic violence, as well. In his book, The Inner World of Abraham Lincoln, Michael Burlingame reveals the repeated severe assaults that President Lincoln suffered at the hands of his wife, Mary. These incidents forced President Lincoln to set up a couch in his office where he sometimes spent the night. But attacks on men have long been viewed as a lesser cause for social concern.

Philip Cook's book, Abused Men: The Hidden Side of Domestic Violence, documents the experiences of dozens of men who suffered repeated partner assaults, only to encounter disbelief, hostility, and outright rejection when they sought help.

One director of a Washington shelter admitted, whenever I speak of male abuse, I am met with disbelief and, even worse, laughter…I notice in talking with other shelter staff throughout the state that this attitude prevails in the other shelters, too.

This early example reveals how that attitude had become pervasive throughout many sectors of American society: A father of two endured repeated physical assaults by his substance-abusing wife, including thrown objects, hitting, and kicks. After years of abuse, he finally called the local police. He was advised that since women don't beat up men in this state, the officer would likely discard the complaint. Or worse, the man might be arrested.

The man then telephoned the local shelter to ask for help. The woman who took his call scolded him, saying, Only men perpetrate domestic violence.

The father then sought the assistance of a divorce attorney. The lawyer explained to the father that he would probably lose custody of his children, because men are not victims of DV. Shortly after that conversation, his drunken wife attacked him with a baseball bat, cracking three ribs and causing him to black out. Although he gave the emergency room nurse a detailed account of what had happened, the nurse wrote in the medical record simply, household accident.

Following years of physical and psychological abuse, and after the divorce had been finalized, the man sought counseling. The therapist asked him, what did you do to provoke this?

Anti-Discrimination Requirements

All grants administered by the Department of Justice are governed by the Omnibus Crime Control and Safe Streets Act of 1968, which states, No person in any State shall on the ground of race, color, religion, national origin, or sex be excluded from participation in, be denied the benefits of, or be subjected to discrimination under or denied employment in connection with any programs or activity funded in whole or in part with funds made available under this chapter.

The penalties for violating these requirements are described in Section 3789d. (c)(2) Of the law. These non-discrimination requirements apply both to direct recipients of Department of Justice funds as well as to sub-contractors:

Federal agencies shall apply the provisions of the sections of this Circular to non-Federal entities, whether they are recipients expending Federal awards received directly from Federal awarding agencies, or are sub-recipients expending Federal awards received from a pass-through entity (a recipient or another sub-recipient).

Thus if a state domestic violence coalition receives federal funds and awards the funds to an abuse shelter or other agency, those groups must comply with anti-discrimination requirements. In response to complaints of sex-based discrimination by VAWA-funded programs, Senator Orrin Hatch made the following statement in 2000 to clarify Congressional intent:

Despite the need to direct federal funds toward the most pressing problem, it was not, and is not, the intent of Congress categorically to exclude men who have suffered domestic abuse or sexual assaults from receiving benefits and services under the Violence Against Women Act.

The Act defines such key terms as domestic violence' and sexual assault,' which are used to determine eligibility under several of the grant programs, including the largest, the STOP grant program, in gender-neutral language.

Men who have suffered these types of violent attacks are eligible under current law to apply for services and benefits that are funded under the original Act—and they will remain eligible under the Violence Against Women Act of 2000—whether it be for shelter space under the Family Violence Protection and Services Act, or counseling by the National Domestic Violence Hotline, or legal assistance in obtaining a protection order under the Legal Assistance for Victims program.

We anticipate that the executive branch agencies responsible for making grants under the Act, as amended, will continue to administer these programs so as to ensure that men who have been victimized by domestic violence and sexual assault will receive benefits and services under the Act, as appropriate. Senator Joseph Biden, who first championed the Violence Against Women Act, later confirmed Senator Hatch's statement, remarking, Nothing in the act denies services, programs, funding or assistance to male victims of violence. The 2005 renewal of VAWA added this requirement:

Nothing in this title shall be construed to prohibit male victims of domestic violence, dating violence, sexual assault, and stalking from receiving benefits and services under this title. Despite those statements of congressional intent, sex-based discrimination continues to the present time. Indeed, the exclusion of men appears to be the norm.

Government- and State-Level Discrimination

Discrimination begins at the highest levels—the federal and state governments, national domestic violence organizations, and state domestic violence coordinating councils. This problem is detailed in the three sections that follow.

Governmentally-Sanctioned Discrimination

The Department of Justice's Office on Violence Against Women (OFFICE ON VIOLENCE AGAINST WOMEN) is the principal federal agency that administers VAWA funds. On several occasions the OFFICE ON VIOLENCE AGAINST WOMEN has issued directives or established funding mechanisms that openly discriminatory in nature:

In 2002, the OFFICE ON VIOLENCE AGAINST WOMEN instructed the Delaware Domestic Violence coordinating council that, states must fund only programs that focus on violence against women.

Department of Justice (Department Of Justice) research solicitations have explicitly excluded applications that focus on male victims. One Solicitation for Proposals from the Department Of Justice National Institute of Justice specifically prohibited proposals for research on intimate partner violence against, or stalking of males of any age...

The webpage of the Office on Violence against Women provides this perspective: Although both women and men may be victims of domestic violence, sexual assault, and stalking, women are the victims of the vast majority of these crimes. According to the Bureau of Justice Statistics, more than 85% of violent victimizations by intimate partners between 1993 and 1998 were perpetrated against women.

Women are between 13 and 14 times more likely than men to be raped or sexually assaulted; for instance, in 1994, 93% of sexual assaults were perpetrated against women.

Four of five stalking victims are women.

Data on male victimization do not show that males experience comparable victimizations and injury levels, do not account for women who act in self-defense, and do not measure financial control, intimidation, and isolation used by perpetrators of domestic violence against women.

For these reasons, this application kit may refer to victims as women and perpetrators as men. However, applicants who receive grants under this program must serve all victims regardless of gender. By citing outdated crime statistics that are known to underestimate the extent of male victimization and by not mentioning its own National Violence Against Women Survey, the real message appears to be, men need not apply.

Given these federal actions, it is not surprising that state-level governmental programs follow suit: In Texas, an application for a program serving male victims was turned down because programs that focus on children and/or men were ineligible, despite Senator Hatch's reassurances. The next year, a grant application kit from the Texas Criminal Justice Division used identical words to reiterate the exclusion:

Programs that focus on children and/or men.

In California, male victims are excluded by definition. Section 124250 of the state's Health and Safety Code defines domestic violence as follows:

The infliction or threat of physical harm against past or present adult or adolescent female intimate partners, and shall include physical, sexual and psychological abuse against the woman, and is part of a pattern of assaultive, coercive, and controlling behaviors, directed at achieving compliance from or control over, that woman.

Likewise, the OFFICE ON VIOLENCE AGAINST WOMEN awarded $3 million to Baylor University to establish the Faith and Community Technical Support (FACTS) program designed to reduce domestic violence in rural communities. In 2006 the FACTS program issued a grant solicitation stating, As with previous VA-WA methods, it is assumed that … all victim data reported is about victimized women.

One of the questions on the FACTS grant application asks, Number of year's organization has spent working on violence against women issues.

National Domestic Violence Organizations

Several national organizations coordinate the efforts of state-level DV service providers. Through their mission statements, announcements, and pictures, national organizations make it clear that their focus is solely the female abuse victim. For example, one major organization, the National Network to End Domestic Violence provides money to domestic violence victims through its Amy's Courage Fund.

The NNEDV describes the fund this way:

We all know an Amy – she's the girl next door, the woman standing in front of you at the grocery store. She's your sister, your mother, your friend, your coworker or maybe even you. The NNEDV makes no mention about the boy next door, the man at the grocery story, or your brother or father who may have suffered from domestic violence.

The National Coalition Against Domestic Violence (NCADV) features a number of position papers, including a Women's Statement, Women in Afghanistan, and Women of Color Caucus. But the NCADV has no position papers on male victims of domestic violence.

State Domestic Violence Coordinating Councils

The Violence against Women Act provides for the establishment of state-level DV coordinating councils. These groups are charged with allocating federal grant monies to local service providers. But the committees that make funding decisions are composed of persons representing the same groups that are receiving the monies, an obvious conflict of interest. According to Boston Globe columnist Cathy Young, these coordinating councils formally require member organizations to embrace the feminist analysis of abuse as patriarchal coercion. An example of that perspective came from the director of the Massachusetts Coalition Against Sexual Assault and Domestic Violence, who made this dismissive comment about male victims: Sometimes it snows in Florida … but we don't make public policy around it.

These coalitions have not been welcoming to organizations that serve male victims. In Maine, the Maine Coalition to End Domestic Violence refused to approve the application for membership from the Domestic Abuse Helpline for Men, explaining that our current criteria require that membership be organizations whose primary purpose is to provide a full range of services to battered women and their children.

In Fort Morgan, Colorado. Carolyn Fox is both a supervisor of the department of human services —The child Protective services division —and —Carolyn Fox is also on the board of directors for the local women's crisis center. The shelter also refused to return survey papers on the research of domestic violence which was worded as gender neutral.

In New Hampshire, the New Hampshire Coalition against Domestic and Sexual Violence likewise refused membership to the Violence Intervention Program – New Hampshire, on the grounds that VIP-NH, which had a predominantly male clientele, duplicated the services already provided by A Safe Place, a domestic violence crisis center located in the same area. But Ann Venier, the center's education and out-reach coordinator, had a different story to tell: We did not provide shelter to any men.

The West Virginia Coalition against Domestic Violence has published a judicial education handbook titled, For a Safer State of Family. The handbook all but ignores male victims and is adamant in discounting female aggression:

Domestic violence educators are often challenged to use gender-neutral language when talking about intimate partner abuse. However, domestic violence is not gender neutral. The fact remains that the vast majority of heterosexual victims are women and the vast majority of heterosexual perpetrators are men.

Shelters, Hotlines, and Other Services

Not surprisingly, the actions detailed above eventually bias the provision of shelter services, outreach, and other services at the local level. These problems are documented below.

Shelters

Although the exact number of women's shelters in the United States is unknown, it is estimated that some 1,200–1,800 are currently in operation. It's no secret that these shelters routinely turn away male DV victims or provide them a substantially lower level of service.

One former shelter director revealed, The shelter did not provide services to male victims of domestic violence, even when the men had suffered physical abuse similar to what women had experienced. Instead the men were referred to a local police station to request a restraining order. Some shelters only provide men a voucher for them to stay at a local motel or informally restrict their services to homosexual males.

Psychologist David Fontes noted that when he advised male victims to call local domestic violence programs for help, his clients found that either the shelters and centers never returned their calls, or they were told by the workers that they really don't have the services for male victims of domestic violence. In those cases when men in desperate straits showed up at their door for help, Fontes noted that some of the men felt they were treated at these shelters and centers more with suspect than respect.

Ironically, not only do shelters discriminate against male victims, they also treat female batterers as victims. In one case a female abuser called wanted to get help with her anger management problem, but the local domestic violence center tried to convince her that she was a victim and not a perpetrator.

In a more egregious case:

A woman was arrested and ordered out of the house following her assault against her husband. She was referred to a shelter. Her attorney provided the shelter counselor with a detailed account of what had transpired: Mrs. C. grabbed Mr. C. by his necktie (and) he pushed her away. Mrs. C. then punched his face and her fingernail cut his neck. And how did the shelter workers assess the situation in its records? Physical abuse of the woman by her husband.

In 2002, abuse victim Ray Blumhorst contacted 10 shelters in southern California to request services. All 10 shelters turned him down, offering a variety of explanations:

Ben Schirmer, of Rainbow Services, reasoned, We have limited resources and it's all we can do to try and keep up with the demand for services for women and children.

A lawyer representing several of the shelters claimed, Women's shelters receive funding from the state pursuant to a gender-specific funding statute.

Kathie Mathis, of the Domestic Violence Center, noted, we're all in a network. No one is turned away; they're just referred.

The referral shelter that Ms. Mathis was talking about was the Valley Oasis shelter, located 80 miles away in Lancaster, California. To date, the shelter has served more than 400 abused men. The Valley Oasis shelter is the only shelter in the United States that provides the full range of services to male victims.

One survey of 26 domestic violence shelters in California openly acknowledged that most shelters do not admit males. The former director of a shelter in the mid-Atlantic likewise revealed, the shelter did not provide services to male victims of domestic violence, even when the men had suffered physical abuse similar to what women had experienced. 35 Complaints of sex-based discrimination by VAWA-funded programs continue to the present time. The following report comes from a service provider in southern California:

Every week abused men seek the services of the San Diego Men's Center. Recently, one of these men was seriously injured after his wife kicked him in the groin and clubbed him in the head with the phone when he tried to call 911.

Another man came with his arm in sling after his girlfriend attacked him. Like many others, these men were denied shelter services, and then subsequent restraining orders forced them from their homes and children. When discrimination against male victims becomes the norm, abused men stop asking for help.

They may become victimized three times:

First by a violent partner, then by a treatment program that denies their existence, and finally by a bogus restraining order that ejects them from their own home.

Ruth Woods repeatedly assaulted her husband, David, with punches, kicks, and knives. On one occasion, she tried to shoot him with a shotgun. On four separate occasions, David sought protection and services from WEAVE, a domestic violence agency in Sacramento. He was turned away every time with the curt explanation, we don't help men. But Michelle Coleman, Director of Crisis Services, insisted, we do provide shelter services. At WEAVE we provide services to everyone.

Hotlines

Outreach services such as hotlines are important because they help domestic violence victims find the services they need. But VAWA-funded hotlines ignore an important underserved population: men. One woman from Washington State recounts the experience of an abused male friend. The man called the state's Domestic Violence Hotline, the one MY tax dollars pay for, and because he is male, they told him he was probably a batterer and a liar.

The National Domestic Violence Hotline (NDVH) published a Decade for Change Report designed to create a unified, national movement in ending domestic violence in America. Although the report makes the statement that men in heterosexual relationships can also be victims, the remainder of the 40-page document focuses on females. One wonders how a report can succeed in creating a unified, national movement in ending domestic violence when it all but ignores male victimization. One study documents the experiences of 190 abused men who sought assistance from a hotline.

One man reported, I called 11 different numbers for battered women and got no help. Another man called a helpline to locate couples counseling services, only to hear thinly veiled accusations that he was a batterer. The supervisor subsequently confirmed her agency's dismissive attitude: Why would a man call a helpline if he were not the abuser? One wonders how many abused men would be willing to call a hotline that doesn't recognize the existence of their plight.

Law Enforcement, Prosecution, and Adjudication

Male victims not only face systematic barriers when they seek to obtain treatment and help from hotlines, they also experience discrimination from law enforcement and legal services. In one Ohio case a woman violently attacked her husband, breaking three of his ribs. Falling to the ground, his head banged into hers.

When the police arrived, she was bragging how she had assaulted her husband. Despite the fact that she was the aggressor, the man was also arrested. The injured male victim was required to post a

$10,000 bond. But the woman was released from jail on her own recognizance. And even when the police know the aggressor is female, the man may be forced to pursue the case on his own.

The director of a crisis intervention program in New Hampshire explains:

Most often when women are arrested and jailed for domestic violence, and a no contact order or restraining order is issued, the Domestic Violence crisis centers will appear in Court to represent the interest of, and offer support to the batterer…simply because she is a woman…while a male victim can place a call to his local crisis center, most often upon referral by the Police, and, at best, be offered minimal if any support and often turned away or not taken seriously.

Other RADAR Special Reports have documented widespread gender bias in this area:

Without Restraint: The Use and Abuse of Domestic Restraining Orders

Justice Denied: Arrest Policies for Domestic Violence

Bias in the Judiciary: The Case of Domestic Violence

National Utilization Data

In 2007 RADAR sent a letter to the Office on Violence against Women under the Freedom of Information Act (FOIA) requesting the OFFICE ON VIOLENCE AGAINST WOMEN provide sexspecific utilization data for each of the following grant programs:

1. Transitional Housing Program

2. Rural Domestic Violence and Child Victimization Enforcement Grant Program

3. Legal Assistance for Victims Program

4. Stop Violence Against Indian Women

5. Grants to Encourage Arrest Policies and Enforcement of Protection Orders

6. Grants to Reduce Violent Crimes Against Women on Campuses

7. Services, Training, Officers, and Prosecutors (STOP) Violence Against Women

Formula Grant Program

Overall, only 9.7% of persons receiving help were male victims, the remaining 90.3% being female victims. The percentages of male victims for the Legal Assistance for Victims and Transitional Housing programs were much lower – 3.9% and 0.4% respectively. The complete data can be found on the RADAR website. It should be noted, however, that these numbers may overstate the true extent to which male victims are being served, for two reasons:

1. Even though a male victim may receive help, these services may be less extensive than services provide to a female victim, e.g., providing only a hotel voucher to a man who requires shelter services.

2. Boys who accompany their mothers to abuse shelters are counted as male victims, even though they were never physically abused.

Equality under the Law

Equal treatment under law is one of the bedrock principles of the American legal system. The concept is so important that those words are boldly inscribed on the face of the U.S. Supreme Court building. Most of the examples of discrimination documented in this Report occurred after 2000, the year that Senator Hatch directed that, Executive branch agencies responsible for making grants under the Act, as amended, will continue to administer these programs so as to ensure that men who have been victimized by domestic violence and sexual assault will receive benefits and services under the Act. But equal treatment under the law does not yet exist within the purview of the Violence against Women Act.

CHAPTER 9
Without Restraint: The Use and Abuse of Domestic Restraining Orders

Restraining orders are a law enforcement tool that is granted to provide emergency relief in the event of imminent or actual serious physical harm. Restraining orders (also known as orders of protection or emergency protective orders in some states) are typically issued by following a two-step process:

1. A claimant seeks a temporary restraining order.

2. Ten to fourteen days later, a hearing is held to determine whether to continue the order against the accused.

The original idea behind restraining orders was sound. But as the following example involving a well-known media personality illustrates, restraining orders are now issued on even the most unusual grounds:

On December 15, 2005, Santa Fe District Court Judge Daniel Sanchez issued a temporary restraining order to protect Colleen Nestler. According to Nestler, for the past 11 years a man had been sending her unwanted coded messages over the air-waves expressing his desire to marry her.

Her alleged harasser: CBS talk show host David Letterman. Asked to explain why he had issued a restraining order on the basis of such an unusual complaint, Judge Sanchez answered that Ms. Nestler had filled out the restraining order request form correctly.

If this case represented an unusual occurrence, it would simply become fodder for another late-night comedy routine. But as this Special Report documents, Letter-man's unfortunate experience reveals a serious civil liberties violation currently affecting hundreds of thousands of law-abiding American citizens.

Temporary Restraining Orders

Temporary restraining orders (TROs) are usually issued on an emergency ex parte basis. The judge issues the order without the accused having legal representation, being allowed to present opposing evidence, or even being aware of the allegation. It has been estimated that about 85% of such orders are issued against men, with the remaining 15% issued against women.

Clearly, ex parte orders violate several of the recognized elements of due process, including advance notice of the pro-posed action, the right to present evidence, and the opportunity to present reasons why the proposed action should not be taken.

Police intervention often accompanies a restraining order.

One study interviewed 227 Massachusetts women who had experienced interpersonal violence within the previous 5 years. Of those women, 34.4% had requested a restraining order. In three-quarters of those cases, the woman had also summoned the police. Restraining orders have serious consequences for the respondent. First, they require the person to immediately vacate the house, allowing the claimant to take possession of the property. When children are involved, TROs usually have the effect of separating them from one of their parents.

Nonetheless, restraining orders have long been considered lawful when there is a need for emergency relief in the presence of a direct threat of physical harm. Proponents assert that within 2 weeks the man will have the opportunity to present his case and justice can be served. But the David Letterman saga raises the question, how could the New Mexico judge issue an order in the absence of any direct threat of physical harm? After all, Mr. Letterman lived thousands of miles away and had never met Ms. Nestler.

The answer is simple: restraining orders are easy to obtain because state laws define domestic violence so broadly.

In Massachusetts, the legal definition of abuse includes placing another in fear of imminent serious physical harm. But judges seldom request any objective proof of fear or imminent serious physical harm, so requests for orders are routinely granted.

Likewise, in Oregon, merely claiming a fear of violence is considered grounds for issuance of the order.

In New Jersey, a judge may issue a restraining order when necessary to protect the life, health, or well-being of a victim. Obviously, any lover's quarrel or marital tiff could be interpreted as causing emotional distress or somehow affecting a person's wellbeing.

That broad definition led to the following unfortunate case:

A New Jersey woman repeatedly voiced her disapproval of her estranged husband's newfound romantic interest, which resulted in the imposition of a restraining order on her.

When she later called the new girlfriend a slut, which was ruled to be a violation of the restraining order. She was sentenced to 6 months' probation and community service.

The relevant Michigan law is similarly broad, and contains a troubling loophole.

The law describes domestic violence as:

(i) Causing or attempting to cause physical or mental harm to a family or household member.

(ii) Placing a family or household member in fear of physical or mental harm.

The statute then goes on to exclude any act of self-defense from its definition. Thus, if one party made a remark that caused any sort of mental harm, the second party could presumably retaliate with legal immunity. Once the law defines almost any interpersonal maladjustment as domestic violence, the courts then establish procedures to expedite the issuance of these orders.

For example, in California, it appears to be as easy to obtain a restraining order as a hunting or fishing license.

The Sacramento Superior Court's website instructs TRO applicants as follows:

Please present the completed domestic violence forms to the Family Law Filing Window in Room 100 of the William R. Ridgeway Family Relations Courthouse. The clerk will conduct a mini-interview with you to clarify your request and to ensure that you filled out the forms correctly.

Final Restraining Orders

In most states a temporary order is followed by a full hearing 10–14 days later; at that time, a final determination is reached. In theory, the person accused of domestic violence is entitled to full due process protections. But in practice, it may not work out that way. In modern America, the mere accusation of domestic violence serves to stigmatize and demoralize a person. It becomes the modern-day equivalent of the old joke, So when did you stop beating your wife?

The man, now homeless and distraught, has only a few days to find a lawyer and prepare his defense (assuming that he has the money for a lawyer). He may find it difficult to pay his bills, since the protective order may have precluded his taking his checkbook with him.

He may have evidence in the family home that supports his case, but access to that evidence is now difficult, or perhaps that evidence simply becomes lost. If he requests a continuance to prepare for the hearing, that means he is separated from his home and children for an even longer period of time. Since the incident is addressed under civil proceedings, he has no right to be provided with free counsel if he cannot afford an attorney.

In contrast, the woman may enjoy the benefit of free legal assistance that is underwritten by domestic violence programs. Attorney Miriam Altman observes that the deck is often stacked against the man because the mere allegation of domestic abuse… may shift the burden of proof to the defendant.

In Washington State, for example, the Temporary Order for Protection reads as follows:

IT IS THEREFORE ORDERED THAT…The respondent is directed to appear and show cause why this temporary order should not be made effective for one year or more and why the court should not order the relief requested by the petitioner or other relief which may include electronic monitoring, payment of costs, and treatment.

The wording of the Order is clear: the burden of proof rests on the respondent to prove that the order should not be extended for a full year. In other words, *guilty until proven innocent.*

In New Jersey, the defendant is not allowed to depose the alleged victim because, according to the statutory wording, this perpetuates the cycle of power and control whereby the perpetrator remains the one with the power and the victim remains powerless.

It is troubling that the law itself does not use the word alleged to qualify the terms perpetrator and victim. In some cases, the plaintiff may introduce hear-say evidence and examples of prior actions that should not be allowed under the rules of evidence. But if the man is representing himself, he is unlikely to object. Al-though the woman may have had months to prepare for the case, the man may have only two weeks.

This guilty-unless-proven-innocent logic becomes rooted in judicial thinking as well. It has been one family attorney's experience that the first question a judge some-times asks is, Well, why shouldn't I enter this order against your client? This is the court transcript from a Massachusetts hearing in which the respondent's attorney requested the court to vacate (i.e., discontinue) the order: Mr. Hession: Can you please state your name and your address for the record?

[The Court argues with counsel as to whether Mr. L can testify.]

The Court: —I don't believe I need to hear any evidence from your client. I'm going to deny your request to vacate the restraining order.

Attorney David Heleniak sums up the process this way: In ten days, the hypothetical husband has gone from having a normal life with a wife, children and home to being a social pariah, homeless, poor, and alone, trapped in a Kafkaesque nightmare. That experience can ultimately have disastrous consequences, as the following case reveals:

Lewis Barber, of Alexandria, Virginia, was considered a loving husband and father by his neighbors. Mr. Barber was issued a protective order directing that he not contact his wife or 9 year old son. The judge's decision to grant the order was based on the fact that Mr. Barber owned a collection of Civil War firearms at the time and that 7 years earlier he had fired shots in his attic. On April 26, 2005, a distraught Lewis removed his son from his wife's possession and brought him to his own house. After an 18-hour standoff, Mr. Barber was shot to death by the local police.

Gender Bias in the Issuance of Restraining Orders

If a man has been assaulted by his intimate partner, he should be able to obtain an order of protection. But a double standard may thwart this request. This is borne out by research. In Massachusetts, one analysis examined all domestic ex parte hearings held in the Gardner District Court in 1997. The analysis found that 34% of requests from men were deferred or turned down, compared to only 10% of requests from women.

According to Oregon attorney Ron Johnston, I believe many general practice attorneys who don't specialize in domestic relations would hesitate before trying to get a restraining order for a man, whereas there would be no hesitation at all for a woman under the same set of circumstances. Mr. Johnston's statement is based on the fact that in Portland, the protective orders once featured the following gender-based language: The respondent in this order is the natural/legal father of the below named minor children.

A father suffered repeated assaults by his wife, on one occasion requiring medical treatment for his injuries at the local emergency room. Afraid for his children and for himself, he sought a restraining order. At the time of court hearing, he brought photographs of his injuries, medical documentation of his emergency room visit, and a copy of the police report. The judge's explanation for denying the man's request was: Well, you have to expect one knock-down drag-out fight per divorce.

When Abuse Victims Themselves Are Accused of Being Perpetrators

Legal bias is not the only reason that male victims are often reluctant to seek restraining orders. There have been reports of abused men who, upon requesting help from law enforcement officials, found them accused of being the perpetrator.

In one case, a woman severely bit her husband on the shoulder and chest. After showing the judge pictures of his injuries, the man was granted a restraining order.

The next day the woman went before the same judge and, even though she had suffered no injuries, she claimed to be in fear for her life, saying that the man was the real abuser. On the basis of that unsubstantiated allegation, the judge reversed the original order against the wife and issued an order against the husband.

As family violence expert Murray Straus put it, there are a growing number of complaints that attempts by men to obtain police protection may result in the man being arrested.

A Washington State attorney gives this advice with regard to domestic violence: Don't call 911 unless you are bleeding and she still has a weapon in her hand. Too many men who have called 911 for help have ended up being arrested for DV.

When government programs ignore the actions of perpetrators and encourage the arrest of victims, that's a sure sign of a justice system turned upside down.

Restraining Orders Break Up Families

Allegations of abuse and restraining orders are often used as part of the gamesmanship of divorce-a tactic that is generally unavailable, however, to men. In-deed, divorce attorneys have been known to offer to drop the allegation of abuse in exchange for financial concessions.

This section of the Report uses two actual cases from Illinois to illustrate how restraining orders serve to disrupt normal family bonds. The problem begins with the legal definition. The Illinois Domestic Violence Act's definition of domestic violence encompasses any type of emotional distress. How does that play out in the event of a marital conflict?

An actual Order of Protection issued in Illinois is shown on the next page (the red markings were added later). In this case, there was not even an allegation of physical assault. Rather, the wife accused her husband of harassment and interference with personal liberty (box #1). Both allegations are subjective and vague. On the basis of those claims, the petitioner was granted physical custody of the children (box #5). Additionally, the children were removed from their father and allowed to see him only every other weekend until 6:00 p.m. on Sunday (box #7).

Another Illinois case reveals how these restraining orders soon become the legal foundation for long-term family disruption. The following case is recounted from the perspective of Mrs. Arlene Soucie, a grandmother: In November 2002, Mrs. Soucie's daughter-in-law moved out of the family home, taking her 9-month-old son with her. For more than 3 months, the father, who worked in law enforcement, and the grandmother were not informed about the child's whereabouts.

They were finally granted child visitation rights, but even though the two were careful to be considerate when picking up and returning the child, the mother apparently became irate. So the mother went to a judge and claimed that she was experiencing emotional distress when the father and grandmother picked up the child. As a result, in October 2003, Mrs. Soucie and her son were placed under an order of protection prohibiting them from having any contact with the child. The mother has learned the system and uses it to her advantage, concluded the distraught grand-mother.

How common are Frivolous Restraining Orders?

Concerns that restraining orders violate due process protections have been voiced in the legal community for years.

Elaine Epstein, former president of the Massachusetts Bar Association, admitted, Everyone knows that restraining orders and orders to vacate are granted to virtually all who apply…In many cases, allegations of abuse are now used for tactical advantage.

In Connecticut, attorney Arnold Rutkin charged that many judges view temporary restraining orders as a rubber-stamping exercise and that subsequent hearings are usually a sham.

In Missouri, a survey of judges and attorneys yielded many complaints of blatant disregard for due process and noted that allegations of domestic violence were widely used as a litigation strategy.

Nationally, domestic violence has become whatever the woman wants to allege, with or without evidence.
But how many restraining orders are indeed issued without good cause? To answer that question, an estimate is made of the total number of retraining orders issued each year. Then the proportion of those that are frivolous is calculated.

Annual number of restraining orders

Analyst Neal Miller compiled data on final restraining orders (mostly in 2002) from 29 state court systems, and found that rates varied widely across the states. Florida issued such orders more than four times more often (504 per 100,000 population) than in Tennessee (115 per 100,000 persons). On average, Miller found that 342 final restraining orders were issued per 100,000 persons. When extrapolated to the entire US population, an estimated 860,000 final orders were granted.

That number parallels data from the FBI National Crime Information Center (NCIC), which includes a national registry of restraining orders. Each year 600,000 to 700,000 permanent orders are entered into the registry.

However, eight states do not participate in the NCIC registry at all, and many other states have incomplete coverage. For example in Texas, 25 counties do not report. In California, 17 counties do not have a reliable procedure to enter orders into their database. Given the trend to increasing numbers of restraining orders, the best estimate of final restraining orders now issued each year is 900,000. The national number of temporary restraining orders is unknown.

But break-downs on temporary vs. final orders are available from three states:

In Connecticut, 9,390 restraining orders were issued in 2004, of which 66.5% were temporary and the remaining 33.5% were permanent.
In Pennsylvania, 57,316 Protection from Abuse orders were issued in 2004, consisting of 39,997 temporary orders and 17,319 final orders, either by stipulation/agreement or after a hearing.
In Virginia, 84% of all restraining orders are emergency or temporary, 16% are permanent.
In Connecticut and Pennsylvania, two temporary restraining orders are issued for every final order.
In Virginia, the ratio is over five to one.

On the basis of that information, we estimate that 2-3 million temporary restraining orders are issued each year in the United States.

Non-meritorious orders

What percentages of all restraining orders are issued without sound basis? Restraining orders were originally designed to protect individuals from physical harm. So, by any reasonable standard, a restraining order—especially when issued on an ex parte basis that does not even allege violence is non-meritorious.

A 1995 study conducted by the Massachusetts Trial Court reviewed the domestic restraining orders issued in that state. The study found that less than half of the orders involved even an allegation of violence.38 In other words; the order was issued solely on the basis of alleged fear or emotional distress, or even on the basis of a desire to seek retribution not because of actual or imminent violence.

Likewise, Dorothy Wright, a New Jersey attorney and former board member of a women's shelter, has estimated that 40%–50% of all restraining orders are requested purely as a legal maneuver. One analysis examined the allegations listed in 288 abuse prevention orders issued in the Massachusetts Gardner District Court in 1997 that were requested by women.

In 41% of these cases, fear was the sole allegation listed. Furthermore in only 34% of the 288 orders did the woman claim that any harm had occurred. A more recent analysis of domestic violence restraining orders issued in 2006 in Campbell County, West Virginia concluded 81% were unnecessary or false.

Based on those reports, it is estimated that at least half of all restraining orders are issued in the absence of direct injury or harm.

Orders Issued with an Evil Eye or a Heavy Hand

The original idea behind domestic restraining orders may have been sound. But over the years, state definitions of abuse were widened, the types of partner relationships were broadened to include cohabiting and dating couples, and evidentiary requirements relaxed.

The Fourth Amendment affirms the right of the people to be secure in their persons, houses, papers, and effects, against unreasonable searches and seizures shall not be violated. It is those rights to be secure in their houses and to be protected from unreasonable seizures that are violated by unjustified restraining orders.

The U.S. Supreme Court once commented that the Fourteenth Amendment is violated by legal procedures that appear fair on their faces, but are administered with an evil eye or a heavy hand. The same could be said about restraining orders that are freely granted without even an allegation of physical violence.

CHAPTER 10
Justice Denied: Arrest Policies for Domestic Violence

Domestic violence is a widespread problem in the United States, endangering the safety of victims and weakening families. This is the profile of domestic violence:

Men and women are equally likely to initiate and engage in partner aggression. In about half of all cases, the aggression is mutual, meaning that there is no clear-cut initiator of the altercation.

Although women are more likely to be harmed, males represent 38% of those who suffer an injury from partner aggression. For many years, advocates have pushed for the strengthening of arrest laws and policies as a deterrent to domestic violence. But these persons have had to over-come a number of legal objections. In both the Fifth and Fourteenth Amendments, the government is commanded to not deprive any person of liberty without due process of law. Arresting a person for allegedly committing domestic violence has a profound impact on personal liberty men who are arrested for domestic violence are detained an average of nine days. Arrest has serious legal and social effects as well.

For that reason, police officers traditionally were not allowed to make an arrest for a misdemeanor most instances of domestic violence are legally classified as misdemeanors unless the officer actually witnessed the event or had an arrest warrant from a judge. That policy, the hallmark of a civil and just society, served to protect law-abiding citizens from arbitrary and unfair arrest. But over the past two decades, states have enacted domestic violence laws that increasingly departed from these time-honored protections. This Special Report documents how arrest policies driven by the Violence against Women Act violate fundamental notions of due process and equal protection under the law.

The Evolution of Arrest Policies for Domestic Violence

Over the last 20 years the criteria for arrest have experienced a remarkable evolution. They have evolved from warrant-required arrest to warrantless arrest, then to mandatory arrest, next to arrest only of the primary aggressor, and more recently back to pro-arrest. This transformation is discussed in the following sections.

Warrantless Arrest

Originally when law enforcement personnel were summoned for a domestic incident, the most common police responses were to mediate the dispute, recommend a referral for counseling, and/or separate the parties. Arrest was a relatively uncommon action. But advocates began to allege police leniency. In response states began to pass laws in the mid-1980s that allowed for so-called warrantless arrests for domestic violence cases. These laws still required police officers to have probable cause to believe the person they are about to arrest initiated the violence, even though the officer did not actually witness
the incident.

But exactly what is probable cause?

Probable cause suggests more than a suspicion, but less than a certainty. The broad latitude of the concept renders probable cause open to a wide range of interpretations. In particular, the vague meaning of probable cause places law enforcement personnel in a difficult situation, especially when neither party has suffered a visible injury. That subjectivity was revealed at one judicial education seminar where judges were instructed, So if anybody ever came back at you and said, Well, gee, that's a real reach in terms of probable cause,' you have the legislatively mandated response, which is, I erred on the side of caution.'

In other words, judges were advised to flatly discard the notion of probable cause in favor of the decidedly non-legal notion of better to be safe than sorry.

Nonetheless, advocates continued to push for warrantless arrest laws, citing a Department of Justice study from the mid-1990s that revealed the police arrested the suspected abuser in only 20% of domestic cases. And eventually they succeeded. By 2000, advocates had persuaded the legislatures of all 50 states to enact such statutes.

Requests for Police Assistance

Passage of the Violence against Women Act in 1994 triggered an increase in calls for police help. The Department of Justice National Crime Victimization Survey (NCVS) revealed that female victims of intimate violence became more likely to report partner assaults to the police over a four-year period:

1993: 48%
1994: 50%
1995: 53%
1996: 56%

Unfortunately, the Department Of Justice survey did not provide corresponding information for male victims. It is interesting to note, however, that the 1985 National Family Violence Survey found that women were nine times more likely than men to call for police help, even though women were just as likely to initiate the aggression. Obviously, the more often police are summoned, the more arrests will be made.

Mandatory and Pro-Arrest

One of the key provisions of the 1994 Violence against Women Act went beyond merely allowing police officers to make warrantless arrests. VAWA now began to actually encourage such arrests. That represented a complete departure from the traditional legal presumption of innocent until proven guilty. Now the assumption became, guilty unless proven innocent.

Relying on VAWA funds, states began to pass mandatory and pro-arrest laws:

Mandatory arrest requires a police officer to detain a person based on a probable cause determination that an offense occurred and that the accused person committed the offense. Thus the standard normally reserved for felonies began to be applied to misdemeanors.

Pro-arrest laws consider arrest the preferred, but not required action. An officer who fails to make the arrest must then file a written incident report justifying why no arrest was made.

One female officer revealed the dilemma of mandatory arrest policies: If we don't make the arrest, even if it's against our instincts, if something should happen, or if somebody else is reading the case and disagrees, you could be jammed up big-time.10 Mandatory arrest laws do not distinguish between one-time vs. chronic, or minor vs. severe violence.

In one Wisconsin case, a woman who slapped her 18-year-old son was detained because he sassed her and made an obscene gesture. Courts soon found themselves flooded with cases involving shoving, hair-pulling, and even yelling. One former prosecutor in Hamilton County, Ohio, complained, In the past, the officers would intervene or separate the parties to let them cool off. Now these cases end up in criminal courts.

It's exacerbating tensions between the parties, and it's turning law-abiding citizens into criminals. Jurisdictions responded to their rapidly-growing domestic violence docket with two strategies: establish fast-track prosecution and adjudication procedures, and implement the primary aggressor concept. Prosecution and adjudication procedures are analyzed in RADAR's Special Report, Bias in the Judiciary: The Case of Domestic Violence. The primary aggressor concept is the focus of the next section.

Dual Arrests and Primary Aggressor

Studies have repeatedly documented that in at least half of all cases, partner aggression is mutual. For example, a recent survey of dating couples in the United States found that 70% of couples who engage in violence do so is on a mutual basis. Not surprisingly, mandatory-arrest triggered sharp increases in the number of arrests of both men and women.

In New Jersey, enactment of a mandatory arrest law in-creased arrests for domestic violence by 33%. In California, mandatory arrest policies caused the number of arrests of men to increase by 37%, while the number of women arrested soared by 446%.

Hirschel and Buzawa examined the number of domestic violence arrests as a percentage of all incidents reported to the police in a number of jurisdictions. Before pro-arrest laws and policies, DV arrests represented 7-15% of all arrests; afterwards they rose to over 30% of all such incidents. But advocates began to complain that the law was being enforced too aggressively.

They argued that women who were arrested were being re-victimized by the system, seldom mentioning that false arrests of men might also be of concern. In response to these concerns, the Department Of Justice Violence Against Women Office modified its grant requirements.

Application kits for VAWA funding began to claim that dual arrests trivialize the seriousness of domestic violence and potentially increase danger to victims, so grant recipients would need to demonstrate that their laws, policies, or practice and their training programs discourage dual arrest of the offender and the victim.

As a result of these new requirements, the concept of the primary aggressor was introduced.

As a result, 24 states now have primary aggressor laws: Alabama, Alaska, California, Colorado, Florida, Georgia, Iowa, Maryland, Missouri, Montana, Nevada, New Hampshire, New Jersey, New York, Ohio, Oregon, Rhode Island, South Carolina, South Dakota, Tennessee, Utah, Virginia, Washington, and Wisconsin.
Which raises the important question, how does a police officer responding to a call determine who is the primary aggressor?

The Alabama Coalition against Domestic Violence developed these criteria:

1. Likelihood of future injury

2. Whether one of the persons acted in self-defense

3. Prior complaints of domestic violence

4. Relative severity of injuries to each person

5. Physical strength of the parties

But these considerations are riddled with legal and practical flaws:

1. Based on a quick assessment of the situation, how is an officer supposed to determine the likelihood of future injury?

2. How can the officer determine who acted in self-defense, unless there was an objective eyewitness to the event?

3. Knowing that women are far more likely than men to summon help, relying on the record of prior complaints typically disadvantages the man.

4. Relative severity of injuries may not be a good indicator of who is the primary aggressor, since a victim may retaliate with greater force.

5. Since women are just as likely as men to instigate DV, relying on the determination of physical strength is almost as arbitrary as relying on skin color or hair length.

The New Hampshire Department of Justice established a Law Enforcement Protocol that provides this advice:

When the officer has probable cause to believe that the persons are committing or have committed abuse against each other, the officer need not arrest both persons, but should arrest the person whom the officer believes to be the primary physical aggressor. In determining who is the primary physical aggressor, an officer shall consider the intent of the statute to protect victims of domestic violence, the relative degree of injury or fear inflicted on the persons involved and any history of domestic abuse between these persons, if that history can reasonably be ascertained by the officer

The New Hampshire criteria are similar to those in the Alabama list, except that the concept of fear is introduced. But experience reveals that men may be adept at hiding their fears.

Hence, the primary aggressor concept becomes a form of gender profiling, as the following case illustrates:

Susan Finkelstein and her boyfriend got into a heated argument while riding in the car. The argument escalated, so he pulled over to get out and walk home. She scratched him and he pushed her. The police spotted the incident and began to arrest the man.

Finkelstein told the officer that she was as much the aggressor as her boyfriend in their altercation. The officer responded that policy required arresting the larger of the two parties.

Current Status of Arrest Provisions

As of 2004, the following 22 jurisdictions had implemented mandatory arrest laws:

Alaska, Arizona, Colorado, Connecticut, District of Columbia, Iowa, Kansas, Louisiana, Maine, Mississippi, Nevada, New Jersey, New York, Ohio, Oregon, Rhode Island, South Carolina, South Dakota, Utah, Virginia, Washington, and Wisconsin.

In the following eight states, arrest is preferred but not mandated: Arkansas, California, Florida, Massachusetts, Michigan, Montana, North Dakota, and Tennessee.
As a result of the problems outlined above, the 2005 Violence Against Women Act mollified its position to promote pro-arrest rather than mandatory arrest policies. It is now estimated that each year about one million persons are arrested under criminal law for intimate partner violence,1 of whom 77% are male. A disproportionate number of arrestees are Black.

Ineffective at Best, Harmful at Worst

For some, the civil liberties concerns that surround mandatory arrest are still justifiable if, in fact, mandatory arrest can be shown to substantially reduce offender recidivism. Initial evaluations conducted in six states suggested that mandatory arrest initially deterred violence in employed men, but not among unemployed men. But in the long run, the incidence of physical abuse actually increased.

Furthermore, surveys of abused women reveal higher satisfaction with police actions when the officers complied with the woman's request that they not arrest the alleged offender.

In many cases the woman does not want the offender to be arrested; she just wants to stabilize the immediate situation. In light of these findings, the original research team that evaluated mandatory-arrest policies concluded that the policies should be repealed.

Christopher Maxwell and colleagues then examined evidence from five jurisdictions.30 They found that, according to police records, for 70% of men, whether they were arrested or not did not affect subsequent assaults on their wives or girlfriends. And the 8% of men who engaged in chronic domestic violence did not seem to be deterred by having been arrested.

Recently Harvard economist Radha Iyengar analyzed the impact of the passage of mandatory arrest laws in 15 states. Her conclusion: Intimate partner homicides increased by about 60% in states with mandatory arrest laws, which means that, Mandatory arrest laws are responsible for an additional 0.8 murders per 100,000 people. Thus, the weight of evidence reveals mandatory arrest policies are often harmful. And female abuse victims indicate a preference to have some say over whether an arrest is made.

As the Ms. Foundation for Women notes, victims want their voices to be heard, not silenced.

According to the FBI National Incident-Based Reporting System, 106,962 persons (58,113 spouses and 48,849 boyfriends/girlfriends) were arrested for violent crimes in 2000 (as reported by Durose et al, 2005, Table 5.8). This number is an underestimate for two reasons:

It does not include divorced couples, which account for about 18% all intimate partner violence (as reported by Catalano S, 2006).

The NIBRS receives data from only one-quarter of law enforcement agencies in the United States, which collectively have jurisdiction over 13% of the crime.

Therefore it is calculated that 1,003,392 persons are arrested each year for intimate partner violence:

106,962/0.82 = 130,441
persons from areas covered by reporting agencies; 130,441/0.13 = 1,003,392 total.

Arrests for Violations of Civil Restraining Orders

Civil and criminal laws were traditionally regarded as being separate and distinct. A civil offense was viewed as a lesser infraction that was committed against an individual citizen. In contrast, a criminal offense was an action committed against both an individual and society. A person charged with a criminal offense is subject to greater penalties, in particular, incarceration. Accordingly, the accused is also entitled to greater protections, including free legal counsel, trial by jury, and a higher level of proof required to convict clear and convincing evidence, not just a preponderance of evidence. But domestic violence laws blur the distinction between a civil and criminal offense.

The 2-3 million domestic restraining orders issued each year underscore this problem. Restraining orders are issued under the aegis of civil law, so a temporary re-straining order can be granted less regard for due process protections. But the violation of a restraining order issued for a civil offense carries the penalty of arrest, which is a criminal penalty.

That's like arresting someone who didn't pay a traffic ticket and putting him in jail.
The problem worsens when persons inadvertently engage in minor or technical infractions of restraining orders.

A rigid one-size-fits-all mandate overrides the commonsense discretion of police officers and judges:

Harry Stewart, a Massachusetts lay minister and father of two, dropped off his 5-year old son at the home of his ex-wife. He got out of the car to help open the front door to the apartment building, even though the restraining order required him to stay in his car when dropping off his children. When he later refused to sign a confession stating that he was a batterer, Mr. Stewart was forced to serve a 6-month sentence.

According to Hirschel and Buzawa.

The following 33 states have laws that mandate arrest for violation of a restraining order:
Alaska, California, Colorado, Delaware, Iowa, Kansas, Kentucky, Louisiana, Maine, Maryland, Massachusetts, Minnesota, Mississippi, Missouri, Nebraska, New Hampshire, New Jersey, New Mexico, New York, North Carolina, North Dakota, Oregon, Pennsylvania, Rhode Island, South Carolina, South Dakota, Tennessee, Texas, Utah, Virginia, Washington, West Virginia, and Wisconsin.

These cases represent a significant number of all criminal DV cases. One analysis in New York City found that 15% of all domestic violence cases that went to criminal court involved criminal contempt, typically arising from restraining order violations.

A Double Standard for Arrest

The Equal Protection Clause of the U.S. Constitution directs law enforcement personnel to enforce the law without bias or pre-conception. But cases have been reported of police officers who failed to take appropriate protective measures for male victims.

In one California case, a father of two was married to a physician who was physically abusive to him. On several occasions he called the police, but although they took a report each time, they refused to arrest her. On one occasion, she fractured one of his ribs with her kicks and then beat him over the head with his cell phone, causing him to bleed.

But when the police arrived, they refused to arrest the woman, telling the man, we ain't taking no report from you, buddy.

In another case, as a man opened the door into his house, his wife hit him over the head with a frying pan, causing a large gash. When the police arrived, they acted as if it were a joke. When the man said he planned to file a complaint, the officer rep-lied,
There's nothing to press charges on. She's half your size.
The judge won't even look at it.

In some cases, the civil rights concerns double when the police first refuse to arrest the female Perpetrator, and then proceed to arrest the male victim:

Baltimore Orioles pitcher Scott Erickson was arrested after an altercation with his girlfriend, Lisa Ortiz, in 2002. The local police found that she had initiated the fight by hurling objects that caused injury to Erickson. To prevent further attacks, Erickson carried his girlfriend out of the apartment. Ortiz suffered no injuries during the altercation. Still, the police viewed Erickson's actions as excessive and charged him with second-degree assault. Ortiz later admitted that Erickson has never been physically abusive toward me, and in no way do I feel threatened or have I felt fear from Scott.

The following case is equally disturbing:

A mentally ill woman attempted to shoot her husband with a shotgun. After the husband succeeded in wresting the weapon away from her, she summoned the police, admitting that she wanted them to come because she wanted to kill her husband. Despite this explicit statement, when the police arrived, they immediately grabbed her husband, wrestled him to the floor, and handcuffed him. They uncuffed him only when the daughter repeatedly explained that it was her mother who had instigated the incident.

Biased Training of Law Enforcement Personnel

The previous examples of law enforcement bias do not appear to be the isolated actions of a few over-zealous police officers. Rather, they stem from ideologically driven training programs and policies. In Massachusetts, a training manual advises officers to be wary of a male victim's excuses such as, She hit me first. In addition, the manual encourages officers to downplay the significance of a man's injuries, warning that injury alone doesn't determine who is the abuser. In New Hampshire, the Department of Justice Prosecution Protocol advises officers that alleged DV offenders may claim to be the victim of an assault by the victim. In other words, claiming to be innocent should be interpreted as evidence of guilt.

—You Call, We Haul Justice

The United States justice system is based on the notion that a person cannot be punished without due process of law. Traditionally, American jurisprudence allowed warrantless arrests only in the event of a serious crime, especially a felony. But domestic violence incidents are generally misdemeanors, which represent a lesser severity of crime.

Nonetheless, 29 states and the District of Columbia now have laws that mandate or encourage arrest. As a direct result, hundreds of thousands of persons are arrested each year. This represents a disregard of the principle of innocent until proven guilty. Abuse advocates justify such policies on the basis that they serve to deter future violence, a belief that is not supported by research data.

Perhaps the greatest distortion is VAWA's stance against dual arrest. First, that policy ignores the reality that half of all partner aggression is mutual. Second, it renders a person unable to defend himself from a violent attack, other than fleeing the scene. Any attempt to restrain the assailant or move her to a safe location is likely to be later construed as the man initiating the assault.

The Violence against Women Act, and the state laws it has engendered, turns every act of family conflict—a shove, a thrown pillow, or even a sharp word into a potential crime. The government is now authorized to intrude into the most private affairs of its citizens. Arrests serve to escalate partner conflict and restraining orders deter mediation or partner counseling. As a result, VAWA-driven policies and programs lead to family dissolution. The 2005 Violence against Women Act authorizes up to $75 million annually to encourage arrest and enforce protection orders.

Taxpayers' money would be better spent on programs that actually help to solve the problem of domestic violence without trampling on persons' civil rights.

CHAPTER 11
Bias in the Judiciary: The Case of Domestic Violence

Could this happen in America?

John Fleming of New Brunswick, NJ was repeatedly assaulted by his wife. When restraining orders proved to be ineffective in stopping the attacks, Mr. Fleming initiated lawful video surveillance of their home. One 4-minute clip revealed the mother caught in an abusive rage, physically assaulting both Mr. Fleming and their children. John Fleming did not retaliate. Even though the video was shown to the police and judge, a restraining order was issued against Mr. Fleming. Mrs. Fleming was never criminally charged.

Profile of Domestic Violence

Each year about 16% of American couples experience some form of intimate partner aggression. Over 200 studies show that domestic violence is an equal opportunity problem. Studies typically reveal that half of all abuse is mutual and is initiated equally by males and females. This holds true for couples who are married, co-habiting, or dating; for all racial and ethnic categories; and across all economic strata. About one third of those cases involve severe incidents such as being kicked, hit with a fist, threatened or attacked with a gun or knife, or beat up. The remaining two-thirds of cases represent minor incidents such as a shove or a slap.

The Role of the Judiciary

And each year about one million persons are arrested under criminal law for intimate partner violence, of whom 77% are male. It falls to the judiciary system to assure that justice is served. But many are wondering whether this goal is being achieved. To some, the judiciary has embraced conceptions of sexual assault and domestic violence that are vague, overly-broad, and one-sided.

For example, the web page of the Judiciary of Rhode Island explains, Domestic violence is not just a shame … It's a crime.

The page then lists several criteria for DV, including:

Are you concerned about your relationship?

Does your partner tell you what to do?

These criteria blur the distinction between normal partner discord and true physical violence. Others believe the prosecution of domestic violence cases has become tainted by the presumption of guilt.

In New York, Chief Judge Judith Kaye explained that the purpose of its integrated domestic violence courts is to make batterers and abusers take

According to the FBI National Incident-Based Reporting System, 106,962 persons (58,113 spouses and 48,849 boyfriends/girlfriends) were arrested for violent crimes in 2000 (as reported by Durose et al, 2005, Table 5.8). This number is an underestimate for two reasons:

1. It does not include divorced couples, which account for about 18% all intimate partner violence (as reported by Catalano S, 2006).

2. The NIBRS receives data from only one-quarter of law enforcement agencies in the United States, which collectively have jurisdiction over 13% of the crime.

Therefore it is calculated that 1,003,392 persons are arrested each year for intimate partner violence: 106,962/0.82 = 130,441

persons from areas covered by reporting agencies; 130,441/0.13 = 1,003,392 total.

responsibility for their actions, omitting any mention of meting out impartial justice or protecting the falsely accused from frivolous claims. This Special Report examines these concerns. Previous RADAR reports have examined the abuse of restraining orders and sex bias in domestic violence arrest policies. This report examines judicial bias in the domestic violence criminal justice system.

Steps in the Judicial Process

As the following discussion reveals, bias plagues every step of the judicial process.

Initial Prosecutorial Actions

At the outset, the prosecutor must decide whether to pursue a case. Sex bias has been detected at this stage. In Iowa, the Attorney General's Crime Victim Assistance Division has openly admitted, The prosecutors we fund are prohibited from prosecuting female cases. At the arraignment, defense attorneys have noticed that compared to other crimes, domestic violence defendants are more likely to be jailed rather than released on bond.

This impedes the attorney's negotiating leverage, since some persons will agree to a disadvantageous plea bargain in order to get out of jail. In one Massachusetts case, a man accused of partner assault requested an evidentiary hearing. The judge responded, I don't need a full-scale hearing…I don't care about that.

Why?

Because, as the judge stated, the issue was not who's telling the truth.

No-Drop Prosecution

Domestic violence is probably the only area of criminal law where the majority of claimants later decide to recant or refuse to cooperate with the prosecutor, occurring in about 80% of cases.
There are a number of reasons for this:

1. The claimant called the police to stabilize the situation, but did not want the abuser to be arrested.

2. The claimant wants to maintain a relationship with the abuser, believing the aggression was a one-time event and expecting the situation will improve.

3. The claimant was equally involved in (or even instigated) the violence, and does not want this fact to come out in court. One survey of dating couples in the United States found that 70% of all physical abuse was mutual.

4. The allegation is non-meritorious.

In response to claimants' refusal to cooperate, many jurisdictions have implemented so called no-drop programs (sometimes referred to as evidence-based prosecution) in which prosecutors decide whether to pursue the case, regardless of the claimant's wishes One survey found that about two-thirds of prosecutors' offices around the country have implemented such no-drop policies.

The New Hampshire Prosecution Protocol for domestic violence provides a revealing example of the mindset that no-drop prosecution can instill. The Protocol re-minds the prosecutor, A case should not be declined solely on the basis of reluctance expressed by the victim. Driving home the point, the Protocol further advises, During every phase of the prosecution of a domestic violence case the focus must remain on the offender's criminal behavior.

Nowhere in the Prosecution Protocol is the word offender qualified by the word alleged. The phrase due process is never mentioned. There is no hint that a person may falsely file a claim. So, not surprisingly, the document contains no reference to the notion of innocent until proven guilty. Despite the widespread adoption of no-drop policies, there is no evidence that such policies work, and they may deter victims from seeking police assistance in the future.

One research team concluded, We do not know whether no-drop increases victim safety or places the victims in greater jeopardy. The value of no-drop policies is further discussed in the RADAR Special Report, Why Have Domestic Violence Programs Failed to Stop Partner Abuse? Instances have been reported in which the prosecutor has threatened the woman with child abuse for failure to cooperate.

In one California case, the county prosecutor put a woman in jail for 8 days after she refused to testify against her boyfriend. She later won a $125,000 settlement for false imprisonment.

In some cases, no-drop prosecution results in the wrong party being charged with the crime:
Former NFL quarterback Warren Moon got into an argument with his wife, Felicia. Against her wishes, the case went to trial. Placed on the witness stand, she testified that she had started the fight by throwing a candlestick at her husband. Mr. Moon was acquitted.

Jury Selection

For cases that go to a jury trial, additional bias is introduced if the prosecutor uses unorthodox jury selection procedures. The National Center on Domestic Violence and Sexual Assault has published a list of questions to ask potential jury members.

Many of the questions are phrased in a way to prime potential jury members to presume the defendant's guilt: All of the questions refer to the alleged perpetrator using the male he pronoun, e.g., Do you think you can tell an abuser by how he looks or acts?

Some questions are inflammatory, e.g., how many of you understand that nobody is allowed to commit murder, even if they believe their wife is getting too modern?

Most disturbing is the question that begins with this claim: With domestic violence as the number one cause of injury to women in this country… That last statement is flatly false. According to researcher Richard Gelles, the claim that domestic violence is the leading cause of injury to women appears to be a fact from nowhere. The FBI has published no data that support this claim.

Evidentiary Standards

Innocent until proven guilty is a bedrock principle of the American criminal justice system. But many attorneys say that tenet has become compromised. Now, court procedures have been devised to save the few complainants who are in imminent physical danger, at the expense of many defendants who are wrongly accused. Referring to his experience in a domestic violence court, one New York City attorney commented, *my client is guilty the minute he walks in the door.*

Other attorneys have noticed a tendency to refer to complainants as victims, a term that can prejudice the outcome of the case. One article in the William and Mary Law Review highlighted the fact that evidentiary standards for proving abuse have been so relaxed that any man who stands accused is considered guilty. These concerns are heightened in specialized domestic violence courts that appear to care more about conviction counts than due process.

Conviction or Acquittal

In criminal cases other than domestic violence, about 90% of persons charged are eventually convicted. But when mandatory arrest and no-drop policies are implemented, cases of questionable merit are brought into the judicial pipeline. As a result, court dockets become backlogged, prosecution becomes more difficult, and conviction rates fall.

One review of 88 studies found that on average, only 47% of prosecuted cases resulted in a conviction. Likewise an analysis of adjudication outcomes in New York City found that on average, 58.7% of all cases were dismissed or adjourned in contemplation of dismissal.

Prosecutors justify these dismissal rates with the explanation that prosecution of questionable cases nonetheless provides the assumed victim with opportunities and services that would advance their safety. In other words, it's acceptable for an accuser with an unsubstantiated claim to be rewarded with services that he or she would not otherwise be entitled to.

Not to mention the pernicious effects of the false allegation on the person wrongly accused.

Sentencing

There is evidence that the sentencing of persons found guilty of domestic violence is gender-biased, as well. Donna LeClerc, director of a Florida-based domestic abuse treatment program, once observed, I think there's a lack of equality in the justice system. Women serve half of the sentence a man does for the same crime, if she serves time in jail at all.

That assertion actually understates the true extent of bias. According to the Department of Justice, the average prison sentence for men who have killed their wives is 17.5 years, compared to 6.2 years for women who have killed their husbands.

Alternative Adjudication Procedures

In many jurisdictions, mandatory arrest and no-drop policies have triggered an influx of cases that threaten to overwhelm court dockets. In some jurisdictions, alternative adjudication procedures are being implemented.

Bench Trials

As an alternative to using the criminal courts, some jurisdictions have created programs that issue retraining orders issued following bench trials in family courts. The practice of depriving a defendant of a jury trial and the other protections typically afforded a criminal defendant short-circuits due process. One attorney complained:

From the perspective of job security, a judge has much to lose and little to gain from ruling in favor of the defendant.

If he rules against the defendant, and the defendant is really innocent, so what? The defendant's life might be ruined for something he did not do, but who cares? There will be no headlines, no angry activists protesting on the courthouse steps.

Court Diversion Programs

Court diversion programs have been established in which the alleged abuser agrees to admit to a lesser charge and, in return, participate in a rehabilitation program in order to avoid a jail sentence. But these procedures are deficient in their respect for due process.

In Colorado, prosecutors devised a Fast Track system in which accused persons were incarcerated, charged with third-degree assault, and then offered a plea bargain involving a lesser domestic violence charge.

Most troubling, the defendants were not allowed legal representation; hence many did not understand the consequences of admitting guilt to a crime that some did not commit. Defense attorney Kevin Donovan asserts that the Fast Track system violates the right to counsel guaranteed by the Sixth Amendment, and is just butchering the Bill of Rights. One female defendant who went through the kangaroo-court system stated simply, It ain't about justice, that's for sure.

In Portland, Oregon, the deferred sentencing program has developed literature explaining the program procedures. The literature always refers to the perpetrator as he and the victim is denoted as she. An administrator for the Portland program defends this bias with the dubious claim that using gender-neutral language would devalue the fight against domestic violence in the overwhelming majority of cases.

In Warren County, Pennsylvania, a person who is arrested on a charge of domestic violence can choose between two possibilities: Go to jail, or sign a preprinted admission of guilt that reads, I have physically and emotionally battered my partner...I am responsible for the violence I used.

My behavior was not provoked. Observers suggest that these procedures are tantamount to extracting a forced confession.

In Lexington County, South Carolina, a diagram outlining program procedures reveals that all persons who are arrested for non-felony battery cases of domestic violence are meted some sort of punishment: treatment, fine, and/or jail.

There is no legal option that allows a person arrested for a domestic violence offense to be found innocent of the allegations.

Further Evidence of Bias

Gender ideology views domestic violence as a tool of patriarchal domination over women. Thus it is sometimes asserted that women never commit domestic violence, or if they do, they are acting solely in self-defense—even though research reveals that self-defense accounts for less than one-fifth of female partner aggression.

Nonetheless, that belief has inured itself into legal thinking, creating a double Standard. One prosecutor admitted, If I were the defense lawyer that [judge's attitude toward domestic violence] would be my concern. In one case a woman had a lengthy history of violence, including punching her husband in the nose and chasing him with a baseball bat, and later threatening to burn his house down. But when the man sought protection from the court, the judge ordered, *You must be 225 pounds, don't tell me you're afraid of that little thing, get out of my court.*

Prosecution of False Allegations

Some allegations of partner violence are non-meritorious. One former DV prosecutor in Georgia revealed:

As politically incorrect as it is to say, many women file charges against boy-friends/spouses on a routine basis, and then recant the charges when the cases come to trial. Some of the alleged perpetrators are really guilty, and [a] very large percentage (though not majority) are not guilty of anything except making the woman in their life angry.

But few district attorneys prosecute false allegations. Casey Gwinn, a well-known San Diego prosecutor, has acknowledged: If we prosecuted everybody for perjury that gets on a witness stand and changes their story, everybody would go to jail...I would say it's in the thousands of people who take the witness stand and somewhat modify the truth.

Battered Woman Syndrome

The controversial battered woman syndrome (BWS) provides further evidence of a judicial double-standard. The term battered woman syndrome is used to describe women who are subjected to repeated domestic violence, yet are disinclined to leave the relationship.

Battered woman syndrome was initially proposed by psychologist Lenore Walker. Erin Pizzey, founder of the world's first battered women's shelter, visited with Lenore Walker in 1977 during Pizzey's tour of the U.S. In her memoirs, Pizzey writes: I spent many hours with Lenore explaining my theories about domestic violence. I explained to her that after six years of taking in women and children and seeing many of their partners, I knew that domestic violence was not a gender issue. ... She [Lenore] was avid to hear of my experiences.

It was only later on that I discovered that she took much of what I had to say and recreated her own version of violence towards women which did not allow for the fact that both men and women can be violent. ... She knew and even then agreed with me that women could be violent. She knew that the cycle I explained to her was used by both men and women but she preferred to create her career based on false information.

Given that history, it's not surprising that psychologists disagree on how to diagnose the syndrome, and many believe it is more a product of political advocacy than of sound science. Thus, BWS fails to meet the minimum legal requirements for admissibility as evidence into a criminal trial.

Nonetheless, one review found that the vast majority of jurisdictions admit both expert and opinion evidence on the effects of domestic violence on victims of battering as part of a self-defense. Psychologists Joe and Kim Dixon conclude, The discrepancy between the low level of scientific support and the high level of admissibility suggests the courts may be attending to factors other than a valid scientific basis in reaching their decisions to admit BWS testimony. In California, state law has long recognized the existence of battered woman syndrome as grounds for commutation of a sentence. So when California socialite Betty Broderick went on trial for the double-murder of her ex-husband and his new wife, she claimed that as an abused woman, the law should protect her from a prison sentence. In this case, however, the jury disagreed with that line of reasoning.

More recently, the California statute was modified to encompass the effects of physical, emotional, or mental abuse upon the beliefs, perceptions, or behavior of victims of domestic violence where it appears the criminal behavior was the result. In short, a person can get out of prison for any crime if she can convincingly claim that she was subjected to emotional or mental abuse.

In 1990, Ohio Governor Richard F. Celeste granted clemency to 25 women who were serving time in prison for murdering their husbands. Governor Celeste's official explanation for the pardon? They were all suffering from battered woman syndrome. Each year many men are accused of domestic violence, some of whom no doubt were acting in self-defense. But no man so charged has been known to qualify for battered man syndrome.

Justice Unblinded

The King of England's Council once met in a room in the Westminster Palace where a star was painted on the ceiling. Intended to be a fast-track alternative to the criminal courts, the phrase star chamber eventually became a byword for judicial proceedings lacking due process. A new star chamber has emerged in the United States, one that is designed to make alleged abusers take responsibility for their actions, rather than meting out impartial justice.

As documented in this report, the modern-day Star Chamber prosecutes domestic violence cases against the wishes of the victim, side-steps recognized due process protections, and acquiesces to a gender-based double-standard. Attorney Mace Greenfield writes, as an officer of the Court sworn to seek the truth, I am offended and appalled at the truth being ignored in favor of the media-sexy political correctness. It only erodes the integrity of our justice system.

In front of many courthouses around America, a statue stands guard. Lady Justice, as she is known, is depicted as a blind-folded woman holding scales in her left hand and a sword in the right. The scales stand for the need to balance competing interests, the blindfold represents objectivity, and the sword reminds of us punishment. These are the moral principles that under gird the American legal system.

In recent years, Lady Justice's image has become tarnished. Her blindfold and scales have been removed, leaving only a sword to wield. That sword has rent families asunder, while unfairly punishing the innocent and excusing the criminal conduct of the guilty. What's more, that heavy-handed approach has turned out to be ineffective in stopping partner victimization.

It's time to restore the luster to Lady Justice.

CHAPTER 12
Education for Injustice

The Realities of Domestic Violence.

An article in the Daily Herald in Austin, Minnesota, described a domestic violence training program: Local law enforcement agents, social workers and county employees sat by helplessly Thursday night as Lenny savagely punched and pulled Maria's hair, then kicked her while she was on the ground.

Did anyone who attended this program notice the gender bias? Would they have been surprised if the roles had been reversed if Maria was shown pummeling a prostrate Lenny? Or if it turned out that Maria had provoked the incident by attacking Lenny with a kitchen knife? Each year millions of dollars, many of them monies from the Violence Against Women Act, are spent on education and training. These activities shape the understanding of judges, prosecutors, legislators, and others regarding domestic violence. These perceptions eventually influence legal decisions, government policies, legislative initiatives, and funding priorities.

Many VAWA-funded activities are educational in nature.
The following sections of VAWA refer to information, education, or training in their titles:

Section 105: The Violence against Women Act court training and improvements

Section 111: Grants for law enforcement training programs

Section 204: Training and services to end violence against women with disabilities

Section 205: Training and services to end violence against women in later life

Section 302: Rape prevention and education

Section 303: Services, education, protection, and justice for young victims of crime

Section 403: Public awareness campaign

Section 503: Training and education of health professionals in domestic and sexual violence

Section 833: Domestic violence information and resources for immigrants and regulation of international marriage brokers.

But what if these educational efforts were one-sided and misleading in their content?
What if they provided a systematically biased depiction of the partner abuse issue?
Would that undercut the effectiveness of efforts to curb domestic violence?
Could that undermine judicial impartiality?

What the Research Says

Hundreds of studies have analyzed the extent, nature, and causes of domestic violence. With remarkable consistency, research demonstrates the following: Each year one in seven American couples experience some form of intimate partner aggression.

Women are at least as likely as men to engage in partner aggression.
In about half of all cases the aggression is mutual.
Self-defense accounts for only 10-20% of female partner aggression.
About 38% of persons who suffer an injury from partner aggression are male.

Some studies have found that women are actually more likely than men to engage in physical abuse. Psychologist John Archer's meta-analysis concluded, Women were slightly more likely than men to use one or more act of physical aggression and to use such acts more frequently.13 Likewise, researcher Renee McDonald noted in her study, Differences were observed in the rates of male and female partner violence, with female violence occurring more frequently.

Most Male Victims Are Missed by Crime Surveys

A number of crime surveys have purported to pinpoint the prevalence of domestic violence. But their findings are misleading. For example, the Department of Justice has conducted two major surveys of intimate partner abuse:

National Violence Against Women Survey (NVAWS)

The NCVS reported that men represented 16% of all victims of physical abuse, while the

NVAWS pegged the male victimization rate at 39%.

Which study is correct?

Neither—for the simple reason that men are far less likely to consider a shove, slap, or a kick to be a crime, especially when the act is perpetrated by a wife or girlfriend. Thus, men report the incident less frequently.

One study found that male domestic violence victims are nine times less likely than female victims to summon the police.

As researcher Donald Dutton explains, these surveys, in turn, tend to filter out male reports of victimization. The following sections assess whether domestic violence education and training programs are consistent with established research findings.

Department of Justice Office on Violence against Women

The Department Of Justice Office on Violence Against Women (OFFICE ON VIOLENCE AGAINST WOMEN) website features information about domestic violence. One page encourages men to take the pledge to stop violence against women.19 Nowhere does the OFFICE ON VIOLENCE AGAINST WOMEN website invite women to take a pledge to cease violence against men.

More ironic is the OFFICE ON VIOLENCE AGAINST WOMEN page on teenage dating violence, which states, Twenty percent of teenage girls and young women have experienced some form of dating violence. Female victims of teen dating violence are also at greater risk for many other issues, such as substance abuse, sexual activity, pregnancy, and suicide.

That OFFICE ON VIOLENCE AGAINST WOMEN page also highlights the federally sponsored Choose Respect Initiative, which is based on a 2003 survey of high school students. The survey found that 8.9% of males and 8.8% of females reported that they had been a victim of physical dating violence during the previous year.

But the OFFICE ON VIOLENCE AGAINST WOMEN page contains no mention of the fact that teenage boys are victims of dating violence to the same extent as teenage girls.

Judges

Judges play a pivotal role in the interpretation, implementation, and enforcement of the nation's laws. Their rulings not only determine the outcome of the case at hand, they also send a signal to law enforcement personnel and prosecutors regarding the types of cases deemed worthy of judicial action.

Training Courses

Curricular materials designed to train judges have been found to present a misleading depiction of domestic violence. The National Family Violence Prevention Fund has developed a national judicial education curriculum, which states that its purpose is to help state court judges assess cultural dynamics that cause women to hide domestic violence and understand the potential dynamics between immigrant battered women and their abusers. The book's description does not mention immigrant battered men or indicate that half of all abuse is mutual.

The West Virginia Coalition Against Domestic Violence has published a judicial education handbook titled, For a Safer State of Family. The handbook all but ignores male victims and is equally adamant in discounting female aggression:

Domestic violence educators are often challenged to use gender-neutral language when talking about intimate partner abuse. However, domestic violence is not gender neutral.
The fact remains that the vast majority of heterosexual victims are women and the vast majority of heterosexual perpetrators are men. In its section on homosexual relationships, the handbook notes that saying women cannot abuse women are a form of psychological denial.

The book never acknowledges that ignoring female-on-male abuse also represents denial. The book simplistically asserts that domestic violence is a pattern of coercive control used by one person to maintain power and control in a relationship. That statement ignores the large body of research that shows that partner aggression is caused by many factors, including unemployment, history of childhood abuse, and alcohol and drug abuse. Given the gender bias found in training materials, it is not surprising that the actual presentations made to judges are also slanted.

For example, judicial education programs typically refer to the perpetrator as he, while victims are designated as she. One former court counselor in Wisconsin remarked that, despite his initial disbelief in the presenters' standard formulation (i.e., domestic violence is a by-product of male abusers' need for power and control), he found that the presentations still shaped my deeper mindset.

One New Jersey training program went beyond mere one-sidedness it explicitly instructed judges to ignore due process protections. One presenter, a sitting judge, dispensed this advice: Your job is not to become concerned about all the constitutional rights of the man that you're violating as you grant a restraining order. Throw him out on the street, give him the clothes on his back, and tell him, See ya' around.

If there were any doubts about his intentions, the judge further emphasized, So when you say to me, am I doing something wrong telling these judges they have to ignore the constitutional protections most people have, I don't think so.

The programs stress that judges should issue restraining orders liberally in order to keep their names out of the newspapers. Another judge says he warns his judges, If you don't follow the law after I told you what to do, I will guarantee that your name will be in the headlines. That's not a threat. That's an absolute promise on my part. Attendees were given additional warnings that lacked any notion of judicial impartiality and restraint:

If you've got any hint whatsoever there's a problem, sign the TRO. Don't take the chance.
Quite frankly, the standard really is by a preponderance of credible evidence. That's what the law is.

But what he's saying to ya, Don't make that mistake at three o'clock in the morning. 'You may be a little tired. Err on the side of being cautious.

So don't get callous about the fact that these people are pestering you again. You know, grant the restraining order.

Benchbooks

Many judges rely on benchbooks to summarize state laws and other key information about domestic violence.

A review of these books reveals widespread bias:
Alabama's Domestic Violence Benchbook contains the long-discredited claim, National crime statistics show that about 95% of spouse-abuse victims are women.29 No citation is given for those national crime statistics.

The benchbook from the New Mexico Judicial Education Center opens with this openly distorted explanation: The discussion in this chapter will assume a heterosexual relationship with a male abuser unless otherwise indicated.

The cover of the Ohio Domestic Violence Benchbook shows evocative photographs of five abused females, but none of abused men.
The Tennessee Domestic Abuse Benchbook includes demonstrably false statements such as Women are unlikely to commit homicide except in self-defense.

The West Virginia benchbook states unequivocally that women are overwhelmingly the typical victims of domestic violence and features the controversial Power and Control Wheel the same diagram that appears in the previously discussed handbook by the West Virginia Domestic Violence Coalition.

National Council of Juvenile and Family Court Judges

The National Council of Juvenile and Family Court Judges is an association of over 1,800 judges and judicial officers who work in juvenile and family courts. The NCJFCJ has established a Family Violence Department that has released a number of publications, including Managing Your Divorce: A Guide for Battered Women34 but no guides to help battered men.

The NCJFCJ's page on Family Violence states one-sidedly, Domestic violence puts millions of women and their families at risk every year. The page about its Green-book project refers to battered mothers, but makes no mention of battered fathers.

With the help of a grant from the federal Office of Violence Against Women, the NCJFCJ is now developing a curriculum that, according to its website, engages a critical mass of state court judges and judicial officers in:

1. learning how to identify and resolve issues that arise in court cases involving violence against women and children,

2. exercising leadership to end and prevent violence against women and children in the community, and

3. advancing the state of knowledge about how the justice system can intervene in and prevent violence against women and children.

One wonders how the NCJFCJ can turn its back on nearly 200 studies that show that women are as likely as men to engage in domestic violence, and that half of all partner aggression is mutual. And one worries how a one-sided curriculum endorsed by a national organization of judges could sway judicial decision making and under-mine the legal presumption of innocent until proven guilty.

Therapist Edward Dunning recounts his experience with a male client who was punched repeatedly by his wife. She was arrested twice on domestic violence charges and was later convicted. Although the man had no history of domestic violence, the divorce court judge somehow regarded the wife as the true victim and granted her sole custody of their son. Dunning notes, It's not unusual for violent women to be granted custody of the children.

Lawyers

The American Bar Association, the national trade organization for attorneys, has openly advocated for the Violence Against Women Act. The ABA has also published a report with the provocative title, When Will They Ever Learn? Educating to End Domestic Violence.

The report opens with this claim:

Experts estimate that 2 to 4 million American women are battered every year, a statement attributed to former Surgeon General Antonia Novello.

But family violence researcher Richard Gelles has debunked the 2 to 4 million battered women statistic, as well as other faulty claims made by Novello. Ignoring the well-known fact that domestic violence is concentrated in low-income populations, the ABA report warns, Law students and law professors are just as likely to be victims or perpetrators of domestic violence as other members of society.

The report makes this emotional plea: It is time for law schools to fill this desperate gap in legal education by incorporating domestic violence law into core curricula courses, upper level courses, and clinical programs. The ABA Commission on Domestic Violence has also published a fact sheet, 10 Myths about Custody and Domestic Violence and How to Counter Them, which has been found to filled with more half-truths and misrepresentations than truthful state-ments.

Law Enforcement Personnel

The Violence against Women Act also funds training programs for law enforcement personnel. Again, serious bias has been documented.

One police officer from New York discovered that the training in his state was run by the Office for the Prevention of Domestic Violence, not the Division of Criminal Justice Services, the state agency that is responsible for setting police training standards.

Why?

The DV people didn't want the police control over the training because police training is heavily influenced by the Constitution and constitutional protections in the areas of arrest and reporting in other words, the DV training session espouses arrest procedures that ignore due process protections.

A California-based officer described the domestic violence training classes he had attended as so dripping with male hatred that everyone in the class felt uncomfortable, male and female officers alike. He also criticized his state's must-arrest laws:

They also removed arrest decisions from the responding officer and we repeatedly had to arrest the man, whose only crime was physically repelling the woman attacking him. In the hundreds of domestic violence phone calls, perhaps 90% to 95% were false, yet I saw children's and men's lives destroyed irrevocably due to vindictive, greedy, spoiled, mentally imbalanced, and/or drug-infested women perverting the judicial system.

One retired police officer from Illinois explained, I recall the indoctrination seminars'that I was required to attend during our yearly police in-service updates. The State's Attorney would send a domestic violence advocate to deliver their Catherine MacKinnon-inspired policy speech. This person was usually someone who worked for a DV shelter or hotline.

Biased training can translate into inappropriate police response, as this case reveals:

David Woods of Contra Costa, California, was repeatedly assaulted by his wife, including having a liquor bottle cracked over his head, being kneed in his groin 16 or 17 times, and having a shotgun pointed under his chin. At one point, his wife called the police requesting protection from herself. When the police arrived, they promptly wrestled Mr. Woods to the ground. Despite his protests, the police would not release him until the couple's daughter informed the police, No, it's not my daddy. It's Momma.

Other Professionals

Training manuals, curricula, and courses have been developed for other professionals as well. This is only a partial listing:

The Simmons School of Social Work in Boston has developed a domestic violence training program that misrepresents the research by making statements such as, Between 21% and 34% of all women will be physically assaulted by an intimate male during adulthood.

The Department of Justice has funded a curriculum for dentists that makes the statement, 9.2 percent of women who sought care for physical assault by a partner saw a dentist, but makes no corresponding statement about male victims of physical assault.

Even journalists are instructed on how to properly cover the DV issue. The Washington State Coalition Against Domestic Violence has developed Covering Domestic Violence: A Guide for Journalists and Media Professionals.

The guide carefully avoids any mention of female-initiated aggression.

Public Information and Education

The Violence Against Women Act and other governmental programs also support informational programs and services designed for the general public. Several examples follow:
The Minnesota Advocates for Human Rights has a training module called Myths and Realities of Domestic Violence. The module consistently refers to battered women but makes no reference to battered men, and, additionally, makes the false claim that research shows that women are victims in 95% of domestic violence cases. It's ironic that a training program designed to counter myths would end up endorsing them.

The Judiciary of Rhode Island has a web page that explains, Domestic violence is not just a shame … It's a crime. The page then lists several criteria for DV, including:

Are you concerned about your relationship?

Does your partner tell you what to do?

These statements blur the distinction between normal partner discord and true physical violence.

In one West Virginia case, the presenter at a public lecture first made light of a young male who had been molested by a female teacher. He then went on to denigrate a male abuser in another incident, calling him a scum bag. When an attendee approached the presenter, suggesting that his comments were inconsistent with research, he was ordered to leave the session.

Hotlines

The Violence against Women Act also supports hotlines designed to assist abuse victims. These hotlines exist at both the national and state levels. The National Domestic Violence Hotline has a fact sheet called Abuse in America. In 13 of the 17 bullets listed, men are characterized only as perpetrators and women as victims.

None of the bullets refer to males as victims or give any indication of the mutual nature of many abusive incidents. One bullet makes the disturbing claim, 1 out of 3 women around the world has been beaten, coerced into sex or otherwise abused during her lifetime. That global statement is supported by a single American study on dating violence among adolescent girls.

By any standard, the NDVH fact sheet is lacking in factual content. At least part of the bias that exists at domestic violence hotlines can be traced to the training their counselors receive. In one case, the director of the California-based Rainbow Services admitted that trainers had instructed them to profile callers based on gender, treating all male callers as perpetrators, regardless of the actual circumstances.

Injustice in the Pursuit of a Moral Agenda

This Special Report has reviewed a variety of training manuals, curricula, educational programs, and other informational resources directed at judges, lawyers, law enforcement personnel, the lay public, and others. Many information sources make no concession to the problem of female aggression. For example, the Department Of Justice Office for Violence against Women website implies that only girls are at risk of teenage dating violence, while carefully avoiding any mention of a federal survey showing that teenage boys are equally likely to be victims.

Websites like these call to mind the Yiddish proverb, A half-truth is a whole lie. Some of the materials and programs acknowledge that women sometimes are aggressors, but then claim that women constitute the overwhelming majority of abuse victims, thus implying that the problem of male victimization is so rare as to be unworthy of further discussion. Some use phrases like research shows or studies indicate, but cite only crime surveys or studies that interviewed only women, never mentioning that such studies are inherently flawed. Often the statements are mutually contradictory, and the re-search citations are outdated or simply wrong.

In sum, not a single educational program identified in this report reflects the well-established research findings on intimate partner aggression—that women are at least as likely as men to engage in abusive behavior.

It should be noted that many of these programs are supported by grant monies from by the Violence against Women Act. But the biases go beyond misrepresentations of fact. Often materials employ emotionally charged phrases like battered women. In some cases, training programs refer to men in ways designed to elicit contempt or with such epithets as scum bag.

One training program was described by an attendee as dripping with male hatred. The misrepresentations contained in this report go beyond the occasional misstatement or overzealous claim. Rather, this analysis documents a consistent disregard for the truth, a campaign of willful disinformation.

This report is not the first to reveal the falsehoods that permeate the domestic violence industry. Family researcher Richard Gelles has noted that policy and practice seemed to be more influenced by ideologies and political values than actual re-search and evidence. Journalist Phil Cook has documented how industry advocates have resorted to threats of physical violence against researchers who reported their findings on female abusers. How did this situation come about?

Family violence expert Murray Straus offers this explanation: ... social scientists tend deliberately to close their eyes to excesses and incorrect statements by feminists because they do not want to undermine feminist efforts to bring about a more equitable society. Thus, avowedly feminist scholars have suppressed data on violence by women. ... History is full of atrocities carried out in the service of a moral agenda.

In far too many cases, female aggressors are denied help, male victims are treated as perpetrators, restraining orders are issued with no claim of physical violence, persons are falsely accused and arrested, and constitutional protections are circumvented all in the name of curbing partner abuse.

CHAPTER 13
A Culture of False Allegations: How VAWA Harms Families and Children

Families are the cornerstone of an orderly, prosperous, and free society. Families provide the environment in which children are nurtured and protected. In all countries and cultures, families constitute an important social welfare net for its members. Over the last 30 years, the American family has grown progressively weaker. Now, persons are far less likely to wed. From 1970 to 2002, the annual number of marriages dropped by 40%. When persons do marry, their risk of divorce is almost 50%. Non-marital births represent a growing concern. In 2004, a record high 1.5 million babies were born to single mothers, representing 35.7% of the total. Among Blacks, the number reaches 69.2%. Father absence is another indicator of family dissolution. Now, 34% of American children live away from their biological father, placing these children at higher risk for a broad range of social pathologies, including academic difficulties, conduct issues, and involvement with the criminal justice system.

The Violence Against Women Act (VAWA) was first passed into law by President Bill Clinton in 1994 and was extended by George W. Bush for five more years in 2006. VAWA (and companion laws such as the Victims of Crime Act and Family Violence Prevention and Services Act) funnel about $1 billion a year to provide victim services and enhance law enforcement efforts. The Violence Against Women Act has also spawned the passage of about 1,500 state-level laws. This Special Report analyzes how the Violence Against Women Act establishes the legal framework to create perverse incentives, make false claims of abuse, escalate partner conflict, and discourage partner reconciliation. The end result is to break up families and separate children from one of their parents.

Dynamics of Partner Abuse

Domestic violence programs often portray partner abuse as men assaulting their wives or girlfriends. This depiction is one-sided and misleading. Research reveals these dynamics of partner aggression:

About two-thirds of partner abuse cases are minor (e.g., shoving, throwing a pillow), while the remaining one-third involve severe incidents (kicking, punching, and choking).

Men and women are equally likely to initiate and engage in partner aggression.

In about half or more of abuse cases, the aggression is mutual, meaning that there is no clear-cut initiator.
Due to differences in size and strength, women are more likely to be harmed during an altercation. Nonetheless, 38% of persons who suffer an injury from partner aggression are male. The following discussion details how VAWA weakens families and harms children.

Legal Framework

The nation's domestic violence laws create a legal framework that serves to facilitate allegations of abuse that often lead to family break-up and harm children. The framework has five components.

1.Broad Definitions of Domestic Violence
The Violence Against Women Act defines domestic violence this way:

The term domestic violence' includes felony or misdemeanor crimes of violence committed by a current or former spouse of the victim, by a person with whom the victim shares a child in common, by a person who is cohabiting with or has cohabited with the victim as a spouse,... *Good laws rely on definitive and unambiguous definitions.* But VAWA employs the vague term includes, a word that opens the door to broad interpretations. State legislatures have used that loophole to enact domestic abuse statutes that allow persons to claim they are merely afraid or fearful as the basis for a domestic restraining order. Now, 63% of all states'definitions of domestic abuse include psychological distress and 33% incorporate the ill-defined allegation harassment. The result is that in many states, almost any action, violent or not, can be construed as domestic violence.

2. Incentives to Make Allegations of Abuse

State domestic violence laws provide for a variety of remedies to persons who claim to be abuse victims. These remedies, awarded as part of a restraining order, typically include sole control of the family residence and temporary custody of the children. Most states also allow for a broad range of other benefits, such as reimbursement for medical expenses, counseling costs, attorney's fees, and, in some cases, even punitive damages. These remedies are granted following a brief ex parte hearing. In many cases the defendant is not invited to present his side of the case, and indeed may not be aware that the hearing is taking place. Even though a final hearing is held 10–14 days later, such proceedings are considered by many to be a rubberstamp exercise. The allure of extensive remedies with minimal attention to due process protections and no penalties for perjury serves as a powerful incentive to make questionable allegations.
2005 Violence Against Women Act, Section 3(A)(6)

3. Aggressive Law Enforcement and Prosecution Measures

Communication break-downs and conflict are inherent in all human relationships. Most couples resolve misunderstandings on their own; police and legal intervention is seldom necessary. But most states have instituted intrusive pro-arrest or mandatory arrest laws, even when a brief cooling-off period will suffice.

Many jurisdictions have instituted no drop prosecution policies. No-drop means that even if the alleged victim recants the allegation and requests that the case be dropped, the prosecutor must still pursue the case. These programs operate under the doubtful assumption that most partner conflict requires heavy-handed legal intervention.

4. Child Custody Laws

Domestic violence advocates have pushed to enact laws that govern how allegations or findings of domestic violence should be considered in making determinations of child custody.

Twenty-six states require the divorce court to regard domestic violence as a best interest of the child consideration, 23 jurisdictions have a rebuttable presumption against shared parenting, and four states have an outright prohibition on shared parenting in such cases.15 At first these may appear to be reasonable provisions, until one begins to consider the previously discussed problems of open-ended definitions and perverse incentives. For example, the Kentucky statute defines domestic violence as:

*physical injury, serious physical injury, sexual abuse, assault, or the infliction of fear of imminent physical injury ... between family members or members of an unmarried couple.*16

The law also governs the impact of DV allegations on visitation arrangements:

If domestic violence and abuse, as defined in KRS 403.720, has been alleged, the court shall, after a hearing, determine the visitation arrangement, if any, which would not endanger seriously the child's or the custodial parent's physical, mental, or emotional health.

Thus simply claiming to be fearful may be sufficient to remove the other parent's child visitation rights.

5. Politicization of the Judiciary

One might expect the judiciary to serve as a buffer against unfounded claims of partner abuse. But the Violence Against Women Act funds judicial education programs that have been shown to be ideological and one-sided.18 Rather than helping judges to balance the legitimate needs of the accuser with the due process rights of the accused, the training sessions do the opposite, instructing judges to grant a re-straining order if there is any hint whatsoever that there's a problem.

At one New Jersey program, a trainer openly advised judges to ignore due process protections:
Your job is not to become concerned about all the constitutional rights of the man that you're violating as you grant a restraining order. Throw him out on the street, give him the clothes on his back, and tell him, See ya' around.' The Judiciary of Rhode Island has a web page that explains, Domestic violence is not just a shame … It's a crime. The page then lists several criteria for DV, including: Are you concerned about your relationship? and Does your partner tell you what to do? The Rhode Island Judiciary apparently believes that's domestic violence.

False Allegations of Domestic Violence

These five factors—broad definitions, powerful incentives, aggressive law enforcement and prosecution efforts, laws that link child custody to domestic violence charges, and the politicization of the judiciary create a nexus that gives rise to all-too-common allegations of domestic violence in which no violence actually occurred.

Criminal Law

Each year about one million persons are arrested under criminal law for intimate partner violence, of whom 77% are male.

A disproportionate number of arrestees are Black.

One report by the Ms. Foundation for Women expressed the concern that overly aggressive law enforcement has led to mass incarceration of men, especially young men of color, decimating marginalized communities.

Many persons assume a criminal charge of domestic violence involves an actual assault. But about one-third of domestic violence criminal prosecutions do not arise from a physical at-tack. One analysis in New York City found that 15% of the cases that went to criminal court involved criminal contempt (typically arising from restraining order violations) and 20% included crimes such as harassment, criminal mischief, and larceny.

According to the FBI National Incident-Based Reporting System, 106,962 persons (58,113 spouses and 48,849 boyfriends/girlfriends) were arrested for violent crimes in 2000 (as reported by Durose et al, 2005, Table 5.8). This number is an underestimate for two reasons:

1. It does not include divorced couples, which account for about 18% all intimate partner violence (as reported by Catalano S, 2006).

2. The NIBRS receives data from only one-quarter of law enforcement agencies in the United States, which collectively have jurisdiction over 13% of the crime.

Therefore it is calculated that 1,003,392 persons are arrested each year for intimate partner violence: 106,962/0.82 = 130,441 persons from areas covered by reporting agencies; 130,441/0.13 = 1,003,392 total.

It is not known how many domestic violence arrests involve allegations that are frivolous or false, but one former DV prosecutor in Georgia wrote, As politically incorrect as it is to say, many women file charges against boyfriends/spouses on a routine basis, and then recant the charges when the cases come to trial. Some of the alleged perpetrators are really guilty, and [a] very large percentage (though not majority) are not guilty of anything except making the woman in their life angry.

Or a person can be arrested for simply acting in self-defense:

Lisa Ortiz attacked her boyfriend, Baltimore Orioles pitcher Scott Erickson, by throwing objects at him. To protect himself, Erickson carried Ortiz out of his apartment. Even though Ortiz suffered no injuries, the police arrested Erickson. Ortiz later ad-mitted that Erickson has never been physically abusive toward me, and in no way do I feel threatened or have I felt fear from Scott.

A vindictive motive can be discerned in some cases:

Sally of Vallejo, California, had been ordered by the court to vacate the family home. But the day she was supposed to move out, she accused her husband Joe of pushing her. Joe spent the night in jail. The judge later dismissed the charges. Even the cop was apologetic, said Joe. She told me she didn't believe (my wife), but that she had to arrest me because the accusation had been made.

Two New York City attorneys have claimed the local police policy is to arrest every-one and let the prosecutor sortem out. Whatever happened to the legal requirement for probable cause? Thus, a significant number of criminal prosecutions for domestic violence do not include any allegation of physical violence, and some claims are actually frivolous and false.

Civil Law

It has been noted that allegations of domestic violence tend to cluster around partners with children and no prior history of violence. Such domestic violence al-legations are made to gain a legal advantage during a divorce proceeding, many believe. With remarkable candor, one legal expert advised, With child abuse and spouse abuse you don't have to prove anything. You just have to accuse. These tactics have become so widespread that divorce lawyers euphemistically refer to them as silver bullets, slam-dunks, or divorce planning. Legal commentators have expressed alarm over the perversion of justice:

Elaine Epstein, former president of the Massachusetts Bar Association, once revealed, Everyone knows that restraining orders and orders to vacate are granted to virtually all who apply...In many cases, allegations of abuse are now used for tactical advantage. In California, the State Bar admits that protective orders are almost routinely issued by the court in family law proceedings, even when there is relatively meager evidence and usually without notice to the restrained person...it is troubling that they appear to be sought more and more frequently for retaliation and litigation purposes.

New Jersey attorney David Heleniak sums up the process this way: In ten days, the hypothetical husband has gone from having a normal life with a wife, children and home to being a social pariah, homeless, poor, and alone, trapped in a Kafkaesque nightmare. By any commonsense definition, violence involves the perpetration of a physical assault that may result in injury. Each year 2-3 million civil restraining orders are issued in the United States. But analyses by the Massachusetts Trial Court and others reveal that half of those orders are not based on even an allegation of physical violence. Thus each year, at least one million civil restraining orders are issued without any allegation of violence - often with serious consequences for families and children.

Impact on Families

The current epidemic of domestic violence claims weakens the American family by promoting family dissolution and discouraging men from marriage.

Family Dissolution

Our nation's domestic violence system often portrays intact families as violent, escalates partner conflict, imposes separation, thwarts reconciliation, leads to divorce, and blocks pro-family reform.

1. Portrays Intact Families as Violent: According to the Department of Justice, only 2% of DV incidents involve currently married couples who live together.38 But the domestic violence industry often makes dishonest claims such as, women are safer in the streets that they are in their own homes. Likewise, training videos and TV documentaries (such as Lifetime's Terror at Home) often depict domestic violence as a problem mostly of married couples.

2. Escalates Partner Conflict: In the past, police intervention encouraged the parties to calm down and made amends. But now, a call to the police has the opposite effect. One former prosecutor in Ohio notes, In the past the officers would intervene or separate the parties to let them cool off. Now these cases end up in criminal courts. It's exacerbating tensions between the parties, and it's turning law-abiding citizens into criminals. Indeed under the laws of most states, any marital tiff can be considered domestic abuse and a single incident of physical aggression can deemed to be full-scale battering. There are
cases of pushing and shoving that are treated like crimes of the century, relates California attorney John Digicianto. Thus, state intrusion into the matter only serves to heighten the dispute.
Imposes Separation: One California assistant public defender complains that the district attorney pushes a particular point of view: separation. Likewise, women's shelters, sometimes criticized as one-stop divorce shops, discourage clients from reuniting with their partners, even when the abuse is minor.

One woman's account illustrates how a shelter's false police report impacted the family:

Following several heated arguments with her husband, Susan went to her local shelter for get counseling for herself. She emphasized to the shelter worker there had been no physical violence. Nonetheless, the shelter called the police. The police report stated—falsely—that Susan's husband had threatened to rape her and to kill the children. As a result, the husband was ordered out of his house. Two days later, the Child and Protective Services worker came to the house and detained the children, claiming the mother had not adequately protected her children. The children were placed in foster care for 38 days. Then Susan's husband was arrested and bail was set at $350,000. Because he worked as a truck driver, he couldn't afford an attorney. So he agreed to a plea bargain with 3 years' probation-even though no physical violence had ever occurred.

4. Thwarts Reconciliation:

VAWA-endorsed treatment programs likewise stymie reconciliation. One analysis of 30 states that have implemented standards for offender treatment programs found that 42% of states actually prohibit couple's counseling. A study by the National Institute for Justice observed, Restrictions on couples therapy and individual psychotherapy for battering are a point of contention between feminist oriented batterer intervention providers and mental health providers in many communities.

5. Leads to Divorce:

As a result of aggressive law-enforcement and prosecution efforts, our nation's domestic violence system amounts to state-imposed de facto divorce, explains Harvard Law School professor Jeannie Suk. The government initiates and dictates the end of the intimate relationship as a solution to DV.

6. Blocks Pro-Family Reform:

Efforts to reform divorce laws or promote marriage are often opposed by domestic violence industry advocates at both the state and national levels.

Men Reluctant to Commit

—*Hence the term Marriage strike.*

Most young women hope to eventually settle down and get married. But given the number of fathers who have lost their homes and children to false allegations of domestic violence, it is not surprising that many single men are now opting to forego family life altogether. According to a national Rutgers University survey, 22% of single heterosexual American men 25–34 years old indicate that they do not plan to ever marry.

And 53% of these men say that they are not interested in getting married anytime soon. Hence the term marriage strikes. These figures translate into many millions of families that will never come into existence. In sum, there is very little that is family-friendly in our nation's domestic violence system.

Effects on Children

More than one million American children experience divorce each year. How often is a false allegation of DV made during the course of the divorce proceeding? One study of divorcing couples with custody disputes found that DV allegations were made in 55% of the cases, 59% of which could not be substantiated as true.

Thus, each year, many thousands of children experience divorces in which false allegations of partner violence are made, allegations that often serve as the basis to deprive children of contact from one of their parents. Even after the divorce, allegations of domestic abuse may be used to separate children from a parent:

My ex-wife used a domestic violence charge against me so that she could take the children out of state. It worked great for her. The judge automatically granted a restraining order so that I had to stay away from her and my children (no more visits with my children). My ex-wife had no proof and actually told the judge that I was OK but she didn't like my [new] wife. After a year and 25K in ex-

penses, and almost losing my job and my license for being an accused domestic violence offender, I gave in and let her take my children out of state. And she agreed to drop the charges.

The all-too-common result of these laws is a weakening or severing of the child-parent bond. I've run into hundreds of fathers who've been falsely accused of domestic violence and can't see their children because of it, notes one shared-parenting proponent. These non-custodial fathers experience a range of emotional and psychological problems, ranging from a sense of displacement and loss, depression, and even suicide.

Four decades ago, Daniel Patrick Moynihan foresaw the impact of fatherless families:
From the wild Irish slums of the 19th century eastern seaboard to the riot-torn suburbs of Los Angeles, there is one unmistakable lesson in American history:

A community that allows a large number of young men to grow up in broken families, dominated by women, never acquiring any stable relationship to male authority, never acquiring any rational expectations about the future—that community asks for and gets chaos. Moynihan's prediction is now confirmed by dozens of studies that gauge the effects of separating children from their fathers. These are some high-lights:

Child Abuse

As discussed above, most states have enacted laws that restrict shared parenting, based on the belief that abusive husbands are also likely to be abusive fathers. However, the advocates of such laws rarely mention that the perpetrators of child mistreatment and homicide are more likely to be mothers than fathers - not because women are more abusive, but because single parents, who are usually mothers, lack the social supports that intact families have. Extensive research shows that when a couple separates, the risk of physical and sexual child abuse increases dramatically. For example, one national survey found that 7.4% of children who lived with one parent had ever been sexually abused, compared to only 4.2% of 235children living with both parents.

The most recent National Incidence Study (NIS) of Child Abuse and Neglect found that, compared to children living with both parents, children living with a single parent were placed at substantially higher risk of abuse. These children have a:

64% greater risk of experiencing emotional neglect 165% greater risk of experiencing physical neglect 77% greater risk of being harmed by physical abuse Approximately 80% greater risk of suffering serious injury or harm from abuse or neglect.

But these statistics actually understate the risk, because the NIS combines co-habiting and married parents into one group—and child abuse is substantially higher among cohabiting parents.

A better gauge of the risk that single parenthood places on children comes from a large British study. The research found that, compared to married biological parents, children with single mothers have a 14-fold higher risk of experiencing serious child abuse, and a 7- fold higher risk of suffering fatal child abuse.

Other Indicators of Child Welfare:

Children who live apart from their fathers are at risk for a broad range of social pathologies, including educational, behavioral, and health problems:

School performance:

Academic performance: A study of Black children ages 6–9 showed that children living with both parents scored significantly higher on tests of intellectual ability than children in mother-only households.

School drop-out rates: Fatherless children are twice as likely to drop out of school.

School disciplinary problems: Only 13% of 6th to 12th graders living with both parents have had behavior problems that resulted in suspension or expulsion, compared to 27% who lived in mother-only families.

Behavioral issues:

Among young adolescents, only 10% living with both parents had had sexual relations, compared to 23% who lived with a single mother.

Suicide: Only 9% of high school students from intact families reported suicidal behavior, compared to 20% of teens from single-parent homes.

Injuries:

A study of 17,110 children showed that children who lived with their divorced mothers had risks of injury that were 20–30% higher than children who lived with both biological parents.

Longevity: Children who experienced parental divorce had a lifespan 4 years shorter than children who did not experience divorce.

Poverty:

In 1999, the poverty rate for children living in single-mother families was 50%, compared to only 9% of children in married-couple families.

During the first 4 months of a father's absence, the chances that the child's family would fall below the poverty line increased from 18.5% to 37.6%

Of all children in TANF (Temporary Assistance to Needy Families) families, 71.8% lived with a single parent in 1998.

Juvenile delinquency:

The chances that a young male will engage in criminal activity doubles if he is raised without a father.

Violent crime:

Low percentages of father-absent households were associated with lower rates of homicide among black and white men.

Children are our Future

Tim Russert, former moderator of NBC's Meet the Press, wrote a sleeper best-seller. Wisdom of Our Fathers consists of dozens of poignant letters from children to their fathers. Most letters are edifying, some are amusing, a few are sad.

All of them drive home the same essential message: children need and want their fathers. Some may dispute the value of aggressive law enforcement measures. Many believe that restraining orders are ineffective and even counter-productive. And there may be controversy as to whether the Violence against Women Act can be credited for reducing overall levels of partner abuse.
But there can be little doubt that VAWA has contributed to our culture of false allegations. Each year, at least one million false allegations of domestic violence are made, often in the context of a divorce.

The resulting separation of children from one of their parents is linked to higher child abuse rates and the worsening of a broad range of indicators of child well-being. Any society that aspires to survive and prosper must be careful to place our children first.

CHAPTER 14
Has VAWA Delivered on its Promises to Women?

The Violence Against Women Act was enacted in 1994 by President Bill Clinton to prevent and treat intimate partner abuse. Since that time, many abused women have received sorely needed services and public awareness of the problem has been raised.

But has VAWA reduced the overall level of partner abuse?

Have VAWA programs paid heed to the needs and wishes of abused women?

Have they respected and supported the families and communities in which women live?

Have VAWA pro-grams balanced the needs of victims with the due process rights of alleged offenders?

In short, has the Violence against Women Act delivered on its promises to women?

To answer those questions, we first need to understand the dynamics of partner aggression. Over 200 scholarly studies of domestic violence reveal that:

Women are at least as likely as men to engage in partner violence.
In about half of all cases, the aggression is mutual and there is no clear-cut initiator.

About two-thirds of those cases are minor (e.g., shoving, throwing a pillow), while the remaining one-third involve severe incidents (e.g., hitting with a fist or attacking with a weapon).

The Violence against Women Act provides funding to develop counseling, medical, and other services for victims of domestic violence; to step up law enforcement programs to prevent partner assault; and to aggressively prosecute perpetrators.

As a result, 1,500 domestic violence laws have been passed at the state level that over-hauled the legal framework for addressing partner abuse.

These laws:
Provide for a broad range of benefits to domestic violence victims.
Mandate treatment programs for abuse perpetrators.
Allow for the easy availability of domestic restraining orders.
Encourage or mandate arrest.
Encourage jurisdictions to adopt no-drop prosecution policies.

But many of these laws are based on questionable assumptions and may infringe on civil liberties. A sizeable number of VAWA-funded services lack evidence of effectiveness. Indeed, VAWA programs have been criticized for ignoring a large segment of the domestic violence problem.

These issues are examined in the next 10 sections.

1. No Proof that VAWA Has Reduced Intimate Partner Abuse

Violent crime of all types—robberies, simple assaults, and aggravated assaults—has been falling in the United States for many years. That long-term decline also has been observed for intimate partner crimes. In 1976, 2,944 men and women were victims of intimate partner homicide. By 1994, the year that VAWA was enacted into law, that number had fallen to 2,087 per-sons—a 29% drop. So fatal partner crime began to fall long before VAWA had been passed:

Intimate Partner Homicides, 1976-2004   *1976/ 1980/ 1985/ 1990/ 1995/ 2000/ 2004*
Number of Victims   *500/ 1000/ 1500/ 2000/ 2500/ 3000/ 3500*

Hence, there is no evidence that VAWA-funded programs have accelerated the decline in intimate partner homicides. We have no evidence to date that VAWA has led to a decrease in the overall levels of violence against women. —Angela Moore Parmley, PhD, U.S. Department of Justice

2. Aggressive Prosecution Policies Place Women at Greater Risk

Three studies reveal that get-tough prosecution measures may actually make things worse for female victims of partner aggression: Mandatory Arrest for Restraining Order Violations: Many states have enacted laws that mandate arrest and prosecution in the event of a restraining order violation. One Department of Justice-funded project studied the effectiveness of such prosecution policies and con-cluded, Increases in the willingness of prosecutors'offices to take cases of protection order violation were associated with increases in the homicide of white married intimates, black unmarried intimates, and white unmarried females.

Mandatory Arrest for Assault: Another analysis of arrest policies found that women whose partners were arrested under mandatory arrest laws were far less likely to request police assistance in the event of future of violence. This is worrisome be-cause if persons don't report the abuse, the criminal jus-tice system is of only marginal relevance to persons who need help.

No-drop Prosecution: Sixty-six percent of prosecutors' offices have implemented so called no-drop prosecution, in which the prosecutor continues the case despite the victim's stated wishes to the con-trary. But one National Institute of Justice analysis warns, We do not know whether no-drop increases victim safety or places the victims in greater jeopardy.

3. Real Victims Have To Compete with Minor Cases to Get Help

Our nation's broadly defined domestic abuse laws have opened the flood gates to minor allegations of domestic violence. Currently, half of all restraining orders do not include even an allegation of physi-cal abuse.13 Elaine Epstein, former president of the Massachusetts Bar Association, once revealed, Everyone knows that re-straining orders and orders to vacate are granted to virtually all who apply … In many cases, allegations of abuse are now used for tactical advantage.

A case involving a well-known media personality illustrates the problem:

New Mexico Judge Daniel Sanchez issued a restraining order to protect Colleen Nestler. According to Nestler, a man had been sending her mental telepathic messages over the past 11 years expressing his desire to marry her. Her alleged harasser: CBS talk show host David Letterman.

One commentator deplored the questionable basis of the Letterman case, arguing that the abuse of temporary restraining orders endangers real victims. Likewise, one National Institute of Justice report questioned the wisdom of mandatory arrest laws, saying that arrests for all suspects may unnecessari-ly take a community's re-sources away from identifying and responding to the worst offenders and victims most at risk.

In short, court dockets have become choked with minor and even vindictive complaints of abuse. As a result, the voices of the real victims of violence often go unheard.

Judge Rucker Smith, of Sumter County, Georgia, was assaulted by his ex-girlfriend. Even though she had instigated the incident and he did not retaliate, he was charged with battery. A jury later acquitted Smith of all charges. The judge subsequently recounted, For someone to falsely accuse another out of anger and vengeance silences the voices of the many real victims.

4. No-Drop Prosecution Ignores Women's Wishes

The majority of abuse cases involve disputes in which the conflict is a minor, mutual, and/or one-time occurrence. Women often believe these situations can be handled better through counseling rather than legal intervention. So in about 80% of cases, women who request police assistance later recant or decide to drop the charges.

As discussed above, no-drop prosecution policies often discourage women from seeking police help in the event of future violence. No-drop is controversial for other reasons, as well. If the woman refuses to testify, the prosecutor may charge her with obstruction of justice and threaten to take away her children. In one case, the county prosecutor put a woman in jail for 8 days after she refused to testify against her boyfriend. She later won a $125,000 settlement for false imprisonment.

New York University professor Linda Mills explains it this way: Mandatory policies turn professionals away from women in abusive relationships by focusing so exclusively on arrest and prosecution and ignoring the opportunity, through human contact, to nurture a relationship with the victims.

In short, mandatory arrest and prosecution policies silence women's voices. And sometimes no-drop policies turn out to be embarrassing to all parties concerned:

Former NFL quarterback Warren Moon got into an argument with his wife, Felicia. The police were summoned and, against her wishes, Mr. Moon was arrested. When the case went to trial, Felicia Moon admitted that she had instigated the altercation by kneeing him in the groin and throwing a candlestick at him. Mr. Moon was acquitted of all charges.

5. Lulled into a False Sense of Security

American taxpayers pay hundreds of millions of dollars each year for domestic violence treatment programs and law enforcement and prosecution policies. Yet there is considerable doubt about the effectiveness of these programs.

Treatment: Offenders are often ordered to undergo treatment programs based on the Duluth model. But psychologist Donald Dutton, PhD notes, Research shows that Duluth oriented treatments are absolutely ineffective, and have no discernible impact on rates of recidivism. The National Research Council explains that these programs lack effectiveness because they are driven by ideology and stakeholder interests rather than by plausible theories and scientific evidence of cause.

No-Drop Prosecution: Only one randomized study has been conducted that evaluates the effectiveness of no-drop prosecution. The research found that only one factor reduced abuser recidivism rates—allowing the victim to select whether and how aggressively the prosecutor would pursue the case. But by their nature, no-drop prosecution policies eliminate the ability of abused women to make that choice.

Restraining Orders: Restraining orders do not appear to be effective in deterring subsequent physical violence. One study concluded that restraining orders were flatly ineffective in stopping physical violence. Similarly a second report concluded that having a permanent order did not appear to deter most types of abuse. One review concluded that such interventions may, in fact, lull women into a false sense of security.

6. Rigid Law Enforcement Programs Ensnare Women

The Violence against Women Act encourages states to enact get-tough laws that promote the issuance of restraining orders, promote arrest, and facilitate prosecution efforts. But these laws may be going too far.

Restraining Orders: State laws have been broadened to the point that almost any action can be viewed as domestic violence. Once a restraining order is in place, a vast range of ordinarily legal behavior becomes criminalized. As a result of open-ended definitions, almost any lover's quarrel or marital spat now qualifies as domes-tic abuse. 2-3 million temporary restraining orders are currently issued each year—15% of them against women, and many of them for trivial incidents:

In August 2006, Saturday Night Live comedian Joe Piscopo obtained a restraining order against his wife, Kimberly.

The allegation?
She was using foul language and spitting at him.

Arrest: Thirty states have now enacted laws that promote or mandate arrest for domestic violence. As a result, the number of female offenders in domestic violence arrests rose by 10–25% in many areas. In California, the number of women arrested soared by 446% as a result of mandatory arrest policies, even though a number of those arrests may have been considered unnecessary by the woman's partner.

Prosecution: In Colorado, a Fast Track prosecution system put accused persons in jail, charged them with third-degree assault, and then offered a plea bargain involving a lesser charge. In exchange, the defendant agreed to not seek legal representation—a transparent violation of due process protections. One woman who went through the system stated, It ain't about justice, that's for sure.

7. Female Abusers Can't Get the Help They Need

Research shows that women are at least as likely as men to engage in partner aggression.
This is one example:

On November 10, 2006, Krystle McGlothin of Peoria County, Illinois, rammed the pickup truck of her ex-husband, Dennis, smashed its windows, and then ran him down, all the while yelling obscenities. Ms. McGlothin was charged with six counts of first-degree murder.

Most abusive women do not take their anger to the point of killing their partners.

But where can violent women get the help they need?

Violence initiated by a woman increases the chances of retaliatory aggression against that woman. But experience reveals that when abusive women request help from VAWA funded agencies, they learn that female-specific treatment pro-grams are almost nonexistent, and their requests for treatment may be dismissed with comments such as, I'm sure you're under stress, or He must have provoked you. Or if these women do find services designed specifically for women, they may find that female offenders are actually treated as the victims, which allows the abuse to continue.

Researcher Susan Steinmetz tells of receiving letters from violent women who recognized that they needed help, but were turned away or being offered no help when they called a crisis line or shelter. As attorney Linda Kelly puts it, Today's treatment denies the possibility that women can be violent. When government policies neglect the problem, it's often children who pay the price:

Socorro Caro of San Fernando Valley, California, had repeatedly attacked her husband. But her husband, a well-known physician, was reluctant to report the incidents because he thought that the authorities wouldn't believe him. On November 22, 1999, Mrs. Caro shot their three sons with a .38-caliber handgun. Two years later she was convicted of first-degree murder.

8. Abuse Shelters Do Not Meet Victim's Needs

Abuse shelters are considered to be a mainstay of treatment services for domestic violence victims. But evidence supporting the effectiveness of these shelters is not persuasive. Whether the outcome measure is recurrence of the violence, long-term separation of the abuser and victim, or victim satisfaction, the results have been found to be mixed. One survey of shelters found that half of them stressed feminist political activism over providing women with practical solutions to their problems. An example of such bias came from a former volunteer who was told by her supervisor to not ad-vise an abused woman to learn self-defense techniques.

Why?

Because such advice could be interpreted as blaming the woman for not protecting herself.

In Massachusetts, one mother was pressured to attend a group for abused women run by volunteers with no professional qualifications. She claimed that the clients were coerced by use of threats, intim-idation, and fear of losing their children. In the end, she filed a lawsuit against the shelter alleging a variety of civil rights violations.

Marilyn Hooks, 25, and Milaus Almore, 8 weeks pregnant, were residents in the SafeSpace shelter in Stuart, Florida. On October 31, 2007, the women fell into an argument. Hooks pulled out a knife and fatally stabbed Almore. Hooks was later charged with second-degree murder.

Before the incident, Hooks had made death threats to a staff member and resident, but the shelter manager ignored staff recommendations to evict the woman. The manager was later terminated from her position.

9. System Removes Children from Their Homes

In many states, the definition of child abuse has now been expanded so if a child simply observes partner aggression, it is deemed to constitute child abuse. The mere accusation of partner aggression means that that parent will also be suspected of child abuse and the other parent may be charged with child neglect. That be-comes grounds for removing the child from the family home.

In one case, a shelter held meetings for abused women and promised their statements would be kept confidential. In spite of assurances to the contrary, however, one woman's comments were passed along to the state child abuse agency. Shortly afterwards, the agency ordered the woman's daughter be removed from the home, accusing the mother of neglectfully allowing the girl to be exposed to domestic violence. The daughter, who had never suffered any physical abuse, was returned home 13 months later.

This is another example:

A couple had several heated arguments, but neither had suffered any physical abuse. When Susan began to think about striking her husband with an object, she realized that she needed to get help. So she went to her local shelter to seek counseling. The shelter called the police to take a statement. The police report stated—erroneously—that Susan's husband had threatened to rape her and to kill the children. On the basis of that faulty report, the husband was arrested and bail set at $350,000. He was eventually placed on 3 years' probation. The children were placed in foster care for 38 days. The woman concluded, these people have no idea of the damage they have done. I compare it to someone coming into your home and
ransacking it.

In addition, when a restraining order is issued, it forbids contact not only between the alleged offender and the victim, but also between the alleged abuser and the children. This restriction extends to the couple's parents and extended family members as well. As a result, grandmothers and grandfathers may be prohibited from seeing their own grandchildren.

10. Policies Break Up Families and Harm Children

Research shows that the safest place for women is in the intact family. According to the Department of Justice, only 2% of partner aggression involves currently married couples who live together. The majority of domestic abuse incidents are minor, such as a shove or one-time slap. In such cases, reconciliation is preferable. But no-contact restraining orders and policies of women's shelters preclude persons from receiving couples' counseling.

Harvard law professor Jeannie Suk argues that restraining orders amount to state imposed de facto divorce in which the mere presence of the accused offender in the family home becomes a proxy for the crime of domestic violence. As a result, the government initiates and dictates the end of the intimate relationship as a solution to DV. Suk wonders whether such orders violate persons' fundamental right to marry. Some VAWAfunded programs appear to actively promote divorce. Abuse shelters have been referred to as one-stop divorce shops. The website of one Department Of Justice-funded program includes an advertisement for a divorce lawyer matching service.

Thus, a mere allegation of domestic violence—substantiated or not—can lead to family break-up. As a result, the child often loses regular contact with his or her non-custodial parent. Research shows that children who grow up in a one-parent family are at greater risk of child abuse, and fare worse on a broad range of indicators of academic, emotional, and social well-being.49

Women Speak Out

Women's groups are saying that our domestic violence laws may be hurting families more than they are helping:

Independent Women's Forum: Men may become alienated from and hostile toward the system in the conviction that it is stacked against them and unjustly favors women.

Eagle Forum: VAWA funds the reeducation of judges and law enforcement personnel to teach them...how to ride roughshod over the constitutional rights of men.

Ms. Foundation for Women: Unfortunately, when state power has been invited into, or forced into, the lives of individuals, it often takes over.

And a growing number of women are now calling for change:

There is no compassion without justice for all perpetrators and victims of domestic violence. All victims and perpetrators should receive help from VAWA programs.

Sheila Smith, LCSW, board member, Stop Abuse for Everyone

Research suggests that men and women in heterosexual and same-sex relationships are both perpetrators and victims of intimate partner violence.

If we as a society hope to end violence in our families, the feminist perspective needs to be replaced with a more holistic approach. —Jan Brown, executive director, Domestic Abuse Helpline for Men and Women

Regrettably, some State Institutions collude in the dishonest representation of domestic violence as consisting only of violent men abusing innocent defenseless women.

Now that equality is deemed to be a worthy aspiration, government agencies must openly reject the myth that domestic violence is a gender issue.

Mary T. Cleary, director, Amen (Abused Men), Ireland

A Time for Reform

This Special Report documents how the Violence Against Women Act and the state level laws it has engendered are ineffective in reducing abuse, may place women at greater risk of violence, make it difficult for real victims to get help, ignore the wishes of abused women, lull women into a false sense of security, ensnare women in a rigid law enforcement bureaucracy, neglect the needs of female aggressors, fail to provide needed services at abuse shelters, remove kids from their homes, and harm families and children.

Previous Special Reports have documented other problems with our nation's domestic violence system, including discrimination against male victims, politicization of the judiciary, and violations of due process and civil rights. Scientific research, expert panels, and individual cases all point to a singular conclusion:

Our nation's domestic violence system, once conceived with high hopes and the best of intentions, is now in need of reform.

CHAPTER 15
Perverse Incentives, False Allegations, and Forgotten Children

The family is the bedrock of society. The family socializes the young, provides economic security to its members, and allows for emotional fulfillment. But what happens to a society when a law provides incentives to file false claims of abuse that then become the basis for family dissolution? The following case involving a Major League baseball player illustrates the problem:

Southpaw pitching ace Chuck Finley was married to actress Tawny Kitaen, whose prescription drug addiction and erratic behavior once placed the lives of their two daughters at risk. One night Kitaen turned on the gas in the fireplace without lighting it and then called the girls to come to bed to go to sleep. On another occasion, she was charged with vandalizing a woman's car in a parking lot. On April 1, 2002, Kitaen attacked Finley while he was driving the car, kicking him with her high-heeled boots, which left abrasions and scrapes on his body. Kitaen was arrested by the Newport Beach, California police. Three days later,

Finley filed for divorce and was granted temporary custody of their children. But in a move to gain custody of the two girls, Kitaen retaliated, accusing Finley of domestic violence because he had allegedly started the argument. Finley had no prior record of physical violence.

Following passage of the Violence Against Women Act in 1994, states began to overhaul their domestic violence statutes by enacting some 1,500 civil and criminal laws.

These laws:
Ensure the easy availability of restraining orders, resulting in 2–3 million temporary orders being issued each year Strengthen arrest and prosecution efforts Allow domestic violence (DV) victims to receive a range of legal, counseling, medical, and job training services, and Make it easier for alleged DV victims who are going through divorce to gain custody of their children It is believed that many, perhaps the great majority of, allegations of domestic violence are false. For example, in half of all restraining orders, violence is not even alleged. And in those states with dominant aggressor laws, men are often arrested as a result of sex-biased criteria, such as physical size or which person appears to be more in control of the situation. One reason for the rash of false allegations is the fact that civil and family law statutes now provide for a broad range of property, monetary, and child custody benefits, referred to in the law as remedies or relief. These benefits serve as incentives to file false allegations.

This Special Report analyzes the remedies described in the domestic violence and family law statutes in the 50 states and the District of Columbia.

Restraining Order Procedures

In most states, judges issue a temporary order to the alleged victim (referred to in legal parlance as the petitioner or claimant) on an emergency ex parte basis. The order is followed by a hearing 10–14 days later, at which time a permanent order can be awarded. In about 85% of cases, the claimant is female.

Since restraining orders (sometimes referred to as orders of protection) are issued under civil law, the preponderance of evidence standard applies. Unlike the beyond a reasonable doubt standard used in criminal cases, this means that even if the man accused has a credible case, the alleged victim will prevail if she appears to have a slightly stronger case. The most basic element of a restraining order is the prohibition of contact between the two parties.

The California statute is typical: An order may be issued under this part, with or without notice, to restrain any person for the purpose of preventing a recurrence of domestic violence and ensuring a period of separation of the persons involved. This means that the accused (legally referred to as the respondent or defendant) is prohibited from entering the claimant's place of residence or employment, approaching them within a prescribed area, or telephoning the claimant.

When restraining orders involve couples who reside together or have children, three additional issues arise:

1. Use of the couple's residence,

2. Temporary custody of the children, and

3. Financial support for the children's caregiver.

Even though denying the respondent access to his own home and children are serious penalties, such restrictions are imposed relying on broadly worded definitions of abuse6 and based on the unsupported assertions of the claimant. If a couple is going through a divorce, the temporary restraining order issued in civil court is then filed by the attorney in divorce court, requesting that the judge grant child custody as part of the divorce decree.

By invoking continuity and best interests of the child, the temporary restraining order becomes a de facto permanent award of child custody and child support payments to the mother. Other incentives are available, as well. In many states, judges can order that the alleged victim receive a variety of additional remedies and types of relief. The incentives fall into the two categories listed below, both of which are discussed in the sections that follow.

1. Property and monetary benefits

2. Final child custody awards

Property and Monetary Benefits

In most states, the judge has the discretion to award a broad range of benefits to an alleged domestic violence victim. These benefits are summarized in this section. The information in this section is extracted from WomensLaw.org, a website that com-piles civil domestic violence laws.

Property

As noted above, states allow the judge to award the exclusive use of the family residence to the alleged victim. In many states, the judge can award other types of property as well. In Missouri, for example, the judge can order that the petitioner be given temporary possession of specified personal property, such as automobiles, checkbooks, keys, and other personal effects.

In Idaho and other states, the judge can even restrain the respondent from taking more than personal clothing and toiletries and any other items specifically ordered by the court. One wonders how the person, now evicted from his home, can be expected to go about his normal activities with only clothing and toiletries to his name.

Monetary

In most states, the judge can also require the defendant to pay for a variety of expenses, including attorney's fees, suitable alternative housing, alleged property damage, moving expenses, and medical

and psychological services for the alleged victim. In Illinois, for example, the judge may: Order respondent to pay petitioner for losses suffered as a direct result of the abuse, neglect, or exploitation. Such losses shall include, but not be limited to, medical expenses, lost earnings or other support, repair or replacement
of property damaged or taken, reasonable attorney's fees, court costs and moving or other travel expenses, including additional reasonable expenses for temporary shelter and restaurant meals.

Open-Ended Statutes

The statutes in many states include open-ended language such as including, but not limited to and other relief deemed necessary.

In Nebraska, for example, the law permits Ordering such other relief deemed necessary to provide for the safety and welfare of the petitioner and any designated family or household member.

In Massachusetts, the wording of the law is more generous in ordering the defendant to pay the person abused monetary compensation for the losses suffered as a direct result of such abuse. Compensatory losses shall include, but not be limited to, loss of earnings or support, costs for restoring utilities, out-of-pocket losses for injuries sustained, replacement costs for locks or personal property removed or destroyed, medical and moving expenses and reasonable attorney's fees.

Summary of Property and Monetary Benefits

The Incentives for Allegations of Domestic Violence table contains tabulated information for each state and the District of Columbia:

Number of Remedies (column 1) lists the number of benefits allowable under the statute.

Type of Remedies (column 2) indicates the kind of remedies that can be awarded.

Because all states allow the judge to award temporary child custody, use of the family residence, and temporary financial support, these remedies are not cited in the table. The number of allowable remedies (in addition to the three benefits mentioned in the paragraph above) ranges from 0 to 14, with an average of 3.1 remedies per jurisdiction, as follows:

No additional remedies are specified in the following nine states: Connecticut, Florida, Hawaii, Kentucky, Maryland, Michigan, Rhode Island, South Dakota, and Vermont.

Twenty-three states allow for 1–2 additional benefits, the most common being legal fees/court costs, personal property, and other relief.

In 14 states, 5 or more extra remedies are enumerated. There, the list of possible benefits begins to resemble a restraining order sweepstakes. Those states are: Alaska, California, Delaware, Illinois, Indiana, Maine, Massachusetts, Mississippi, Missouri, New Hampshire, New Jersey, New Mexico, Pennsylvania, and West Virginia.

New Jersey has the largest number of additional allowable remedies—14. The New Jersey statute reads as follows (remedies beyond basic spousal and child support are indicated in italics):13 (4) …Compensatory losses shall include, but not be limited to, loss of earnings or other support, including child or spousal support, out-of-pocket losses for injuries sustained, cost of repair or replacement of real or personal property damaged or destroyed or taken by the defendant, cost of counseling for the victim, moving or other travel expenses, reasonable attorney's fees, court costs, and compensation for pain and suffering. Where appropriate, punitive damages may be awarded in addition to compensatory damages.

(8) An order requiring that the defendant make or continue to make rent or mortgage payments on the residence occupied by the victim.

(9) An order granting either party temporary possession of specified personal property, such as an automobile, checkbook, documentation of health insurance, an identification document, a key, and other personal effects.

(10) An order awarding emergency monetary relief, including emergency support for minor children, to the victim and other dependents, if any.

The New Jersey statute is excessive for two reasons.

First, it enumerates a large number of remedies.

Second, it allows for compensation for pain and suffering and punitive damages, remedies that are generally awarded only after a jury has reached a decision following a full evidentiary trial.

Child Custody

Wives are more likely to engage in partner abuse than husbands, according to the latest research. Fewer than 5% of domestic violence incidents involve currently married couples, whereas in about 60% of cases, the alleged incident occurs between partners who are currently separating.15 This reveals that partner aggression occurs predominantly during times of relationship break-up. The American Bar Association has completed a compilation of the way divorce courts treat domestic violence allegations or findings in child custody decisions.16 That listing was published in 2004 and is still considered to be largely accurate. The information is presented in the Incentives for Allegations of Domestic Violence table:

Court Must Consider Evidence of DV/Best Interest of the Child (column 3) is the weakest type of law that can be used to prevent an award of joint custody.

Twenty-six states have enacted such laws.

Rebuttable Presumption against Joint Custody (column 4) means that joint or sole custody should not be awarded to the abuser unless that person is able to produce compelling evidence that the allegation of domestic violence is false. In other words, the burden of proof rests on the defendant.

Twenty-three jurisdictions have such statutes.

Prohibition of Joint Custody (column 5) indicates that the statute actually precludes a joint custody award in the event of an allegation or finding of domestic violence.

Four states: Arizona, Pennsylvania, Texas, and Washington have such provisions.

Two states: Connecticut and West Virginia have no statutes that address this is-sue. The irony is that an allegation of partner abuse may become the basis for a father losing custody of his children even if he never abused his children, or such abuse was never alleged.

Remembering the Forgotten Children

Each year, one million children experience the divorce of their parents. Often allegations of domestic abuse are made during the divorce proceedings to gain a legal ad-vantage. In 85% of all cases, custo-dy is awarded to the mother. Now, 34% of all American children do not live with their biological fa-ther.
The effects of removing children from their fathers are well-documented as they are profound.

These include a higher risk of academic difficulties, drug and alcohol abuse, mental health problems, conduct problems, teenage pregnancy, and involvement with the criminal justice system. In some studies, paternal involvement has been shown to have more impact than maternal love on delinquen-cy, substance abuse, and overall mental health and well-being.

Living in a single-mother household places a child at greater risk of physical mistreatment. In 2004, 57.8 % of child abuse and neglect perpetrators were females and 42.2 % were males, according to the federal Administration for Children and Families. Likewise, one Gallup Survey found that mothers were twice as likely as fathers to report ever physically abusing a child.

Father-absence is also linked to economic well-being. One report noted that in 1999, 8% of children in married-couple families were living in poverty, compared to 42% of children in female-headed families.

Clearly, removing a father from the family has highly detrimental effects on children, and eventually on the social order.

This Special Report has reviewed the statutes in all 50 states and the District of Columbia. This report documents that in only five states Connecticut, Maryland, Michigan, Rhode Island, and Vermont do the statutes contain no undue incentives to make claims that are trivial or unwarranted. By legislative design, 46 jurisdictions have created incentives to file false allegations of domestic violence.

So an allegation of domestic violence is often the first step in an inexorable cascade of legal actions and judicial decisions that each year results in hundreds of thou-sands of children losing daily contact with their fathers. Ten-year old Josh has these simple words to say about his father:

Dad is my buddy. And six-year-old Amanda looks forward to her nightly bedtime stories: At the end of the day when I go to bed, Daddy tucks me in. We talk together about our day. He reads me a story to help me sleep. We pray together. That is my favorite part. It's the Joshes and Amanda's who have been forgotten by the people who have crafted our nation's domestic violence laws.

CHAPTER 16
Fifty Domestic Violence Myths

Effective abuse-reduction programs need to be grounded in verifiable facts about the nature, extent, and causes of domestic violence. An early incident reveals this may not always be the case:

On January 28, 1993, a press conference was held in Pasadena, California to issue an ominous warning that the upcoming Super Bowl would be the biggest day of the year for violence against women. Based on that dire prediction, an article in the Oakland Tribune warned the event could cause men to explode like mad linemen, leaving girlfriends, wives, and children beaten.

A national advisory was issued with this blunt advice: Don't remain at home with him during the game.

Three days later the Washington Post ran a front-page story revealing there was in fact no evidence to support such claims. A representative of the Massachusetts Coalition of Battered Women's Services later decried to the Boston Globe how the Super Bowl story sensationalized and trivialized the problem of domestic violence.

This episode later came to be known as the Super Bowl hoax. It would not be an isolated event. Indeed, rogue abuse statistics have become sufficiently widespread that researchers have published articles designed to refute such claims.[1,2,3] These myths have been disseminated by well-known political figures, government agencies, the mass media, and advocacy groups. Respected professional organizations such as the American Bar Association, American Psychological Association, and the American Medical Association have become parties to the disinformation, as well.

This Special Report compiles and analyzes 50 domestic violence (DV) claims made by various organizations and in legislative bills. But first we discuss the fundamental premise of domestic violence advocates that patriarchal dominance lays at the root of partner aggression.

Does Patriarchy Cause Domestic Violence?

Domestic violence programs often make the claim that domestic violence is all about power and control. Indeed, it appears that our entire approach to stopping domestic violence programs has been premised on the belief that patriarchal dominance is the fundamental cause of the problem.

Lenore Walker once explained, The causes of men's violence against women include preservation of men's need for power and status. Likewise two leading practitioners have posited that men in contrast [to women] appear to use violence to dominate and control.

The Power and Control Wheel, which depicts strategies that persons can use to exert influence over another, is an educational tool used widely by domestic violence advocates.

But research paints a very different reality:

One study found Mexican men who valued dominance and independence were less likely to resort to partner aggression.

One review concludes, When comparing men's and women's use of controlling behaviors, research using non-selected samples has found that there are no differences in their overall use.

Meta-analyses found no consistent link between traditional gender attitudes and partner assault.

A 32-nation survey documented a link between dominance and physical aggression, but the connection turned out to be stronger for female-initiated than male-initiated aggression. So interpersonal dominance has been found to have less impact, greater impact, or no impact on partner aggression, depending on the population surveyed and the way dominance is measured.

Psychologist Donald Dutton has termed the patriarchal dominance model a fallacy. and clearly the patriarchal dominance theory cannot account for the existence of female initiated violence, in particular the higher rates of partner aggression among lesbian couples. Despite the remarkable absence of scientific verification; many of the myths discussed in this Special Report can be traced back to a presumed power imbalance between intimate partners.

Analysis of Domestic Violence Myths

Below are 50 domestic violence claims organized into eight categories, along with an analysis of each claim. Most of these assertions appear widely in domestic violence programs and presentations.

A. Incidence and Nature of Domestic Violence
No. Claim Analysis

1 Violence against women... Many DV claims begin with this phrase, implying intimate partner violence against men is so infrequent as to be unworthy of mention. Nearly 250 scholarly studies show women are at least as likely as men to engage in partner aggression and that partner violence is often mutual.

2 According to the FBI, a woman is beaten every (fill in the blank) seconds. The FBI does not tabulate information on domestic violence.

3 One in four women experience domestic violence sometime in their lifetimes. Approximately equal numbers of men and women experience domestic violence during their lifetimes.
The reported number of victims varies depending on how aggression is defined.

4 Women are victims of 85% of all cases of domestic violence. This statistic from the National Crime Victimization Survey understates and distorts the true incidence of domestic violence, since victimized men are less likely to view partner aggression as a crime.

5 Domestic violence kills as many women every five years as the number of U.S. soldiers killed in Viet Nam. This number is nearly eight times greater than the true figure, according to Department of Justice data.

6 When women engage in domestic violence, it is only for reasons of self-defense. Self-defense accounts for only 10-20% of female partner aggression.

7 The fact that only one in four victims of partner homicide is male shows that domestic violence by women is a negligible problem. A woman's initiation of violence is the strongest predictor of her subsequently becoming a victim of intimate partner aggression.

8 92% of homeless women experience severe physical or sexual abuse at some time in their lifetimes. This figure, cited in HR 590, comes from a single study done in Massachusetts and ignores the existence of domestic violence against homeless men.

9 Minor incidents of domestic violence always escalate to full-scale battering. In the majority of cases, partner aggression does not escalate, and in many cases attenuates without external intervention.

10 A marriage license is a hitting license. Fewer than 5% of domestic violence incidents involve couples in an intact married relationship. Marriage is the safest partner relationship.

11 At least 40% of law enforcement families experience domestic violence. This claim, made by the National Center for Women and Policing, is based on studies that surveyed all forms of family conflict, including arguments and loss of temper. Most instances of family conflict do not involve physical violence.

12 Batterers are not fringe characters, but rather persons whom society regards as normal. Studies of both male and female offenders show personality disorders are far more common among these persons. As violence becomes more chronic and severe, the likelihood of psychopathology approaches 100%.

B. Causes of Domestic Violence
No. Claim Analysis

13 Domestic violence is all about power and control. This mantra-like assertion was analyzed in the Does Patriarchy Cause Domestic Violence? section of this Special Report.

14 Men who assault their wives are living up to cultural prescriptions that are cherished in Western society.35 This gender-baiting claim is contradicted by the fact that domestic violence generally is not condoned in American society. Only 2.5% of US males approve of slapping a wife to keep her in line, whereas many more persons believe that a wife slapping her husband is acceptable.

15 Men are controlling in their relationships with partners. A need for control is not a common cause of domestic violence, and when it is, women are as likely as men to be controlling.

16 Domestic violence committed by women is justifiable, while partner aggression by men is not. This claim represents an obvious double standard.

17 Domestic violence is not caused by poor anger management, communication problems, jealousy, stressful living conditions, childhood experiences, or economic conditions. All of these have been found to be important risk factors for domestic violence. For example, partner aggression is far more common among low-income partners.

18 Men and women engage in domestic violence for fundamentally different reasons.
A study of causes of domestic violence found that 12 of the 14 reasons applied to both men and women.

C. Consequences of Domestic Violence
No. Claim Analysis

19 Domestic violence is the leading cause of injury to women. According to the US Department of Health and Human Services, the leading causes of injury to women are unintentional falls, motor vehicle accidents, and overexertion. Domestic violence doesn't appear on the list of leading causes of injury.

20 22% of all visits by females to emergency rooms are for injuries from domestic assaults. This figure comes from a now-outdated study of an inner city hospital in Detroit, which found over one-third of the victims were actually men. The actual national figure is less than 1%.

21 The March of Dimes reports that battering during pregnancy is the leading cause of birth defects. The March of Dimes has never conducted such a study.

22 Women can't walk out on an abusive relationship because they are fearful of losing their home and means of financial support. This claim is true in some cases, but is one-sided because it ignores the fact that men can't leave an abusive relationship because they may fear for their child's safety or worry about losing the relationship with their children.

23 The annual cost of domestic violence is $13 billion. This figure, cited in HR 739, has never been verified by a reputable researcher. According to the Centers for Disease Control, the annual cost for female victims of domestic violence is about $5.8 billion.

The cost for male victims is unknown.

24 The annual medical costs for domestic violence are $31 billion. This figure, cited in HR 739, has never been verified. According to the Department of Justice, the correct number is about $2 billion.

D. False Allegations
No. Claim Analysis

25 False allegations of domestic violence are almost nonexistent. One study found 71% of civil re-straining orders were unnecessary or false. Another analysis found over half of re-straining orders did not involve even an allegation of violence.

26 If we were to prosecute persons who commit perjury, true victims would be less likely to come forward. False allegations weaken the credibility of true victims, making it less likely they will file a complaint. False allegations also undermine public support for the national effort to stop domestic violence.

27 Even if they are not true, allegations of domestic violence help assure the domestic violence issue remains in the public eye. False allegations divert needed services and resources away from true victims of violence. This claim reveals an easy disregard for the rights of the falsely accused.

E. Sexual Assault
No. Claim Analysis

28 According to Government estimates, approximately 987,400 rapes occur annually in the US. This statement was made in HR 739. The actual number of rapes reported by the FBI is 90,427, one-tenth the number claimed in the bill.

29 One in four women has been a victim of rape or attempted rape. This claim by Mary Koss has been criticized on many grounds. For example, only 27% of women classified by the researchers as rape victims actually viewed themselves as victims of rape, and 42% of the putative victims later had sex with their attackers.

30 Since 2001, rapes have actually increased by 4 percent. This claim was made in HR 739. The FBI reports that female rapes have fallen dramatically since the 1970s. From 2001 to 2005 the rate of rapes continued to decline (0.6/1,000 women in 2001 to 0.5/1,000 women in 2005).

31 89 percent of rapes are perpetrated against female victims. This claim from HR 739 ignores the problem of male rape in prisons. A Human Rights Watch report cites a study that found 140,000 male inmates are raped each year in the United States, a number that is higher than the FBI report of female rapes.

32 Almost 50 percent of sexual assault survivors lose their jobs or are forced to quit in the aftermath of the assaults. This statistic from HR 739 is an incidental finding from a non-representative sample of 27 women in the Atlanta, GA area. This figure has never been replicated.

33 One in four teenage girls has been in a relationship in which her partner pressured her into performing sexual acts. This claim was made in HR 590. The actual percentages are 11.9% of teenage girls and 6.1% of teenage boys.

F. Legal/Law Enforcement Response to Domestic Violence
No. Claim Analysis

34 From the very beginning, American jurisprudence has viewed wife beating as an acceptable practice. The Body of Liberties adopted in 1641 by the Massachusetts Bay colonists' states, every married woman shall be free from bodily correction or stripes by her husband, unless it be in his own defense from her assault.

35 The expression rule of thumb refers to the diameter of a stick or rod for which wife beating was considered legal. The phrase rule of thumb does not appear in legal treatises on English common law.

36 Domestic violence is such a heinous crime that it warrants harsh criminal justice measures. There is no good evidence that a draconian criminal justice response deters domestic violence, but a get tough on crime approach may in fact place persons at greater risk of victimization.

37 Restraining orders should be made freely available to victims of abuse. There is little evidence that restraining orders prevent future violence and sometimes they escalate the conflict.

38 Mandatory arrests have been proven effective in stopping future violence. Mandatory arrest laws increase, not reduce, the risk of subsequent partner violence.

39 Domestic violence cases are treated more leniently than other types of crime. Felony domestic assaults are less likely, not more likely, to be dismissed by the court than nondomestic assaults.

40 Women who kill their batterers receive longer prison sentences than men who kill their partners. The average prison sentence for men who have killed their wives was 17.5 years; the average sentence for women convicted of killing their husbands was 6.2 years.

G. The Workplace
No. Claim Analysis

41 According to the General Accounting Office, between 1/4 and 1/2 of domestic violence victims reported that they lost a job due, at least in part, to domestic violence. The GAO report cited in HR 739 states a very different conclusion: we cannot conclude that being a victim of domestic violence changes the likelihood that a woman will work.

42 35-56% of employed battered women are harassed at work by their abusive partners.70 This claim from HR 739 is based on three small, uncontrolled, and outdated studies that lack scientific validity. The respondents represent a highly selected population (women from abuse shelters) and the results are based on unverified self-reports.

43 Female victims of intimate partner violence lose 8,000,000 days of paid work each year. This one-sided statistic from HR 739 comes from Centers for Disease Control report that omits consideration of male victims of domestic violence.

44 Homicide is the leading cause of death for women on the job. This claim was made in HR 739. The leading cause of fatal workplace injuries to women is actually transportation incidents (43%). Homicides represent 35% of all fatal workplace injuries to females.

H. Children and Custody
No. Claim Analysis

45 Abusive parents are more likely to seek sole custody than nonviolent ones. This claim is derived from an American Psychological Association publication containing numerous claims that lack a scientific basis.73 The task force that produced this publication was headed by Lenore Walker, who was instrumental in organizing the Super Bowl hoax. The APA publication has now been withdrawn.

46 25–50% of disputed custody cases involve domestic violence. Many custody cases involve an allegation of domestic violence. However, only a minority of these allegations are substantiated as true.

47 False allegations are no more common in divorce or custody disputes than at any other time. False allegations of sexual abuse in fact appear to be far more common during custody disputes.

48 Children are safer with their mothers than with their fathers. Data from the Department of Health and Human Services shows that 71% of children killed by one parent were killed by their mothers.

49 Abusive fathers are successful in winning sole child custody about 70% of the time. This figure appears to be an embellishment of a claim in a 1989 report by the Gender Bias Committee of the Massachusetts Supreme Judicial Court which claimed that in 70% of cases, fathers (not abusive fathers) were successful in winning some form of child custody, though not necessarily physical custody or sole custody.

A re-analysis of the data concluded that when mothers sought sole custody, the court granted the request at a rate 65% higher than it did when fathers made the same request.

50 Allegations of domestic violence have no demonstrated effect on the rate at which persons are awarded custody of their children. This claim is refuted by a study that found judges were more likely to award sole custody to the non-perpetrator. 79 1 The claims in this section come from the American Bar Association's sheet, 10 Myths about Custody and Domestic Violence and How to Counter Them.

Twelve Strategies to Disguise the Truth

In reviewing the 50 domestic violence myths, the distortion strategies are found to fall into one of 12 categories:

1. Make evidence free claims.

This is the most common way the truth is distorted. Perhaps the most common example is, Men are overwhelmingly the perpetrators of domestic violence, an assertion routinely made without evidence or proof.

2. Use definitional ruses

Some persons use studies on verbal disagreements and arguments to claim the study results are indicative of physical violence. Other persons use the word battering to refer to any form of partner conflict, physical or not.

3. Rely on information from crime surveys

Domestic violence programs often use results from the National Crime Victimization Survey, even though it is known that the NCVS underestimates and distorts the true extent of partner abuse.

4. Make faulty generalizations

Persons often take information from a single incident or from a self-selected group such as abuse shelter residents, and then generalize this to the entire community.

5. Collect information only on male-on-female violence

This is a commonly-employed strategy. For example, the World Health Organization did an international survey on domestic violence, but neglected to interview men or to inquire about female-initiated aggression.

6. Withhold data on female-perpetrated violence

Some studies have collected information on female-perpetrated aggression but then withheld that data when reporting the research results.

Examples include:

a. A survey for the Kentucky Commission on the Status of Women collected information on both male and female perpetrators, but only the data on male abusers was published. 82

b. One study of intimate partner terrorism ignored its own data on female-perpetrated violence. 83

7. Misrepresent the findings of prior research

Examples include:

a. The WHO World Report on Violence and Health claims, where violence by women occurs, it is more likely to be in the form of self-defense.84 but the three studies cited by the report actually show self-defense is an infrequent explanation for female violence.

b. One author stated her previous research showed Males and females were found to differ in their motivations for using violence in relationships. But her actual findings reveal males and females have very similar motivations for partner violence.

8. Publish factually deficient fact sheets

Many domestic violence fact sheets purport to debunk misconceptions, but in fact create new myths and reinforce old ones. For example, the American Bar Association's 10 Myths about Custody and Domestic Violence and How to Counter Them has been found to contain many more misrepresentations than true statements of fact.

9. Reject grant applications that propose to study male victimization

Two documented cases illustrate that the grant award process has become biased:

a. A 2005 solicitation from the Department Of Justice National Institute of Justice prohibited proposals for research on intimate partner violence against, or stalking of males of any age

b. In one case, a reviewer gave a lower score to a proposed study because the application described partner violence as a human problem of aggression, not a gender-based problem.

10. Instigate legal action

A Florida researcher planned to evaluate the effectiveness of an abuser intervention program. But a zealous prosecutor took her to court, charging the study was unethical because they already knew such programs work.

11. Resort to defamatory gender stereotypes

When Erin Pizzey, founder of the first abuse shelter in the world, toured England to publicize her book Prone to Violence, she was met by angry demonstrators carrying placards that read, All men are rapists, All men are batterers.

12. Employ pressure tactics

Family violence researchers have been subjected to slander campaigns, denial of promotion and tenure, and more for presenting information about female-initiated violence. Erin Pizzey once described how persons tried to deny the existence of aggressive women: Abusive telephone calls to my home, death threats, and bomb scares, became a way of living for me and for my family. Finally, the bomb squad asked me to have all my mail delivered to their headquarters. Researchers worry such tactics have created a climate of fear that has inhibited re-search and publication in this important field.

Nine of Ten Claims are False

This Special Report identifies 50 domestic violence claims and reveals how these assertions are false. But the concern is not merely the large number of dishonest assertions. The problem is, the widespread existence of such myths has come to overshadow the truth of domestic violence. Three examples illustrate this phenomenon:

1. The American Bar Association's flyer, 10 Myths about Custody and Domestic Violence and How to Counter Them, contains 19 claims, of which 89% are unsupported, misleading, or wrong.

2. House Resolution 590 contains 22 findings. Twenty of them – 91% — were found to be one-sided, misleading, unverifiable, or simply false. Only two findings (pertaining to the need for abuse education programs in schools and to the risks to children exposed to domestic violence) were true.

3. The Security and Financial Empowerment (SAFE) Act, HR 739, contains 53 findings, of which 92% are found to be misleading, outdated, unverifiable, exaggerated, or wrong. Overall, nine out of 10 claims made in these documents are myths, what professor Richard Gelles has somewhat whimsically referred to as factoids from nowhere.

Myths Don't Help True Victims

This Special Report documents how exaggerated, misleading, and false statements about domestic violence have become commonplace. Indeed, many of these misrepresentations appear to be intentional.

Journalist Philip Cook has analyzed the widespread existence of these myths and reveals how resistant these myths are to correction. Cook concludes, there is more false, falsely framed, or disingenuously deceptive information about domestic violence than any other significant public and social issue.

These myths exert a myriad of harmful effects. In legal jurisprudence, such bias creates unsupported presumptions of blame, presumptions of merit, and presumptions of what may be in the best interests of children. The myths also impede the ability of programs to respond to the needs of victims and offenders.

As researcher Miriam Ehrensaft explains, findings from recent studies remain largely overlooked or discounted. In particular, these myths have served to divert our attention away from female-instigated and mutual violence. The cumulative effect has been to hamper the overall effectiveness of abuse reduction programs. The National Research Council has expressed its concern that most domestic violence programs are driven by ideology and stakeholder interests. As a result, we have no evidence to date that VAWA has led to a decrease in the overall levels of violence against women, decries one Department of Justice official.

Even worse, these factoids and theory might actually be harmful to women, men, children, and the institution of the family, explains researcher Richard Gelles. In-deed, there is evidence that abuse-reduction programs are escalating partner conflict and discouraging victims from getting the help they need.

The choice is clear: Either we continue to disseminate misleading and false information that conforms to a self-serving ideological agenda.

Or we move forward in our shared goal to help families become violence-free.

The Realities of Domestic Violence.

True stories from men or their friends.

Men's Stories - 2012

Many stories here ...
"A single death is a tragedy; a million deaths is a statistic." -- Joseph Stalin

---

You see on January 1, 2012 Bobby was shot in the head by his live in girlfriend and mother to his child Adeline Isaacson. ... My son is dead and Adeline Isaacson is still out on the street doing what she wants with whom she wants. She brags about shooting Bobby and how tough she is.

Please help us **my brother was murdered by the mother of his child.** We have been trying to get help from anyone possible. No one will listen to us. Detectives will not return our calls, States at tony claims they don't have the case yet.NCRA was no longer interested in speaking with me as soon as I told them we didn't have an attorney.The problem we are having is finding an attorney to deal with this sort of case, We have contacted every person we can think of to guide us in how to proceed on this, i have been ignored by everyone turned away by all media groups, news paper reporters claiming there is no story, Bianca Prieto reported Bobby as being first homicide in 2012, but has since told us When we get juicier info on the case let her know. i have included a letter from my mother posted on a petition she started on change.org also i added the link to the petition where you can see community responses, the prior artical written for the previous baby daddy of Ms. Isaacson whom was also murdered by a self defense claim, she has told several people she set up. I included a link to the blog also showing community concern. Please if you could help us or recommend how we should proceed or any suggestion, they would be greatly appreciated.

This is my son Bobby W Root. This is the vision I deal with every single time I close my eyes. I hear the beeps of the machines that were trying to keep him alive every time the noise of the day has stopped. I still see the tears sliding from his eyes when I talked to him, even though he could not understand anything I was saying.

You see on January 1, 2012 Bobby was shot in the head by his live in girlfriend and mother to his child Adeline Isaacson. They had been to a New Years Eve party and were very well intoxicated. Also using recreational drugs. They had been arguing the entire day and at one point, we know Adeline had slapped him across the face. When they got home, they continued to argue and fuss with each other. He had no weapon of any kind but she had her pistol in her waistband. She pulled it out and shot him in the head. When she shot him, the bullet severed the blood supply to his brain and then went into the part of his brain that let him speak and understand speech. So all the time I was trying to tell him that I loved him and beg him to fight he could not understand me. He died on January 4, 2012.

The day before he died Adeline moved in with her ex boy-friend.

My son is dead and Adeline Isaacson is still out on the street doing what she wants with whom she wants. She brags about shooting Bobby and how tough she is. All she had to do is say self-defense. They did not drug test her give her any kind of sobriety test to see if she was over the limit for intoxication. An Orange County officer told us that in the state of Florida it is not illegal to have drugs in your system, just on you person. If she had been caught with the drugs on her then it would have warranted a drug test. On the other hand, if she had shot him by accident it would have been wrongful death so she would have been drug tested. Even better, if they would have been getting along and she would have wrecked the truck on the way home and killed him, It would be deemed manslaughter; she would have already been in jail. In addition, drug tested.

The only thing that was noticed was that Bobby had a prior arrest for domestic battery against her. It didn't matter that the arrest was made when she came to where he was again intoxicated and high on drugs and started hitting him, with the baby in his arms, or that she ran him over with the car. Even the fact that there were people there that wrote statements of what really happened,. Bobby, being the guy, went to jail and Adeline, being the female, went home to sleep off her high. When everything was said and done they offered him, plead guilty go home on probation or fight the charge and sit in jail until trial. He was 24 years old with three kids. He chose what anyone would, the probation.

The fact is that the drugs and the alcohol took over the situation that night. Even with all the fighting and fussing they have done the past three years neither of them every hurt the other enough to warrant a band aid or even an ice pack. Other than on the 4th of July when Adeline busted Bobby's face open with a pistol, again drugs and alcohol.

The Realities of Domestic Violence.

In one case I recall a man had been out drinking and came home to fall asleep on the couch. His wife took an iron skillet and beat him. He was taken to the emergency room of the hospital and stitched up. He was taken there by police, but no charges were filed against his wife. My heart goes out to the men who call because no services are available to them, other than with a psychologist or psychiatrist. I have some doubts about many of them [therapists] as I feel they are back in the dark ages of how they stereotypically view males.

(Excerpt from Philip A. Cook, **_Abused Men: The Hidden Side of Violence_**, pp. 157-8. Interview with the author, 1994) (Kelso and the Valley Oasis Shelter program in Lancaster CA and "a few other places" are the only programs Mr. Cook found in the U.S. that serve men.)

Whenever I speak of male abuse, I am met by disbelief and, even worse, laughter. We are looked upon as being friends of the perpetrators rather than friends of the victims, because all males are supposed to be evil and bad. I notice in talking with other shelter staff throughout the state that this attitude prevails in the other shelters, too- men are the perpetrators, women are the victims.
-- Jan Dimmitt, Executive Director of Kelso's Emergency Support Shelter

Our son, nor his dad and myself can afford legal representation for him or his 3 year old son. The child is the result of their short lived marriage. Our family is large and so unfamiliar with abuse that we didn't see the signs or start to connect the dots until the past year of how dangerous and serious it is. The mother's dad and step mom have deep pockets and the mother has now went from supervised visits (originally ordered by child services because she was diagnosed manic depressive and admitted to other episodes), to unsupervised visits--(this is when the abuse against the child really started to get worse), and now our son has temporarily lost the right to visit with his son outside of paying someone to supervise the visits. The mother is blaming the abuse on his daddy. The two attorney's the daddy did have for a short time only took his money and did not get enough of the facts and the truth out that the judge see what is really going on. It seems no one wants to believe the mother is the abusive one... Even when there is a history of abuse and violence in her family.

When our son first started bringing her to our house and she would punch him in the arm jokingly, it did make me uncomfortable, but I had no idea that it was one of those earmarks that people need to be aware of. Is there any help available? Even an attorney to represent the child's best interests and his safety would be something. Anyone that knows how to play detective and connect the dots? It has been so much drama, it is almost unbelievable. It seems like the more she gets away with the more cruel her abuse to this three year old boy. The child is starting to talk and that may make things worse for her, and therefore she could get worse with the child. They had to do the baby exchanges in front of the police station so she would quit calling the daddy names in front of the child. Some of the incidents are out of this world... that a mother could or would really do such things to her own child.

If you can help, thank you in advance. We have reached out to dept. family and children services, law enforcement, the judge, etc... and there has been no help or deliverance for our son and his baby. The mother hates her birth mother and is/has been estranged from her. It would not be good for the baby to grow up and hate his mother.

BATTERED BY BAD PRESS: MEN ARGUE THAT WOMEN ARE VIOLENT, TOO

John Marshall
Seattle Post-Intelligencer
7/22/94

... a 30ish Seattle therapist who, under physical attack by his lover, was fending off her blows while trying to shield his two young children.

The man finally called 911 to report the attack, then left the house with his kids after striking back once at the woman. He says he was never interviewed by either police or prosecutors, but was later charged and convicted of assault and required to pay a $500 fine, perform 100 hours of community service and have absolutely no contact with the woman. His conviction is now under appeal, which is why he asked that his name not be published.

"I was dumbfounded from the very start of the incident," the man says. "I was getting struck by this woman while I was holding my daughter and I was the one who called the police."

I am currently sitting in a crisis recovery center because I was unable to cope with just everyday life anymore and I didn't know why. now after being here a few days away from her I have been able to sort through my thoughts and learn more about the abusive cycle that many men including me, must endure from living with an abusive partner. I couldn't understand why all of a sudden I just couldn't handle normal everyday stress and that was very disturbing to me. I knew for a while before my breakdown something just wasn't right and I wasn't my self anymore. I felt alone, lost, angry, confused, un-motivated, and basically like the world was just closing in and I was trapped. its all apart of the abuse cycle and I was so beaten down physically, emotionally, and my spirit and fire also. my wife was so possesive of me, and jealous of everyone I paid any attention to. including family, friends, and even my own two kids back home. she would go to extremes lengths to control my behavior. she swallowed a bottle of sleeping pills one night because after blowing up irrationally over something so small, I went for a drive to let her cool down. she then sends me a text message saying "this is what you get for leaving me". needless to say I myself started changing my own behaviors just to avoid an unavoidable conflict with her. its no wonder I broke down and ended up here in the recovery center. I was literally cut off from all my normal support. my friends, my family, everyone. the normal things I would do to cope with stress and blow off steam, gone. if I showed any attention to a game, internet, book or whatever, she would blow up. it was like a sin just to have or need time to my self. I wasn't allowed to lock the bathroom door while using it, I couldn't have my phone without her being present to watch me and hound me who am I texting?, what am I doing? etc... her behavior was just like a two year olds. name calling, belittling, spiteful. but I was always the one acting immature according to her. all of her behaviors and actions were my fault. I felt so worthless, so weak, and had virtually no self esteem at all. I could never make her happy and the things I would do for her stopped being cause it felt good to do them for my love. i t became me doing them just to avoid a fight. I kept making excuses for my wife, she just needs help she will get better, she was drunk, she is just stressed, she has been through a lot. then it started rationalizing such irrationable behavior which led into me thinking im the crazy one. she would alienate me from my step son and teach him to disrespect me also. I was walking on eggshells at home. I hated waking up, but also hated going to sleep cause it would just bring tomorrow even quicker. I was just so low and beaten down I just broke one day at work. I snuck away found a truck at back of the motor pool and just cried, I couldn't stop. I was so lost, I had no idea who I was anymore. it hurt knowing I couldn't cope anymore. im normally a strong person. im a soldier and a paratrooper, I swallow my fear and it ignore it when it comes to the moment I have to jump from the plane. I have been through afghanistan and rocket attacks constantly and made it through. im constanly away from home and family and my kids but I manage to cope. this though was so different, I had no way to cope, she cut all that out of my life. its only after I finally admitted to myself that I am in fact a victim of spousal abuse. me, a victim, its such a hard thing to do but when you just ignore it and downplay the seriousness of the emotional damage and harm abuse causes, eventually your going to break. im so grateful that my breaking point only landed me here in a recovery center and not in a coffin. im learning now why I had the disturbing change in behavior and emotions. its all apart of the methods and process of an abuser and its not my fault. everyone deserves to be treated with respect and if you are in this sort of situation you need to understand that you cant fix crazy, you can either try to cope with it, or save yourself and get out. now im on to my next challenge and that's finding support to help on my path to recovery. people tend to downplay the hurt, and damage you suffer emotionally. I used to take it jokingly also about wifes abusing husbands. that was until I found myself breaking down because of it. its not a joke and can have very serious effects on a mans well being. don't make excuses, don't lie to yourself and say I can handle it or im overeacting......your not. women can abuse, do abuse, and will abuse you not all women but it can happen to you is my point. men arent the only abusers. get help and as fast as you can!

I have had an experience with a woman that is something out of a horror movie. And while I am no longer in the relationship with her it is still severely affecting my life. The telling of this is going to take some time. And will not be done in this one email. But I need to do something, to get started somehow. I woke up from a dead sleep thinking about this and

some searching found the battered mens website.
I met Laura Stewart Deronde at a party. Over 6 months we had a passionate and tumultuous relationship. We always argued, yelling. She lied and manipulated. She was hyper sexual, needed very little sleep. She drank stronger things than I could handle as if it was nothing. She went through severe emotional swings. She could be very caring and loving and giving. She would blame me for everything and never take any responsibility. I refused to back down on my own part. And I responded to her verbal abuse with my own. And i had some unresolved issues from a recently ended relationship that I took into this one. I was always fighting against her trying to control me. She awoke me from sleep several times hitting me and screaming at me. I left several times, but she would stalk me and become apologetic and I would eventually give in, because she wanted me and I wanted her, I fell in love with her against my own better judgement. Eventually our relationship escalated into a fight that I could not get out of, which led me to a conviction, time in jail, and I am now going through probation and programs. Somehow through it all I am the one who got portrayed as the way she is. No matter that everyone who has ever known me says otherwise, but that was not allowed into trial. The police and prosecutor did not bring the evidence from the apartment into court that would have shown her story to be a lie. No matter that I have never been in trouble in my life. No matter that she has a history. She has ruined my reputation in my career field, blasted my name across the internet, posed as fictitious people, cost me and family countless amounts of money now, and of course all the emotional difficulty. And I seem to have no recourse except to go on with my life.

I am sending this partially to date some accounts and I do have pictures and more to show it. I want a peaceful divorce but she is putting on her "victim" hat even though she freely admits in counseling she is the violent one. I sense some bad behavior possible and along with her malignant narcissism and possible bi polar mixed with the abuser mentality I worry about losing my kids. **She has abused hitting,spitting ect my son too. What happens when my 7 yo girl the wife wants to homeschool starts into teens? God and love are the only true help**

Hello. I am married for 16 years and have been suffering with abuse for 16 yrs. **I always in my mind came to her defense and justified the abuse by saying it's her period or a pregnancy or just stressed out.** My wife continually uses the children as a tool to hurt me. I'm very tight for money, have a large family and she refuses help. I don't know where to turn. I will not divorce my wife as I wont leave the children with her alone. Can anyone help me. Plz keep anonymous -(

My name is Xxxxx Xxxxx and I am responding to you from the Battered Men website. I will try to make this a succinct as possible, as it's quite a long story.

Two years ago I had a female roommate who was/is, quite literally, insane. While she was on her medication we became mutually attracted to one another and one thing led to another. Three months later her doctor took her off these meds and her multiple psychosis became apparent. I tried to help her for a six month period, to no avail. **In this time frame I was hospitalized twice. Dodged flying knives, pots, pans, glassware, etc. I had an oak dining room chair broken over my back. Was struck over the head with a stack of hardcover books and had a water bed's frame cushion "jousted" into my lower spine at a full run.** I had to call the police on 8 occasions over this 6 month period and having been an EMT, understand the depth of Domestic Violence calls on first responders. She was arrested only once for DV. I finally left my home during one of her "episodes" under a "civil assist", leaving everything behind that I could not load into a truck with 4 guys in 20 minutes (2 bedrooms, furniture, dining room set, kitchen, 17 years of my career Film Industry memorabilia, my whole life)... Furthermore she has 5 dead exes, ie; 2 husbands and 3 past boyfriends. She also told me of a woman she killed in a bus station.

I moved from Denver to Loveland, CO to stay with friends while I regrouped. There I received help from a local agency Alternatives For Violence (ATV). They were a wonderful resource and helped me put my life back together by assisting with housing, furniture, kitchenware and such. I was the first man they had assisted and I tried to return any favors, in any way I could. Things were very hospitable until I was asked by the director, a victim herself, to edit a video designed to assist in her fund raising presentations for a new Safe House. While researching this, I came across valuable information about violence against men and when I compiled this into the edit, I was instructed to remove it. This is when things began to get cold. Also, the staff who had originally assisted me, were fired at roughly the same time. There is more here, but I will move on...

Within my first month at ATV I was asked to attend a community event at their location, to show a males face. Here I met a female client and a local pastor who is also on the ATV Board. She (client) and I became fast friends and we also attended the pastor's church for many months.

I'll skip all the details, but will confide that after several months,

> I called police and talked to the DA and they refused to even file charges of anykind and then both hung up the phone on me!!! I called the national domestic violence hot line and basically the only thing they did was give me the number to internal affairs and told me to do a self help stay away order!!! In other words none of them was any help cause I'm a man complaining of Domestic abuse and abuse by the law!!!
> ... anonymous e-mail

I had a very very hard time in life and tried burying myself in a bottle. Suffice it to know that I had: 1) diagnosis with terminal Beryllium Granulamatosis Aug. 2010 2) Broken engagement Nov. 19, 2010 3) Terminal automobile breakdown Nov. 20, 2010 4) Resultant lob loss Nov 22, 2010 5) Eviction due to job loss Feb. 2011.

Please know here that I NEVER mentally, emotionally, or psychically abused this or any other woman. However; while I was in a detox center and seeking treatment, asked her to leave my apartment (where she was packing my belongings for my eviction) and told her I "felt like I could no longer trust her". This after I had learned she had requested an Involuntary Commitment upon me. (Overthrown by DA) Three hours later and 8 days after I had been in the center, I received a phone call from a police officer in her home town, threatening me with heavy repercussions if I contacted her in any way. At this point I knew she had filed a restraining order against me.

Through this rough period her lifelong history of domestic abuse (by alcoholics) was pushed to the limit as she dealt with having to watch me fall apart and self medicate with a bottle. I'm sure her reaction to my statement broke her down emotionally, resulting in her false statements to police, our pastor, my family and my friends. I also know that ATV advised and helped her to file the restraining order. I spent 5 months at a recovery center and met with the ATV board member/pastor 1 month after leaving. I also met with him today to discuss the restraining order which was filed nearly a year ago. He believes all that this woman has falsely alleged against me. And that regardless of the fact that one with a DV restraining order cannot be hired into the public sector, that I deserve it.

After all that... Where do I go? What do I do from here? This "man hating" (their own words - not mine) institution has aligned against me and I am currently unable to find a job in any field I have worked within, in the last 33 years. I AM a victim of domestic violence NOT an abuser. Yet this reverse abuse continues by cohesive alignment, conceptual stereotyping and manipulation through false allegation of the legal system. This itself should be criminal. She has lied and defamed me and yet I do not hold this against her. I would like to be able to make amends, get a job in my field, go hunting with my dad again, etc. I know after talking to the pastor that this is a personal issue with me, derived from those in charge at ATV, not through the woman who tried to help me through the toughest time in my life. Due to her dependence upon ATV, she is either unable or unwilling to endanger her position with them. She shouldn't. She needs their assistance. But again, what can I do to clear my name? How can the financial, emotional and psychological damage that ATV has caused and continues to cause, be remedied?

The Realities of Domestic Violence.

Men are also less likely to call the police, even when there is injury, because, like women, they feel shame about disclosing family violence. But for many men, the shame is compounded by the shame of not being able to keep their wives under control. Among this group, a "real man" would be able to keep her under control. Moreover, the police tend to share these same traditional gender role expectations. This adds to the legal and regulatory presumption that the offender is a man. As a result, the police are reluctant to arrest women for domestic assault. Women know this. That is, they know they are likely to be able to get away with it. As in the case of other crimes, the probability of a woman assaulting her partner is strongly influenced by what she thinks she can get away with.
  -- family violence re-searcher Murray A. Straus

My thought on this issue is in-line with your research that we, as a public needs to be aware of the statistics on domestics violence, but I believe the numbers do not tell the whole story. **I have been a victim of domestic violence. I did not report it because I felt that a man should deal with this issue on his own. Maybe this thinking process is a bit prejudice, but if I report this incident; my co-workers would have a field day with it. I really only thought that fatal attraction happened with the women being the victim, but I realized that men are victims of spousal abuse and elect not to report the issue in fear of ridicule from peers.** As men, we are brought up to "handle" situations such as these. I met a woman that was nice and found out that this was not the case after a few months within the relationship. I had dinner thrown at me, I was beaten across the yard on the way to her sisters house, and lost my friends that I had at the time because of her actions towards me. I could not believe that her sister actually told me that she could not believe that I did not take action while she witnessed her sister beating me while I tried to walk across the lawn to get to her house. Sometimes the statistics do not tells the whole story. I would love to support your research, but I would really like to tell my story on reverse spousal abuse if it would help anyone else. I moved several times only to have her find me, and ultimately had to transfer and move out-of-state for this situation to finally end.

Domestic abuse to men happens more frequently than is report-ed. I have had a fully-adorned Christmas tree thrown down a stairwell at me (just one of many objects), a girl break into my house and try to beat me up with a hockey stick while I slept, and left my home countless times to avoid confrontations and police paperwork. I can attest to the plight of "reverse" domes-tic violence... I have plenty of stories. With the physical ability to beat up any of those females, I chose to avoid confrontation. As a guy, you learn that hitting a woman is poor judgment, and you suck it up. Of course, my personal taste in women could have been fine-tuned a bit...

You state "With the physical ability to beat up any of those fe-males, I chose to avoid confrontation. As a guy, you learn that hitting a woman is poor judgment, and you suck it up. Of course, my personal taste in women could have been fine-tuned a bit". You couldn't have stated it better when you state that you could have beat up any of those females, but chose to avoid confrontation. I physically could have taking matters into my own hands (no pun intended), but chose to suck it up, also. And, of course, I could have had a better judgement of women, also. These things helps us later in life. I finally found my soul-mate seven years ago. My past experiences allowed me to un-derstand and appreciate a "good thing" when it finally happened, but I will admit that my personal taste in woman could have been better in the past, I have been having trouble in my relationship of 5 years we have one son together and for the past 4 years of our relationship I've been battered. Whenever my wife gets mad all she does is scream and starts hitting me with her hands I have Bruises and scratch marks all over my arms and I blame them for work injuries I've never told anyone about my problem I don't have anyone I can really talk to about my problems. I love her though I try to explain how she makes me feel and she won't listen she takes it as a joke and tells me I need to grow up. What she doesn't know is that every time she hits me or calls me every other bad word in the world she puts me down I've stuck with her this far because she was my first real love but I just can't take living like this I feel depressed at all times the worst thing of all is recently she said she wished I was dead and that made me feel bad I felt like the only Person that should be there for me is just sinking me down! Any advice?

I couldn't believe my eyes when I came across your article—someone actually acknowledges that there is a problem here! I appreciated the tone and balance of your article, and the only problem I had was with the headline, namely use of the term "battered men.": That conjures up visions of men in the emergency room with black-and-blue marks on their bodies, when (I suspect) that is rarely the true nature of the problem. Most of us "of a certain age": were taught a couple of absolutes: "boys do not hit girls": and "men do not hit women.": Most men can defend themselves against their female attackers, but the real problem is the violence that has been initiated, not whether the man can defend himself. The answer is not to respond with violence (unless physical action is absolutely necessary for self-protection), but to respond in other ways — namely, seeking outside help.

Unfortunately, that doesn't necessarily include the police. When I was living in Connecticut, my wife—in one of her drunken rages—took our daughter's baseball bat and used it to smash the locked door to my study, where I was trying desperately to meet a deadline (I was a writer, working at home). Mind you, she is 5'2" tall and petite in size, so that shows what a person consumed by rage can do. And since I'm over 6 feet tall and muscular, I wouldn't get much sympathy posing as a "battered man!":

Anyway, I had thought of calling the police that night. When I recalled this incident to my divorce lawyer some time later, his response was: "It's a good thing you didn't, because the police probably would have arrested you.": He explained that my wife probably would have claimed that I bashed the door to beat her, and the police would have taken her side because of the "Torrington case": in Connecticut.

Well, a job brought me to the Washington, D.C., area. The first thing I did was contact a lawyer there, who happened to be female—and the local leader of one of the most prominent feminist organizations. She took this seriously, and told me I wouldn't face the same attitude from police down here. She taught me to leave a "paper trail": every time my wife went into a drunken rage. Call the police on 911, and get your side officially recorded by the police and social workers. I did this, and the response by both police and social workers was totally professional and helpful. My wife couldn't believe that I was actually doing this, and after a couple of visits from the police fled back to New England one day while I was at work—unfortunately, with our daughter.

I have two main pieces of advice for anyone—male or female—faced with domestic violence:

(1) Get help. It may be best to start with a family counselor active in domestic violence cases, rather than to start with the police, but get help! When (as in my case) you are white, middle class and living in the suburbs, there is often a surreal aspect to calling the police—we say to ourselves, "This doesn't happen to people like us.": When we see scenes on TV, it's usually poor people and/or minorities. Well, get rid of those stereotypes and realize that, yes, this is a problem that is present EVERYWHERE in our society!

(2) Do not put up with the violence, as I did, hoping to work things out and telling yourself that you are "doing this for the children.": The situation can only get WORSE with time—for you, for your abusive partner, and for the children.

I'm sorry to go on at such length, but the mere existence of your article really released a flood of emotions, 10 years after all this happened in my life. Thank you for daring to report on this subject, and for doing so in such a balanced, positive way.

I am glad to see some attention to the idea that domestic violence goes both ways. Last year, my son was married to a violent young woman for a few months before he left her. He is much larger than her and is a one time amateur boxing champion. But he never did anything more to her than push her away and restrain her to defend himself. Nonetheless, neighbors hearing her screams got the impression that he was beating her. We have at least one independent witness to one of their arguments who confirms my son's story. But I lived in fear that he was going to be arrested as long as they were together.

She never used weapons, so she never came close to hurting him physically. But she hit him whenever she got the notion to, she cut up his clothes and threw them in the yard, she destroyed the trophies he had accumulated in various sports competitions since childhood, and she destroyed a wedding album my wife had made for them.

Neither party was blameless, but the physical violence was

all hers. If my son had ever hitten her, there would have been evidence for weeks.

Women do not have the right to use their relative smallness and weakness, and the fact that decent guys are brought up not to hit them under any circumstances, as an excuse to declare open season on the men they live with. No one deserves to be hit or to have their valuables destroyed.

I was in a hellish marriage with a woman who had difficulty controlling her rage, which would frequently erupt with her hitting, verbal abuse, and screaming. If fighting with her did occur, it was self-defense; if she threw a punch or kicked, I defended myself. In one particular case, after she initiated a fight by kicking and throwing punches, she called the police to report me as the violent abuser! When they responded, I was seen as the bad guy, she was the victim!

Attempts at counseling did not work, only separation and eventually divorce finally extracted me from this nightmare.

I think the macho in males puts them in denial mode that they were attacked or abused. Society naturally assumes that the men will "take care of themselves": and continues to focus on the problems of battered women. However men are also the victims. Society tolerates violent behavior in females while for men it is not. Take for example, the classic television or movie scene of the angry wife/girlfriend throwing dishes at the hapless male victim. No one gets hurt; it's supposed to be funny. Is this domestic violence? Would a relative or neighbor who witnessed a real situation like this laugh and shrug it off? I hope not, but they probably wouldn't consider this domestic violence, either. Is the woman in this scene accountable for unacceptable or violent behavior? Of course not! It's considered cute and humorous!

The recent report of violence against women should be taken seriously. However, it would be of interest to know who initiated the violence and what events occurred prior to the victim seeking a remedy. Violence in our society must be dealt with regardless or gender. Sexist attitudes add to the difficulty by creating conflicts between groups that should join to focus on solving the problem.

I saw your website and have been on other website dealing with the aftermath of the **worst relationship in my history without doubt.**

The tragedy of this relationship, which I take responsibility for at my end, is that I had worked all my life to grow beyond the dynamics of my family home. I had dated girls and had four or five relationship, each one improving, all with a loving, trusting base and all with amicable break ups.

Then, I met a BPD. We knew each other for three years in total. For over a year, just as acquaintances. I could never understand the strange rhythm of her calls or moods to call it a friendship but in some way, she struck a chord with me. Her description of the family she came from hit home, and I found myself opening up to what I thought was some sort of kindred spirit. How many times have you heard that one? Or the "soul mate" line. By the time I opened up to this woman, I was past magical thinking and soul mates, so she got me with other tricks.

To cut a long story short. **I was in a relationship with this woman for almost two years and it was abusive to my core. I am certain that I have PTSD and depression but have managed to lift myself out of it** and exist through a healthy routine of exercise, good diet, no alcohol or drugs etc. I almost lost my business and she tried to have me charged with a crime I did not commit and ended our relationship with a restraining order. This was her second order in a row as she also broke up with her ex husband before me, the same way. She has two kids to him and one to me. I haven't seen my child for almost two years. I sometimes think I am going crazy as there have been some calls over the two years from unknown numbers and attempts to befriend me on facebook from fake profiles using my school of origin. I could be wrong about this but I feel like I'm being watched. It makes me want to take a long shower.

The amount of break ups were insane and the gaslighting, smear campaigns were brilliantly executed. I have documented every detail of her behaviour and recording over 1700 phone calls from this relationship because by the time I was starting to become aware of this crazy woman, she fell pregnant with my child.

I have posted over 500 threads on a BPD site also which has helped me to process this nightmare although when I am touched by my current partner, in a loving fashion, I cannot accept it anymore. I never had a problem with intimacy or closeness ever, now I feel like a prostitute. I feel that I want detached sex. I can't explain it to well I'm sorry. I do attend therapy so have taken every step to be pro active about dealing with this relationship. I even took the hard line of deciding not to pursue her through the court system as she had already screwed over her ex this way and bragged to me about how she would destroy me.

For thirty three years I have been physically and emotionally abused by my wife. Divorce is out of the question. Divorce would mean fighting a no-win battle resulting in humiliation with vicious reprisal. I strongly believe the court system is biased against men to begin with painting a slanted stereotyped image that paints men as large brutes who victimize poor, puny help-less women. Addionally both phone directory and on-line que-ries only seem to yield only help geared toward men that are batterers or homelass. Battered Men appeares to be the first instance that seems to understand the plight of men. I am at my wits end and don't know where to turn. It has gotten me so depressed that I found myself contemplating suicide. Upon this realization, I flushed all of my sleeping pills down the toilet.

please help me.

I came across your website and figured to send you an e-mail since nobody else aside my family is willing to listen to me.

All in all, I'm just amazed that nobody is willing to listen. Not the police, not child services not ANY-BODY! I have tons of in-criminating texts and a telephone recording in which it is very clear that the incident she called the cops on me did not go down the way she says it did. I'm screaming that i have this evidence at the top of my lungs and no-body will listen. WHY?????

I became involved with my ex-partner in 2010 and in mid 2011 we had two beutiful baby girls. We moved in together after they were born and that's when all the problems began. The very first day she was there, she went into a fit of rage and through 3 or 4 unopened glass beer bottles in my direction because she thought i was drinking too much while trying to mount our new TV on the bedroom wall. I guess i should have known that was going to be a sign of things to come. About a month later, we got into an argument in which she repeatedly shoved and scratched me, ripped my shirt and basically attempted to hold me hostage In our apartment preventing me from going to work. This led me to call the Police and when they arrived at the scene she made up a story of how i was out of control and at-tacking her and since she had a couple of bruises on her which may have been caused when i tried to throw her off me, they arrested the both of us! They result of these arrests were cross limited orders of protection, meaning we can live under the same roof but just not fight, harrass, etc.

Fast forward a month later and we are having another argument on my birthday weekend, this time it's because she thinks i was looking at another girl at a party. She went completley ballistic, punching me in the face, giving me a fat lip and a bloody nose. My friends had to restrain her from further attacking me.

Fast forward a couple of months later and we get into an argu-ment again and i try to leave as i usually do when she gets up-set, she follows me to my car and prevents me from closing the door and after some shouting back and forth she punches me in the mouth. After she does that, i push her away from the car door to try and escape. Well after i leave (and she knows im not around) she calls the cops and files another false Police Report without even telling me. She called me later on and said "one of the neighbors called the cops, they came by and i told them nothing happened".

So as a result of this false Police Report i was arrested and ordered to stay away from my kids and apartment, Child Services got involved and are getting her all this help for "domestic violene victims" and the Family Court is only going to give me supervised visits. Meanwhile, im sleeping on the floor in my mom's living room and while paying the rent and all the bills for the apartment i'm not allowed to go to.

Everyone always asks me why i kept going back and, well, the main reason is that she always threatened to take the babies 6 hours away from me to make it very difficult for me to see them. I also like to think that if there is even the slightest bit of chance she could change, i out to my daughters to give it a shot so that they have both parents in their lives every day. But i just cant take anymore.

The abuse is not just physical but it's psychological as well. Her constant suicide threats (she actually tried hanging herself in front of me once) have taken quite an emotional toll on me.

Right now, she's back to her old tricks, trying to reel me back in. Although she told the cops she was afraid of me, she's constantly calling me and sending texts, with these crazy stories about how the babies are so sick or that she thinks she's pregnant or some other emergency that i have to come see her. I've caved in on a couple of times and gone even though I'm not supposed to (order of protection from the false police report) and it's always nothing. She just wants to "work things out".

All in all, I'm just amazed that nobody is willing to listen. Not the police, not child services not ANYBODY! I have tons of incriminating texts and a telephone recording in which it is very clear that the incident she called the cops on me did not go down the way she says it did. I'm screaming that i have this evidence at the top of my lungs and nobody will listen. WHY?????

"So I ask ... what do I **do**?
(One thing we can do is tell our stories ...

I have been verbally and psychologically battered and abused, I've been threatened with bodily harm, I've been threatened to be shot right between the eyes, I've been kicked in the groin, I've had to watch while my ex sexually molested my daughter often! If you have other ideas, <u>e-mail me</u> and I'll forward them to this man.)

and not dare interfere for fear of retaliation.

Then 1 day, while my ex was grabbing and hurting my daughter, I reached out and grabbed her, telling her to stop. Well, there ended up being a red mark on her neck. She called 911 so fast and had me arrested, my head was literally spinning with disbelief. When trying to tell the officer that I was provoked and that she was hurting my daughter and that I was protecting my daughter, he told me that I had better keep quiet, I'd charge you with a felony if I could, he said.

We met at a singles get together in July, 1995. She seemed very friendly and outgoing and liked a variety of activities. We began dating, and in a few months we were getting pretty serious. In December, 1995, we became engaged. In March, 1996, when we went to get our Marriage License, she informed me that she wasn't 'officially' divorced, and had to file those papers first, then we could apply for the Marriage License. She never mentioned to me that she wasn't divorced or free to marry....I was a bit shocked. We went ahead with the wedding in April, 1996. Right before the wedding started,her friend Susan whispers in my ear that she would kill me if I did anything to her. I thought the comment was a bit inappropriate, but I smiled at the cameras as I walked down the aisle.

Just a few weeks after the wedding is when the big change seemed to appear. I had 10 acres of land that I lived on for 6 years. I was in the process of building a house on it when I met her. And it so happened that I had completed it just in time for us to move into a brand new house. Two months into the marriage, she becomes pregnant. What should have been an extremely joyous celebration for us, was tainted by the fact that she chose to take the EPT (early pregnancy test) at work with her boss and friends instead of with me, and only when I noticed an used EPT, that she told me that the test was positive.

At first, she adored the house and the country setting. But soon, she began complaining of the design......"I sure wouldn't have done it this way". She started complaining of the 50 mile drive to work. She started bad-mouthing the neighbors. Then she started bad-mouthing the land, then the local church, it's members, the music, the smell of the church. Then it was me. After she insulted and degraded everything that I built, my friends, the church.......I guess it was my turn. I was stunned at first, just trying to understand what could be going through this woman's mind. She no longer would do any housework. I would get up at 5am just to do laundry, clean the floors, clean the toilets, sweep the porch, feed the cats, and get breakfast ready for us. I wouldn't go to bed until 12midnight, because she wanted me to do extra things around the house, like change the light fixtures, change the electrical outlet color, paint cabinets. Soon I decided to hire a housekeeper once a week to help out. Now I'm lazy, because I won't do the housework.

In October, 1996, she was about 4 months pregnant, she informed me that she is moving out and getting a divorce unless I sell the house and move to her hometown 60 miles away. All during these months, I was keeping my mouth shut, trying to be the good and understanding husband. She now reveals to me that she works out with police officers, practices regularly at shooting guns. She tells me that she will have me killed or better yet she will shoot me between the eyes herself because she is a sharpshooter. She says that she doesn't believe in wounding a person.....she would shoot to kill. I have no response to this except to say that I don't believe in guns or violence, but I would just try to defend myself the best I can. She says that she would hunt me down wherever I was and "take care" of me.

You may be asking me why did I stay in this relationship of threats. Well, my answer is that I believed in the bonds of matrimony, and since she was pregnant, I would tolerate this as long as possible. Yes, I probably was a bit naive......but I was trying to keep loving this woman. Yes, I was depressed at this time and sought counseling. The counselor was understanding, and said, try to keep your chin up, it won't last forever. So I stayed in the relationship, constantly being bombarded with insults like, "you're worthless, you're a quitter, you're a loser, you're stupid, so fucking stupid". What was I supposed to do? I had already been through a divorce, I didn't want another one. i wanted a family, not a war zone, but what was I to do? I know how men are looked at by society. Men don't dare accuse a woman of threats or violence, or they'll be ostracized by the world.

Well, I sold the house. The very next week, she secretly, while I was asleep, takes the child in the middle of the night and moves 60 miles away, claiming that she was kicked out with only the clothes on her back. The attorney and judge give her everything she wants, and I don't even get to see my daughter. Nearly every single visitation, I was insulted and degraded in front of my daughter. On the day mentioned above, I go to pick up my daughter. The ex yanks her out of my arms, twisting her legs and making her cry. She then kicks me in the groin. I grab hold of my daughter with one arm, and grab my ex with my other hand on her neck. I tell her to stop hurting the child. She kicks me again in the groin, I fall to the ground, my daughter falls, too, and my ex falls on top of me. She kicks me again. Being stupid as I've been told, I get up, help her up to the sofa, pick up my daughter to see if she is ok(she is, thank God). I tell her that I should just go.....sorry that all this happened. 911 is called and arrives within minutes. I tell my story, she tells hers. I get the handcuffs and a ride to jail for 48 hours. Now I can't see my daughter at all. The police don't believe me, the judge doesn't, and I can see in the faces of others that all this is questioned also.

I would like to stay anonymous if possible. This is a terrible injustice.

I have 2 police reports of Communication to Threats, I have a Sprint Carolina Telephone File on 7 harassing telephone calls. I approached the magistrate with this. This woman magistrate told me that there was nothing to do because I waited too long. A days later, I approached another magistrate, a man. He sent me to a shelter for the abused for a Restraining Order and possible criminal charges. The lady at the shelter said that she appreciated all the work it took me to gather all this information, but there was nothing that she could do because between the police reports and the telephone file, it was several months. But she did say that she would keep my name on file for the future.

So now what do i do? Tell my story in hopes that others may see that this really does happen to men...that there truly is gender discrimination. I'm almost at the point of going public, even at the risk of being humiliated by many.

So I ask again.......what do I do?

Thanks for your website. I'm sharing my story below.

I've had an extraordinary year (2011) where my wife verbally & physically attacked me by hitting me on my arms and chest on 4 separate occasions, then kicked me out of the house, and ultimately deprived me from seeing our 1 and 4 year olds for 6 straight weeks, and then I could only see them under supervised visitation for 2 more months. After locking me out, she got a temporary restraining order by saying I was said I was planning to sexually abuse the kids. During this abusive time, I became very disoriented, and she took something I said and twisted it around. I finally got a good lawyer, she backed down, and we have settled on 50/50 custody. Now she says she wants to get back together, and told me our situation was so crazy that the normal rules shouldn't apply to us. I can see that as classic abuser language now. Looking back I realize she was controlling throughout the relationship, as early in the relationship she threw a block of cheese and a cheese grater at me (which hit my ankle). Although I was never seriously hurt, it set a "unwritten" rule that she would go there, and kept me in a submissive position. Her ultimate abuse was hurting the children when she kept them from seeing me as I am a very hands on dad, and they were very sad when I was not seeing them. It was amazing how much influence she had over our friends and the court commissioners just by acting scared and claiming fear without ever having to have proof -- just hearsay. She wrote things like: there was a suspicious car parked outside the house, so she called the police, and the neighbor wrote that I had made a joke about serial killers, and so she stayed clear of me. It's comical now that it's resolved but was horrible at the time. I also know of two of my male friends who's spouse hits them, and so I know it's very common, but just not talked about in our culture. I never even thought of calling the police, since I rationalized her behavior was reasonable (even though I've never hit anyone) and I should be understanding, and also I thought we needed to work it out for the benefit of the kids.

It actualy just happened last night. My wife came home and I had just woke up to go to work and she was ignoring me. I asked what the problem was and she started yelling at me saying she hates me and that I am evil and that I am the reason she is unhappy and everyone would be better without me and she doesn't care if I live or die. I walked away and she followed screaming at me about something we have talked about. She called me a bad father and evil and I told her to back away from me. She continued to yell at me and when I attempted to get my keys to leave she punched me in the mouth causing me to bit through my lip. As I proceeded to the bathroom to try and see the damage she grabbed me and pushed me into the wall.

I did not seek help as the week before she was punching me in the face while I was pinned against the wall and I lost it and pushed her away and pinned her to the ground and she said she would have me arrested because I had abused her.

My wife told me that she was sorry but she wouldn't get so angry with me if I was more attentive and treated her better.

I don't know what to do. I am trying to figure it out I want her to get help but she said it is all my fault so she doesn't.

I would like to thank you for the web site. There is very little out there for men that have been abused. This is more therapeutic of me telling my story.

I was raised with strong moral beliefs and one was that man

should never hit a woman.

For 12 years I was married and abused by my now ex-wife. I am a survivor and not a victim.

When we were first started dating she stated that she had been abused prior by her partners. She became physically abusive in the early stages of dating. I thought that this was because she had only know this in response to her previous relationships. I sadly thought that if I just showed her that two people could have a discussion if I just acted right.

If I just showed her that if I remained calm and took it she would see that physical, verbal and emotional abuse would stop.

We married a little later because she was pregnant. During these first several years I called the police because I was scared for my sons life and my own when she became violent.

I was told by a police officer on the last time I called for help. If I called the police again to stop the violence that they would have to inform the state Child Protection Agency and my son would be taken.

Well that was the last time I called the police for help. Now there was no one to stop her because I feared that our son would be taken away. I would leave when I saw that an incident was about to happen or if one happened.

One day everything was going well when all of sudden she became upset. She started a physical attack on me. She would block the door so I could not leave. I tried to hide but she broke down the door to the bathroom and then the bedroom. I was scared for my life and our sons. I grabbed our sleeping son and him in my arms and she was still hitting and biting my arm to escape I bite her arm. I had tried to get to the car several times before but could not make it because she blocked me. Now I ran with our son but I did not have the key to the car because she took the key away from me on one of prior attempts. I sat in the car with our son on my lap holding the car door lock down so she could not open it with the key. When she ran to the other side I would hold the passenger door lock down. She was pounding on the car the windows. I was scared that she may break a window with a rock.

I did not know this lunatic person with the crazy look in her eyes. How can someone say that they love you and deliberately hurt you.

She continued beating on the car and screaming at me for 20

minutes. She went back into the house and I waited 4 to 5 hrs in the car before I thought that it was safe and she was a sleep.

The next day she asked me if I was going to divorce her. I told her that I was honestly thinking of it and I was not sure and I was scared for the safety of our son and my own safety.

As I was pondering life the next several days and no one to talk to. The Police Chief pulled me over and informed the was arrest warrant out for domestic abuse against my wife. Of course this was a curve ball of being abused and never lifting a finger against her or any women. She had suffered a cracked rib, scuffed elbow and bite mark. She fell and hit a door knob in her ribs and elbow hit the heating vent on one of her attacks. I admitted to biting her to get away from her.

The Chief of Police allowed me several hours to take care of things. There is no place for anyone to run to and he had me give him my word that I would not contact my wife.

Several hours later I put my affairs in order and turned myself in at the Police station. In horror and disbelieve I was booked. As they were booking me I had small scratches on my face from her ring when she was punching me. My back still had fading bruises and scratches on it. They took pictures of my face, back and arms.

I was in total shock and horror my abuser is out there and I am behind bars. How was this that the truth will prevail and the innocent will be not found guilty.

She pleaded with the police to see me in jail but I would not give them permission. The four months until the trial of course my visitation to my son did not happen with what the court ordered but when she allowed. I was just a shell in total shock

.

Two days before trial of Domestic abuse my lawyer told me the police lost the photographs of all my bruises, scratches and bite marks.

He said they offered me a plea deal or I could fight it and if I lost I would face 1 year in prison. Every fiber of my being screamed. The courts are to protect the innocent. How can God be so unjust. How can I being the victim be convicted of abuser. I was the man and women are the abused is all heard.

I pleaded no contest at my lawyers advise at this point with everything that happened this killed me inside.

Several months later my wife promised it would never happen again and I went back and she was scared I was going to get a divorce from her and that is why she lied to the police.

The abuse turned from physical and emotional to financial, sexual, isolation, intimidation and using our son.

A person feels they are at fault and caused the problems if only they did or did not do something. No one else would could love them. You become numb and they find another way to hurt you. You bury the bad things because you cannot face or deal it. There is no hiding or not facing it though.

As I finally got away from the abuse I was diagnosed with Post Traumatic Stress Disorder. I was a wreck with nothing. Sleeping, eating and functioning in life was a challenge. I was lucky to find a counselor that saved me from myself.

Society still is under the perception that a man is suppose to be in control and how can a man be abused by a women.

I hope my story may help someone or be a inspiration that they will make it.

My best friend was repeatedly physically abused by his fiance. Once, she called the police with a false claim and then punched and kicked him, when the police arrive they arrested him. Two long years later, he was acquitted of the charges. What a relief. Two weeks after that, after drinking, she starts a fight that ended with him shot dead. He never reported her abuse. His neighbors and close friends knew of it. She is going to get away with it because of the doubt from the previous charge, even though he was cleared of it. He was abused as a child by his father and was ex-military so he, like many others thought he could handle it, that he didn't need to report it, how far would it really go..

I am looking for some resources about battered men and court cases where they may have actually prevailed, a lawyer who has handled cases.. They are about to wrap up the investigation, and I fear that she will get off scott free. This is horrifying.

---

ive been a victim of Abuse from one samantha wheeler my ex

and mother of our two children.she was arrested for assualting me and my mother since she was pregnant with my daughter i decided to not persue the charges.that was 3 yrs ago and now the tables have turned since i have a criminal record she has been able to lie and get me charged with acrime i never committed.she also has our two kids and was granted a no contact order from me and im unable to see them.i decided the best thing was to move to bozemen mt and go back to school since she was sending the police to arrest me for violating a nocontact order also untrue.i came home for cristmas and was contacted by her and she came to my parents home with our children.her main goal was to get pain pills from my parents she made that clear to us.since i returned i found out that there is ten people living in the small 3 bedroom home i rented for us before things got bad.one of whome is a convicted felon and on parole.also when she was here she approached my sister and asked if she knew were to get methamphetamines im in fear for my two small children but am helpless and dont know what i can do.shes a very skilled liar and knows how to manipulate police and the courts i read a article on your site that sounded all to familiar.if you can help guide me on what to do id greatly appreciate it.

More Personal Stories
Before 2012

A man from Washington state---
I am 6'2" and about 200 lbs. I have a solid background in wrestling and have dabbled in TKD and Judo. I am also a DV survivor. I am NOT a "victim"! ... I was awakened by her screaming as she came through the bedroom door swinging a baseball bat. She brought it down across my legs. I managed to avoid most of the blow and took the bat away

At age 42, I am 6'2" and about 200 lbs. I have a solid background in wrestling and have dabbled in TKD and Judo. I am also a DV survivor. I am NOT a "victim"!

In the summer of 1993 my X came home drunk and on pain pills. I was asleep in "our" bed having returned from a charity event earlier that evening. I was awakened by her screaming as she came through the bedroom door swinging a baseball bat. She brought it down across my legs. I managed to avoid most of the blow and took the bat away from her by twisting it out of her hands. She went to the kitchen and got a marble rolling pin. She stood above me in the bed and swung the pin down at my head shattering the light fixture above us. I managed to block that blow with a pillow and trapped the rolling pin. Again I twisted the object out of her hands.

She left the room and I got up to get dressed to leave. As I started to get dressed I could hear her screaming as she approached the bedroom door "I'm going to kill you, you son of a bitch!" Instinctively I knew that she had retrieved my 357 handgun and I was prepared as she entered the bedroom. No, I from her by twisting it out of her hands. She went to the kitchen and got a marble rolling pin.

didn't hit her with the bat or rolling pin, and in fact, that option did not occur to me until I wrote this. No, I "locked" the cylinder and hammer with both hands so the gun wouldn't discharge... and I twisted it out of her hands. She suffered a minor sprain to her wrist at that point as I was a bit "motivated".

I unloaded the gun, finished dressing and left the house. I called her father from a pay phone in the hopes that he might be better able to deal with her. I did not call the police and I did not call a "shelter". I stayed with family that night. The next day I went home and cleaned up the mess from the broken light fixture. Her response to the event was that she was giving me a "pretty major plea for a hug". I guess I missed it in the translation.

Since we separated she has tried to run me down with her car. I did not report it to the authorities as I was afraid that the judge would further limit my contact with my child.

We've tried to find help for him but all of the shelters just answer in silence. It's a shame how he was treated by the police and that there are no shelters or groups to help men, they need it every bit as much as women. It's time to stop offering help to someone just because they are a women. Abuse is abuse, it does matter how the abuser is or how the abused is.

These people need help and I suppose the only to change things is to speak out and to speak out often and loudly. Tell every one you can and bring it to the worlds attention, so if this story helps please us it any way you can. Thank you for having this place

I am telling this for my brother. I am a woman and I have to say that I know all too well that abuse happens to men, too. It all began about 9 months ago, but it's been a long 9 months. She only started out being verbally abusive at first, but the things she said were so sick and discusting,every other word was the "F" word. She would accuse him of doing all kinds of sick things with everyone from my mother to the friend of my brothers that she had just met. She would go into wild rages in public places and scream and throw food. It didn't matter where they were or who was there she would go off for no reason.

We (my mother and I) would plead with him to leave her but he felt like he could help her. She had had a troubled child hood,don't really know exactly what, she lies so good and about everything. Four months ago they moved in together. After about a week after the abuse grew into physical attacks. They included scracthing, burning with cigeretts,hitting with anything she could get her hands on, and biting. She would blow up and then be somewhat good for 6-12 days and it would start all over again. I'v seen him with scracthes down both sides of his face,she tried to ripe his ear off once and has burnt him on several occassions.

He never hit her back but would try to hold her of by grabbing wrists when she came after him, these were the only marks he ever left on her. He was bigger than her,he's about 5'11" and she about 5'4",that just goes to show size doesn't matter. Things kept going like this until about a week ago,she got really mad because he stopped by mom's to move a tv for her. She bit him 10 times including twice on his genital area and his nose. As he tried to get out of the door she jumed on his back,as he to speak out.

threw her to the ground the police bust in the door. They throw him to the ground and slapped the cuffs on him. They took her to the hospital even though she had no marks on her. Luckily they arrested her too.

We got my brother out the next morning, she had to spend three days there. The jugde ordered both of them to stay away from each other. My brother is doing that although she's been trying to find him. I moved all of his things out of the apartment while she was still in jail. He quit his job so she couldn't find him there and it was a good thing, she's been there 4 times trying to find him. I just hope and pray that she never does, she won't stop until he's dead. this little gal is going to kill somebody I just hope it's not him.

I would like to say he's been to hell and back but he's still got a long way to go to get back. We've tried to find help for him but all of the shelters just answer in silence. It's a shame how he was treated by the police and that there are no shelters or groups to help men, they need it every bit as much as women. It's time to stop offering help to someone just because they are a women. Abuse is abuse, it does matter how the abuser is or how the abused is.

These people need help and I suppose the only to change things is to speak out and to speak out often and loudly. Tell every one you can and bring it to the worlds attention, so if this story helps please us it any way you can. Thank you for having this place to speak out.

I know the terror that comes from domestic violence, in this case perpetrated by my mother.
-- a Seattle man

Exposure to public discussion, pamphlets, posters, movies, and other media promoting awareness of domestic violence is a difficult for me. Invariably I experience a whole range of emotions: sadness, anger, cynicism, desperation. The whole of scenario of domestic violence is biased toward making males the sole source of the problem.

From personal experience I know the reality is quite different. I know the terror that comes from domestic violence, in this case perpetrated by my mother.

My mother's anger was intense. She obviously became out of control. The violence was manifested in both mental and physical actions.

I will enumerate several events I can remember.

My mother went on a screaming spell that was of such intensity and duration that it ended only when she had fainted.

Another episode ended when she threw something which ended up breaking a window.

We had a heavy duty set of matching restaurant dishes. In one of her fits of rage, she systematically took stack after stack of these dishes and forcefully flung them to the floor.

My brother was trying to get his studying done for college. Her yelling went on and on without slowing even with his appeal for some quiet. The only thing that stopped it was my brother bringing the police in the front door.

The domestic violence involved mental cruelty also. I can remember no positive statements by her toward or about my father. This usually took the form of criticism or putting him down for the lack of ability of different kinds. She criticised as nothing special the string of Christmas lights he strung up every year on the house trim. She put him down as lacking mechanical/fix-it or monetary talents. And weaved in these comments was a reference to his gender.

In a fit of rage, she picked up a bowl and cracked it against my leg. I required several stitches.

I'm not a wimp. But what can I do? Some time I have to take physical abuse, like getting kicked in the back, or having my electronic equipment over turned and destroyed. Sometimes things get a little terrifying, such as the time she broke my bedroom door off it's frame so that she could accuse me of "not loving her." ... But, as I judge the situation, it is still better than the result of a divorce for my daughter Laura.

One man posted: I can't see all this battering business. Are we becoming a nation of wimpy men? If any man will stand up and let a woman abuse him physically or mentally deserves what he gets. If a woman comes at a man cursing and wanting to fight has a right to defend himself. In our schools if a small crisis arises we have to call in the counselors. Half of these counselors can't run their life much less advise our children. Is it any wonder men are being battered? I think if men would stand up and be a man instead of a cry baby it would solve a lot of problems. *His reaction is similar to that of many who hear about battered men.*

Hi everyone. I haven't been around in a while, but I took the time today to set up my news reader, and decided to look through things. I saw this message from Doc and thought it might be a good one to reply to.

In my situation, the issue about my own manliness is not a question in my mind, but the problem of what to do when my wife begins to get hysterical is still a genuine problem. I realize that it might be hard to see through all of the catch-22 situations that men are typically put into in a wife-battering-husband situation, but they are very real.

If my wife were a mature adult, a maturely done divorce might be a workable solution. However, I can see from when that question has arisen that she will call Laura into the room against my protests, and insist upon asking her all manner of adult questions.

Typically, the episode will start with her being tired, and then verbal abuse starts. Any question even politely stated may tick her off. She may direct her anger toward me, or it might get directed toward our daughter. Now, I have experimented with various ways of handling it and I think I can answer fairly informatively all of the questions of the form: "Why don't you just .... in order to handle the situation ?"

In the end, there is no good answer.

For example, you asked if we are becoming a nation of wimpy men. I think that on a social level, the answer to that might honestly be yes. Of course, the way your question is worded, if I answer merely "yes", then that would seem only to impugn the individual man at the individual level. Really that's not where the blame wholly lies. To understand that, really follow through the courts and media all of the cases where the men have decided "not to be wimpy". Your wife throws a telephone at you, and hits you in the head, what do you do? 1) Call the police ? 2) Throw the phone back at her ? 3) Try to "talk it out" with her ? 4) File for divorce?

Let's just go through the options. I have called the police, and I have thrown the phone back at her. I've tried talking it out with her. I have tried taking the baby and getting away from her until she became calmer. All of these backfired to either a greater or lesser extent. The least of all the evils was #3, try to talk it out with her. The end result of using this method as a policy leads to a tyrannical situation in the marriage where you literally have worse than a slaves life, constantly jumping to her every whim, and if she is really clinically unbalanced, then even total obedience to her will will not satisfy what it is that she really needs from you. She MUST hurt you somehow, and obviously so in order to be satisfied.

Filing for divorce might be a good option, if you have no children, or you can PROVE that your wife is sick, or has a flawed character. I must caution you on what constitutes PROOF, however, since video and audio evidence will in all likelihood get YOU locked up as either a pervert, or a felon, long before it will ever do it's proper work in the divorce proceedings. It will not end up giving you custody of your child so that you can protect your child from her mother.

Calling the police will get you locked up, if your wife is willing to tell the police that you abused her. Whatever you say in that case will not matter. If she does not say this, then it will depend on her admitting to the police that SHE abused YOU. If she admits to it, then they MIGHT take her into custody, or they MIGHT not, depending on other particulars. If she denies everything, or will not talk, it does not matter what you say, the police will never take her into custody on any statement that you, as a man, allege. Or at least that's how it worked in September of 1996 in a suburb of Atlanta, anyway. I think you will find this to be typical of all police department policies. In either case, your child will be AT LEAST as unprotected as she ever was.

If you throw the phone back at her, or man handle her in anyway, will she call the police ? Oh, you might be able to disconnect the phone, but who are you kidding, she WILL get to a phone sometime. You WON'T keep her kidnapped forever. And if she is clinically ill, it is doubtful that under such circumstances that she will ever calm down. It is also doubtful that your in-laws will be of any help to you whatsoever, even if they are generally normal people. In-laws tend to harbor suspicions about your ultimate intentions. It is doubtful that they would take the position that you are trying to "help" your wife.

Hence, you are back to the default answer. Try to ride out the hysteria. Take the bumps and brusies, the cuts and the scraps that she dishes out, and do not return them. If she responds to logic, then use it, otherwise, merely be silent. It is your child that you are doing this for, not yourself. When your child grows up, it is likely that you will then be able to get a divorce, and be treated fairly by the courts.

THAT is about the only solution that I see. If you choose to call a man who commits himself to such a life a WIMP, then so be it. But I am no wimp. I have more stamina than 99% of all other men could have in this situation. I can endure for the next 11 years, just as I have the past 5. As far as I am concerned, this is the most manly choice that I or anyone could have possibly made, and the most intelligent one besides.

I have certainly considered divorce. But, unfortunately, after 11 years of having been married to her, though there is nothing I would selfishly like better than to get a divorce, I can predict her reaction to that fairly accurately. She was raised to believe, that once the marriage contract was signed, that I somehow took delivery of some kind of "goods", and just payment for those goods is that I owe her everything. By this, I mean that she thinks that if life ever hands her a dirty deal, that I must somehow, find the power within myself to change the world, and to right the wrong done to her. Obviously, I cannot do this. All I can offer is my psychological support to her, and apparently, that is not good enough. In her eyes, I am less than a man.

She also has other expectations that I fall short of, but I'd rather not go into all that right now. I have expectations too, but after the second year of marriage I began to realize that she must be sick, and that I was going to have to put these expectations on the shelf indefinitely. After the fifth year, we became totally physically separated in the same house, because after having been thrown out of the bedroom under threats a few times (several) I could not find within myself the power to keep crawling back. So now, for the past 5 years, I have lived on a cot in the basement.

We still have a kind of family time together, and I stay just out of sight, but within earshot so that when I hear her begin to lose control, and do what I'll call "borderline abuse", then I involve myself as a kind of "bullet shield". I have gotten fairly good at redirecting her hatred away from Laura, and onto myself. Once I have accomplished this, the pattern is fairly set now. I am the big brute, and the "abuser" or the "wife-beater" (no I do not beat her). Something protective in her nature kicks in, and she feels that suddenly she must protect Laura. Once that happens, I ease myself out of the picture. Some time I have to take physical abuse, like getting kicked in the back, or having my electronic equipment over turned and destroyed. Sometimes things get a little terrifying, such as the time she broke my bedroom door off it's frame so that she could accuse me of "not loving her".

But, as I judge the situation, it is still better than the result of a divorce for my daughter Laura. If my wife were a mature adult, a maturely done divorce might be a workable solution. However, I can see from when that question has arisen that she will call Laura into the room against my protests, and insist upon asking her all manner of adult questions.

Every day, every week, Laura matures, and the situation for her gets better. At this point Laura desperately needs her mother. Of course, she needs her mother to act like an adult mother should act, and she needs her mother's approval. I would judge that it would be a little worse to disturb the current relationship, unless I had some assurance that she would not withdraw all of her affections from Laura entirely as a punitive measure against me; something she has done in the past.

Whether this becomes slow suicide for me or not remains to be seen. Currently I have my honor which sustains me. It would be nice, toward the end of my life to also retain the respect of my daughter, but that, in itself is not a requirement of mine. It will be sufficient that I stayed and was a good father to her. Or, at least as good a father as I can be.

I know your web site is for men, but I cannot begin to tell you how much good you are doing for women (or possibly girls too) like

I've read many articles on your most excellent web site - in fact I have linked to many of them from my Web Site 'Abuse Hurts Everyone' at:
http://www.stirling.u-net.com/abuse.htm

I know your web site is for men, but I cannot begin to tell you how much good you are doing for women (or possibly girls too) like my-

myself who have nowhere to go - Like the men on your Web site, I know women abuse - our mother abused me and my three sisters but like men also, no one believed us. I'm 48 now, but it angers me so much that for your friends and folk like me - nothing has changed.

...

What makes me so angry are all those information sites listing 'a batterer's profile' - everything listed to 'describe' a violent man fits my mother also.

...

I've found, to my cost, that women survivor places don't like folk like me - I've been wiped off message boards inviting women to 'share and care' because my abuser was a woman.

self who have nowhere to go - Like the men on your Web site, I know women abuse - our mother abused me and my three sisters but like men also, no one believed us. I'm 48 now, but it angers me so much that for your friends and folk like me - nothing has changed.

You just can't know how empowering it is to find there are people in the world who 'know' we'd not been lying - I don't know why it should be, but I find it makes me still cry with relief just to know someone knows that we'd not been 'bad girls for telling such nasty stories about your own mother' you know what I mean?

I just feel that everyone who can deny women are violent, controling, cruel, malicious, and capable of carrying out such soul-destroying inhumane acts against others, yet say they are 'working to end abuse' are morally bankrupt.

I've not been able to talk of such things until the last year - I think, because when we were children no one believed us and it really did make me feel 'it was my fault' I mean we must have deserved it or why didn't anyone help us? Anyhow, now I'm staying silent no longer - I know I wasn't lying then and I'm not lying now - I know what happened and don't care who believes me or not I know it was not my fault and I have nothing to be ashamed of - I also know that because folk like me keep silent it helps the feminazi to win and the general public to believe their lies.

I just wondered if it would be of any benefit to you if I wrote an article or some of my experience of abuse at the hands of a woman for your Site.
[**Yes!** - Ed.]

What makes me so angry are all those information sites listing 'a batterer's profile' - everything listed to 'describe' a violent man fits my mother also. She killed and abused our pets - and took great pleasure in destroying our things. Even sometimes giving them away in our presense saying something like "Well, take these records for your daughter, Susan doesn't play them anymore do you Susan" Of course, one then had to smile and say, "No Mum." but not mention you'd saved up for months for every one because you never got any spends - nor did you have a record player - but you bought them because the words meant so much to you and you knew you could sneak them out the house and play them at your friend's house. There honestly isn't one section on any of those profile things that either myself or my sisters didn't suffer through.

I can honestly say that if it hadn't been for people like you, and Senator Anne Cools of Canada, I would never have started speaking out. I guess, although my past has been long behind me - I'd still so desperately needed to be believed. That knowledge shocked me so much and I know I cannot keep silent so no one else will have to suffer their secrets alone.

I've found, to my cost, that women survivor places don't like folk like me - I've been wiped off message boards inviting women to 'share and care' because my abuser was a woman. I feel that it's immoral - to say 'we're here to help women' but - it seems - only women we feel won't upset our totally stupid and lying version of the world. I'm dangerous I guess, because I know that women can be and are abusers.

Anyway, I won't take up any more of your time, even if I can't help you in any way, I'm so glad of the opportunity to thank you very sincerely for helping me to feel okay about myself.

Woman seeks help for boyfriend

I have a friend named [deleted] and we have been trying to find help for him. He is in an 11 year emotionally abusive relationship and he is not sure if he should leave. Can you email him and/or call him> He gave me permission to find help for him. He drinks a lot and he is depressed. He feels there is no way out. She confuses him when he states his mind and she tells him to shut up and she doesn't want to hear it. Please help him get some respect back. He is begging for help and I need someone else like a man to help him help himself.

Dear [deleted],

It's fortunate you have a loving, caring friend like [deleted].

One of the biggest issues that men face is that they feel they are alone ... that other men don;t go through this. A second is the shame that men often feel. They don't want to talk about it.

But it's important to find someone to talk to, to confide in, to re-confirm for you that no, you are not "crazy."

This doesn't deserve to happen to you ... or to ANYONE!

I wish there were a place to send you. But most domestic violence programs don't serve men. These programs are not just shelters. Their main service is help in getting a protection order, a friendly ear and counseling, a friend in court, and other social type services.

I'd urge you to check out our Battered Men page ... ideas on what to do, a listing of the resources around the country I know about, and page after page of other men;s stories. Ordinary men ... just like you. Not "wimps" or "victims."

http://www.menweb.org/battered.htm

I'd encourage you to also become involved in a local men's group. Not necessarily one for survivors of DV. Any men's group. A local gathering of men or wisdom council, a church-related men's group, a "leaderlesss" men;s group, or maybe even a therapist's men's group. Get to know the guys and hear them tell their own stories.

We list some men's groups at:

http://www.menweb.org/menscoun.htm

Bert

Daughter seeks help for father after pastor-mother put her in the hospital

My mother is verbally and emotionally abusive to my father and I. She is a pastor, and they live in a small enough town that everyone knows where they are, and when they were at such and such intersection. Luckily, I'm away at school. My parents just moved to this town from a big city, and over the summer, my mom was particularly bad.

Now I am searching for help for dad.

I am getting help at school, and making plans to avoid coming home. Christmas scares me. The bad part of this is I miss dad. Over the years we have been each other's support group. After mom is no longer a part of my life, my dad, who despite many failings in life has always been a terrific, wonderful, fantastic father, will still have a part. Dad and I are both bipolar, and only our therapists knew until this summer, when some, but not all, of the family started to believe us. My mom has managed to convince almost everyone—including my doctors and counselors—that we were the problem and she was perfect.

This summer, her abuse landed me in the hospital, and my doctor finally believed me. I felt for dad—he had just been diagnosed with thyroid cancer and been released from the hospital after having the rest of his thyroid removed when he had to take me to the hospital. This summer we ran and hid from mom together.

When ever I needed support or encouragement, he was there to provide it and make sure I was safe. I only wish I could protect him now. I don't know why my parents don't get divorced. Dad has given me silent permission to seek help for him. He is in a situation where it is hard for him to do this for himself, but he knows there is a problem and mom won't get help. We made a deal that he would allow me to look for help for him if I got help myself.

I don't know why I'm writing all of this. I think I'm just frustrated that there isn't more help for men victims of verbal and emotional abuse in general. No one believed us. No one. Dad is past the "I'm a man and I don't want anyone to know my wife hurts me because they might think I'm not man enough"—He's taught me that real men are good fathers, and that to help me, he has to admit it and get help himself.

Dear [deleted]

Thanks for writing on behalf of your Dad.

Yes, men are reluctant to seek help, for the reasons you talked about. I'm glad yours has shown some willingness.

One thing about men - it's often hard or impossible to *get* them to go, unless they reach that decision themselves. Telling them to, and pointing out the harm they're enduring, isn't enough, sometimes. Openning up and listening—giving him a safe space for him to talk about this stuff himself—is a big step. Men are sometimes ashamed to talk about it - I'm glad he's past that "I'm not manly enough" stage. They can also think it's not that bad, or not realize how bad it is. Talking to someone about it and hearing from "outside" that yes, it is bad, Comedian Phil Hartman said he had a good marriage - he just had to leave the house for a while when his wife was angry. That was shortly before his wife shot and killed him.

I'll say what many people in AA and ACOA (Adult Children of Alcoholics) say. *She* needs the help. What your Dad needs is to *take care of himself* and protect himself. Sometimes leaving the abuser (the abusive person or the substance abuser) is just the sort of "push" the abuser needs, to get the help she needs.

Bert

After a while it came to hitting me and biting me more and more....I would take it until I started fighting back against her....she started calling me an abuser for that after everything she did. She said I was the one who was controlling....I was the one who was abusive after she spent a year hitting me and biting me.

Hi,

I don't know who else to tell....My wife had been hitting me, biting me, spitting on me for a year. She prevented my son from seeing my father who died in May...She tried to prevent me from going to my brothers wedding...Anyway, in the beginning I did nothing I would sit and take her abuse. I have had my eyeglasses broken by being accused of looking at porn web sites on the internet--she punched me in the face. Anyway, after a while she started taking money out of the account when I wouldn't do what she said. After a while it came to hitting me and biting me more and more....I would take it until I started fighting back against her....she started calling me an abuser for that after everything she did. She said I was the one who was controlling....I was the one who was abusive after she spent a year hitting me and biting me.

Anyway, on May 25th 2001 my father died and on June 10th I went to jail for domestic abuse because she had the mark. I got angry because she was so selfish and did not let my son see my father. He was 3 yrs old and saw my father twice.

I made a video of some of the marks she caused and it meant nothing. I have had to plead guilty to domestic abuse. The prosecuters were so desperate to get a guilty plea out of me they didn't care about what happened to me in the past all they cared about was their guilty plea. I tried to use that video to get charges filed against her, but they wouldn't.

I even have bank records with her signature on it showing that she was taking huge chunks of money out all the time, but it meant nothing since I was the man. I know there is nothing that can be done...all I have now is 1 year of pobation, 1000 in fines, 30 hrs of community service all because I didn't report my wife a long time ago for biting hitting controlling everything in my life. I know have a class B misdemeanor and there is nothing I can do about it all because of a law our lawmakers passed saying it doesn't matter who throws the first punch as long as there is a mark, not only that it doesn't matter what happened in the past, as long as the arresting officer notices a mark. It's truly a shame that laws like this are passed.

Thank you.

... I've seen her punch him as if she were a man.

I was with this guy who I loved quite a bit. I did everything for him, my mom got him a job, etc. I never, ever hit him or treated him badly. He was wonderful to me, always gentle, always kind. I'd been in abusive relationships before, so he was Heaven - sent, or so I thought. After being screamed at, beaten, etc., he was so wonderful to me, always buying me things, taking care of me when I was sick. After being alone all my life because my father beat me and my mom let him, I was so happy, I was grateful for him, I loved him so.

Well, he left me for my next door neighbor. The man she left said, at the time, that my boyfriend was going to regret leaving me, because Janice was really hard to live with. I found out within a few months that her ex was understating the problem.

A month later, which was the next time I saw him, he had three perfect half-moon shaped scars on his right forearm from her digging her nails into his arm when she got mad at him. I saw them together and she did it right in front of me, digging her nails into his arm, drawing blood.

We'd go to Perkins, and if she got peeved at him, she threw food and dishes at him, scream at him a little, then storm off like he provoked her. He didn't say or do anything to her at all. I was there; I saw the whole thing. In December of 2000, she had been badgering him so long he tried to kill himself. She actually encouraged him to do it; then, when he took the pills, all the sudden she was concerned and made him go to a hospital emergency room to save his life.

The next time I saw him after that was two months ago (September 2001). He had three more scars on his left arm from her clawing him. I should mention that she tells everyone what a lousy guy he is and how he does nothing but make her miserable, how he's not a man, how he's lousy in bed, puts him down, etc. I've seen her punch him as if she were a man.

He left me and our daughter so he could be with her, and he's still with her. It breaks my heart to know that the father of my baby is with a woman who abuses him physically and emotionally, and that it's only going to get worse. I should also mention that she tells everyone that he abuses her, but I have seen absolutely no evidence of it. I've seen her punch him, claw him, slap him, and otherwise treat him like he's worth nothing, but I have never seen him do anything to her. I've seen bruises on him but none on her. I do not understand why he's still with her after all this time, when she abuses him like that. Apparently I should have treated him like crap too, he'd still be with me then. And if you don't think that it hurts like hell to write that, think again.

My son has been abused during his eight years of marriage more so as I can tell at the moment Emotionally. He has been degraded, not able to have money or food for lunch, not able to shower, have new work boots, NO FAMILY OR FRIENDS, etc. We received a phone call last Fri. (11-9) He was terrified. I think he had been threatened by her family. We rescued him from WV and he is now home with us in NY.

There are children involved...one he adopted and his own who is a boy 10 months old. The mother -- in -- law had the father- I-law beat up and tossed aside in the hills but found by passerby's almost dead. I do believe that my son was also threatened. I worry for my grandson as they may treat him the same when he is older.

The daughter-in-law filed for a legal separation without my son there. She just asked for the money to pay for it. He is so uncivilized and needs to learn social skills as he has NOT been allowed to have any stimulus whatsoever. He has been sleeping on the couch for 9 months. He worries about his son also.

Could I please talk with you one on one? I would appreciate it and as soon as possible as I believe the legal separation papers should arrive sometime within the next few days and therefore we only I have 30 days to file charges or whatever we can for his purpose. Please contact me!

Breaking the cycle of abuse

Thank you so much for the links. I am a survivor of abuse from childhood to the man that is the father of my children. I grew up being abused and seeing my parent abuse each other. That's why I divorced my children's father because he didn't want them growing up in what I did and wanted to break the chain. I have experienced every kind of abuse you can think of and am constantly telling my children, I have a girl and a boy, that its not right. Even though they were 3 and 1 when I made him leave, the abuse didn't stop and they went through so much and I had to put them both in therapy in fear they would repeat my mistakes. It makes me mad that there is only information for women 95% of the time. I have had the hardest time finding resources for men. Please keep up the good work in helping men find them. Thank you so much and have a blessed day.

Brother's ex-wife used court system to further batter husband

I was on your web site today. My brother lived in a home that was constantly controlled by his wife. She would throw him out of his home after a rage attack against him. Slapping him in the face, telling him he was no good, tearing up sentimental things by stepping on them or throwing them. He has been also now tormented by the court system. For two years, she has had all her living expenses paid and receiving child support. You see, she put him out the last time and then filed a protection order against him. He was unable even with his attorney to look at her at defend himself. She also took control of the children by saying that he molested the oldest child so that he has to have supervised visits now for two years. I hope soon the truth will come out and this case can come to a peaceful end for all involved. Thanks for your site.

Every agency I contacted let me and my family down. ... She cut my chest open with her fingernails in front of our 5 year old daughter.

I am so impressed!

For 7 or 8 years, my kids and I lived in constant fear of their Mother.

I would fax and call the shrinks to no avail. I called the Police and the Coroner, and she conned them all.

Every agency I contacted let me and my family down.

I eventually walked out and divorced her.

She had beaten me on numerous occasions. She refused my 4 year old son medical attention. She cut my chest open with her fingernails in front of our 5 year old daughter.

The list goes on.

She now is a working Lawyer for a respected Hospital/University

The Realities of Domestic Violence.

in New Orleans.

Unreal!

She told me that violence toward me is justified. She said that it is a way of getting my attention and it is away of punishing me.

I have been in a battered relationship with my wife. She has a problem with anger. She would hit me a throw things at me. She told me that violence toward me is justified. She said that it is a way of getting my attention and it is away of punishing me. Violence has escalated. through 4 years of violence I did the most violent thing. I though a bowl of salad at her. it was a big mistake. I regret it now. I am planning to get on with my life and make it better. I am going to counseling and I am going get better and be a better person. I know that future relationships would be better for me. I hope that it would be better for my wife in the future.

Mother wants kids to see her hitting him: *As fast as she cut me down she started hitting me. I asked her to stop, but she kept on swinging. The kids came out of their rooms and were told by me to go back in their rooms, their mother said "no I want them to see this!"*

To begin. I went to bed and was awakened by my wife screaming and telling me to go outside and bring the kids back inside, they were camping in the back yard. Rather than argue with her I went out and brought them back inside. After tucking my daughter in bed I went to tuck my Step son in bed only to find his mother standing if front of the door telling me I am no good, he doesn't love you, he doesn't want anything to do with you. I am a disabled veteran and I stay home and raise the kids, I have for 4 years.

As fast as she cut me down she started hitting me. I asked her to stop, but she kept on swinging. The kids came out of their rooms and were told by me to go back in their rooms, their mother said "no I want them to see this!"

My daughter came running to me and I picked her up, my wife drew her arm back and I said don't you hit our daughter again, she hit her in one of her previous rages. I turned to leave and she fallowed taunting me and fell down the stairs. I put my daughter down and went to see if she was ok. She jumped up and started hitting me again. I told her to leave, she said NO you leave. She then went to get her car keys, I said you are not taking the car your drunk, so she grabbed her son's hand and went out the front door saying he is not yours she is you can have her. I said to her that I am going to make sure that her son went back to his father. She came running back at me swinging again. This time she also told her son to start hitting me. I told her to stop, she wouldn't.

I realized the only way to get her to stop was to defend myself and hit her. I did. She still didn't stop she started to throw things at me. The neighbors knocked at the door and she said Now you are going to jail. She ran out with the neighboors and the police came.

The police arrested me and charged me with assult 4 DV. for defending myself. Now it is going to trial, even though my wife has a previous history of battering, she was hitting me broke my nose, scrached my back and arms, bloodied me up, I called the police, the police took her to the hospitol for sucide watch, no charges were filed, and admitted to causing the whole incident.

The state still wants to prosecute. My wife knows about her problems and is seeking help for them. I just want to state that the system is supposed to help families not destroy them. It would seem that the state has a one size fits all kinda attitude. It is not the truth. This is another reason why men do not report abuse by their wife.

Woman seeking help for brother: *I called the local phone book number for domestic violence to look for a support person or group for him and learned from the lady on the phone that there is not a spouse abuse hotline for men, only for women. I was appalled at the discrimination against men. Then she told me that many men don't report it and they didn't feel there was a need for a hotline. I thought a lot about what she had to say after we hung up. I began to think, well, if they would establish a support hotline, men may begin to call. If there isn't one, how do they know men won't report it or call for support? ... I have spoken with my local church about*

Hello,

Thank you so very very much for posting information about battered men. My brother is suffering from abuse from his live in girlfriend of approximately 3 years. I called the local phone book number for domestic violence to look for a support person or group for him and learned from the lady on the phone that there is not a spouse abuse hotline for men, only for women. I was appalled at the discrimination against men. Then she told me that many men don't report it and they didn't feel there was a need for a hotline. I thought a lot about what she had to say after we hung up. I began to think, well, if they would establish a support hotline, men may begin to call. If there isn't one, how do they know men won't report it or call for support?

My brother has been facing 2 recent charges from Vicki for crimes. In research of Vicki's past, she has a history of man abuse of former husbands, one which had to go to jail for a year because she accused him of abuse. In actuality, she is the abuser. She told my brother this summer that she hates men (she was abused as a child by the males (brother and possibly father, in her home).

My brother was recently relieved of her accusation of sodomy. I sat in the courtroom during the case. The judge apparently saw right through the lies.

Now he faces another charge on Nov. 7 in court, in which she claims he threw her across the room and she fell and hurt her wrist. My brother said she pulled the phone out of my brother's hand, fell over the chair. The police officer she called, claiming my brother threw her, says she saw a bruise on her wrist. The officer apparently arrived within approximately 10 minutes from the call. We are wondering how a bruise could form that quickly from a minor injury. It was apparently healed quickly, no fracture, sprain, etc. from what I understand. We think she may *the possibility of helping establish a support group for men.*

have 'doctored' up her arm with black and purple makeup such as eyeshadow makeup just prior to the officer's arrival. She apparently "stages" appearances for officers.

My brother has said she frequently has sudden outbursts, is an alcoholic, has beat her teenage daughter on more than one occasion, almost smothering her to death in one instance. My brother has witnessed her slapping her daughter.

My brother spoke of many abuses by Vicki, however, he said he loved her and wanted to help her. He knew she had no family support (they had disowned her previously). He tried to convince her to get help. She would say she would, then would come up with a reason why she didn't.

Do you know where any information can be found regarding how long it takes for a bruise to form from falling onto the floor?

My brother spoke with a dentist friend who said he felt a bruise could appear within about 15 minutes but it would only happen from a very severe injury, of which Vicki did not sustain.

Thank you so much!! I have spoken with my local church about the possibility of helping establish a support group for men. I plan to speak with another person today that has returned my call and said she is very anxious to hear what I have in mind about helping the support/recovery ministry.

My brother will face one year in jail if there is a guilty verdict on Nov. 7. My sister and mother and I have been trying to figure out how to help. He has an attorney however, the attorney tells my mother that we shouldn't worry. How can we not? He is my only brother. We would love him even if he was one of 5 brothers. We don't want to see him suffer from Vicki's fraudulent claims. We have no where to turn since there is not a men's support group. Vicki has the help of the women's spouse abuse group (they accompanied her to the court for the sodomy charge last month) since she is claiming he is the abuser- how discriminatory is that? My brother said Vicki learned a while ago that sodomy carries a 5 to 10 year prison term, so we think she wanted to get him in the worst way by charging him with something that has a lengthy prison term. Thank God the judge felt is was not a valid charge at the court hearing.

I want to commend you for your efforts to get a church men's support group started! The attitude of the woman on the hot-line is typical. I agre with you that if there were a hot-line for men, more men would call and seek the services they need.

Bert

I came upon your site while trying to find information for a report for an oral communications class. I am hoping that even though I am only speaking to my class, someone will be helped by the information I provide. It is so sad to see that this is an one-sided situation. There should be no difference of your sex if you are abused, physically or emotionally.

Hi, I was an abused female. I have been out of the relationship for some years now. I have been in counseling for over a year and have just sucessfully finished it up. I was abused emotionally and phycically. My reosources were for help were all there. Everyone was wonderful, I came in, told my story and the people were right there to help me fill out the paperwork and send me to the right places. I had a temporary PFA before the day was out. I assumed this is how the system worked for everyone, male or female.

One of my good friends, male, came to me one day for help. His ex-girlfriend had shut his head in the car door. He had, I think, 14 stitches to his ear. He was told to go and file a PFA against her, as this was not the first incident. He went to the exact same place that I had got mine. He was told they didn't have time to help him feel out his paperwork. Take it home, have someone help him and bring it back. Of course, he felt as if they didn't care about him or what happened to him and never went back.

My ex-boyfriend, who is wonderful and would never hit a woman, was somewhat in the same situation. His ex-girlfriend tried to shove her way in the bathroom while he was getting ready for work. She had already hit him and was verbally abusing him. He shoved the door hard to get it shut nad keep her away from him. In the process, she got shoved by the door. She called 911 and told them he was abusing her. When the state police got there, she told them he had hit her. She also told them that it was her place of residence. He was taken into custody and booted out of his own residence. His sister had the title to the home, once it was found, then he was allowed back into HIS home. However, he did end up with court cost and fines. Nothing happened to her. She played the victim and won. He had no support, other than family and friends that knew he was the abused and not her. The system is definetly there for women, but not men.

I came upon your site while trying to find information for a report for an oral communications class. I am hoping that even though I am only speaking to my class, someone will be helped by the information I provide. It is so sad to see that this is an one-sided situation. There should be no difference of your sex if you are abused, physically or emotionally.

You have my permission to post this, but I wish to remain anomonous.

Hopefully someday, the same help and understanding abused women get, men will too.

The Realities of Domestic Violence.

The mistake I made was defending myself and restraining my partner of the time.

Hello

I am from Central Australia my name is Will Rogers

I am a man who has a reason to believe in abuse towards men, I lived with a woman for about 4 years and suffered both physical and mental abuse throughout the relationship. I will be attending a trial this up and coming Thursday to defend my self in court against allegations of assault.

The mistake I made was defending myself and restraining my partner of the time.

After abusing one of her children for wetting her bed at 3am my partner returned to bed, I was appalled at the way she had abused her daughter by calling her names and yelling until her child was cringeing into a corner. I told my partner that, the way she talked to her children was off and that I was sick of her behaviour. She replied by punching me square in the face. This was in a dark room and I was totally un aware that she would punch me. I made the mistake of trying to restrain her so I wouldnt receive any other blows. I sat on top of her and yelled at her that she shouldnt do that and stuck my finger in her ear. She attacked me more and I pulled away from her. She lunged at me and I warded off her blows, The altercation stopped shortly after and we both returned to bed. I went to work the following day and nothing more was said about the incident. A few weeks later The police came and visited me and said that my parrtner wanted the police to have a talk to me andthat she didnt want to press charges. I told the Police my side of the story and they left. My partner went away to her family for holidays for a month and nothing else was said

.

When my partner returned we had futher arguments and I decide that I wanted to leave and take the child we had together. I have been succesful in the Family Court and have kept my child in my care for the last 14 months.

Since then she has abused me the people at my work harassed me in the street.......and so on.

I m not a lawyer and have spent most of my savings in the Family Court and dont have the money needed to hire another Lawyer to defend me at this hearing.

I was hoping that somebody could give me advice on how to handle this in the next few days.

In fact, during our

In my previous marriage, I was the "victim" of domestic vio-

marriage I never thought of myself as abused, although I was afraid of her.

lence. I don't think I was a stereotypical "battered husband" in that my spouse was not a heavy drinker or consistently throwing the dishes at me. In fact, during our marriage I never thought of myself as abused, although I was afraid of her.

She was manipulating, and controlling. Finances, sex, holidays, the weekend calendar, which relatives we could see and what not. My opinions seldom entered into the picture.

During the divorce, she humiliated me -- made me feel that all was my fault. And in the process did manage to control that as well (quitting her job and asking for alimony, demanding full custody, siphoning off our assets to god knows where prior to the divorce).

I attempted suicide twice in the process. Removed from my children, financially destroyed, humiliated.

But what I learned was this. She WAS abusive, but I was far too WEAK. I had accepted things for years. Gave in rather than pushed back -- complied rather than participated. I too had abandon the relationship. Choosing to abdicate rather than accept responsibility for the relationship with her.

She is still volitle, threatining, and sometimes I do worry for the kids. However, I have been able (successfully) to challange the visitation times with my children, and to have a better relationship with them.

I still find elements of fear in my being. But I realize that strength is not what force we apply to a situation, but force (as my ex-wife had applied) is a weakness for those who do not have the inner fortitude to cooperate and work. I try to deal with her on that ground now on issues regarding the children, and I think my last victory in court (if a legal decision can be called a victory) helped drive that point home.

I am not a changed man, but I no longer tollerate her controlling behavior.

If you can, direct that message to other men. The process of becoming a peer in a destructive relationship (or just getting out) means that you have to become assertive, and communicative. It also means that you have to be tempered, consistent, and stable. They are hard things to do -- without your spouse jumping out and trying to kill you. Threaten you, or what ever.

The other option of course, is get out when you can.

Sadly it depends on what can be repaired and what will never be repaired.

But the repair starts inside.

I was unable to communicate the humiliation I endured over the years with my ex-wife. I was unable to communicate the fears I felt. I was unable to respond in the divorce process. I was unable to face the humiliation I received in the settlement.

But the key was communication all along. I was unable to face myself. Face my own fears. And once those had been controlled. I was no longer dealing with those issues.

Battering begins within ones self.

She would go into these rages and when I wouldn't do what she wanted, or threaten to leave she would file either child abuse or PFA's against me.

I left my wife two years ago because of her abuse. She would punch, scratch, kick, pull my hair. Thats not the worst of it. She would go into these rages and when I wouldn't do what she wanted, or threaten to leave she would file either child abuse or PFA's against me. I have proof by witness that she did these things. Anyway to make a long story short, after I left she filed for spousal support. Her two children are from her prior marriage. The courts didn't want to hear about a man being abused and granted her support. It's in appeal now, six months old and the judge has not made a decision yet. I'm paying this women 780.0 a month for spouse support because she abused me. Right before left she pulled a loaded gun on me. I'm very bothered by all of this and it seems their is nothing I can do.

This has been going on for over 10 years. Almost every aspect of my normal life or way of living has been systematically challenged or threatened with divorce. Stories are told to her family members that then stop speaking to me and treat me disrespectfully, in public. Neighbors and friends are next and I never know who has been told what story. The extent of our disagreements has escalated to name calling only, which is bad enough. I had an order of protection filed against me, we live in Illinois. Anyone can file an order and get away with it. The Judge dismissed it because it was determined to be inaccurate. Then divorce papers were drawn up about 3 months ago and signed but not filed to add pressure. I do not know what this person is trying to do to me. I have suspected another man. She wants more time alone and goes out with single friends until 2-3am and tells me she was with other men. She likes attention, her mother rules her father and the entire family. Her mother calls me names as well as her sister, vulgar names. She has gone on Caribbean Cruse this year with her sister, men again and no details of cruise. She is a NON at-home-mom, playing tennis twice a week, bunko 3 times a month, Tea's, lunches with friends, always something or some reason not to be at home with the 2 boys and/or me. Asks for more time away alone. Heavy phone usage, 8/23/99 - 9/22/99 a total of 544 phone calls. This is more than I use and I run a business out of the house. I have sought help, she is a master of derailing counselors. We normally spend 60-70% of the time listening to her complaints. We never seem to be able to move forward with working on a solution. According to Mary, all of the problems or at least 99.99% are due to me and I am incorrect or lying about everything else. She committed to working on the relationship 100% but refuses to drop the divorce papers and retainer of her attorney. I finally retained an attorney last week and will file for divorce next week. I did not know what else to do. We have 2 boys and I am already overwhelmed at the grief, hurt, pain, and confusion they will go through. I will suggest joint custody with me being the residential parent. I am now doing research via the internet to help myself in this next most difficult struggle.

I apologize if this seems like rambling but there is an enormous amount of psychological baggage to go through. Please feel free to forward any info you think might help me in my situation.

He didn't get out soon enough. ... She killed him.

My brother was the victim of domestic abuse. Unfortunately he did not get out soon enough. He always said he would-- sometimes he did, but he always went back. She killed him. Now we are dealing with a DA who says, "It's just different, we don't put women in jail for killing men when they claim self-defense." Please, I would like to visit with you about the entire story; it is one of disbelief. If you are interested, please e-mail me back. I would like to talk more.

So what's the big deal? I never really got close to a man I didn't want to slap the crap out of every now and then.

I have visited your site a few times and find it fascinating! I am a 42 year old female that has pretty much been abusing the men in my life since I was a teenager. Boyfriends, spouse etc, for a long time it was just the "significant others" , recently I lash out at male clients and male business associates. It seems as if a large percentage of my victims enjoy it! So what's the big deal? I never really got close to a man I didn't want to slap the crap out of every now and then.

The Happy Slapper

I finally did something about the abuse. The other night I went to the police department to report my wife.

Hey Bert,

I finally did something about the abuse. The other night I went to the police department to report my wife. She twisted the skin on my arm, scratched my arm, bit my hand and clocked me in the head. It all started when I was feeding our son a bottle of milk and he started to cry a little bit. She told me that my son didn't like me, and called me an imbecile. So, I told her that I didn't like that and to shut up. She came over and started kicking my shins. She just wouldn't stop it. So, I left and went to the police department. They came and arrested her. That night they took her to the hospital to be seen by a doctor. I told the police that she was suffering from post-partum depression. Her first appt. with a psyche doctor is this week. Since the incident she has been to her OB/GYN doctor and is taking Sarafem. It works quite well. What a difference a drug makes. She has totally changed. That's good for me.

Thanks,
Dale

She has tried to strangle me, chased me out the house twice with knife, spilt hot tea on me, spat at my face in front of 7 year son, many more.....

I have been battered husband for a year. I did not where to turn who to contact, but showed my injuries to my doc in May/June 2001. Thank heaven I found your site. My wife has turned the tables 180 degrees on me!!!

I love our 3 children, and I love my wife Susan. Susan is a very angry woman for some reason. She hates my side of family. If I go see my mum or sisters, Susan will swear at me at least 30 times, kick me, scratch me, bang her head against door etc. She say the ultimatum is either her or them (my mum/sisters)!!! It is a stupid situation. She does not want me to see my mum/sis nor are kids allowed to see them!! Susan opens all our mail, she even takes phone with her when she goes out. She has tried to strangle me, chased me out the house twice with knife, spilt hot tea on me, spat at my face in front of 7 year son, many more.....

Now she is asking for separation, and she wants custody of kids, and me to pay maintenance, she has lied and got a restraining order on me. Why does she want to split our family....can any-one help. She will not go see doctor or counsellor....I have been many times over last 2 years. She did see a phsyciatrist 3 years ago for one brief session, he wanted to keep her overnight in hospital, but due to shortage in beds, I had to take Sue home. He said to bring her back in a week...but she never went back.

Please please help us. My mum & sisters have not been to our house for 3 years, this is not fair. We are in our 40's. Kids are 19y, 15y & 7y old.

Colin.....HELP!!!!!

I even had two therapists tell me that the abuse I went through was good for me.

I can give you several cases to document where the local police and the local mental health counselors just totally blew me off and refused to help me. I even had two therapists tell me that the abuse I went through was good for me. The others I saw were just totally hateful and made it clear that they had no intention of helping me. There is something VERY wrong with the local mental health community here in Escambia/Santa Rosa county florida (the two counties have the same program together). Theres something even more wrong with the cops in Escambia county. Its like they think their job is to harras people and never help anyone. But I sure can't do anything about it. I'm to worn out and tired to even clean my house.

I wish someone would intervene and do something about how these "professionals" treat people around here. I went to the neighboring county of Okaloosa and talked to the people at the "Okaloosa/Walton Mental Health Agency" and they flat out refused to give me any helpful information at all. They refused to even tell me if there are any abuse support groups in the area. It was like all this information was a big secret or something. I guess because it was all women working there. When a man gets treated for abuse by a woman the abuse statistics that feminists use to vilify men get farther out of their favor. I've learned something in all of this though. There are not more male criminals than female criminals in this country, its just that the women get away with violence and men don't. Dont tell that to a feminist though, she'll probably try to destroy you.

I love him very much and want to help him however I can..whether that be end our relationship, or whatever. I just don't know how to help and I'm afraid he's going to lose all hope and do something stupid. What can I do?

Bert, I'm emailing you about an abusive situation that I am aware of that I am very concerned about. Your website said you wanted personal stories, but since this is written by me instead of the victim himself you may refer me somewhere else. I am open to any suggestions.

I am a female who had been in a verbally abusive relationship myself until 6 months ago..was married for 24 years and near the end of my marriage had tried everything to make my marriage work. In fact, I only realized after reading some of your information that I truly was in an abusive relationship and understood for the first time why it was so difficult for me to get out of that relationship.

Back to my reason for writing...about 2 years ago, myself, desperate for help and/or understanding of my own situation, I started searching the web for sites..I was looking for a message board or a chat area to find someone that was experiencing similar problems as myself. I answered an ad written by a gentleman..the two of us eventually met and became lovers...but we also became very good friends and have continued to share our problems with one another. After having read from your website, I feel quite stupid for not having realized his true problems...I suppose its because I was refusing to see that I, myself, was suffering from abuse. His story...

Simon was single, having been through a nasty divorce. He had a very good job, had a nice home. He was dating another woman when Gwen came along...Gwen saw what she wanted and conquered...basically, moving into his home uninvited... She is 15 years younger, was divorced with 2 small children that her husband had custody of. I suspect that the abuse happened pretty much from the start, but from what I understand she started withholding sex from him after about the first year they were together. Simon never intended to have a permanent relationship with her and she was aware of that but kept hanging in there.

They live in England...there are no common law marriages (as of yet) and according to the law if there is no monetary input by one party towards household expenses, then that party has no claim against the household. Thus, Simon has been paying all household expenses, although she lives there and works...she spends her money any way she sees fit. He pays for everything...and from my understanding she controls his money as well.

Several years into their relationship, Simon developed colon cancer, which his mom had died from only 4 months earlier. His cancer was malignant and even though his prognosis was very good, he was afraid he was going to die. Well...I suppose in an effort to "cleanse his soul" he divulged some information to her that was very personal and would be very damaging to him personally if it were revealed. HUGE MISTAKE...but, he recovered from the cancer and has gotten a clean bill of health.

She totally controlls him and regularly threatens him to divulge the information she knows. He has told me that it could ruin him personally, professionally... She has been physically violent with him, although I don't think that's the normal behavior. Because of her indifference to sex, or because of her only wanting it when she wanted it and the way she wanted he quit trying..they've not had a sex life in several years. He finally told her he was impotent and she has put him down, humiliated him in front of other people, telling them that he is impotent.

She is never satisfied with anything, continually bitches at him to do more around the house, bitches and complains when everything is not just the way she wants it, continually wants to blow his money ie. remodelling the house, wanting cars, expensive gifts. She regularly has temper tantrums, is very rude to his family members, has very little to do with his family or friends, always has to have things her way. He has told her that he didn't love her, told her he'd like for her to move out, but she hangs on - and ignores his wishes.

She had put him down so badly that by the time we met, he had almost no self-esteem, didn't think he could perform sexually, really felt totally worthless as a human being. We were able to meet and spend a few days together last year. Recently, we had another visit, spent some wonderful days together. We've fallen in love...the problem is that he has lost all hope of being able to get her out of his life. He is absolutely miserable, and I'm afraid our seeing each other again made things worse for him...He has been suffering from depression which seems to be growing more severe and I've gotten quite worried about him.

I was aware of his problems with Gwen from the beginning, although I didn't know how severe they were...I'm afraid I've not understood until now all his fears...and always thought maybe he was exaggerating a bit...I'm beginning to realize the full implications of the emotional damage that a battered relationship leaves you with.

I love him very much and want to help him however I can..whether that be end our relationship, or whatever. I just don't know how to help and I'm afraid he's going to lose all hope and do something stupid. What can I do?

If there is anything you might could suggest, I am certainly willing to try it...

Your website is most informative and I'm very grateful I found it. I work for social services and plan to give your web address to some of the social workers who regularly deal with abuse issues. Thank you so much for your time and your effort!!! Keep up the good work - it gives people encouragement and hope!!!

My mother routinely threw things at my father, my brother and myself. This was in addition to the verbal abuse. An acquaintence's wife took a shot at him with a pistol she stole. Fortunately she missed. He never reported the incident. A boss had his wife chase him around the house with a butcher knife.

Its not uncommon. My mother routinely threw things at my father, my brother and myself. This was in addition to the verbal abuse. An acquaintence's wife took a shot at him with a pistol she stole. Fortunately she missed. He never reported the incident. A boss had his wife chase him around the house with a butcher knife. He called relatives and they subdued her.

A woman I briefly dated chased her early teen-aged boys out into the street because they were "evil" males. Fortunately they located their father and moved In with him. She was taking a masters in Social Work and planned on getting into "family counseling." A friend's wife refuses to talk to her 20 something son for roughly the same reason. She's convinced that he beat his ex-wife even tho both deny it absolutely. She also is a social worker.

[The author adds: *I would also suggest that these are not ordinary women and that there are men who are equally abusive. The vast majority of women and men that I've met are decent, non-abusive people.*]

Don't psychologists have a code of ethics? Even prisoners of war must be treated according to certain guidelines. How can we

She is a professor of child psychology with a Ph.D.. I had no idea people like this existed and had no idea that someone in her position could get away with it. I cannot believe no one has caught on to her. She is mean, abusive, threatening, manipulative and cruel.

As an example, she tells us she is sending their adopted daugh-

diffuse this? Doesn't she have to abide by some ground rules? She doesn't have a right to verbally abuse us does she?

ter to us because she can no longer deal with her. We agree,are thrilled, get her room ready, then out of the blue she calls and begins threatening my husband with made up stories and issues that happened years ago. She threatens to black mail him.

Their oldest daughter is 13 and has been diagnosed as being emotionally and mentally ill. She has told so many lies about us it is un believable. Even though her mother knows she has been diagnosed, she chooses to believe any lie the child tells and then calls us to rant and rave over something that never happened.

I truly believe her only concern is that as a child psychologist she is more afraid of being embarrassed by her emotionally ill daughter than she is in getting help for her.

Your article are right on target. My husband is afraid to stand up to her because he is afraid of losing his children. We have become imprisoned at times by her nastiness and fear that we might upset her. She does not communicate, she talks a hundred miles an hour or rants and raves.

I have had it and will take it no more. I want to protect and educate my husband because he cannot protect himself - your article is right - she has trained him so well and knows is vulnerable spots so well she can take advantage of any situation. I do not want him to lose his beautiful children, but acceptance of her verbal abuse is no longer OK.

Don't psychologists have a code of ethics?

Even prisoners of war must be treated according to certain guidelines.

How can we diffuse this? Doesn't she have to abide by some ground rules? She doesn't have a right to verbally abuse us does she?

[Bert replies:]*I'm always leery in a relationship when someone says they have the "right" to do something, or that someone else doesn't have the "right." You may have the "right" to nag at me, and I have the "right" to be angry about it. A simplistic analogy, to be sure.*

The main thing for a person in an abusive relationship is to protect yourself. Over a long period of time, you get worn down and get "used to it." (That happened to me in my prior marriage -- and I can't tell you what a relief it was when it was over - like a gigantic weight had been lifted off my shoulders!)

One would hope that a child psychologist would comport herself or himself on the lines of what they help others with—"walk the walk" or "mirror" in their own lives how things should be done. But I know too many counselors to believe that's true. Too, too many don't do this.

*If she's working with a caseload concerned with abuse, there's always the chance to file a complaint with the licensing authority. But that is way, **way** secondary. The **first** and **most important** thing is that he take care of **himself**. Anything you can do to help and support him in that would be great.*

I was the most positive happy person always caring, never hit or pushed my weight around. I cherrished her and the more I cherished her the more lethal her words became. till she started hitting me.

All my friends are on her side. I still love her and it's literally making me bleed to death inside. I'm hemoraging internally. and she won't let me go. I have no-oe to talk to. My businesses have gope under. Even my counselor is on her side. The police, the courts, women helping women, And I was the most positive happy person always caring, never hit or pushed my weight around. I cherrished her and the more I cherished her the more lethal her words became. till she started hitting me. Till now I have never raised a hand to her. I have a restraining order and can't see her or my son And I feel like I'm going to die without them. No one believes me. This one is very serious her whole family is violent all in and out of prison. She seemed like a little angel I just wanted to take her away from all that hatred and lies. I'm afraid she will manipulate her family to come after me she has done it to others since childhood.

I am currently getting a divorce,,,she filed,,,,,,,I relapsed back to drinking and using drugs. Which I know I can't keep clean around her ,,,,she is a codependent and the adult child of alcoholic parents,,,,,and I don't want to die,,,so I accept the divorce as a healthy step in my recovery.... oops I also had a homosexual event with a man while I was dressed as a woman,,,,,,Yes I told her,,big mistake....I don't think it bothered her as much as she let's on,,,,,,,It was part of my self destructive nature. I am a crosdressor ,, infact I slept in nighties for the past 5 years, with her ofcourse,,,,,I had also other fetishistic behaviors, infantisim,bd, s&m (me submissive),,,, she would spank me, if I asked her to....However a couple of times, during the spanking,(with her sitting on my back while I was laying face down, she is twice my body weight,) I asked her to stop and she wouldn't she continued inspite of my pleading,,,,once whipped my penis and testacals,,,,breaking small blood vessels, creating blood blisters on both......is this considered abuse?,,,,spanking my behind she would leave huge black and blue bruises........ Most severe of all is the verbal abuse,,,,,,,"you're not a man", ,, then infront of other women,,, "stop acting like a man",,,constantly berating me in front of strangers,family(HERS AND MINE), my employees,,,and worst of all my daughter,,11 years old .... The last time I relapsed I sobered up to get back together with her,,,,this time I was doing it for myself,I didn't want her involved in my counseling etc.,,,,,,Which I am sure pissed her off,,,,Wee have been separated for 9 weeks now,,,,,,,she also had stopped me from going to our church, telling the elders she wouldn't go if I was there,,,even though I have confessed and repented of my sins,,,,,,through much insistence I have finally been allowed to return,,,,firsat time will be Nov. 18,,,,I am looking forward to it,,,though I expect a few dirty looks...I have viewed the church thing as another part of her controling,,,,,,,,,I believe she has told my daughter everthing,infact I am certain,,,needless to say my daughter doesn't want to see me,,,,,My daughter is very angry with me,,,I expect that from the using,,,,,the other stuff ,,, well I don't know. My daughter hates me now and I am enduring yet broken hearted, because of my wife's treatment of me, my daughter hasn't respected me for the past 18 months...I am fighting for some counseling and visitation for me and her .....

I am interested in some comments.
Clean and sober
And so happy to still be alive.

I just found this site, and I must say - Thank God!!! It's your site (and others) that has inspired me to seek my dream. I've just enrolled in a local college to become an attorney - practicing father's and men's rights. I know this will be a long road, but I have the strength and determination to follow through. I have much support through many men going through similar tribulations such as mine.

Two years ago I discovered my wife's affair. Since that time, my life has become a living hell. Her lover lives in the Caribbean, and that's where she wishes to live. It's surprising how easy it is to be a woman, pick up the phone, dial 911, and have a man arrested. It wasn't until I went to Radio Shack and bought a small tape recorder, that my arrests ended. After 4 arrests for 'harassment' I'd had enough. The last 3 time the Sheriffs knocked on my door, I was able to avoid arrest by simply replaying the actual conversation, on magnetic tape (complete with my voice stating time and date), to prove my ex-wife a liar. (I RECOMMEND A TAPE RECORDER FOR ALL GOING THROUGH THIS TYPE OF SITUATION.)

During my marriage, I was subjected to constant verbal and physical violence. I never reported it. After all, I'm 6'3", 240 lbs and a loving, devoted husband and father of two boys! I just wanted to make my marriage work!!! The sad news is, it takes two.

At the time that my marriage started falling apart, I was working at a career that paid me $40,000 a year. Sadly, a year before that, I managed to get my wife a position with my company. In just a few months, I was terminated - due to "problems on the job with my ex-wife". I immediately took a job that paid $8.00 per hour. My weekly Child Support was $93.00 a week. After C.S. and typical expenses, I was left with about $30.00 a week to live on. Live? Come on!!! And the worst part? I have my children 50% of the time!!!

Two months ago, I accepted a job with Syracuse University. I work

During my marriage, I was subjected to constant verbal and physical violence. I never reported it. After all, I'm 6'3", 240 lbs and a loving, devoted husband and father of two boys!

It's surprising how easy it is to be a woman, pick up the phone, dial 911, and have a man arrested. It wasn't until I went to Radio Shack and bought a small tape recorder, that my arrests ended. After 4 arrests for 'harassment' I'd had enough. The last 3 time the Sheriffs knocked on my door, I was able to avoid arrest by simply replaying the actual conversation, on magnetic tape (complete with my voice stating time and date), to prove my ex-wife a liar. (I RECOMMEND A TAPE RECORDER FOR ALL GOING THROUGH THIS TYPE OF SITUATION.)

in food service. That's a far cry from utilizing my A.S. in Criminal Justice!! When I had the opportunity to join the local Sheriffs Dept., I allowed my wife to talk me out of it. She said it would be too dangerous. (What a fool I was! I became a garbage man instead!)

I am now proud to say, that I'm starting my first class next week. But - before I become an attorney, I will have already started my first "Men's Group". The injustice against men has gone on too long. I guarantee, you will hear my name, and read about my group in less than two years.

I have concerned myself with justice for most of my life. I now have a reason to fight!!! I may not change the world - but one fight at a time, I will help change the system!! God Bless and Good Luck!!!

The final thing is that now a days I cannot think of anything else as I am always afraid that my wife may not call the police again for nothing.

Sir,

I went through your website and find it greatly satisfying and have lot of things common to the views expressed.

I would like to be involved in this move to help men as I know a lot of men who just do not say anything against there wives because they feel ashamed of the society.

Couple of months back I was arrested by the police and charged with domestic battery.

I requested the police officer to reconsider my arrest and charging me with that crime as I had done nothing. But instead another police officer came in and started pushing me around.

I was let off only after I payed a cash bond of $2500 and my finger prints my photographs were taken at the police station.

On the intial hearing date I went to the court and told the Judge and the prosecuter that I was innocent and had done nothing but they wanted an attorney to represent me.

I searched for an attorney and talked to them all of them said that if your wife calls the police they have to come and arrest you and charge you with domestic battery.

So they suggested me to hire them to fight my case otherwise I may land in jail and serve even a year.

Now whom so ever I talk to tells me that I have been booked under a very very serious crime but I do not understand why? Is there no place for men in this kind of a situation.

So what I am wondering that is it so easy in America for a wife to call the police and get the husband arrested and then the police takes a cash bond and then the husband has to hire a attorney to fight the case.

Is there any way that I can get some help in my present circumstances and in future if this kind of thing happens to me.

I am afraid that as this case has already been put on my record next time if my wife calls the police the police will not even think twice because they will always give the reference of this case.

The final thing is that now a days I cannot think of anything else as I am always afraid that my wife may not call the police again for nothing.

Can you suggest me some real solution as I have never been in my life been into any situation involving the police and the court like this.Can my life straighten out again , is it possible to remove this thing from my record . Where should I go whom should I seek help from. Why am I made to spend so much money and time even when I am innocent.

I am on medication for an ulcer. Recently one night, I left my ulcer pills on top of the bathroom medicine cabinet and had to go upstairs to get them. In doing so, I accidentally knocked a can of shaving cream off the shelf and onto the floor. This woke up our toddler son in the adjacent bedroom after which my wife stormed out of our bedroom in a violent rage. She began beating on me with her fists while yelling at me through clenched teeth and wild eyes because I woke up our son after it took her "a solid hour" hour to put him to sleep.

I went downstairs to get away from her but she followed me all over the house ranting, raving, punching, scratching, with ever increasing anger. When she came at me with a rolling pin I was forced to defend myself. I shoved her against the doorjam so hard that it knocked the breath right out of her while letting the rolling pin fall to the floor. Meanwhile, our three year old son was standing at the foot of the stairs yelling for his mother to stop. At that point, she finally did.

And all of this because I inadvertantly woke up our son while going upstairs to retreive my ulcer medication. The next morning I woke up and my wife was sitting apologetically/sympathetically, by the foot of the bed, as if nothing had ever happenned...

This is a typical example of my wife's Jeckel & Hyde behavior which, incidentally, began shortly after our son was born and has carried on (more or less) over the last three years. If it weren't for our son I would've left a long time ago. However, he needs me and I can't bring myself to let go of him. And who would my wife vent her rage against if I were gone? I know these are lame excuses to some but they are valid when in the position described.

Any advice appreciated.

The only reply I could think of was to refer him to our page on Borderline Personality Disorder. "Jeckel & Hyde behavior" is something spouses of BPD people frequently mention. Any other suggestions? Pass them along and I'll forward them.

She beat me during the course of the marrage and I went for help. People could of helped but no one did. Finally in December 95 she attacked me in three diferent rooms even carried a picture taken of the wall to throw at me but because I was the man I was arrested.

My story is involved . However ther are simple facts that are presant .My wife now EX has lived her adult life by having men take care of her while she seeks her next mate. Furthermore she uses control to get what she wants including violence, threats, and false reports to police. In my case she used all three and more. I did not know these things when we got married only after searching for the truth and investagting the crimes comited aganst me did I uncover a definite pattern to her actions aginst men. THERE IS ALLWAYS SOMEONE AFTER HER, AND ALL FORMOR RELENSHIPS HAD VIOLENCE AGINST HER. What I have discovered is that she was instionalized as a child for mental problems. She has for a long time claimed people are after her. My marrage to her should not be upheled. She was living with another man while dating me. We lived three miles apart yet nether of us know. She pulled this off by lying about a former relenship that she claimed she was stalked. THerefore she did not want her address or phone known.

She beat me during the course of the marrage and I went for help. People could of helped but no one did. Finally in December 95 she attacked me in three diferent rooms even carried a picture taken of the wall to throw at me but because I was the man I was arrested. My wife convinced me to stay in the marrage and take the plea so that we could get on with our lives and I could avoid the posibaly of a record. Faced with moving from my home paying to support her while tring to win a case that never should have seen me arrested in the first place I gave in. Little did I know that when she talked to the DA she lied to them and me. She told me she was going to tell what happened her attacking me and that she needed help but that not what she said to them. She is a master manipulator and can cry on cue. She lied in the divorce did not have to pay any of the bills in both names.

The most damaging thing is she set out to intentionally hurt me. By geting a restraning order and by making false actulations aginst me in court. I have proven that she lied to the DA but they wont take any action aginst her becaues the police wont charge her. The law is not about truth any more. BUT I deserve the truth to be herd and my records to be free from fraud and lies. MY rights have been denied through the cases in court. The most damming evidence I have aginst her is the fact that she approached me while I was in a girlfriend's SUV and then moved next to her at the same time she told the court she was afaraid of me and was hiding and moving to keep her wearabouts secret from me. If you just read all the divorce papers you can see by her actions that is is bold and uncooperative to a fair settlement. When she was asked about the approaches to me in court she lied. She won her restraining order on lies.

During the course of a seven year marriage I was hit, scratched, gouged, bit, kicked and beat in the head with a high heel shoe until blood ran down my face. Another time I cooked her breakfast early on a Sunday (just because I wanted to) and when I told her "Honey! Time to get up. I made breakfast!" she went into a rage and told me that I was trying to "control" her by making breakfast. And then when she came into the kitchen and saw that I was finishing with the eggs, she screamed and called me a liar ("You fucking liar!

I first shared this story on an e-mail list I participate in. I was held up to ridicule and disbelief by some of the other men on the list. Comments like "Yeah, right" and even outright accusations of being a liar were made. People just have a hard time believing that a man can be on the receiving end of abuse.

One of the participants there (Tad) started a thread about a friend of his (female) that had been abused and he was promoting the idea that abusive men (not women, just men) be put on some sort of national register. So I replied with an offer to send links to research that shattered the popular stereotypes and showed that abuse was a two way street.

Tad took this to mean I was defending abusers and must be a wife beater myself. I am always amazed at how many men respond this way. Oddly enough I had some fairly supportive public posts and private e-mail but is all came from other women on the list. Go figure...

The plain and simple fact is that domestic violence is not an either/or issue. Men and women both abuse each other and at roughly equal numbers Hard to believe? Yes. True? Also yes.

I have had exactly two black eyes in my life. Real shiners they were. Both came from my first wife. And both times she knew, I mean she just knew, that I would not hit her back.

During the course of a seven year marriage I was hit, scratched, gouged, bit, kicked and beat in the head with a high heel shoe until blood ran down my face. Another time I cooked her breakfast early on a Sunday (just because I wanted to) and when I told her "Honey! Time to get up. I made breakfast!" she went into a rage and told me that I was trying to "control" her by making breakfast. And then when she came into the kitchen and

Breakfast isn't ready!) and in retaliation picked up a pot of boiling hot grits and hurled it at me while my five year old son looked on.

saw that I was finishing with the eggs, she screamed and called me a liar ("You fucking liar! Breakfast isn't ready!) and in retaliation picked up a pot of boiling hot grits and hurled it at me while my five year old son looked on.

During that marriage I went into counseling. At one time when I was talking with a counselor I spoke of how I felt a need to "walk on eggshells" with my wife and to think long and hard before I spoke to her to be sure that what I had to say would not cause her to be angry. My counselor, a woman, told me that I (a man) was exhibiting behavior associated with "battered woman's syndrome"! She went on to tell me that was a misnomer and that it really ought to be called battered spouse syndrome because it affected men and women who were being abused physically, mentally or both in a relationships.

There were a lot of times during that marriage where I left the house with my son and went to stay with friends. They would see the bruises and the scratches and the bites. For me it was absolutely humiliating.

The only marks that anyone ever saw on my ex was redness around her wrists where I would restrain her. I can remember it like it was yesterday! I would be saying "Charlene, please just stop! Promise you will stop and I will let you go." And she would promise and it would be a lie. I'd let her go and often as not she would immediately punch me or kick me or look for a weapon.

There were times later when she would come to me and apologize and break down in tears and tell me she didn't know why she did these things. She would tell me that she just got so angry that she couldn't help it but then she would promise me it would never, ever happen again and I would hold her and tell her I loved her and that it would be OK and we would both cry together.

But it never lasted.

There were other methods of abuse too. Like the time after a relatively sane and normal argument that did not really escalate but where the tension was so thick you could cut it with a knife. After it had calmed down somewhat I told her maybe she would feel better if she went for a drive just to get out of the house for a while. So she did. And hours later she came back after midnight and I told her I had been worried. Se said "You didn't need to worry. I went to a bar and found someone to take care of me." I asked her "What do you mean?" And she told me that she had gone to Bennigans (a bar/restaurant chain) and a guy bought her a drink. She said later she went outside with him and walked up the hill behind the restaurant and there se fucked him on the ground. When she took off her clothes to get ready for bed her back was covered with scratches from the pine straw and leaves and she smelled of his semen.

I was shocked and hurt. I asked her to please take a shower because I could not stand that she "smelled" like this man. Which erupted into another argument because "Hell, I like the smell" and "It's too damn late to shower."

So when people ask why do people stay in abusive relationships, I know the answer. And when people try to make it out like women are helpless, I know it's a fallacy.

My experience with court in Gwinnett County, Georgia also makes me sensitive. If not for a letter written by my ex and the testimony of my (then) five year old son, I would be a convicted abuser today.

See, at the time my marriage finally broke up, my ex hired scum bag attorneys and what did they recommend? You guessed it! They told her to bring charges against me! So there I am....blood dried in my hair, tooth marks on my arms and scratches on my face getting a first person view of the inside of the county jail.

At arraignment I was offered a bench trial. The judge said "We don't take to wife beaters here in Gwinnett County." Needless to say, I took the jury trial instead.

What happened in between is what saved me. My ex wrote me a long letter, six or seven pages as I recall, in which she admitted that she was violent and out of control. She apologized over and over. All I can say is that it must have been a weak moment for her.

Later she broke into my home and tore that letter to a thousand pieces. If she had not been worried about getting caught maybe she would have taken the time to burn it. Or flush it. But she didn't. Instead she threw the pieces in the trash.

Well, I took em out and spent days painstakingly taping all pieces back together and my attorney introduced the letter at trial and had her read it out loud.

And my five year old son was also found competent to testify and testify he did.

The jury returned a not guilty in about twenty minutes. My attorney told me that without that letter and the testimony of my son, I would have stood about a 95% chance of conviction.

Oddly enough, before trial the DA interviewed my son and read the same letter. He told me that he was convinced that I was

NOT guilty but that with political pressure brought by the "battered women's movement" he had no choice but to try and make me look like scum and convict me. He said that dropping the charges was a death knell for chances at re-election and until the political climate changed that was just the way things were.

Some justice huh?

Impact of not speaking out on female violence ... young men shy from relationships

My mother was my first "battered," She gave me violent, overwhelming enemas as a child, despite my screams of terror and begging. When she whipped me (when I showed some independence) it was with forsythia switches that form painful welts. Her friends used to a pass me around for greasy kisses and handling, despite my screams of terror. I was taught never to hit and woman (and never have) but women took advantage of that. I dated a woman, idiot that I was, who regularly slapped me, pretending it was a "game>'

I am very good looking and find that women here in San Francisco go out of their way to push me., even bump me off of the street (I am now an older man.) I do think San Francisco has the meanest women in the world - there were outreach posters up a few months ago for women who were raped or battered by another WOMAN. What a world. I am a somewhat oversensitive man now, in relation to women, and find endless female meanness - curt answers, impoliteness, deliberate verbal cruelty, and on and on. The standard things. Nevertheless, I have held to the basic idea that I am a good man, a good human.

This poor, suffering country! Recently I asked a couple of young men dispensing yogurt in a store how younger women were for the, these days. They just shook, their heads, smiled and laughed awkwardly, looked at each other, and said "We just keep our minds on yogurt." They are so frightened and shut down they can't even discuss it! Good luck to men everywhere. We need it. I also see women "pulling tricks" =a bus driver almost hit a man, then when he complained to her she accused him of making a racial slut (he didn't(and of threatening her. She was twice as big as the guy. I understand women's training includes sections of how to lie and make him the abuser, even when you abuse first. I'm sure you have heard all this before. Thanks for the opportunity to send this E-mail.

A wife talks of problems with an abusive 90-year-old mother

I am married to a man who has been abused by his mother all his life. We have been married 13 years; he will be forty years old in July. He is a mental health professional, a field he chose, I think, because somehow he thought he would be able to "cure" his disturbed mother. She is a very small woman, but her rage is enormous. He is her only child. All of her sickness fell on him. She hates so many people--her speech is a foul litany of curses against people who have supposedly insulted her. She is never to blame, rules apply only to others. As a small child, my husband was thrown down stairs, locked in closets, beaten. By the time he was 12, he was an emotional substitute for her spouse. As an adult her abuse has been emotional--threatening to kill herself, belittling him, as well as, paradoxically, insisting that he is wonderful, better than everyone else, etc. etc.--and at times physical.

My husband is wonderful--he takes after his father. He has a heart like an ocean. He is so ready to blame himself for anything that goes wrong, anywhere. She has burdened him with so much guilt and rage. As you can imagine, she's done all she can to break up the marriage, and I've spent thirteen years defending the marriage against her. She was committed last year to a psychiatric hospital, due to suicide threats, because her second husband had walked out on her, saying he couldn't take it anymore. She spent the time in the hospital calling my husband at work and screaming at him to get her out of there. He was worried sick and panic-stricken. "What if they talk to her and find out what she's like--they'll never let her out," he said to me. He did his best to have her discharged, into the care of my husband's father, his best friend.

My father in law stuck with her until February of this year. He did all he could to make her happy, he put up with all her screaming insults, he was terrified every time she threatened suicide. He and my husband, the only people left who cared about her, did all they could. I wasn't worried about her suicide threats. Does that sound cold? She has an absolute loathing of any physical pain, and a total intolerance to medication. I've seen an imaginary sore toe lay her up for a week, and one Tylenol knock her out for a day. I was more worried about my father in law. We had them both to visit for Christmas, and he looked terrible. She ruined the holiday with tantrums, curses, moods, all in front of our two young sons. "She'll kill him before she committs suicide, " I told my husband. But it was a good threat to use on kind-hearted men. As I said, my father in law stayed by her until February. She screamed at him once too often, and he suffered a massive cardiac and died. In the three days following the death my husband was physically and emotionally abused by her.

She has left many bodies in her wake. She is seventy years old, and in excellent health. She takes good care of herself

, has never gone hungry a meal in her life, has never known poverty.

Following the funeral I gave my husband an ultimatum--me or Mom. I don't want to lose him in the way we lost his father. Now she is again threatening suicide, claiming I am forcing him to choose between the two of us. Well, I am. She got away with this behavior for all these years, but no more. But how does he do it? How does an abused man, programmed since birth to pacify Mommy, keep Mommy happy, forgive Mommy, protect Mommy, apologize to Mommy, ever leave Mommy??? As the mother of two sons, as the wife of an abused man, I find your testimonials of great interest. I have no patience with this culture's pro forma idealization of women. Women can be just as vicious, just as heartless, just as violent. But, unlike men, they have a few extra weapons in their arsenal. How can I best save my husband from this woman? Do you happen to know of any web site that could maybe help me?

Man censured for speaking out ...

I just wanted to thank you for your efforts regarding illuminating the subject of domestic abuse, particularly male victims. I am a victim of abuse in a previous marriage, a father of two sons(who spend half their time with each parent) and a mid life career changer. As a non traditional university student (age 43) earning my Bachelors degree in social work, i am amazed at the bias in a field that purports to work towards ending oppression. i have recently been censored for speaking up in a domestic violence course. the instructor took exception to my pointing out that yes, men are victims of abuse too. not that that will stop me! but it does convey the level of institutional bias. in any event, thank you for maintaing this site, i have used materials from it to support my position in various research papers, and i provide the social work faculty with copies to enlighten them.

To start off, my "domestic abuse" was caused by my fiancé. I had met my fiancé in London, England last year at the hotel I was staying at in July 1998. We had corresponded by e-mail for months. Then in November 1998, she came to visit me. As soon as she arrived, we/she had arguments about trivial things, but we worked the problems out. Then in Dec 98 Jan 99, I visited her in England for 2 weeks. During that time, we seemed to argue constantly about trivial things. By that I mean if I made a general statement, she would make a critical remark and that would set off an argument. When I was with her, it seemed to me that she would have what I call "severe emotional swings". She would constantly yell at me, I would try to talk to in a calm manner, but it didn't do any good.

Then she visited me in late March/April, we were planning to get married April 3, 1999. But when she was here, she constantly criticized me for not planning the wedding better etc. She would yell and scream at me, saying that I am, and I quote: "Stupid and Pathetic",, she did this for 3 days prior to the wedding, in addition, she would walk out on me from a restaurant because she was mad at me. Then one evening, April 3, she was again yelling and screaming at me, accusing me of being "stupid and pathetic". So I said " I am stupid and pathetic" etc. Then she jumps in the bed and started clawing at my face, which caused a few cuts and bleeding. Then she makes fun of me bleeding. I did not hit her or do anything abusive to her, I tried to stop her from clawing at me. The next day she apologized for yelling at me, but not for clawing at me. To be honest, I was astounded that she did that. So, I called off the wedding. Then she complains to me about cancelling the wedding. The bottom line is that I was afraid to marry her because I did not want to endure that type of abuse for a lifetime.

I did not report that abuse because like most guys, I was afraid to, and I could have had her deported, that is if the police would have believed me.

Can you reccomend books that I could read on women abuse and what should I do about it? We have talked about our problems, but I have not directly confronted her about her abuse towards me that night. Which I know I should.

We will wonder why so many women in today's, American culture think men are idiots and stupid and deserve to be treated poorly. Why is this discussion taking place on the fringes of society and not in the main stream.....how much of it is the fault of men because we allow it to continue unanswered??? Why aren't we standing up and saying enough is enough? We should not

My, now, ex-wife started showing signs of a violent temper just a few days before we got married. At first they were not aimed directly at me but were kinda scary. I was told by our minister not to marry her (I told him about them), but I thought I could be a good husband and help her through her issues. My first mistake.

About one month after our wedding day, late at night, we had had an argument and she wanted the keys to the car (it was my car before we were married) to drive around to cool down a while. Not a strange request except the following; she is legally blind (but does wear glasses), she did not know her way around Dallas because we had just moved there and it was close to midnight. I told her she was not taking the car out that late because I had already had to go "find" her twice before because she had gotten lost during the day. So I did not think it was safe for her to be out that late at night in Dallas, upset and driving my car. I had the keys in my hand, she jumped on me and started scratching my face and arms and pulling my hair...all the while screaming at me to get off of HER!! I did not hit her but I did try to defend myself as well as keep the keys from her. After we wrestled for about 10 minutes on the floor I got her off of me and called my parents across town to come and get her...I did not want her in the house with me. Just as my dad and mom came in the front door she threw herself on the floor in the bedroom and started screaming and crying that I had hit her. My dad, like the rest of society, took her side immediately *complain if we are not willing to go against the crowd and speak out against all domestic violence. In one form we men have become victims of our own silence on this issue.*

and threw me out of my own home (he's a big man) and started fighting me in the front yard saying he was going to call the police. Oddly enough that night my mom started seeing right through my wife and did not believe her...later of course the truth came out. But I had to live through several more of these violent attacks before people started seeing the truth.

It all came to a climax when my wife, who was expecting our first child at the time, accidentally fell in our basement and bruised her back. I was upstairs in bed when it happened. I immediately took her to the Base hospital terrified that the baby had been hurt too. (I was in the Air Force at the time) A complete change came over her as soon as we got inside the Hospital door. She acted terrified of me, like I had beat her up and she faked not being able to speak... blah blah blah. The nurses immedialty separated us and took her into a different part of the hospital and they called the S.P.'s and I was kept in a room for 4 hours, not allowed to leave and not allowed to know how my baby was or my wife was. I was charged with Assault and Domestic Violence and put under investigation with a possible penalty of Court Martial and time in prison. The investigation lasted 3 months and was a complete nightmare. My wife was admitted to the Hospital and "treated" for DV and underwent counseling for the terror I had been putting her through. All a complete fabrication and false. The charges were dropped after 3 months ONLY because she said she did not want to pursue filing any charges and she left me. I filed for divorce within a few weeks.... the visitation of my son is another horror story I guess is reserved for another group of men who have been screwed by the absurd court system of this up-side-down country.

Until we put a stop to the ridiculous idea that "women cannot abuse men" and "men cannot be victims" and stop supporting television programs that show women slapping men and hitting men (it happens on way too many shows) and making it look okay when it does happen, then men will continue to suffer in silence. We will wonder why so many women in today's, American culture think men are idiots and stupid and deserve to be treated poorly. Why is this discussion taking place on the fringes of society and not in the main stream.....how much of it is the fault of men because we allow it to continue unanswered??? Why aren't we standing up and saying enough is enough? We should not complain if we are not willing to go against the crowd and speak out against all domestic violence. In one form we men have become victims of our own silence on this issue.

I was with her for 3 years, in 3 separate tries at a relationship. I actually got out of it completely twice, finding others to be involved with (that reminded me of what a normal relationship should be) but then went back.

She had been both physically and sexually abused by her father; she has at least one scar from when he hit her.

I only came to understand later, about now as I write this, that he dealt with her anger and abuse simply by hitting her. Often when she was angry at me she'd say that if I hit her she'd leave.

Life with her was being put down all the time, nothing I did was ever good enough except when I spent lots of money (at least several thousand) on something for her, and then I was okay for a day or two. We finally got a new kitchen done, costing 40K; she was happy for 48 hours and then began screaming at me because I said there wasn't money to do 7K in landscaping.

Two other anecdotes, becuase they didn't involve me as a target:

We took a couple of kids (related to her) to the circus; and we had fun mostly. On the way back to drop off the kids I stopped for gas. The little girl wanted to clean off the windshield with the squeegee, and did a decent job for a 6 year old, leaving streaks (;-). She got back in the car and said "So, did I do a good job?" very proud of herself. Before I could answer, she (the ex) snapped "you did a lousy job", and the little girl just wilted.

Other: she had trained as a nurse, but works doing office/clerical work because she can't hold a nursing job: she was fired from the Visiting Nurse Association for throwing an ashtray at an elderly patient.

We were supposed to get married very soon, and it became very clear that it wasn't working. She was taking Accutane (a tetragenic drug, it causes severe birth defects), and doing her best to avoid sex. (we were able to have sex 11 times in the entire 3 years.

She was going to leave a couple of times in the past three months, but each time (just as I was totally relieved that she was finally going) she decided to "try to make it work"; and I didn't have the guts to say again to just go. (I did once the second time, and she was going to, but yet again she tried to make it work.

Of course the verbal abuse got worse and worse. All sweetness and light when anyone else was around, and cold rage as soon as we were alone.

In the end she spent many minutes screaming at her, and I slapped her. I've never done anything like that never will, and never would have had the idea at all if she hadn't kept threatening me "if you hit me, I'll leave." But this time I wanted her to leave.

Instantly she was calm, picked up the phone and called 911, to report domestic violence. She even called it that. Not "He hit me", or "I'm scared", but dead calm, "I want to report domestic violence, would you please send a unit."

I'll skip some sorry details about what followed, you know the story; I was arrested, she stole $10,000 from me during the hours I was in custody, told a friend of mine, quote: "I should have killed him when I had the chance."

I'm assigned to a program for "men who batter", and can escape the A&B charge with a dismissal if I can "successfully" complete the program.

I can't recover the money; the judge and DA didn't even care about that; if I sue, she'll use that as means to endless controlling behavior.

Where do I go now? I went to a program at Fenway, and they told me to get lost. Does anyone know of a program to help, and help me survive the "counseling" I'm going to be subjected to?

DOMESTIC VIOLENCE GLOSSARY

There may be other definitions for these words but these are the meanings used in relation to domestic violence.

Advocate -

A person who works for an organization that provides help to domestic violence victims. The Advocate must have received specialized training in counseling domestic violence victims including completion of state-certified 40-hour training.

The Advocate provides confidential, free help and will go to court with the domestic violence victim.

A Domestic Violence Advocate provides legal advocacy services for victims of abuse. Advocates help victims by:

Notifying them of, and going with them to, court hearings,

Educating them about the court system and domestic violence,

Helping them fill out applications for restraining orders,

Helping them communicate with prosecutors, probation officers, and court personnel and Safety planning.

Anger Management class–

An older term used to refer to what are now called Batterer's Intervention programs. The name has been changed to reflect current understanding that abuse is not only about anger but about control issues with many different causes.

Answer–

In Civil/Family cases, a form the restrained person fills out and files with the court before the restraining order court hearing. This form is sometimes called a "Response" but there are also other forms called "Response."

Batterer–

Someone who abuses another person. Abuse can be physical, financial or emotional.

Batterer's Intervention Program –

By California State law, when a person is convicted of Domestic Violence, they must take a 52 week class to work on
the attitudes and things they did which caused them to abuse their Intimate Partner. The Probation Department makes sure the person who has to go to these classes attends them, pays the fees, keeps records, and makes progress in class.

Batterer's Treatment Program – See Batterer's Intervention Program.

California Law Enforcement Telecommunications System (CLETS) – A statewide computer system that has information about restraining orders issued in California or registered in California from another state. Law Enforcement personnel access the system to respond to and enforce domestic violence orders.

Child Abuse -

Maltreatment or neglect of a child, including non-accidental physical injuries, sexual abuse/exploitation, severe or general neglect, unjustifiable mental suffering/emotional abuse, and willful cruelty or unjustifiable punishment of a child.

Child Abuse Protocol –

The Santa Clara County District Attorney's Office along with Law Enforcement and other government agencies has implemented protocols (rules) where those agencies agree:

1. conduct prompt and thorough investigations of child abuse, endangerment and neglect cases;

2. reduce trauma to victimized children;

3. cooperate effectively to investigate, prosecute and prevent child abuse, endangerment and neglect within Santa Clara County;

4. train employees on recognition and investigation of child abuse, endangerment and neglect.

Civil Harassment restraining order

– A restraining order that protects one person from another. It specifically applies to relationships which are not covered by the Domestic Violence Prevention Act.

Example: neighbor against neighbor, person against ex-spouse/girlfriend/ex-boyfriend's new partner.

Civil Standby –

When a Law Enforcement agency comes to a location (normally the home shared by the protected person and restrained person) to keep the peace. This is usually so that one of the parties may pick up a few personal items or follow another court order.

CLETS

– see California Law Enforcement Telecommunications System.

County Counsel

– The chief legal advisor and representative for the County of Santa Clara, including the Board of Supervisors and County agencies and departments; Represents and advises a county on legal matters.

Court Specialist -

Family court clerks that look over requests for temporary or emergency orders (called ex parte orders) before the judge sees them. They also process fee waivers.

Criminal Protective Order-

An order a Judge makes to protect a witness or victim of a crime.

DA– *see District Attorney*

Dating Violence–

Intimate Partner Violence (IPV) between people who are dating. The abusive behaviors between dating partners include verbal, physical, emotional, sexual, financial and/or electronic harassment. The genders or sexual orientation of the parties doesn't matter.

Defendant–

The person accused of a crime in a criminal case. The person or company being sued in a civil case (Family Court, Civil Harassment, Workplace Violence or Elder Abuse). In a civil case the term used is "Respondent."

Dependent Adult Abuse-

Physical abuse (including sexual), financial abuse, neglect, abandonment, isolation, abduction, treatment that causes physical harm, pain or mental suffering, and withholding of things or services by a care custodian of a dependent adult. *(Adapted from the Elder Abuse Task Force)*

District Attorney–

An attorney who works for the people of the State of California. They bring criminal charges against people who violate the law and then prosecute the resulting case in Santa Clara County Superior Court.

Document Examiner– Now called a "Court Specialist."

Domestic Violence Agency–

A non-profit organization that provides free, confidential domestic violence services to victims. Services include: a 24-hour crisis line, emergency & confidential shelter, legal advocacy, safety planning, peer counseling, therapy, and resource & referral.

Domestic violence agencies have historically offered services including confidential emergency shelter, counseling and education, and legal advocacy. Legal advocacy could mean providing people who go to court hearings with the victim or the help of attorneys, when needed.

Because some victims of domestic violence do not call domestic violence agencies, new types of agencies have started to help clients where they are: in drug rehabilitation, court rooms, jails or prisons. These victims are often referred to existing traditional domestic violence agencies for confidential shelter, counseling or specialized programs.

Domestic Violence Prevention Act restraining order-

This order protects a person from physical violence, a verbal threat of physical violence, or a pattern of harassing behavior by someone the victim has or had a close relationship with (such as husband/wife, family relative, and currently or previously dating or living together). It is free to apply for the order.

DVPA–

Domestic Violence Prevention Act. This is a code section found within the Family Code that is the law related to domestic violence. This section begins at Family Code section 6200 (scroll down to section 6200).

Elder Abuse-

Physical abuse (including sexual), financial abuse, neglect, abandonment, isolation, abduction, treatment that causes physical harm or pain or mental suffering, and withholding of things or services by a care custodian of an elderly person.

(adapted from the Elder Abuse Task Force)

Elder Abuse / Dependent Adult Abuse Restraining Order–

These restraining orders are meant to prevent mistreatment of an elderly person or a dependent adult - an adult who has physical or developmental disabilities, or failing physical or mental abilities caused by age.

Emergency Protective Order (EPRO) –

This is a restraining order requested by Law Enforcement on an emergency basis at a domestic violence scene. The EPRO is approved by a duty judge after s/he receives a phone call from the Law Enforcement officer. An Emergency Protective Order only lasts for 5 court days or 7 calendar days. To get a restraining order or custody/visitation orders that last longer, the victim must file papers in Court or a case may be opened by the District Attorney in Criminal Court.
An EPRO can:

• Protect a victim from stalking, violence, threats of violence or a pattern of harassing behavior,

• Protect the victim, their immediate family and people who live with them,

• Say who has custody as long as the EPRO is in effect. Employers can ask for EPRO's to protect their workplace from someone who is threatening their employee.

Emergency Protective Restraining Order– see *Emergency Protective Order.*

EPO – *see Emergency Protective Order.*

EPRO – *Emergency Protective Restraining Order; see Emergency Protective Order.*

Ex parte order-

An order that the judge makes after meeting with, or reading legal forms submitted by, only one party in a case.

(An ex parte request).

Family Violence–

A general term which includes the categories of Child Abuse, Elder Abuse, Dependent Adult Abuse, Domestic Violence & Animal Cruelty.

Intimate Partner -

Current or former spouses (husband/wife/domestic partner), boyfriends, and girlfriends of any sexual orientation.

Intimate Partner Violence– *Violence between Intimate Partners.*

"Violence" includes physical violence or a verbal threat of physical violence by one intimate partner against the other. It includes death and other crimes - rape, sexual assault, robbery, aggravated assault, and simple assault.

Juvenile Court restraining order–

A restraining order issued by a judge in Juvenile Court that protects one of the parties in the case.

Kick-out order – *see Move-out order.*

Move-out order–

When a judge, through a valid court order, requires the restrained person to move out of the home the restrained person and protected person share for the safety of the protected person(s).

Moving Party –

The party who files a motion in a case asking for a court order. It can be either the Petitioner/Plaintiff or Respondent/Defendant.

No contact order–

A type of restraining order which is given to a person by the court based on the:

1.Domestic Violence Prevention Act (Family Code Sections 6200-6380, scroll down to these sections), or

2.The Uniform Parentage Act (Family Code Sections 7710 and 7720), or

3.In connection with a dissolution (divorce), legal separation or annulment (Family Code Sections 2045, 2047, and 2049),

4.In cases of elder or dependent adult abuse (Welfare and Institutions Code Section 5657.03) or

5.In criminal domestic violence cases (Penal Code Section 136.2).

This order protects the person from any type of contact with the abuser i.e. personal, phone or email. Any contact in violation of this order can lead to criminal charges against the person who violates the order.

Non-CLETS order– *see definition of CLETS, above.*

A civil court order that is intended to protect a person from another person.

Non-CLETS orders cannot be entered into the statewide and national computer databases that all Law Enforcement personnel access to respond to and enforce domestic violence matters. If an order is not in the CLETS system, then the "restrained" person will still be able to have firearms, and Law Enforcement cannot enforce the order in the same way they are required to enforce CLETS orders.

For this reason and others, such as giving DV victims a "false sense of security," non-CLETS orders are disfavored. Santa Clara County's Family Court judges routinely refuse to sign them, especially if they use the language of a CLETS order.

At the statewide level, the DV Task Force recently urged judges not to sign restraining orders that cannot be entered into CLETS.

Opposing Party–

The "other" person in a court case. For example, if you are opening a new domestic violence case, the opposing party is the person you want protection from.

Parenting Without Violence class–

A parenting class taught with an understanding of power and control abuse between parents. This class can empower parents to become more aware in family relationships and to encourage and live a life showing respect and accountability to each other.

PD– *see Public Defender or Police Department*

Peaceful contact order–

A type of restraining order which is given to a person by the court (see all listed Acts and Codes in the definition for "No contact order") which allows the restrained person (abuser) to contact the protected person (victim) as long as all contact is peaceful.

The restrained person can live with the protected person; BUT the restrained person cannot hit, grab, throw things, damage property, or pull the phone cord out of the wall; knock over, or break furniture; swear at, or about, the protected person; tear up important papers; stop the protected person from leaving the house; make threats to hit, harm or kill the protected person; argue with the protected person or a family member; argue or shout so loud that the neighbors are disturbed; have friends come over and do any of the above; and not do anything that makes the protected person, or the family, frightened, hurt, injured, upset, or disturbed.

Petitioner-

A person who presents a petition to the court; person who files legal forms to start a court case.

Plaintiff-

The person or company that files a lawsuit.

Police Department -

A law enforcement agency in any of the 50 states in the united states or abroad.

Probation–

When a defendant who has been found guilty of a crime is released into the community and must follow certain conditions, such as jail time, paying a fine, doing community service or attending a drug treatment program. Violation of the conditions can result in incarceration.

Protected Party-

A person who is protected by a court order(s) that restrains another person (the restrained person) from harassing, annoying, striking, etc. the protected party.

Protective Order– *see Criminal Protective Order.*

Public Defender–

A lawyer who works for a state or local agency representing clients accused of a crime who cannot afford to pay.

Respondent-

If you are the person that answers the original Petition, you are the Respondent. Even if you later file an action of your own in that case, you are still the Respondent for as long as the case is open.

Response-

A Respondent's first answer to the Complaint or Petition that started the case.

Restitution–

When a defendant/abuser/restrained person is ordered by the court to repay financial loss a victim suffered as a result of something the Defendant/Respondent did.

Restrained Party–

The person who cannot contact the protected party when the court makes a restraining order.

Restrained Person– *see Restrained Party.*

Restraining Order–

Common term used to refer to the existence of an Emergency Protective Order, Criminal Protective Order or Civil/Family law Restraining Order After Hearing.

Restraining Order After Hearing–

The form used to write up a restraining order in Family or Civil Court. The order is then igned by the judge, filed with the Clerk's Office and entered into the CLETS system.

Family (DVPA) restraining order, Civil Harassment restraining order, Elder Abuse Restraining Order, Workplace Violence restraining order.

Safety Plan –

A plan created by a domestic violence victim (with the help of an Advocate) that shows the victim ways s/he can prevent or protect her/himself during a violent incident and reduce the risk they are hurt or killed. Safety plans should be prepared for different situations such as:

• During a violent incident,

• When the victim is getting ready to leave,

• After the victim leaves the abuser, and

• At their work.

Each of these situations has different risks. Advocates can help victims weigh the risks to their safety and personal freedom in each of these situations, comeup with options, and evaluate those options.

Evaluating options includes anticipating the consequences of each action and determining which option best increases safety and personal freedom. Safety plans should be individualized and realistic. *(Based on Jill Davies Safety Planning with Battered Women)*

Serve–

When the moving party has someone, not him or herself, give the filed court papers to the other party

Service–

Delivering legal papers to the other party in a case. There are 5 main ways an adult, over 18, who's not involved in the case, can deliver the papers:

• Personal Service is when someone hands the legal forms to the defendant.

• Service by Mail is when someone mails the defendant the legal forms.

• Substitute Service is when another adult is served in the place of the other party; a second copy is mailed to the other party.

• Service by Publication is when someone publishes a Summons and Complaint in a newspaper.

• Service by Posting is when someone posts a Summons and Complaint in a public place. You have to get special permission from the court to serve by Publication or Posting.

You can never be the person to serve papers in your own case.

Not all types of service are allowed for all types of filings. For example, a restraining order application has to be served in person.

Spousal Abuse-

A more narrow term describing abuse between husbands and wives. Currently it is more often called Domestic Violence or Intimate Partner Violence.

Stalking –

Willfully, maliciously, and repeatedly following or willfully, maliciously, and repeatedly harassing another person and making a credible threat with the intent to place that person in fear for his or her own safety, or the safety of his or her immediate family
(Penal Code 646.9).

Teen Dating Violence-

Intimate Partner Violence between teens who are dating. Of concern for young victims is a lack of experience responding to violence and/or sexually coercive behavior. This type of IPV is not limited to any particular sexual orientation or identity.

Victim–

A person who is harmed, physically, emotionally or financially, or killed by another; A person who suffers from a destructive or injurious action; The person against whom a crime has been committed.

Workplace Violence Restraining Order- A restraining order a business applies for if it needs protection for its worker(s).

Chapter References And further information

Chapter 1

1 Gelles RJ. The politics of research: The use, abuse, and misuse of social science data the case of intimate partner violence. Family Court Review, Vol. 45, No. 1, 2007.

2 ABA Commission on Domestic Violence. Quarterly E-Newsletter, Vol. 4, summer 2006. http://www.abanet.org/domviol/enewsletter/vol4/custodymythsandcounter.pdf

3 American Bar Association Commission on Domestic Violence. 10 Myths about Custody and Domestic Violence and How to Counter Them. Chicago: American Bar Association, 2006. http://www.abanet.org/domviol/custody_myths.pdf

4 http://www.abanet.org/abastore/index.cfm?section=main&fm=Product.Search&type=a&cid=25

5 http://www.radarsvcs.org/docs/RADARreport-Myths-of-ABA-Commission-on-DVDetailed.pdf

6 McDonald R. Estimating the number of American children living in partner-violent families. Journal of Family Psychology, Vol. 20, No. 1, 2006. http://www.smu.edu/experts/study-documents/family-violencestudy-may2006.pdf

7 Whitaker DJ, Haileyesus T, Swahn M, Saltzman L. Differences in frequency of violence and reported injury between relationships with reciprocal and nonreciprocal intimate partner violence. American Journal of Public Health, Vol. 97, No. 5, 2007.

8 Arehart-Treichel J. Men shouldn't be overlooked as victims of partner violence. Psychiatric News Vol. 42, No. 15, August 3, 2007, page 31. http://pn.psychiatryonline.org/cgi/content/full/42/15/31-a

9 Follingstad D, Wright S, Lloyd S, and Sebastian J. Sex differences in motivations and effects in dating relationships. Family Relations, Vol. 40, 1991, pp. 51–57.

10 Carrado M, George MJ, Loxam E, et al. Aggression in British heterosexual relationships: A descriptive analysis. Aggressive Behavior, Vol. 22, 1996.

11 Whitaker DJ, Haileyesus T, Swahn M, Saltzman L. Differences in frequency of violence and reported injury between relationships with reciprocal and nonreciprocal intimate partner violence. American Journal of Public Health, May 2007.

12 Straus MA. Gender symmetry in partner violence. In Lutzker JR, Whitaker DJ (eds.): Prevention of Partner Violence. Washington, DC: American Psychological Association, 2008.

13 O'Leary K, Barling J, Aria I, et al. Prevalence and stability of physical aggression between spouses: A longitudinal analysis. Journal of Consulting and Clinical Psychology, Vol. 57, 1989, pp. 263–268.

14 Feld S, Straus M. Escalation and desistance of wife assault in marriage. Criminology, Vol. 1, 1989. pp. 141–161.

15 Archer J. Sex differences in aggression between heterosexual partners: A meta-analytic review. Psychological Bulletin, Vol. 126, No. 5, 2000, pp. 651–680.

16 Catalano S. Intimate Partner Violence in the United States. Washington, DC: Department of Justice, 2006. http://www.ojp.usDepartmentOfJustice.gov/bjs/intimate/table/wommar.htm

17 U.S. Department of Health and Human Services, Administration for Children and Families. Child Maltreatment 2005. Figure 3-5. http://www.acf.DepartmentofHealthandHumanServices.gov/programs/cb/pubs/cm05/cm05.pdf

18 U.S. Department of Health and Human Services, Administration for Children and Families. Child Maltreatment 2005. Figure 4-2. http://www.acf.DepartmentofHealthandHumanServices.gov/programs/cb/pubs/cm05/cm05.pdf

19 Sedlak AJ and Broadhurst DD. The Third National Incidence Study of Child Abuse and Neglect (NIS-3): Final Report. U.S. Department of Health and Human Services, National Center on Child Abuse and Neglect, Washington, DC, September 1996. http://www.healthieryou.com/cabuse.html

20 Whelan R. Broken Homes and Battered Children. London: Family Education Trust, 1993.

21 Nord DW and West J. Fathers' and Mothers' Involvement in their Children's Schools by Family Type and Resident Status. Washington, DC: National Center for Education Statistics, 2001. NCES 2001-032.

22 National Center for Health Statistics: Survey on Child Health. Washington, DC: Government Printing Office, 1993.

23 Flewelling RL and Bauman K. Family structure as a predictor of initial substance use and sexual intercourse in early adolescence. Journal of Marriage and the Family, Vol. 52, 1990, pp. 171–181.

24 Hill MA and O'Neill J. Underclass behaviors in the United States: Measurement and analysis of determinants. New York: City University of New York, 1993.

25 Cubbin C, Pickle LW, and Fingerhut L. Social context and geographic patterns of homicide among US black and white males. American Journal of Public Health, Vol. 90, 2000. pp. 579–587.

26 Dawson D. Family structure and children's health and well-being: Interview survey on child health. Journal of Marriage and the Family, Vol. 53, 1991, pp. 573–584.

27 Rubenstein JL et al. Suicidal behavior in adolescents: Stress and protection in different family contexts. American Journal of Orthopsychiatry, Vol. 68, 1998, pp. 274–284.

28 Duncan WS. Economic impact of divorce on children's development: Current findings and policy implications. Journal of Clinical and Child Psychology, Vol. 23, 1994, pp. 444–457.

29 House Committee on Ways and Means. 2000 Green Book, Washington, DC: U.S. Government Printing Office, 2000.

30 National Academy of Sciences. Advancing the Federal Research Agenda on Violence Against Women. Washington, DC, 2005, p. 97.

31 Babcock JC, Canady BE, Graham K, and Schart L. The evolution of battering interventions: From the Dark Ages into the Scientific Age. In Hamel J and Nichols TL (eds.).

32 Family Interventions in Domestic Violence: A Handbook of Gender-Inclusive Theory and Treatment. New York: Spring Publishing Co., 2007. 32
http://www.radarsvcs.org/docs/RADARreport-Myths-of-ABA-Commission-on-DV-Detailed.pdf

33 http://www.abanet.org/domviol/statistics.html   Accessed April 21, 2008.

34 Sarkadi A, Kristiansson R, Oberklaid F, Bremberg S. Fathers' involvement and children's developmental outcomes: A systematic review of longitudinal studies. Acta Paediatrica,Vol. 97, No. 2, 2008.

35 RADAR Services, Inc. Myths of the ABA Commission on Domestic Violence: Detailed Findings. Rockville, MD: 2008.
http://www.radarsvcs.org/docs/RADARreport-Myths-of-ABA-Commission-on-DVDetailed.pdf

36 Telephone conversations with Dr. Daniel O'Leary, April 4, 2008.

Chapter 2

1 Gelles RJ. The politics of research: The use, abuse, and misuse of social science data, the case of intimate partner violence. Family Court Review, Vol. 45, No. 1, 2007.

2 ABA Commission on Domestic Violence. Quarterly E-Newsletter, Vol. 4, summer 2006.
http://www.abanet.org/domviol/enewsletter/vol4/custodymythsandcounter.pdf

3 American Bar Association Commission on Domestic Violence. 10 Myths about Custody and Domestic Violence and How to Counter Them. Chicago: American Bar Association, 2006.
http://www.abanet.org/domviol/custody_myths.pdf

4 http://www.abanet.org/abastore/index.cfm?section=main&fm=Product.Search&type=a&cid=25

5 http://www.radarsvcs.org/docs/RADARreport-Myths-of-ABA-Commission-on-DVDetailed.pdf

6 McDonald R. estimating the number of American children living in partner-violent families. Journal of Family Psychology, Vol. 20, No. 1, 2006.
http://www.smu.edu/experts/study-documents/family-violencestudy-may2006.pdf

7 Whitaker DJ, Haileyesus T, Swahn M, Saltzman L. Differences in frequency of violence and reported injury between relationships with reciprocal and nonreciprocal intimate partner violence. American Journal of Public Health, Vol. 97, No. 5, 2007.

8 Arehart-Treichel J. Men shouldn't be overlooked as victims of partner violence. Psychiatric News Vol. 42, No. 15, August 3, 2007, page 31.
http://pn.psychiatryonline.org/cgi/content/full/42/15/31-a

9 Follingstad D, Wright S, Lloyd S, and Sebastian J. Sex differences in motivations and effects in dating relationships. Family Relations, Vol. 40, 1991, pp. 51–57.

10 Carrado M, George MJ, Loxam E, et al. Aggression in British heterosexual relationships: A descriptive analysis. Aggressive Behavior, Vol. 22, 1996.

11 Whitaker DJ, Haileyesus T, Swahn M, Saltzman L. Differences in frequency of violence and reported injury between relationships with reciprocal and nonreciprocal intimate partner violence. American Journal of Public Health, May 2007.

12 Straus MA. Gender symmetry in partner violence. In Lutzker JR, Whitaker DJ (eds.): Prevention of Partner Violence. Washington, DC: American Psychological Association, 2008.

13 O'Leary K, Barling J, Aria I, et al. Prevalence and stability of physical aggression between spouses: A longitudinal analysis. Journal of Consulting and Clinical Psychology, Vol. 57, 1989, pp. 263–268.

14 Feld S, Straus M. Escalation and desistance of wife assault in marriage. Criminology, Vol. 1, 1989. pp. 141–161.

15 Archer J. Sex differences in aggression between heterosexual partners: A meta-analytic review. Psychological Bulletin, Vol. 126, No. 5, 2000, pp. 651–680.

16 Catalano S. Intimate Partner Violence in the United States. Washington, DC: Department of Justice, 2006. http://www.ojp.usDepartmentOfJustice.gov/bjs/intimate/table/wommar.htm

17 U.S. Department of Health and Human Services, Administration for Children and Families. Child Maltreatment 2005. Figure 3-5. http://www.acf.DepartmentofHealthandHumanServices.gov/programs/cb/pubs/cm05/cm05.pdf

18 U.S. Department of Health and Human Services, Administration for Children and Families. Child Maltreatment 2005. Figure 4-2. http://www.acf.DepartmentofHealthandHumanServices.gov/programs/cb/pubs/cm05/cm05.pdf

19 Sedlak AJ and Broadhurst DD. The Third National Incidence Study of Child Abuse and Neglect (NIS-3): Final Report. U.S. Department of Health and Human Services, National Center on Child Abuse and Neglect, Washington, DC, September 1996. http://www.healthieryou.com/cabuse.html

20 Whelan R. Broken Homes and Battered Children. London: Family Education Trust, 1993.

21 Nord DW and West J. Fathers' and Mothers' Involvement in their Children's Schools by Family Type and Resident Status. Washington, DC: National Center for Education Statistics, 2001. NCES 2001-032.

22 National Center for Health Statistics: Survey on Child Health. Washington, DC: Government Printing Office, 1993.

23 Flewelling RL and Bauman K. Family structure as a predictor of initial substance use and sexual intercourse in early adolescence. Journal of Marriage and the Family, Vol. 52, 1990, pp. 171–181.

24 Hill MA and O'Neill J. Underclass behaviors in the United States: Measurement and analysis of determinants. New York: City University of New York, 1993.

25 Cubbin C, Pickle LW, and Fingerhut L. Social context and geographic patterns of homicide among US black and white males. American Journal of Public Health, Vol. 90, 2000. pp. 579–587.

26 Dawson D. Family structure and children's health and well-being: Interview survey on child health. Journal of Marriage and the Family, Vol. 53, 1991, pp. 573–584.

27 Rubenstein JL et al. Suicidal behavior in adolescents: Stress and protection in different family contexts. American Journal of Orthopsychiatry, Vol. 68, 1998, pp. 274–284.

28 Duncan WS. Economic impact of divorce on children's development: Current findings and policy implications. Journal of Clinical and Child Psychology, Vol. 23, 1994, pp. 444–457.

29 House Committee on Ways and Means. 2000 Green Book, Washington, DC: U.S. Government Printing Office, 2000.

30 National Academy of Sciences. Advancing the Federal Research Agenda on Violence Against Women. Washington, DC, 2005, p. 97.

31 Babcock JC, Canady BE, Graham K, and Schart L. The evolution of battering interventions: From the Dark Ages into the Scientific Age. In Hamel J and Nichols TL (eds.). Family Interventions in Domestic Violence: A Handbook of Gender-Inclusive Theory and Treatment. New York: Spring Publishing Co., 2007.

32 http://www.radarsvcs.org/docs/RADARreport-Myths-of-ABA-Commission-on-DV-Detailed.pdf

33 http://www.abanet.org/domviol/statistics.html Accessed April 21, 2008.

34 Sarkadi A, Kristiansson R, Oberklaid F, Bremberg S. Fathers' involvement and children's developmental outcomes: A systematic review of longitudinal studies. Acta Paediatrica, Vol. 97, No. 2, 2008.

35 RADAR Services, Inc. Myths of the ABA Commission on Domestic Violence: Detailed Findings. Rockville, MD: 2008.
http://www.radarsvcs.org/docs/RADARreport-Myths-of-ABA-Commission-on-DVDetailed.pdf

36 Telephone conversation with Dr. Daniel O'Leary, April 4, 2008.

Chapter 3

1 Pennell S, Burke C, Mulmat DH. Violence Against Women in San Diego. San Diego: SAN-DAG, 2000, p. 32.
http://www.ncjrs.gov/pdffiles1/nij/grants/191838.pdf

2 Moore N. Inside a batterers program 'for abused' women. Ifeminists.net, July 29, 2003.
http://www.ifeminists.net/introduction/editorials/2003/0729moore.html

3 Koyama E. Abuse of survivors within the domestic violence shelter system. Disloyal to Feminism. Portland, OR: Confluere Publications, 2003.
http://eminism.org/readings/pdfrdg/disloyal.pdf

4 Taylor JS. No shelter from the storm. Accessed November 28, 2008.
http://www.ejfi.org/DV/dv-53.htm

5 Winslow MV, Young C. Suspect in SafeSpace stabbing in Martin County claims self-defense. TCPalm, November 14, 2007.
http://www.tcpalm.com/news/2007/nov/14/30suspect-insafespace-stabbing-claims-self/

6 Gaddis P. In the beginning…A creation story of battered women's shelters. Off Our Backs, Vol. 31, No. 9, 2001.
http://findarticles.com/p/articles/mi_qa3693/is_200110/ai_n8995946/print?tag=art-Body;col1

7 Dorian PN. So who's left? Off Our Backs, Vol. 31, No. 9, 2001.
http://findarticles.com/p/articles/mi_qa3693/is_200110/ai_n8959321/print?tag=art-Body;col1

8 Rosewater L and Walker LE. Handbook of Feminist Therapy. New York: Spring Publishing, 1985.

9 Fontes D. Male victims of domestic violence. In Hamel J and Nichols TL (eds.). Family Interventions in Domestic Violence: A Handbook of Gender-Inclusive Theory and Treatment. New York: Spring Publishing Co., 2007, p. 312.

10 Mitchell SR. Shame ends when women speak out. The Oregonian, November 1, 2004.

11 Dobash RE, Dobash R. Violence against Wives. New York: The Free Press, 1979.

12 Straus MA, Scott K. Gender symmetry in partner violence. In Lutzker JR, Whitaker DJ (eds.): Prevention of Partner Violence. Washington, DC: American Psychological Association, 2009.

13 Epstein S, Russell G, and Silvern L. Structure and ideology of shelters for battered women. American Journal of Community Psychology, Vol. 16, 1988, pp. 345–367. 83

14 Kentucky Domestic Violence Association. Certification Program: Certified Domestic Violence Advocate Level I. 2003, p. 10.
http://www.kdva.org/Level%20I%20Handbook.pdf

15 Marin Abused Women's Services. Mission Statement. Accessed January 7, 2009.
http://www.maws.org/mawssite/mmission.html

16 Florida Coalition against Domestic Violence. Deliverables July 1, 2008 – June 30, 2009.
http://www.fcadv.org/downloads/quality/Exhibit%20A%20Deliverables.pdf

17 RADAR Services. Shelter 990 analysis. Unpublished report based on shelters'most recent 990 tax information provided to the Internal Revenue Service. January 16, 2009.

18 IRS 990 forms for 2006, available at www.guidestar.com

19 Florida Coalition against Domestic Violence. Domestic violence monthly statistical report (ALICE).
http://www.fcadv.org/downloads/quality/Exhibit%20D%20Alice%20Report.doc

20 FCADV Legal Clearinghouse Project. Claim request invoice.

http://www.fcadv.org/downloads/quality/Exhibit%20C%20LCH%20Claim%20Request%20Invoice.doc

21 Florida Coalition Against Domestic Violence. Unit of service payment chart: July 1, 2008 –June 30, 2009. http://www.fcadv.org/downloads/quality/Exhibit%20B%20Payment%20Chart.pdf

22 Florida Coalition Against Domestic Violence. Contract/agreement exhibits FY 08/09. http://www.fcadv.org/quality-contract_fy.php#under25

23 Pennell S, Burke C, Mulmat DH. Violence Against Women in San Diego. San Diego: SANDAG, 2000, Table 4.4. http://www.ncjrs.gov/pdffiles1/nij/grants/191838.pdf

24 Vinton L, Wilke D et al. Florida's Domestic Violence Needs Assessment for 2006–2007. Tallahassee, FL: Florida State University. Undated. http://www.dcf.state.fl.us/domesticviolence/publications/dvna0607final.pdf

25 State of Hawaii, Department of Social Services. FY 2008 Family Violence Prevention and Services Act Grant Application, February 2008, p. 10. http://hawaii.gov/dhs/protection/social_services/child_welfare/FY2008%20FVPSA%20Appl%20wo%20certifications.pdf

26 RADAR. Former shelter director reveals why she left. March 10, 2007. http://www.mediaradar.org/shelterDirectorRevealsWhySheLeft.php

27 Basil. FreeRepublic.com , Posting No. 32, August 4, 2008. 84

28 Comment to Collier clerk's office donates items to abuse shelter. Naples Daily News. October 10, 2008. http://www.naplesnews.com/news/2008/oct/10/collier-clerks-officedonates-itemsabuse-shelter/

29 Pennell S, Burke C, Mulmat DH. Violence Against Women in San Diego. San Diego: SANDAG, 2000, p. 41. http://www.ncjrs.gov/pdffiles1/nij/grants/191838.pdf

30 Associated Press. Police: Shelter refused to accept tortured teen. October 3, 2003. http://fathersforlife.org/fv/women_shelter9.htm

31 Howk A. SafeSpace shelter in Martin County releases plan to increase safety. TCPalm, November 16, 2007. http://www.tcpalm.com/news/2007/nov/16/30safespace-plan-toincreasesafety/

32 http://www.ywcaenid.com/ccemergencyshelter.html .Accessed November 6, 2008.

33 State of Hawaii, Department of Social Services. FY 2008 Family Violence Prevention and Services Act Grant Application. February 2008, p.10. http://hawaii.gov/dhs/protection/social_services/child_welfare/FY2008%20FVPSA%20Appl%20wo%20certifications.pdf

34 Pennell S, Burke C, Mulmat DH. Violence Against Women in San Diego. San Diego: SANDAG, 2000, Table 4.4. http://www.ncjrs.gov/pdffiles1/nij/grants/191838.pdf

35 Vinton L, Wilke D et al. Florida's Domestic Violence Needs Assessment for 2006–2007. Tallahassee, FL: Florida State University. Undated. http://www.dcf.state.fl.us/domesticviolence/publications/dvna0607final.pdf

36 Cedars D. Women's shelters blame stress. 7 News. January 12, 2009. http://www.thedenverchannel.com/money/18467530/detail.html?rss=den&psp=news

37 Kansas Housing Resources Corporation. Kansas homeless shelters and services. Accessed January 2, 2009. http://www.kshousingcorp.org/display/files/ESG/KANSAS%20HOMELESS%20SHELTERS.Pdf

38 Kansas Coalition Against Domestic Violence. Kansas Resources. Accessed January 2, 2009. http://www.kcsdv.org/ksresources.html

39 Bugarin A. The prevalence of domestic violence in California. Sacramento: California Re-search Bureau, 2002, p. 12. http://www.library.ca.gov/crb/02/16/02-016.pdf

40 State of Hawaii, Department of Social Services. FY 2008 Family Violence Prevention and Ser-vices Act Grant Application. February 2008, p. 10. http://hawaii.gov/dhs/protection/social_services/child_welfare/FY2008%20FVPSA%20Appl%20wo%20certifications.pdf

41 Krishnan SP, Hilbert JC, McNeil K. Understanding domestic violence in multi-ethnic rural com-munities: A focus on collaborations among the courts, the law enforcement agencies, and the shelters. New Mexico State University, 2002. http://www.ncjrs.gov/pdffiles1/nij/grants/191863.pdf

42 First Step shelter in Harrisonburg, Virginia proves more dangerous for woman than her home. Ac-cessed November 28, 2008. http://www.ejfi.org/DV/dv-53.htm

43 Straus MA. Dominance and symmetry in partner violence by male and female university students in 32 nations. Children and Youth Services Review, 2008. http://pubpages.unh.edu/%7Emas2/ID41-PR41-Dominance-symmetry-In-Press-7.pdf

44 Whitaker DJ et al. Differences in frequency of violence and reported injury between relationships with reciprocal and nonreciprocal intimate partner violence. American Journal of Public Health, Vol. 97, No. 5, 2007.

45 Pizzey E. Prone to Violence. 1982. http://www.bennett.com/ptv/

46 McDonald R, Jouriles E., Tart C, Minze L. Children's adjustment problems in families character-ized by men's severe violence toward women: Does other family violence matter? Child Abuse & Neglect (in press).

47 Langhinrichsen-Rohling J. An examination of sheltered battered women's perpetration of stalking and other unwanted behaviors. Violence and Victims, Vol. 21, No. 5, 2006.

48 First Step shelter in Harrisonburg, Virginia, proves more dangerous for woman than her home. Ac-cessed November 28, 2008.

http://www.ejfi.org/DV/dv-59.htm

49 Pennell S, Burke C, Mulmat DH. Violence Against Women in San Diego. San Diego: SANDAG, 2000, Table 4.4.
http://www.ncjrs.gov/pdffiles1/nij/grants/191838.pdf

50 McDonald R, Jouriles E., Tart C, Minze L. Children's adjustment problems in families character-ized by men's severe violence toward women: Does other family violence matter? Child Abuse & Neglect (in press).

51 Pennell S, Burke C, Mulmat DH. Violence Against Women in San Diego. San Diego: SANDAG, 2000. http://www.ncjrs.gov/pdffiles1/nij/grants/191838.pdf

52 Vinton L, Wilke D et al. Florida's Domestic Violence Needs Assessment for 2006–2007. Talla-hassee, FL: Florida State University. Undated.
http://www.dcf.state.fl.us/domesticviolence/publications/dvna0607final.pdf

53 McGowan A. Florida domestic violence centers called biased. The Liberator, Fall 2008, p. 4.

54 Panoff R. Report: Driver looked, but failed to see toddler in Stuart. TC Palm, October 26, 2007.
http://www.tcpalm.com/news/2007/oct/26/report-driver-looked-but-failed-tosee-toddler/

55 Personal communication with Brenda Sanchez, January 17, 2009.

56 Communication with Angela McGowan, July 12, 2008.

57 Communication with Angela McGowan, July 12, 2008.

58 McGowan A. Florida domestic violence centers called biased. The Liberator, Fall 2008, p. 4.

59 Cook P. Abused Men: The Hidden Side of Domestic Violence, p. 110.

60 Hamel J and Nichols TL (eds.). Family Interventions in Domestic Violence: A Handbook of Gen-der-Inclusive Theory and Treatment. New York: Spring Publishing Co., 2007, p. 316.

61 Moore N. Inside a batterers program for abused women. Ifeminists.net, July 29, 2003.
http://www.ifeminists.net/introduction/editorials/2003/0729moore.html

62 Bethany House Virginia – A one stop divorce shop. Posted May 22, 2004.
http://www.safe4all.org/forums/message-view?message_id=31905

63 Kentucky Domestic Violence Association. Certification Program: Certified Domestic Violence Advocate Level I, 2003, p. 9.
http://www.kdva.org/Level%20I%20Handbook.pdf

64 Front door. Accessed January 2, 2009.
http://www.safehorizon.org/page.php?nav=bd&page=sheltertour_door

65 Brooks H. American feminists' abuse industry.
www.fathermag.com/205/abuse/

66 Laframboise D. Sheltered from reality. National Post, November 23, 1998.
http://www.fact.on.ca/newpaper/np98112d.htm

67 American Association for Marriage and Family Therapy. AAMFT Code of Ethics. July 1, 2001.
Principle 1.8.
http://www.aamft.org/resources/LRM_Plan/Ethics/ethicscode2001.asp

68 Moore N. Inside a batterers program' for abused' women. Ifeminists.net, July 29, 2003.
http://www.ifeminists.net/introduction/editorials/2003/0729moore.html

69 Communication with Christina Wilson, May 13, 2008.

70 Communication with Desiree Carpenter, July 1, 2008.

71 Koyama E. Abuse of survivors within the domestic violence shelter system. Disloyal to Feminism.
Portland, OR: Confluere Publications, 2003.
http://eminism.org/readings/pdfrdg/disloyal.pdf

72 Florida Coalition Against Domestic Violence. FY08-09 Contract overview. June 9, 2008 Webinar.
https://cc.readytalk.com/play?id=8663ev68

73 De Yoanna M. Larimer County, Colorado, women's shelter loses staff. The Coloradoan, January
22, 2004.

74 Arkansas Council Against Domestic Violence. Shelters by city. Accessed August 7, 2008.
http://www.domesticpeace.com/members.html

75 Florida Coalition Against Domestic Violence. Contract monitoring. Accessed January 13, 2009.
http://www.fcadv.org/quality-contract_monitoring.php

76 Howk A. Report: SafeSpace shelter in Stuart had egregious failure.' TC Palm. November 10,
2007.
http://m.tcpalm.com/news/2007/Nov/10/30report-safespace-hadegregious-failure /

77 Huicochea A. Police: Woman, boy had sex at shelter. Arizona Daily Star, December 29, 2005.
http://www.azstarnet.com/metro/109042.php

78 Communication with Brenda Sanchez, January 17, 2009.

79 McGowan A. Florida domestic violence centers called biased. The Liberator, Fall 2008, p. 3.

80 American Association for Marriage and Family Therapy. AAMFT Code of Ethics. July 1, 2001.
Principle II: Confidentiality.
http://www.aamft.org/resources/LRM_Plan/Ethics/ethicscode2001.asp

81 Black woman finds little succor in shelter. August 14, 2007. http://www.ejfi.org/DV/dv-59.htm

82 Moore N. Inside a batterers program' for abused' women. Ifeminists.net, July 29, 2003.
http://www.ifeminists.net/introduction/editorials/2003/0729moore.html

83 Vinton L, Wilke D et al. Florida's Domestic Violence Needs Assessment for 2006–2007. Tallahassee, FL: Florida State University. Undated.
http://www.dcf.state.fl.us/domesticviolence/publications/dvna0607final.pdf

84 Community Works. Dunn House Shelter Staff, Relief. Accessed January 9, 2009.
http://www.community-works.org/index.php?/cw/victim_services_postings/#

85 Basil. FreeRepublic.com, Posting No. 32, August 4, 2008.

86 Connecticut Coalition Against Domestic Violence. 24/7 signature cards. Accessed January 15, 2009.
http://www.ctcadv.org/WhatYouCanDo/CCADVLegislation/tabid/177/Default.aspx

87 Abuse allegations involving Bethany House Social workers. Posted May 20, 2004.
http://www.safe4all.org/forums/message-view?message_id=31905

88 Shelter needed from shelter. NCFM Transitions, 1995, p. 9.

89 Florida Coalition Against Domestic Violence. SafeSpace, Inc. homicide incident: Management review. November 9, 2007.
http://web.tcpalm.com/2007/11/10/safespace.pdf

90 McGowan A. Florida domestic violence centers called biased. The Liberator, Fall 2008. p. 5.

91 McGowan A. Florida domestic violence centers called biased. The Liberator, Fall 2008. p. 3.

92 Public Order dismissing juvenile action and determining child custody, support, and visitation. December 7, 2007.
http://www.donhaslam.com/cases/documents/Hallfinalorder.PDF

93 Bethany House Virginia – A one stop divorce shop. Posted May 22, 2004.
http://www.safe4all.org/forums/message-view?message_id=31905

94 Arizona Center for Justice. Olga Chaikheeva – Art Smasch – Shield Foundation professional criminals masquerading under the flag of legitimacy. Rip-off Report, July 30, 2007.
www.ripoffreport.com/reports/0/264/RipOff0264095.htm

95 Bethany House Virginia – A one stop divorce shop. Posted May 22, 2004.
http://www.safe4all.org/forums/message-view?message_id=31905

96 Mountain View Voice. Buyer beware before donating cars. May 14, 2004.
http://www.mvvoice.com/morgue/2004/2004_05_14.edit.shtml

97 Internal Revenue Service. Deletions from cumulative list of organizations – Contributions which are deductible under Section 170 of the code. January 14, 2008, p. 269.
http://www.irs.gov/pub/irs-tege/a2008_3.pdf

98 Hawk S. Murder, mayhem no stranger to year. Shawnee (OK) News Star, December 31, 1999.
http://www.news-star.com/stories/123199/com_crime.shtml

99 Theft alleged at abuse shelter. Pioneer Press, February 2006.

100 Former nonprofit official sentenced. NewsOK.com. March 5, 2008.
http://newsok.com/article/3212136/more/headlines/weather

101 Arkin S. Former DOVES director sentenced. Danville News, September 2, 2008.
http://www.godanriver.com/gdr/news/local/danville_news/article/former_doves_director_sentenced/5953/

102 Newsletter of the Florida Coalition against Domestic Violence. Vol. 5, No. 1, p. 6.

103 Nancy S. In search of safer passages: DV, the California social service system, and a suggested blueprint for change. FAVTEA Bulletin, Fall 2004, p. 1.

104 Zabjek A. Domestic violence not a women's issue: educator. Edmonton Journal, September 8, 2008. Reader comment no. 1.
http://www.canada.com/edmontonjournal/news/story.html?id=5c618479-1cce-4b3db04ae5351059c9ec

105 American Humane Society. Pets and Women's Shelters.
http://www.americanhumane.org/homepage/featured-news/paws-program.html
Accessed November 7, 2008.

106 Title IX of the Education Amendments of 1972, 20 U.S.C. 1681, 1682, 1683, 1685, and 1686, cited in HHS Grants Policy Statement, January 1, 2007.
http://www.hhs.gov/grantsnet/docs/HHSGPS_107.doc

107 Omnibus Crime Control and Safe Streets Act of 1968, Section 3789d. (c)(1).
http://www.usDepartmentOfJustice.gov/crt/split/42usc3789d.htm

108 Violence Against Women Act 2005, Section 40002(b)(8).
http://frwebgate.access.gpo.gov/cgibin/getdoc.cgi?dbname=109_cong_public_laws&docid=f:publ162.109.pdf

109 RADAR Services, Inc. VAWA Programs Discriminate Against Male Victims. Rockville, MD: 2008. http://www.radarsvcs.org/docs/RADARreport-VAWA-Discriminates-Against-Males.pdf

110 Deposition of Judy King Smith, September 9, 2008, pp. 16, 18, and 72.

111 Bartley N. Mason County shelter to be state's first to allow victims' teen sons, pets. Seattle Times, November 26, 2006.
http://community.seattletimes.nwsource.com/archive/?date=20061126&slug=turningpointe25m

112 Woods v. Shewry; 3rd Dist. C056072
http://www.courtinfo.ca.gov/cgi-bin/opinions.cgi

113 RADAR Services, Inc. $1 Billion for DV Programs that Misuse Taxpayer Money and Place Victims at Risk. Rockville, MD. 2008.
http://www.radarsvcs.org/docs/RADARreport-DVPrograms-Misuse-1-Billion-Tax-Dollars-Per-Year.pdf

114 National Family Violence Legislative Resource Center. Model programs and legislation: Victim services.
http://www.nfvlrc.org/ModelProgramsLegislation/VictimServices.htm

115 Ensign C, Jones P. Gender-inclusive work with victims and their children in a coed shelter. In Hamel J and Nichols TL (eds.). Family Interventions in Domestic Violence: A Hand-book of Gender-Inclusive Theory and Treatment. New York: Spring Publishing Co., 2007.

116 Howard LW. Shelter an oasis for both sexes. Antelope Valley Press, January 22, 2006.
http://www.ncfmla.org/antelope-valley-press-012206.html

117 Declaration of Patricia Shanley-Overberg. November 1, 2002. www.ncfmla.org/pdf/overberg.pdf

118 South Lake Tahoe Women's Center. Domestic violence against men. Accessed January 21, 2009.
http://www.sltwc.org/dvandmen.htm

119 WTOL. Domestic abuse shelter for men opens in Fostoria. April 2, 2008.
http://www.wtol.com/Global/story.asp?s=8104714

120 The Caring Place: Male victim services. Accessed January 9, 2009.
http://www.thecaringplacenwi.org/MaleServices.htm

121 DASH, Inc.–Domestic Abuse Shelter Homes.
http://findsarasota.com/Listing.asp?id=852

Chapter 4

1 Rubinstein E. The fiscal impact of immigration. The Social Contract, Vol. 18, No. 2, 2007–2008, p. 94. http://www.thesocialcontract.com/pdf/eighteentwo/tsc_18_2_rubenstein_fiscal_impact_report.pdf

2 Department of Labor Inspector General. Restoring section 245(i) of the Immigration Nationality Act created a flood of poor quality foreign labor certification applications predominantly for aliens without legal work status. Report No. 6-04-004-03-321. Washington, DC. September 30, 2004.

3 Government Accountability Office. Immigration benefits: Additional controls and a sanctions strategy could enhance DHS's ability to control benefit fraud. Washington, DC. GAO-06-259. March 2006. http://www.gao.gov/new.items/d06259.pdf

4 Depenbrock T. The danger marriage fraud poses to the national security of the United States. U.S. Department of State, December 9, 2004. http://www.state.gov/m/ds/rls/rm/39620.htm

5 Depenbrock T. The danger marriage fraud poses to the national security of the United States. U.S. Department of State, December 9, 2004. http://www.state.gov/m/ds/rls/rm/39620.htm

6 Legal Momentum. Immigration 101: VAWA, Us and Ts for beginners. Undated.
http://www.legalmomentum.org/site/DocServer/2._Immigration_101_PowerPoint.ppt?docID=1301

7 Catholic Legal Immigration Network. Immigration remedies for abused non-citizens. Washington, DC. March 12, 2002.

http://www.nationalimmigrationproject.org/domesticviolence/OutreachBrochures/CLINIC%20overview%20for%20abused%20immigrants.doc

8 Kinoshita S. Extreme cruelty: What it is and how to prove it. ASISTA newsletter, Fall 2006, pp. 2–4. http://www.asistaonline.org/Public%20Benefits/publications/fall2006.newsletter.pdf

9 Legal Assistance Foundation of Metropolitan Chicago. Obtaining lawful permanent residency through the Violence Against Women Act: A VAWA manual for pro bono advocates. Chicago, IL, 2005. http://files.illinoislegaladvocate.org/uploads/003805Obtaining%20Lawful%20Permanent%20Residency.rtf

10 Immigrant Legal Resource Center. Como solicitar la residencia permanente si su esposo la maltrata. [How to apply for permanent residency if your husband mistreats you] Accessed May 29, 2008. http://www.ilrc.org/vawa/VAWA%20Spanish%20Flyer.pdf

11 INS Memorandum from Office of Programs. Implementation of crime bill self-petitioning for abused or battered spouses or children of U.S. citizens or lawful permanent residents. April 16, 1996.

12 Instructions for Form I-360, Petition for Amerasian, Widowe(er) or Special Immigrant, p. 5. http://www.uscis.gov/files/form/i-360instr.pdf

13 RADAR Services, Inc: Expanding definitions of domestic violence, Vanishing rule of law. Rockville, MD, 2008. http://www.radarsvcs.org/docs/RADARreport-Vanishing-Ruleof-Law.pdf

14 RADAR Services, Inc: Without restraint: The use and abuse of domestic restraining orders. Rockville, MD, 2008. http://www.radarsvcs.org/docs/RADARreport-VAWARestraining-Orders.pdf

15 Committee on the Impact of Domestic Violence and the Courts and the Domestic Violence Benchbook Workgroup. Domestic violence benchbook (civil). November 2006, p. 25.

16 Kinoshita S. Extreme cruelty: What it is and how to prove it. ASISTA newsletter, Fall 2006, pp. 2–4. http://www.asistaonline.org/Public%20Benefits/publications/fall2006.newsletter.pdf

17 Immigration and Naturalization Act, Section 212(a)(6)(A)(ii).

18 Memo from Michael L. Aytes regarding Adjustment of status for VAWA self-petitioner who is present without inspection. April 11, 2008 http://www.uscis.gov/files/nativedocuments/VAWA_11Apr08.pdf

19 DHS Q & A Sessions. Irvine, CA. November 9 and 11, 2005. http://www.tomesparza.com/documents/DHS%20QA%20202005.DOC?docid=18617

20 Legal Assistance Foundation of Metropolitan Chicago. Obtaining lawful permanent residency through the Violence Against Women Act: A VAWA manual for pro bono advocates. Chicago, IL, 2005. p. 57. http://files.illinoislegaladvocate.org/uploads/003805Obtaining%20Lawful%20Permanent%20Residency.rtf

21 Kinoshita S. Extreme cruelty: What it is and how to prove it. ASISTA newsletter, Fall 2006, pp. 2–4. http://www.asistaonline.org/Public%20Benefits/publications/fall2006.newsletter.pdf

22 Rosenberg LD. Doing the right thing in immigration law practice. ASISTA newsletter, Fall 2006. http://www.asistaonline.org/Public%20Benefits/publications/fall2006.newsletter.pdf

23 DHS Q&A Sessions. November 9 and 11, 2005, Irvine, CA. Questions 3 and 10.

24 Government Accountability Office. Immigration benefits: Additional controls and a sanctions strategy could enhance DHS's ability to control benefit fraud. Washington, DC. GAO-06-259. March 2006, p. 37. http://www.gao.gov/new.items/d06259.pdf

25 Communication with Elizabeth Howard, August 28, 2007.

26 Mann J. Beware illegal alien women! (and men). August 4, 2003. http://www.vdare.com/Mann/illlegal_alien_women.htm

27 Voices of American Immigration Fraud Victims. Premeditated Green Card marriage. Case of Lidiia Kolisnichenko vs. Michael Wnuk. http://www.immigrationfraudvictims.us/stories.html

28 Tsering L. Indian husbands fall victim to dowry-immigration fraud. New American Media, January 19, 2005. http://news.ncmonline.com/news/view_article.html?article_id=768649893bc5975ce97b6bff5354c210

29 Department of State. Dowry/visa demands. 2004.

30 Quoted in Tsering L. Indian husbands fall victim to dowry-immigration fraud. New American Media, January 19, 2005. http://news.ncmonline.com/news/view_article.html?article_id=768649893bc5975ce97b6bff5354c210

31 Whitaker DJ, Haileyesus T, Swahn M, Saltzman L. Differences in frequency of violence and reported injury between relationships with reciprocal and nonreciprocal intimate partner violence. American Journal of Public Health, Vol. 97, No. 5, 2007.

32 Straus MA. Dominance and symmetry in partner violence by male and female university students in 32 nations. Children and Youth Services Review, 2008. http://pubpages.unh.edu/%7Emas2/ID41-PR41-Dominance-symmetry-In-Press-7.pdf

33 Questions for Q&A panels with DHS. December 2003. http://www.nationalimmigrationproject.org/forMembers/U%20Visa%20Documents/DHS%20Q%20&%20A.doc

34 Porter E. Law on overseas brides is keeping couples apart. New York Times, October 17, 2006. http://www.nytimes.com/2006/10/17/us/17brides.html?ref=business

35 Questions for Q&A panels with DHS. December 2003. http://www.nationalimmigrationproject.org/forMembers/U%20Visa%20Documents/DHS%20Q%20&%20A.doc

36 Foster BP. Analyzing the cost and effectiveness of governmental policies. Cost Management, Vol. 22, No. 3, 2008.

37 Rubinstein E. The fiscal impact of immigration. The Social Contract, Vol. 18, No. 2, 2007–2008, p. 143.
http://www.thesocialcontract.com/pdf/eighteentwo/tsc_18_2_rubenstein_fiscal_impact_report.pdf

38 Personal communication, Natasha Spivack, Voices of American Immigration Fraud Victims, August 30, 2008.

39 Battered Immigrant Women Protection Act of 2000. P.L. 106-386. Section 1502(a). Findings and Purposes.

Chapter 5

1 Criminal law comes home. Overlawyered.com. Posted December 12, 2006.
http://www.overlawyered.com/2006/12/criminal_law_comes_home.html

2 Lininger T. Bearing the cross. Fordham Law Review, Vol. 74, 2005, pp. 1353–1364.

3 RADAR Services, Inc: Without restraint: The use and abuse of domestic restraining orders. Rockville, MD: 2008. http://www.radarsvcs.org/docs/RADARreport-VAWARestraining-Orders.pdf

4 Office of the Commissioner of Probation, Massachusetts Trial Court: The tragedies of domestic violence: A qualitative analysis of civil restraining orders. October 12, 1995.

5 Leving JM and Sacks G. Some progress for California fathers, but still a long way to go. Ifeminists.net, July 5, 2006.
http://www.ifeminists.net/introduction/editorials/2006/0705sacks.html

6 Kasper T. Obtaining and defending against an order of protection. Illinois Bar Journal, June 2005.
http://www.ancpr.org/obtaining_and_defending_against_.htm

7 Epstein E. Speaking the unspeakable. Massachusetts Bar Association Newsletter, 1993.

8 Atty. Casey Gwinn, part 2 admits perjury not prosecuted. July 6, 2006.
http://www.youtube.com/watch?v=UOClDr5DviU

9 RADAR Services, Inc: A culture of false allegations: How VAWA harms families and children. Rockville, MD: 2008.
http://www.radarsvcs.org/docs/RADARreport-VAWA-ACulture-of-False-Allegations.pdf

10 Atty. Casey Gwinn, part 2 admits perjury not prosecuted. July 6, 2006.
http://www.youtube.com/watch?v=UOClDr5DviU

11 RADAR Services, Inc: Education for injustice. Rockville, MD: 2008.
http://www.radarsvcs.org/docs/RADARreport-Education-For-Injustice.pdf

12 ABA Commission on Domestic Violence. Judicial checklist. 2008.
http://www.abanet.org/domviol/publications/187815-ABA_Checklist-FINAL.pdf

13 Raskin-Zrihen R and Brown JM. Domestic abuse: Does money fuel false allegations? Times-Herald (CA), December 17, 2006.
http://www.timesheraldonline.com/ci_4857258

14 Stoddard T. U.S. State Department behind international child abduction scandal. Price of Liberty, June 16, 2008.
http://www.thepriceofliberty.org/08/06/16/stoddard.htm

15 Statement by Karl Hindle. July 1, 2008.
http://emilyrosehindle.blogspot.com/2008/07/application-for-directions-british-igh.html

16 RADAR Services, Inc: $1 billion for DV programs that misuse taxpayer money and place victims at risk. Rockville, MD: 2008.
http://www.radarsvcs.org/docs/RADARreport-DVPrograms-Misuse-1-Billion-Tax-Dollars-Per-Year.pdf

17 Department of State. Dowry/visa demands. 2004.

18 Quoted in Tsering L. Indian
husbands fall victim to dowry-immigration fraud. New Ameri-can Media, January 19, 2005.
http://news.ncmonline.com/news/view_article.html?article_id=768649893bc5975ce97b6bff5354c210

19 Foster BP. Analyzing the cost and effectiveness of governmental policies. Cost Management, Vol. 22, No. 3, 2008. Exhibit 1.

20 Foster BP. Analyzing the cost and effectiveness of governmental policies. Cost Management, Vol. 22, No. 3, 2008. Exhibit 2.

21 FY 2006 Office on Violence Against Women Grant Activity by State – West Virginia.

http://www.OfficeonViolenceagainstWomen.usDepartmentOfJutice.gov/grant_activities2006.htm#wv

22 USAspending.gov FY 2007.
http://www.usaspending.gov/faads/faads.php?recipient_name=West+VA+Coalition&reptype=r&database=faads&fiscal_year=2007&detail=0&datype=T&sortby=r&Submit.x=9&Submit.y=7

23 Horn WF and Sylvester T. Father Facts. Gaithersburg, MD: National Fatherhood Initiative. 2004.

24 U.S. Census Bureau. Statistical Abstract of the United States, 1999. Tables 155 and 159. Washington, DC: U.S. Government Printing Office, 2000.

25 Allen DW and Brinig M. Anticipated and unanticipated legal changes: The case of joint parenting. Unpublished manuscript, February 2007. Table 7, Column 2.

26 Johnston J et al. Allegations and substantiations of abuse in custody-disputing families. Family Court Review, Vol. 43, No. 2, 2005.

27 Foster BP. Analyzing the cost and effectiveness of governmental policies. Cost Management, Vol. 22, No. 3, 2008.

28 Nock SL and Einolf CJ. The one hundred billion dollar man: The annual public costs of father absence. Gaithersburg, MD: National Fatherhood Initiative. 2008.

29 Scafidi B. Taxpayer Costs of Divorce and Unwed Childbearing. New York City: Institute for American Values, 2008.

30 Schramm DG. Individual and social costs of divorce in Utah. Journal of Family and Economic Issues, Vol. 27, No. 1, 2006.

31 RADAR Services, Inc. VAWA-funded immigration fraud costs American taxpayers $170 million a year. Rockville, MD. 2008.
http://www.radarsvcs.org/docs/RADARreport-VAWAFunded-Immigration-Fraud.pdf

32 Hudson Z. Jury acquits Rucker Smith. Americus Times-Recorder, May 5, 2006.
http://www.americustimesrecorder.com/siteSearch/apstorysection/local_story_125003348.html

33 Lester TK and Haas SM. West Virginia Correctional Population Forecast: 2005–2015. Charleston, WV: Criminal Justice Statistical Analysis Center. 2006. Table 7.

34 Greenfield LA et al. Violence by Intimates. Washington DC: U.S. Department of Justice. NCJ-167237. March 1998, p. vi.

35 The Third Branch. FY2004 Costs of Incarceration and Supervision. Washington, DC: Administrative Office of the United States Courts. Vol. 37, No. 5. 2005.

36 Glaze LE and Palla S. Probation and Parole in the United States, 2003. Washington, DC: U.S. Department of Justice. NCJ-205336. 2004. Tables 2, 4, and 5.

37 The Third Branch. FY2004 Costs of Incarceration and Supervision. Washington, DC: Administrative Office of the United States Courts. Vol. 37, No. 5. 2005.

38 West Virginia Division of Criminal Justice Services: Victim Assistance Grant Program: 2002 West Virginia Grant Program. Accessed June 19, 2008.
http://www.ovc.gov/fund/sbsmap/ovcpfwv1.htm

39 West Virginia Division of Criminal Justice Services: State Compensation Program: 2002 West Virginia Statewide Compensation Program. Column c. Accessed June 19, 2008.
http://www.ovc.gov/fund/sbsmap/ovccpwv1.htm

Chapter 6

1 RADAR Services, Inc. Why have domestic violence programs failed to stop partner abuse? Rockville, MD: 2008.
http://www.radarsvcs.org/docs/RADARreport-Why-DV-Programs-Fail-to-Stop-Abuse.pdf

2 Winslow MV, Young C. Suspect in SafeSpace stabbing in Martin County claims self-defense. TCPalm November 14, 2007.
http://www.tcpalm.com/news/2007/nov/14/30suspect-in-safespacestabbing-claims-self/

3 RADAR Services, Inc. VAWA-funded immigration fraud costs American taxpayers $170 million a year. Rockville, MD, 2008.
http://www.radarsvcs.org/docs/RADARreport-VAWAFunded-Immigration-Fraud.pdf

4 How Do I Apply for Immigration Benefits as a Battered Spouse or Child?
http://www.uscis.gov/portal/site/uscis/menuitem.5af9bb95919f35e66f614176543f6d1a/?vgnextoid=499a6c854523d010VgnVCM10000048f3d6a1RCRD&vgnextchannel=828807b03d92b010VgnVCM10000045f3d6a1RCRD

5 A search of the Department of State Office of International Women's Issues reveals numerous activities pertaining to domestic violence:
http://www.state.gov/g/wi/

6 Housing and Urban Development. Emergency Shelter Grants Program.
http://www.hud.gov/offices/cpd/homeless/programs/esg/

7 Housing and Urban Development. Community Development Block Grants.
http://www.hud.gov/offices/cpd/communitydevelopment/programs/

8 RADAR Services, Inc. False allegations of domestic violence cost taxpayers $20 billion a year. Rockville, MD: 2008.
http://www.radarsvcs.org/docs/RADARreport-False-DV-Allegations-Cost-20-Billion.pdf

9 Government Accountability Office. Services provided to victims of domestic violence, sexual assault, dating violence, and stalking. Report No. GAO-07-846R. July 9, 2007.
http://www.gao.gov/new.items/d07846r.pdf

10 Detailed information on the violence against women programs assessment. Accessed February 9, 2008.
http://www.whitehouse.gov/omb/expectmore/detail/10003814.2006.html#improvement-Plans

11 Department of Health and Human Services. HHS Grants Policy Statement. January 1, 2007.
http://www.hhs.gov/grantsnet/docs/HHSGPS_107.doc

12 Centers for Disease Control and Prevention. Youth Risk Behavior Surveillance System.
http://www.cdc.gov/HealthyYouth/yrbs/index.htm

13 University of North Carolina. National Longitudinal Study of Adolescent Health. Accessed December 26, 2007.
http://www.cpc.unc.edu/addhealth

14 Detailed information on the family violence prevention and services program assessment. Accessed February 9, 2008.
http://www.whitehouse.gov/omb/expectmore/detail/10002150.2004.html

15 U.S. Government Accountability Office. Services Provided to Victims of Domestic Violence, Sexual Assault, Dating Violence, and Stalking. Report No. GAO-07-846R, July 19, 2007, page 3. http://www.gao.gov/new.items/d07846r.pdf

16 Department of Justice. OJP Financial Guide 2006. http://www.ojp.usDepartmentOfJustice.gov/finguide06/index.htm

17 Department of Justice. Other Requirements for OJP Applications. www.ojp.usDepartmentOfJustice.gov/funding/otherrequirements.htm
18 www.OfficeonViolenceagainstWomen.usDepartmentOfJustice.gov/OfficeonViolenceagainstWomeng rantprograms.htm

19 General Accounting Office. Justice discretionary grants: Byrne Program and Violence Against Women Office grant monitoring should be better documented. Report No. GAO-02-25, November 2001. http://www.gao.gov/new.items/d0225.pdf

20 General Accounting Office. Justice impact evaluations: One Byrne evaluation was rigorous: All reviewed Violence Against Women Office evaluations were problematic. Report No. GAO-02-309. March 2002.

21 Office of the Inspector General. Semiannual Report to Congress, October 1, 2004 March 31, 2005. Page 29. http://www.usDepartmentOfJustice.gov/oig/semiannual/index.htm

22 U.S. Department of Justice Office of the Inspector General. The Department of Justice's grant close-out process. Audit Report 07-05. 2006. http://www.usDepartmentOfJustice.gov/oig/reports/plus/a0705/final.pdf

23 Department of Justice. FY 2007 Performance and Accountability Report. Top Management and Performance Challenges in the Department of Justice. http://www.usDepartmentOfJustice.gov/ag/annualreports/pr2007/TableofContents.htm

24 Office of the Inspector General. Grants to encourage arrest policies and enforcement of protection orders administered by Dane County, Wisconsin. Department of Justice Audit Report No. GR-50-04-003. December 2003. http://www.usDepartmentOfJustice.gov/oig/grants/g5004003.htm

25 Office of the Inspector General. Stop Violence Against Women Formula Grant Awarded to the State of Texas Office of the Governor, Criminal Justice Division. Department of Justice Audit Report No. GR-80-05-008. August 2005. http://www.usDepartmentOfJustice.gov/oig/grants/g8005008.htm

26 Office of the Inspector General. Legal Assistance for Victims Grant No. 1998-WL-VX-0023, Legal Aid of Nebraska, Omaha, Nebraska. Department of Justice Audit Report No. GR-60-05- 012. September 2005. http://www.usDepartmentOfJustice.gov/oig/grants/g6005012.htm

27 Department of Justice. Management decisions on audit reports not implemented within one year, as of March 31, 2007. http://www.usDepartmentOfJustice.gov/jmd/alo/may2007/delinquent_audit_reports.pdf

28 Office of the Inspector General. Formula Grant to the Inter-Tribal Council of Nevada, Grant No. 96-WI-NX-0040. March 1998.
http://www.usDepartmentOfJustice.gov/oig/grants/g9098014.htm

29 Office of the Inspector General. STOP Violence against Indian Women Discretionary Grant. Grant No. 96-WI-NX-0035. November 1998.
http://www.usDepartmentOfJustice.gov/oig/grants/g5099002.htm
30 Office of the Inspector General. Formula Grant to the South Puget Intertribal Planning Agency. Grant No. 95-WI-NX-0013. December 1998.
http://www.usDepartmentOfJustice.gov/oig/grants/g9098037.htm

31 Office of the Inspector General. Formula Grant to the Yavapai-Apache Indian Nation. Grant No. 96-WI-NX-0029. December 1998.
http://www.usDepartmentOfJustice.gov/oig/grants/g9098034.htm

32 Office of the Inspector General. Grants to Encourage Arrest Policies. Grant No. 97-WEVX-0043. March 1999. http://www.usDepartmentOfJustice.gov/oig/grants/g8099006.htm

33 Office of the Inspector General. STOP Violence against Indian Women Grant. Grant No. GR-80-00-004. December 1999.
http://www.usDepartmentOfJustice.gov/oig/grants/g8000004.htm

34 Office of the Inspector General. Service, Training, Officers, and Prosecution Grant to the Confederated Tribes of the Chugachmiut Indian Reservation. Grant No. GR-90-00-011. March 2000.
http://www.usDepartmentOfJustice.gov/oig/grants/g9000011.htm

35 Office of the Inspector General. Service, Training, Officers, and Prosecution Grant to the Confederated Tribes of the Umatilla Indian Reservation. Grant No. GR-90-00-012.
March 2000. http://www.usDepartmentOfJustice.gov/oig/grants/g9000012.htm

36 Hawk S. Murder, mayhem no stranger to year. Shawnee (OK) News Star, December 31, 1999.
http://www.news-star.com/stories/123199/com_crime.shtml

37 Theft alleged at abuse shelter. Pioneer Press, Febuary 2006.

38 Office of the Inspector General. Semiannual Report to Congress, April 1, 2007 – Septem-ber 30, 2007. Page 34.
http://www.usDepartmentOfJustice.gov/oig/semiannual/index.htm

39 Former nonprofit official sentenced. NewsOK.com. March 5, 2008.
http://newsok.com/article/3212136/more/headlines/weather

40 Arkin S. Former DOVES director sentenced. Danville News, September 2, 2008.
http://www.godanriver.com/gdr/news/local/danville_news/article/former_doves_director_sentenced/5953/

41 SafeHouse plans last appeal of $483,000 penalty by state. www.mlive.com June 3, 2006.

42 Office of the Inspector General. Semiannual Report to Congress, October 1, 2004 March 31, 2005. Page 29. http://www.usDepartmentOfJustice.gov/oig/semiannual/index.htm

43 General Accounting Office. Justice discretionary grants: Byrne Program and Violence Against Women Office grant monitoring should be better documented. Report No. GAO-02-25, November 2001. http://www.gao.gov/new.items/d0225.pdf

44 Department of Justice. FY 2007 Performance and Accountability Report. Top Management and Performance Challenges in the Department of Justice.
http://www.usDepartmentOfJustice.gov/ag/annualreports/pr2007/TableofContents.htm

45 Government Accountability Office. Services provided to victims of domestic violence, sexual assault, dating violence, and stalking. Report No. GAO-07-846R. July 9, 2007.
http://www.gao.gov/new.items/d07846r.pdf

46 Detailed information on the violence against women programs assessment. Accessed February 9, 2008.
http://www.whitehouse.gov/omb/expectmore/detail/10003814.2006.html#improvement-Plans

47 Government Accountability Office. Services Provided to Victims of Domestic Violence, Sexual Assault, Dating Violence, and Stalking. Report No. GAO-07-846R, July 19, 2007.
http://www.gao.gov/new.itemsd07846r.pdf

48 Detailed information on the family violence prevention and services program assessment. Accessed February 9, 2008.
http://www.whitehouse.gov/omb/expectmore/detail/10002150.2004.html

49 Jackson S, Feder L, Forde D et al. Batterer Intervention Programs: Where do We Go from Here? Washington DC: National Institute of Justice. June 2003. Publication No. NCJ 195079.
http://www.ncjrs.gov/pdffiles1/nij/195079.pdf

50 Babcock JC, Canady BE, Graham K, and Schart L. The evolution of battering interventions: From the Dark Ages into the Scientific Age. In Hamel J and Nichols TL (Eds.). Family Interventions in Domestic Violence: A Handbook of Gender-Inclusive Theory and Treatment. New York: Spring Publishing Co., 2007.

51 RADAR Services, Inc. Why have domestic violence programs failed to stop partner abuse? Rockville, MD: Respecting Accuracy in Domestic Abuse Reporting, 2008.
http://www.radarsvcs.org/docs/RADARreport-Why-DV-Programs-Fail-to-Stop-Abuse.pdf

52 Sherman LW et al. The variable effects of arrest on criminal careers: The Milwaukee Domestic Violence Experiment. Journal of Criminal Law and Criminology, Vol. 83, 1992, pp. 137–169.

53 Berk RA, Campbell A, Klap R, and Western B. A Bayesian analysis of the Colorado Springs spouse abuse experiment. Journal of Criminal Law and Criminology, Vol. 83, 1992, pp. 170–200.

54 Schmidt JD, Sherman LW. Does arrest deter domestic violence? In American Bar Association and U.S. Department of Justice (eds.): Legal Interventions in Family Violence: Re-search Findings and Policy Implications. Washington, DC: U.S. Government Printing Office. NCJ 171666, p. 54, 1998.

55 Iyengar R. Does the certainty of arrest reduce domestic violence? Evidence from mandatory and recommended arrest laws. Cambridge, MA: National Bureau of Economic Research, June 2007.

56 Dugan L, Nagin D, and Rosenfeld R. Exposure reduction or backlash? The effects of domestic violence resources on intimate partner homicide. NCJ Number 186194. 2001. http://www.ncjrs.gov/app/Publications/Abstract.aspx?ID=186193

57 Laney GP. Violence Against Women Act: History and Federal Funding. Washington, DC: Congressional Research Service. Updated June 9, 2005. http://www.ilw.com/immigdaily/news/2005,0802-crs.pdf , Table 3.

58 RADAR Services, Inc: Bias in the judiciary: The case of domestic violence. Rockville, MD: 2008. http://www.radarsvcs.org/docs/RADARreport-Bias-In-The-Judiciary.pdf

59 RADAR Services, Inc: Education for injustice. Rockville, MD http://www.radarsvcs.org/docs/RADARreport-Education-For-Injustice.pdf

60 RADAR Services, Inc: Expanding definitions of domestic violence, vanishing rule of law. Rockville, MD: 2008. http://www.radarsvcs.org/docs/RADARreport-Vanishing-Rule-of-Law.pdf

61 RADAR Services, Inc: Justice denied: Arrest policies for domestic violence. Rockville, MD: 2008. http://www.radarsvcs.org/docs/RADARreport-Justice-Denied-DV-Arrest-Policies.pdf

62 RADAR Services, Inc: VAWA programs discriminate against male victims. Rockville, MD: 2008. http://www.radarsvcs.org/docs/RADARreport-VAWA-Discriminates-Against-Males.pdf

63 RADAR Services, Inc: A culture of false allegations: How VAWA harms families and children. Rockville, MD: 2008. http://www.radarsvcs.org/docs/RADARreport-VAWAACulture-of-False-Allegations.pdf

64 Kruttschnitt C, McLaughlin BL, and Petrie CV (eds). Advancing the Federal Research Agenda on Violence against Women. Washington, DC: National Academy of Sciences, 2005, p. 6. http://www.nap.edu/catalog/10849.html

Chapter 7

1 Parmley A. Violence against women post VAWA. Violence Against Women Vol. 10, No. 12, 2004. p. 1424.

2 Catalano S. Intimate Partner Violence in the United States. Washington, DC: US Department of Justice, 2006. http://www.ojp.usDepartmentOfJustice.gov/bjs/intimate/ipv.htm

3 Nicholls T and Dutton D. Abuse committed by women against male intimates. Journal of Couples Therapy, Vol. 10, 2001, pp. 41–57.

4 Anderson K. Perpetrator or victim? Relationships between intimate partner violence and well-being. Journal of Marriage and the Family, Vol. 64, 2002, pp. 851–863.

5 Williams S and Frieze I. Patterns of violence relationships, psychological distress, and marital satisfaction in a national sample of men and women. Sex Roles, Vol. 52, Nos. 11/12, 2005, pp. 771–785.

6 Whitaker DJ et al. Differences in frequency of violence and reported injury between relationships with reciprocal and nonreciprocal intimate partner violence. American Journal of Public Health, Vol. 97, No. 5, 2007.

7 Straus MA. Dominance and symmetry in partner violence by male and female university students in 32 nations. Children and Youth Services Review, 2008.
http://pubpages.unh.edu/%7Emas2/ID41-PR41-Dominance-symmetry-In-Press-7.pdf

8 Frank PB and Golden GK. When 50-50 isn't fair: The case against couple counseling in domestic abuse. October 2005.
http://www.nymbp.org/reference/5050NotFair.pdf

9 Austin J and Dankwort J. Standards for batterer programs. Journal of Interpersonal Violence, Vol. 14, No. 2, 1999, pp. 152–168.

10 Maiuro R et al. Are current state standards for domestic violence perpetrator treatment adequately informed by research? Journal of Aggression, Maltreatment, and Trauma, Vol. 5, 2001, pp. 21–44.

11 Quoted in Healey, Smith, and O'Sullivan. Controversial approaches in batterer intervention. In Healy KM: Batterer Intervention, U.S. Dept. of Justice, National Institute of Justice, 1998, p. 25.

12 Hamel J. Gender-inclusive family interventions in domestic violence: An overview. In Hamel J and Nichols TL (eds.). Family Interventions in Domestic Violence: A Handbook of Gender- Inclusive Theory and Treatment. New York: Spring Publishing Co., 2007, p. 257.

13 Heyman R and Schlee KA. Stopping wife abuse via physical aggression couples treatment. In Dutton DG and Sonkin DL (eds.): Intimate Violence: Contemporary Treatment Innovations. New York: Haworth Press, 2003.

14 O'Leary KD, Heyman R, and Neidig PH. Treatment of wife abuse: A comparison of gender specific and couple approaches. Behavior Assessment, Vol. 30, 1999, pp. 475–505.

15 Rosewater L and Walker LE. Handbook of Feminist Therapy. New York: Spring Publishing, 1985.

16 Epstein S, Russell G, and Silvern L. Structure and ideology of shelters for battered women. American Journal of Community Psychology, Vol. 16, 1988, pp. 345–367.

17 Dutton-Douglas MA and Dionne D. Counseling and shelter services for battered women. In Steinman M (ed.): Woman Battering: Policy Responses. Cincinnati: Anderson Publishing Co., 1991.

18 Former shelter director reveals why she left.
http://www.mediaradar.org/shelterDirectorRevealsWhySheLeft.php

19 Moore N. Inside a batterers program for abused women. Ifeminists.net, July 29, 2003.
http://www.ifeminists.net/introduction/editorials/2003/0729moore.html

20 Goldner V. Making room for both/and. Networker, March–April 1992, pp. 60–61.

21 Dutton-Douglas MA and Dionne D. Counseling and shelter services for battered women. In Steinman M (ed.): Woman Battering: Policy Responses. Cincinnati: Anderson Publishing Co., 1991.

22 Berk RA, Newton PJ, and Berk SF. What a difference a day makes: An empirical study of the impact of shelters for battered women. Journal of Marriage and the Family, Vol. 48, 1986, pp. 481–490.

23 Follingstad D, Wright S, Lloyd S, and Sebastian J. Sex differences in motivations and effects in dating relationships. Family Relations, Vol. 40, 1991, pp. 51–57.

24 Carrado M, George MJ, Loxam E, et al. Aggression in British heterosexual relationships: A descriptive analysis. Aggressive Behavior, Vol. 22, pp. 401–415.

25 Straus MA. Women's violence toward men is a serious social problem. In Gelles RJ and Loseke DR (eds.): Current Controversies on Family Violence. Newbury Park, CA: Sage Publications, 2004.

26 Gavin C and Puffett NK. Criminal Domestic Violence Case Processing: A Case Study of the Five Boroughs of New York City. New York: Center for Court Innovation, 2005,p.33. http://www.courtinnovation.org/_uploads/documents/Citywide%20Final1.pdf

27 Kelly L. Disabusing the definition of domestic abuse: How women batter men and the role of the feminist state. Florida State University Law Review, Vol. 30, 2003, p. 847. http://www.law.fsu.edu/journals/lawreview/downloads/304/kelly.pdf

28 Cook P. Abused Men: The Hidden Side of Domestic Violence. Westport, CT: Praeger, 1997, p. 110.

29 Pence E. Some thoughts on philosophy. In Shepard M and Pence E (eds.): Coordinating Community Responses to Domestic Violence: Lessons from Duluth and Beyond. Thousand Oaks, CA: Sage Publishers, 1999, p. 30.

30 Rowlands T. The other face of domestic violence. CNN, aired April 7, 2006. http://www.cnn.com/2006/US/04/06/btsc.rowlands.batteredmen/index.html

31 Cook P. Abused Men: The Hidden Side of Domestic Violence. Westport, CT: Praeger, 1997.

32 RADAR Services, Inc. VAWA Programs Discriminate Against Male Victims. Rockville, MD: 2008. http://www.radarsvcs.org/docs/RADARreport-VAWA-Discriminates-Against-Males.pdf

33 Bugarin A. The Prevalence of Domestic Violence in California. Sacramento, CA: California Research Bureau, 2002. http://www.library.ca.gov/crb/02/16/02-016.pdf

34 Former shelter director reveals why she left. March 10, 2007. http://www.mediaradar.org/shelterDirectorRevealsWhySheLeft.php

35 Carnell B. Man files lawsuit over access to domestic violence shelters. EquityFeminism. com, September 24, 2003. http://www.equityfeminism.com/archives/years/2003/000082.html

36 U.S. Congressional Record, October 11, 2000, pp. 10191-92.

37 Fontes DL. Male victims of domestic violence. In Hamel J and Nichols TL (eds.). Family Interventions in Domestic Violence: A Handbook of Gender-Inclusive Theory and Treatment. New York: Spring Publishing Co., 2007.

38 Richard C. An abused man speaks out. FAVTEA Bulletin, Spring/Summer 2004. http://www.favtea.com/news-archives/SpringSum2004.Bulletin.pdf

39 Pence E, Paymar M. Education Groups for Men Who Batter: The Duluth Model. New York: Springer, 1993.

40 Dutton DG, Nicholls TL. The gender paradigm in domestic violence research and theory: The conflict of theory and data. Aggression and Violent Behavior, Vol. 10, 2005, pp. 680–714.
41 Schore AN. Affect Regulation and the Repair of the Self. New York: Norton, 2003.

42 Pence E and Paymar M. Ibid, p. 23.

43 Kline JA. The Whole Truth about Domestic Violence. Dillon, CO: Swan Mountain Press, 2003. p. 147.

44 New York Model for Batterer Programs, accessed August 25, 2007.
http://www.nymbp.org/how_program_works.htm

45 Kruttschnitt C, McLaughlin BL, and Petrie CV (eds). Advancing the Federal Research Agenda on Violence against Women. Washington, DC: National Research Council, 2005, p. 6.
http://www.nap.edu/catalog/10849.html

46 Feder L and Wilson DB. A meta-analytic review of court-mandated batterer interventions programs: Can courts affect abusers' behaviors? Journal of Experimental Criminology, Vol. 1, 2005, pp. 239–262.

47 Dutton D. The Abusive Personality: Violence and Control in Intimate Relationships. New York: Guilford Publications, 1998.

48 New York Model for Batterer Programs, accessed August 25, 2007.
http://www.nymbp.org/principles.htm

49 Babcock JC, Canady BE, Graham K, and Schart L. The evolution of battering interventions: From the Dark Ages into the Scientific Age. In Hamel J and Nichols TL (eds.). Family Interventions in Domestic Violence: A Handbook of Gender-Inclusive Theory and Treatment. New York: Spring Publishing Co., 2007.

50 RADAR Services, Inc: Without restraint: The use and abuse of domestic restraining orders. Rockville, MD: 2008. http://www.radarsvcs.org/docs/RADARreport-VAWARestraining-Orders.pdf

51 RADAR Services, Inc: Expanding definitions of domestic violence, vanishing rule of law. Rockville, MD: 2008. http://www.radarsvcs.org/docs/RADARreport-Vanishing-Rule-of-Law.pdf

52 Finn P. Civil protection orders: A flawed opportunity for intervention. In Steinman M (ed.): Woman Battering: Policy Responses. Cincinnati: Anderson Publishing Co., 1991.

53 Gavin C and Puffett NK. Criminal Domestic Violence Case Processing: A Case Study of the Five Boroughs of New York City. New York: Center for Court Innovation, 2005, p. 30.
http://www.courtinnovation.org/_uploads/documents/Citywide%20Final1.pdf

54 Grau J, Fagan J, and Wexler S. Restraining orders for battered women: Issues of access and efficacy. Women and Politics, Vol. 4, 1984, pp. 13–28.

55 Harrell A and Smith B. Effects of restraining orders on domestic violence victims. In Buzawa C and Buzawa E (eds.): Do Arrests and Restraining Orders Work? Thousand Oaks, CA: Sage Publications, 1996, p. 229.

56 McFarlane J, Malecha A, Gist J et al. Protection orders and intimate partner violence: An 18-month study of 150 Black, Hispanic, and White women. American Journal of Public Health, Vol. 94, No. 4, pp. 613–618.

57 Dugan L, Nagin D, and Rosenfeld R. Exposure reduction or backlash? The effects of domestic violence resources on intimate partner homicide. NCJ Number 186194, 2001. http://www.ncjrs.gov/app/Publications/Abstract.aspx?ID=186193

58 Independent Women's Forum. Domestic Violence: An In-Depth Analysis. Washington, DC, 2005.

59 Berk RA, Campbell A, Klap R, and Western B. A Bayesian analysis of the Colorado Springs spouse abuse experiment. Journal of Criminal Law and Criminology, Vol. 83, 1992, pp. 170–200.

60 Sherman LW et al. The Variable Effects of Arrest on Criminal Careers: The Milwaukee Domestic Violence Experiment. Journal of Criminal Law and Criminology, Vol. 83, 1992, pp. 137–169.

61 Iyengar R. Does the certainty of arrest reduce domestic violence? Evidence from mandatory and recommended arrest laws. Cambridge, MA: National Bureau of Economic Research, June 2007.

62 Hirschel D et al. Explaining the prevalence, context, and consequences of dual arrest in intimate partner cases. Grant No. 2001-WT-BX-0501. April 2007, p. 152. http://www.ncjrs.gov/pdffiles1/nij/grants/218355.pdf

63 Quoted in Sontag S. Fierce entanglements. New York Times Magazine, November 17, 2002, p. 56.

64 Schmidt JD and Sherman LW. Does arrest deter domestic violence? In American Bar Association and U.S. Department of Justice (eds.): Legal Interventions in Family Violence: Re-search Findings and Policy Implications. Washington, DC: U.S. Government Printing Office. NCJ 171666, 1998, p. 54.

65 Hirschel D and Buzawa E. Understanding the context of dual arrest with directions for future research. Violence Against Women, Vol. 18, December 2002, Table 1.

66 Hotaling GT and Buzawa ES. Forgoing criminal justice assistance. Document No. 195667, 2003, Table 1. http://www.ncjrs.gov/pdffiles1/nij/grants/195667.pdf

67 McFarlane J, Malecha A, Gist J et al. Ibid.

68 Dugan L, Nagin D, and Rosenfeld R. Exposure reduction or backlash? The effects of domestic violence resources on intimate partner homicide. NCJ Number 186194. 2001. http://www.ncjrs.gov/app/Publications/Abstract.aspx?ID=186193

69 Miller N. Domestic violence: A review of state legislation defining police and prosecution duties and powers. Alexandria, VA: Institute for Law and Justice, 2004. http://www.ilj.org/publications/DV_Legislation-3.pdf

70 Violence Against Women and Department of Justice Reauthorization Act of 2005, Section 102. http://frwebgate.access.gpo.gov/cgibin/getdoc.cgi?dbname=109_cong_public_laws&docid=f:publ162.109.pdf

71 RADAR Services, Inc. Justice denied: Arrest policies for domestic violence. Rockville, MD: 2008. http://www.radarsvcs.org/docs/RADARreport-Justice-Denied-DV-Arrest-Policies.pdf

72 Buzawa ES and Austin T. Determining police response to domestic violence victims. In American Bar Association and U.S. Department of Justice (Eds.), Legal Interventions in Family Violence: Research Findings and Policy Implications (NCJ-171666, p. 58). Washing-ton, DC: U.S. Government Printing Office, 1998.

73 Erez E and Belknap J. In their own words: Battered women's assessment of the criminal processing system's responses. Violence and Victims, Vol. 13, 1998, pp. 251–268.

74 Hotaling GT and Buzawa ES. Forgoing criminal justice assistance. Document No. 195667, 2003. http://www.ncjrs.gov/pdffiles1/nij/grants/195667.pdf

75 Lininger T. Bearing the cross. Fordham Law Review, Vol. 74, 2005, pp. 1353–1364.

76 Rebovich D. Prosecution response to domestic violence: Results of a survey of large jurisdictions. In Buzawa E and Buzawa C (eds.): Do Arrests and Restraining Orders Work? Thousand Oaks, CA: Sage Publications, 1996.

77 Personal communication from Harry Crouch, Director, San Diego Men's Center, February 20, 2006.

78 Anderson C. Batterer bias? San Francisco Daily Journal, April 4, 2003.

79 Hotaling GT and Buzawa ES. Forgoing criminal justice assistance. Document No. 195667, 2003. http://www.ncjrs.gov/pdffiles1/nij/grants/195667.pdf

80 Crenshaw K. Mapping the margins: Intersectionality, identity politics, and violence against women of color. Stanford Law Review, Vol. 43, 1991, p. 1257.

81 Davis RL. Mandatory arrest and no-drop prosecution. Intellectual Conservative.com. April 7, 2006. http://www.intellectualconservative.com/2006/mandatory-arrest-and-nodrop-prosecution

82 Ford DA and Regoli MJ. The preventive impacts of policies for prosecuting wife batterers. In Buzawa ES and Buzawa CG (eds.): Domestic Violence: The Criminal Justice Response. Thousand Oaks, CA: Sage Publications, 1996.

83 Davis RC, Smith BE, and Davies HJ. The effects of no-drop prosecution of domestic violence upon conviction rates. Justice Research and Policy, Vol. 3, No. 2, 2001, pp. 1–13, (NCJ Number 193235).

84 Violence Against Women and Department of Justice Reauthorization Act of 2005, Section 101. http://frwebgate.access.gpo.gov/cgibin/getdoc.cgi?dbname=109_cong_public_laws&docid=f:publ162.109.pdf

85 Gelles RJ. The politics of research: The use, abuse, and misuse of social science data-The cases of intimate partner violence. Family Court Review, Vol. 45, No. 1, January 2007.

86 Mills LG. Insult to Injury: Rethinking our Responses to Intimate Abuse. Princeton, NJ: Princeton University Press, 2003, p. 6.
87 Hamel J. Gender-inclusive family interventions in domestic violence: An overview. In Hamel J and Nichols TL (eds.). Family Interventions in Domestic Violence: A Handbook of Gender- Inclusive Theory and Treatment. New York: Spring Publishing Co., 2007, p. 247.

88 Hench VE. When less is more—Can reducing penalties reduce household violence? Hawaii Law Review, Vol. 19, Spring 1997.

Chapter 8

1 Tjaden P, Thoennes N. Full Report of the Prevalence, Incidence, and Consequences of Violence Against Women. National Institute of Justice, Publication No. NCJ 183781, November 2000.
http://www.ncjrs.org/pdffiles1/nij/183781.pdf

2 Gelles RJ. Intimate Violence in Families. Thousand Oaks, CA: Sage Publications, 1997.

3 Whitaker DJ et al. Differences in frequency of violence and reported injury between relationships with reciprocal and nonreciprocal intimate partner violence. American Journal of Public Health, Vol 97, No. 5, May 2007, pp. 941-947.
http://www.ajph.org/cgi/content/abstract/97/5/941

4 McDonald R. Estimating the number of American children living in partner-violent families. Journal of Family Psychology, Vol. 20, No. 1, pp. 137–142. 2006.
http://www.smu.edu/experts/study-documents/family-violence-study-may2006.pdf

5 Amy Winehouse beats up her husband when she's drunk. Starpulse News Blog. June 12, 2007.
http://www.starpulse.com/news/index.php/2007/06/12/amy_winehouse_beats_up_her_husband_when
_

6 Roberts C. Women who batter, proudly. Ifeminists.net October 5, 2007.
http://www.ifeminists.net/e107_plugins/content/content.php?content.233

7 Burlingame M. The Inner World of Abraham Lincoln. Champaign-Urbana: Board of Trustees of the University of Illinois, 1994.

8 Cook P. Abused Men: The Hidden Side of Domestic Violence. Westport, CT: Praeger, 1997, p. 157.

9 Parker T. The story of an assaulted man. 2000.
http://www.rhiannon3.net/cs/article6.html

10 Omnibus Crime Control and Safe Streets Act of 1968, Section 3789d. (c)(1).
http://www.usDepartmentOfJustice.gov/crt/split/42usc3789d.htm

11 Office of Management and Budget. Circular No. A-133Revised to show changes published in the Federal Register June 27, 2003Audits of States, Local Governments, and Non-Profit Organizations, paragraph 4.

12 Senator Orrin Hatch, Congressional Record, October 11, 2000, pp. S10191–92.
http://www.menshealthnetwork.org/library/VAWAdocuments2005.pdf
13 Biden pressed to make abuse bill gender neutral, Senator: Bill already applies to both sexes, Hockessin Community News, June 2, 2005, p. 8.
http://www.communitypub.com/WKLYART/HCN_06.02.05.pdf

14 Violence Against Women Act 2005, Section 40002(b)(8).
http://frwebgate.access.gpo.gov/cgibin/getdoc.cgi?dbname=109_cong_public_laws&docid=f:publ162.109.pdf

15 Documentation from the Department Of Justice Violence Against Women Office, quoted in letter from the Delaware Domestic Violence Coordinating Council to David Burroughs, dated October 9, 2002. http://www.menshealthnetwork.org/library/VAWArejectDel1002.pdf

16 National Institute of Justice, Department of Justice, Justice Responses to Intimate Partner Violence and Stalking. November 5, 2005.
www.ncjrs.org/pdffiles1/nij/sl000734.pdf

17 Office on Violence Against Women. Grants to State Sexual Assault and Domestic Violence Coalitions Program.
http://www.usDepartmentOfJustice.gov/OfficeonViolenceagainstWomen/state_grant_desc.htm
Accessed November 23, 2007.

18 Letter to Roy Getting from Robert P. Neff, Manager, Criminal Justice Programs, North Central Texas Council of Governments, dated December 16, 2002.
http://www.menshealthnetwork.org/library/VAWArejectDallas1202.pdf

19 Grant Application Kit – Violence Against Women Act, dated March 10, 2003.
http://www.menshealthnetwork.org/library/VAWAdocuments2005.pdf

20 Usher DR. Baylor comes under attack for VAWA sex discrimination provisions. Human Events, June 21, 2006.
http://www.humanevents.com/article.php?id=15687

21 http://www.nnedv.org/ . Accessed November 21, 2007.

22 http://www.ncadv.org/ . Accessed November 21, 2007.

23 Young C. Ending bias in domestic assault law. Boston Globe, July 25, 2005.
http://www.boston.com/news/globe/editorial_opinion/oped/articles/2005/07/25/ending_bias_in_domestic_assault_law/

24 A search of equality – Domestic abuse groups dispute status of claims by men, Boston Globe, October 28, 2002, p. B1.
http://www.janedoe.org/about/about_news_10_28_02.htm

25 Personal communication from Richard L. Davis, vice-president, Domestic Abuse Hotline for Men and Women, January 24, 2006.

26 DeConto JJ. Advocate for male abuse victims was one himself. Portsmouth (NH) Herald, December 14, 2003.

27 West Virginia Coalition Against Domestic Violence. For a Safer State of Family: A Hand-book for Helpers. Charleston, WV, 2005.

28 RADAR. Former shelter director reveals why she left. March 10, 2007.
http://www.mediaradar.org/shelterDirectorRevealsWhySheLeft.php

29 Fontes D. Violent touch: Breaking through the stereotype. 1998, updated April 15, 2003.
http://www.safe4all.org/essays/vtbreak.pdf

30 Fontes DL. Male victims of domestic violence. In Hamel J and Nichols TL (eds.). Family Interventions in Domestic Violence: A Handbook of Gender-Inclusive Theory and Treatment.
New York: Spring Publishing Co., 2007.

31 Young C. No excuse for domestic violence. Period. Detroit News, May 6, 1997.
http://www.menweb.org/cyoungdn.htm

32 Carnell B. Man files lawsuit over access to domestic violence shelters. EquityFeminism. com.
September 24, 2003. http://www.equityfeminism.com/archives/years/2003/000082.html

33 Howard LW. Shelter an oasis for both sexes: Domestic violence still widespread. Antelope Valley Press, January 22, 2006.
http://www.avpress.com/n/22/0122_s1.hts

34 Bugarin A. The Prevalence of Domestic Violence in California. Sacramento, CA: California Research Bureau, 2002.
http://www.library.ca.gov/crb/02/16/02-016.pdf

35 Former shelter director reveals why she left. March 10, 2007.
http://www.mediaradar.org/shelter-DirectorRevealsWhySheLeft.php

36 Communication from Harry Crouch, director, San Diego Men's Center, January 19, 2006.

37 Angelucci A and Sacks G: California domestic violence lawsuit will help secure services for all abuse victims. Ifeminists.net, January 4, 2006.
http://www.ifeminists.net/introduction/editorials/2006/0104sacks.html

38 Baird J. Men's rights group: Victim support only for women. CBS 13, October 28, 2005.
http://cbs13.com/topstories/local_story_302003457.html

39 Jamieson RL. Battered men are starting to speak up. Seattle Post-Intelligencer, June 14, 2004.
http://seattlepi.nwsource.com/jamieson/177711_robert14.html

40 National Domestic Violence Hotline. Decade for Change Summit. 2007.
http://www.ndvh.org/decadeforchange/Decade%20for%20Change%20SUMMIT%20Report.pdf

41 Hines DA, Brown J, Dunning E. Characteristics of callers to the Domestic Abuse Helpline for Men. Journal of Family Violence Vol. 22, No. 2, February 2007.

42 Groundbreaking study shows need for unbiased domestic violence services. Molokai Times, March 13, 2007. http://www.molokaitimes.com/articles/731312226.asp
43 Pierce M. Home is Where the Hurt Is: Domestic Violence has Unexpected Victims. City Beat September 5, 2007.
http://citybeat.com/gyrobase/Content?oid=oid%3A141329

44 Newman L. Biased courts and traditional' service providers are guilty of allowing abusers to continue. February 20, 2004.
http://www.altrue.net/site/vip/content.php?type=1&id=8034

45 RADAR Services, Inc: Without restraint: The use and abuse of domestic restraining orders. Rockville, MD: 2008.
http://www.radarsvcs.org/docs/RADARreport-VAWARestraining-Orders.pdf

46 RADAR Services, Inc: Justice denied: Arrest policies for domestic violence. Rockville, MD: 2008.
http://www.radarsvcs.org/docs/RADARreport-Justice-Denied-DV-Arrest-Policies.pdf

47 RADAR Services, Inc. Bias in the judiciary: The case of domestic violence. Rockville, MD: 2008.
http://www.radarsvcs.org/docs/RADARreport-Bias-In-The-Judiciary.pdf

48 RADAR Request Reveals VAWA Usage Data by Sex.
http://www.mediaradar.org/OfficeonViolenceagainstWomen _foia_data.php

49 Communication with Lee Newman, executive director, Stop Abuse for Everyone-International, November 23, 2007.

Chapter 10

1 Gelles RJ. The hidden side of domestic violence: Male victims. Women's Quarterly, 1999.

2 Straus MA. Dominance and Symmetry in Partner Violence by Male and Female University Students in 32 Nations. Presented at New York University, May 23, 2006, Table 3.
http://pubpages.unh.edu/~mas2/ID41H3a.pdf

3 Archer J. Sex differences in aggression between heterosexual partners: A meta-analytic review. Psychological Bulletin, Vol. 126, pp. 651–680, 2000.

4 Maxwell CD, Garner JH, Fagan JA. The effects of arrest on intimate partner violence: New evidence from the spouse assault replication program. National Institute of Justice, 2001, p.13.
http://www.ncjrs.gov/pdffiles1/nij/188199.pdf

5 Lane E, Boba R. Police use of dual arrest in intimate assault cases. Police Foundation. June 2002.
http://www.cops.usDepartmentOfJustice.gov/mime/open.pdf?Item=910

6 Judicial Training: Your job is to be a wall. New Jersey Law Journal April 24, 1995, p. 14.

7 Greenfeld LA, Rand MR, Craven D et al. Violence by intimates: Analysis of data on crimes by current or former spouses, boyfriends, or girlfriends. Washington, DC: Department of Justice. NCF-167237, 1998. p. 19. http://www.ojp.usDepartmentOfJustice.gov/bjs/pub/pdf/vi.pdf

8 Greenfeld LA, Rand MR, Craven D et al. Ibid.

9 Stets JE, Straus MA. Gender differences in reporting marital violence and its medical and psychological consequences. In Straus MA, Gelles R (eds): Physical Violence in American Families, New Brunswick, NJ: Anchor Books, 1990, Table 15.

10 Luo M. Domestic violence policy assailed. Newsday (Long Island, NY), August 9, 2000, p. A32.

11 Quoted in Cathy Young, Domestic violations. Reason, February 1998.
http://www.ncjrs.org/pdffiles1/nij/188199.pdf

12 Bias in the Judiciary: The Case of Domestic Violence. Rockville, MD: RADAR Services, Inc. 2008. http://www.radarsvcs.org/docs/RADARreport-Bias-In-The-Judiciary.pdf

13 Straus MA. May 23, 2006, ibid.

14 Ciraco VN. Fighting domestic violence with mandatory arrest, Are we winning?: An analysis in New Jersey. Women's Rights Law Report Vol. 22, 2001.

15 Wells W, DeLeon-Granados W. Analysis of unexamined issues in the intimate partner homicide decline: Race, quality of victim services, offender accountability, and system accountability.
Final report. Document No. 196666, 2000.
http://www.ncjrs.org/pdffiles1/nij/grants/196666.pdf

16 Hirschel D, Buzawa E. Understanding the context of dual arrest with directions for future research. Violence Against Women Vol. 8, pp. 1449-1455, 2002.

17 U.S. Department of Justice, Office of Violence Against Women. Grants to encourage arrest policies and enforcement of protection orders program: Fiscal year 2001 application and program guidelines.
http://www.usDepartmentOfJustice.gov/OfficeonViolenceagainstWomen/grants/arrest/arrest01.pdf

18 Hirschel and Buzawa. Ibid.

19 Alabama Coalition Against Domestic Violence: News: New bill names domestic violence as a separate crime. 2001.
http://www.acadv.org/news.html

20 Stets JE, Straus MA. Gender differences in reporting marital violence and its medical and psychological consequences. In Straus MA, Gelles R (eds): Physical Violence in American Families, New Brunswick, NJ: Transaction Publishers, 1990, Table 15.

21 Governor's Commission on Domestic Violence. Law enforcement: A model for police re-sponse to domestic violence cases. No date.
http://DepartmentOfJustice.nh.gov/victim/pdf/dvlaw.pdf

22 Young C. Domestic violations. Reason Online, February 1998. http://reason.com/9802/fe.young.shtml

23 Miller N. Domestic violence: A review of state legislation defining police and prosecution duties and powers. Alexandria, VA: Institute for Law and Justice, 2004. http://www.ilj.org/publications/DV_Legislation-3.pdf

24 Durose MR et al. Family Violence Statistics. Washington, DC: Department of Justice. NCJ 207846, 2005. http://www.ojp.usDepartmentOfJustice.gov/bjs/pub/pdf/fvs.pdf

25 Durose MR et al. Table 5.9.

26 Schmidt JD, Sherman LW. Does arrest deter domestic violence? In American Bar Association and U.S. Department of Justice (eds.): Legal Interventions in Family Violence: Re-search Findings and Policy Implications. Washington, DC: U.S. Government Printing Office. NCJ 171666, p. 54, 1998.

27 Buzawa ES, Austin T. Determining police response to domestic violence victims. In American Bar Association and U.S. Department of Justice (Eds.), Legal Interventions in Family Violence: Research Findings and Policy Implications (NCJ-171666, p. 58). Washington, DC: U.S. Government Printing Office. 1998.

28 Erez E and Belknap J. In their own words: Battered women's assessment of the criminal pro-cessing system's responses. Violence and Victims, Vol. 13, pp. 251–268. 1998.

29 Schmidt JD, Sherman LW. Ibid.

30 Maxwell CD, Garner JH, Fagan JA. Ibid.

31 Iyengar R. Does the certainty of arrest reduce domestic violence? Evidence from mandatory and recommended arrest laws. Cambridge, MA: National Bureau of Economic Research, June 2007.

32 Davis RL. Mandatory arrest and no-drop prosecution. IntellectualConservative.com April 7, 2006. http://www.intellectualconservative.com/2006/mandatory-arrest-and-no-drop-prosecution

33 Without restraint: The use and abuse of restraining orders. Rockville, MD: RADAR Services, Inc., 2008. http://www.radarsvcs.org/docs/RADARreport-VAWA-Restraining-Orders.pdf

34 Hirschel and Buzawa. Ibid.

35 Peterson R. Comparing the processing of domestic violence cases to non-domestic violence cases in New York City criminal courts. New York City Criminal Justice Agency, 2001. http://www.cjareports.org/reports/dv01.pdf

36 Cook P. Abused Men: The Hidden Side of Domestic Violence. Westport, CT: Praeger Publishers, 1997, pp. 62–64.

37 Ibid, p. 79.

38 Erickson charged with assault. ESPN.com. July 22, 2002.

http://www.espn.go.com/mlb/news/2002/0722/1408560.html

39 Angelucci A and Sacks G. California domestic violence lawsuit will help secure services for all abuse victims. Ifeminists.net, January 4, 2006. http://www.ifeminists.net/introduction/editorials/2006/0104sacks.html

40 Independent Women's Forum. Domestic violence: An in-depth analysis. Washington, DC. 2005.

41 Governor's Commission on Domestic Violence. Law enforcement: A model for police response to domestic violence cases. No date. http://DepartmentOfJustice.nh.gov/victim/pdf/dvlaw.pdf

Chapter 11

1 Accessed April 11, 2006. http://johnflemingmps0.tripod.com/p1.htm

2 Gelles RJ. Intimate Violence in Families. Thousand Oaks, CA: Sage Publications, 1997.

3 Nicholls T, Dutton D. Abuse committed by women against male intimates. Journal of Couples Therapy. Vol. 10, 2001, pp. 41-57.

4 Anderson K. Perpetrator or victim? Relationships between intimate partner violence and wellbeing. Journal of Marriage and the Family. Vol 64, 2002. pp. 851-863.

5 Williams S, Frieze I. Patterns of violence relationships, psychological distress, and marital satisfaction in a national sample of men and women. Sex Roles Vol. 52, Nos. 11/12, 2005. pp. 771-785.

6 Fiebert MS. References examining assaults by women on their spouses or male partners: An annotated bibliography. Long Beach, CA: Department of Psychology, California State University, 2008. http://www.csulb.edu/~mfiebert/assault.htm

7 Ibid.

8 Durose MR et al. Family Violence Statistics. Washington, DC: Department of Justice. NCJ 207846, 2005. http://www.ojp.usDepartment Of Justice.gov/bjs/pub/pdf/fvs.pdf

9 http://www.courts.state.ri.us/domesticnew/ Accessed November 18, 2006.

10 RADAR Services, Inc: Without restraint: The use and abuse of domestic restraining orders. Rockville, MD: 2008. http://www.radarsvcs.org/docs/VAWA-Restraining-Orders.pdf

11 RADAR Services, Inc: Justice denied: Arrest policies for domestic violence. Rockville, MD: 2008. http://www.radarsvcs.org/docs/Justice-Denied-DV-Arrest-Policies.pdf

12 E-mail communication from Marti Anderson to Rick Muller dated January 19, 2005. http://www.vawa4all.org/news/PROSECUTOR%20OFFICE%20SPECIFICALLY%20PROHIBITE D.htm

13 Gavin C, Puffett N. ibid. p. 36.

14 Young C. Hitting below the belt. Salon, October 25, 1999.

http://www.salon.com/mwt/feature/1999/10/25/restraining_orders/ Bias in the Judiciary: The Case of Domestic

15 Lininger T. Bearing the cross. Fordham Law Review Vol. 74, 2005.

16 Straus MA. Dominance and symmetry in partner violence by male and female university students in 32 nations. Children and Youth Services Review, 2008.
http://pubpages.unh.edu/%7Emas2/ID41-PR41-Dominance-symmetry-In-Press-07.pdf

17 Rebovich D. Prosecution response to domestic violence: Results of a survey of large jurisdictions. In Buzawa E and Buzawa C (eds.): Do Arrests and Restraining Orders Work?
Thousand Oaks, CA: Sage Publications, 1996.

18 Governor's Commission on Domestic Violence: Prosecution: Domestic violence protocol. No date. http://DepartmentOfJustice.nh.gov/victim/pdf/dvprosecution.pdf

19 Davis RC, Smith BE, and Davies HJ. The effects of no-drop prosecution of domestic violence upon conviction rates. Justice Research and Policy, Vol. 3, No. 2, 2001, pp. 1–13, (NCJ Number 193235).

20 RADAR Services, Inc. Why have domestic violence programs failed to stop partner abuse? Rockville, MD: 2008. http://www.radarsvcs.org/docs/RADARreport-Why-DV-Programs-Fail-to-Stop-Abuse.pdf

21 Personal communication from Harry Crouch, director, San Diego Men's Center, February 20, 2006.

22 Anderson C. Batterer bias? San Francisco Daily Journal, April 4, 2003.

23 Independent Women's Forum. Domestic violence: An in-depth analysis. Washington, DC, 2005. http://www.iwf.org/specialreports/specrpt_detail.asp?ArticleID=815

24
Buel SM. Voire dire in domestic violence cases. Austin, TX: National Center on Domestic Violence and Sexual Assault. No date. http://www.ncdsv.org/images/VoirDireinDVCases.pdf

25 Gelles RJ. The politics of research: The use, abuse, and misuse of social science data—The cases of intimate partner violence. Family Court Review Vol. 45, No. 1. 2007.

26 Gavin C, Puffett N. ibid. pp. 36-37.

27 Hanna C. The paradox of hope: The crime and punishment of domestic violence. William and Mary Law Review Vol. 39, 1998.

28 Tsai B. The trend toward specialized domestic violence courts: Improvements on an effec-tive innovation. Fordham Law Review Vol. 68, 2000, p. 1286.

29 Garner JH, Maxwell CD. The crime control effects of prosecuting intimate partner violence: A review of empirical research. Presentation at the National Institute of Justice Conference, Arlington, VA, July 25, 2007.

30 Gavin C, Puffett N. Criminal domestic violence case processing: A case study of the five boroughs of New York City. New York: Center for Court Innovation. 2005. Table 2. http://courtbuilders.org/_uploads/documents/Citywide%20Final1.pdf

31 Gavin C, Puffett N. ibid. p. 21.

32 Donna LeClerc, quoted in Karsh D. New program helps women who batter. NBC2 News Online, February 8, 2006. http://www.nbc-2.com/articles/readarticle.asp?articleid=5774&z=3&p=

33 US Department of Justice. Domestic violence: Violence between intimates. Washington, DC, 1994.

34 Heleniak DN. The new Star Chamber: The New Jersey family court and the prevention of Domestic Violence Act. Rutgers Law Review, Spring 2005, pp. 1037 and 1041. http://www.acfc.org/site/DocServer/newstarchamber.pdf?docID=401&JServSessionIdr006=l04p181r 91.app2a

35 Langeland T. Railroaded for domestic-violence defendants, El Paso County's fast track may not always lead to justice. Colorado Springs Independent, August 15–21, 2002. http://www.csindy.com/csindy/2002-08-15/cover.html

36 Cook P. Abused Men: The Hidden Side of Domestic Violence. Westport, CT: Praeger, 1997, p. 136.

37 Baskerville S. Violence against families: Fathers fall victim to domestic-abuse laws. Amer-ican Conservative, August 29, 2005, pp. 23–25. http://www.stephenbaskerville.net/Violence_Against_Families.pdf

38 Gover AR, MacDonald JM, Alpert GP. Combating domestic violence: Findings from an evaluation of a local domestic violence court, Criminology & Public Policy. Vol. 3, No. 1, pp. 109–132, 2003, Table 11.

39 Follingstad D, Wright S, Lloyd S, and Sebastian J. Sex differences in motivations and effects in dating relationships. Family Relations Vol. 40, 1991, pp. 51-57.

40 Carrado M, George MJ, Loxam E, et al. Aggression in British heterosexual relationships: A descriptive analysis. Aggressive Behavior Vol. 22, pp. 401-415.

41 Gavin C, Puffett N. ibid. p. 36.

42 Greenfield MH. Politics of domestic violence. DivorceNet, November 14, 2005. http://www.divorcenet.com/states/new_york/politics_of_domestic_violence

43 Criminal law comes home. Overlawyered.com. Posted December 12, 2006. http://www.overlawyered.com/2006/12/criminal_law_comes_home.html

44 Atty. Casey Gwinn, part 2 admits Perjury not Prosecuted. http://www.youtube.com/watch?v=UOClDr5DviU&feature=related

45 Walker, Lenore E., The Battered Woman Syndrome, Springer, 1984

46 http://www.sossandra.org/2007/05/05/this-way-to-the-revolution-part-6

47 Masson EM. Admissibility of expert or opinion evidence of battered-woman syndrome on issue of self-defense. American Law Review, Vol. 58, 1998.

48 Dixon JW,
Dixon KE. Gender-specific clinical syndromes and their admissibility under the federal rules of evidence. American Journal of Trial Advocacy, Vol. 27, Summer 2003.
http://psychologyandlaw.com/Final Gender Paper.pdf

49 Cited in Pearson P. When She was Bad: Violent Women and the Myth of Innocence. To-ronto: Random House of Canada, 1997, p. 238.

50 Wilkerson I. Clemency Granted to 25 Women Convicted for Assault or Murder. New York Times, December 21, 1990.

51 McElroy W. Battered women's syndrome: Science or sham? Independent Institute. Octo-ber 28, 2002. http://www.independent.org/newsroom/article.asp?id=11

52 Greenfield MH. Politics of domestic violence. DivorceNet, November 14, 2005.
http://www.divorcenet.com/states/new_york/politics_of_domestic_violence
Bias in the Judiciary: The Case of Domestic... 145

53 RADAR Services, Inc. Has VAWA delivered on its promises to women? Rockville, MD: 2008. http://www.radarsvcs.org/docs/VAWA-Has-It-Delivered-on-Its-Promises-to-Women.pdf

Chapter 12

1 Clapper B. County workers get first-hand look at abuse. Austin Daily Herald, April 16, 2007. http://www.austindailyherald.com/articles/2007/04/16/news/news1.txt

2 Violence Against Women and Department of Justice Reauthorization Act of 2005. January 5, 2006.
http://www.naesv.org/Resources/VAWA2005.pdf

3 Fiebert MS. References examining assaults by women on their spouses or male partners: An annotated bibliography. Long Beach, CA: Department of Psychology, California State University, 2008. http://www.csulb.edu/~mfiebert/assault.htm

4 Gelles RJ. Intimate Violence in Families. Thousand Oaks, CA: Sage Publications, 1997.

5 Centers for Disease Control and Prevention. Physical dating violence among high school students – United States, 2003. Morbidity and Mortality Weekly Report, Vol. 55, No. 19, May 19, 2006. http://www.cdc.gov/mmwr/preview/mmwrhtml/mm5519a3.htm

6 Gelles RJ. The hidden side of domestic violence: Male victims. Women's Quarterly, 1999.

7 Straus MA, Gelles R, Steinmetz S. Behind Closed Doors: Violence in the American Family. An-chor Books, 1980, pp. 36–37.

8 Straus MA. Women's violence toward men is a serious social problem. In Gelles RJ and Loseke DR (eds.): Current Controversies on Family Violence. Newbury Park, CA: Sage, 2004.

9 Stets J, Straus M. Gender differences in reporting marital violence. Physical Violence in American Families. New Brunswick, NJ: Transaction Publishers, 1992. pp. 151-166.

10 Follingstad D, Wright S, Lloyd S, and Sebastian J. Sex differences in motivations and effects in dating relationships. Family Relations, Vol. 40, 1991, pp. 51–57.

11 Carrado M, George MJ, Loxam E, et al. Aggression in British heterosexual relationships: A descriptive analysis. Aggressive Behavior, Vol. 22, pp. 401–415.

12 Archer J. Sex differences in aggression between heterosexual partners: A meta-analytic review. Psychological Bulletin 2000, Vol. 126, No. 5, pp. 651–680.

13 Ibid.

14 McDonald R. Estimating the number of American children living in partner-violent families. Journal of Family Psychology, Vol. 20, No. 1, pp. 137–142. 2006.
 http://www.smu.edu/experts/study-documents/family-violence-study-may2006.pdf

15 Tjaden P, Thoennes N. Full Report of the Prevalence, Incidence, and Consequences of Violence Against Women, NCJ 183781, Exhibit 9, p. 26, November 2000.
http://ncjrs.org/pdffiles1/nij/183781.pdf

16 Straus MA. The controversy over domestic violence by women: A methodological, theoretical, and sociology of science analysis. In Arriaga XB and Oskamp S (eds.): Violence in Intimate Relationships. Sage Publishers, 1999. http://pubpages.unh.edu/~mas2/CTS21.pdf

17 Stets JE and Straus MA. Gender differences in reporting marital violence and its medical and psychological consequences. In Straus MA and Gelles RJ (eds): Physical Violence in American Families, New Brunswick, NJ: Transaction Publishers, 1990, Table 15.

18 Dutton D. Transforming a flawed policy: A call to revive psychology and science in domestic violence research and practice. Aggression and Violent Behavior. 2006.

19 http://www.usDepartmentOfJustice.gov/OfficeonViolenceagainstWomen/pledge.htm .
Accessed May 10, 2007.

20
http://www.usDepartmentOfJustice.gov/OfficeonViolenceagainstWomen/teen_dating_violence.htm .
Accessed May 10, 2007.

21 Centers for Disease Control and Prevention. Physical dating violence among high school students – United States, 2003. Morbidity and Mortality Weekly Report, Vol. 55, No. 19, May 19, 2006.
http://www.cdc.gov/mmwr/PDF/wk/mm5519.pdf

22 Family Violence Prevention Fund. Cultural considerations in domestic violence cases. 2001.
http://shop.store.yahoo.com/fvpfstore/culconindomv1.html

23 West Virginia Coalition Against Domestic Violence. For a safer state of family: A handbook for helpers. Charleston, WV, 2005.

24 Hamel J. Domestic violence: A gender-inclusive conception. In Hamel J: Gender-inclusive family interventions in domestic violence: An overview. In Hamel J and Nichols TL (eds.): Family Interventions in Domestic Violence: A Handbook of Gender-Inclusive Theory and Treatment. New York: Spring Publishing Co., 2007.

25 Testimony to the New Hampshire Commission on the Status of Men, June 30, 2004. http://www.nh.gov/csm/dv_straus.html

26 Aronson J. Allegations of DV in custody/placement litigation. FAVTEA Bulletin, Spring/Summer 2007.
http://www.favtea.com/news-archives/Spring07.Bulletin_Single_Page.pdf

27 Bleemer R. N.J. judges told to ignore rights in abuse TROs. New Jersey Law Journal, April 24, 1995. http://www.ancpr.org/amazing_nj_legal_journal_article.htm

28 Judicial Training: Your job is to be a wall. New Jersey Law Journal, April 24, 1995, p. 14.

29 Judicial Benchbook Committee. Alabama's Domestic Violence Benchbook. 2005. http://www.acadv.org/2005benchbook.pdf

30 New Mexico Judicial Education Center. Domestic Violence Benchbook. http://jec.unm.edu/resources/benchbooks/dv/index.htm

31 Family Violence Prevention Center. Ohio Domestic Violence Benchbook. 2003. Public Information and Education
http://www.fvpc.ohio.gov/OCJS%20benchbook.pdf

32 Skaggs K (ed.). Tennessee Domestic Abuse Benchbook. 2003.

33 West Virginia Supreme Court of Appeals. West Virginia Benchbook for Domestic Violence Proceedings. 2004. http://www.state.wv.us/wvsca/DVBenBook/DVMaster.pdf

34 National Council of Juvenile and Family Court Judges. Managing Your Divorce: A Guide for Battered Women. Reno, NV, 1998.
http://www.ncjfcj.org/images/stories/dept/fvd/pdf/managing_divorce.pdf

35 http://www.ncjfcj.org/content/blogcategory/251/299/ . Accessed May 1, 2007.

36 Personal communication from Edward Dunning, Family Interventions Project, Sacramento, CA, May 15, 2007.

37 Goelman D and Valente R. When will they ever learn? Educating to end domestic violence. Chicago: American Bar Association Commission on Domestic Violence, updated March 17, 2007. http://www.ojp.usDepartmentOfJustice.gov/ovc/publications/infores/etedv/welcome.html

38 Gelles RJ. The politics of research: The use, abuse, and misuse of social science data – The cases of intimate partner violence. Family Court Review, Vol. 45, No. 1, January 2007. http://www.blackwell-synergy.com/doi/pdf/10.1111/j.1744-1617.2007.00127.x

39 Rennison CM, Welchans S. Intimate Partner Violence. U.S. Department of Justice, NCJ 178247, Figure 7, May 2000.

40 RADAR Services, Inc.. Myths of the ABA Commission on Domestic Violence: Summary Report. Rockville, MD: 2008. http://www.radarsvcs.org/docs/RADARreport-Myths-of- ABACommission-on-DV-Summary.pdf

41 Personal communication from James Hays, November 28, 2006.

42 Sperry G. Domestic violence from an ex-cop's perspective. San Diego Union-Tribune, April 15, 2006.

43 Personal communication from Gregg Jarrette, November 18, 2006.

44 Simerman J. Domestic abuse role reversal. Contra Costa Times, May 8, 2006. http://www.dhs.ca.gov/director/owh/owh_main/pubs_events/news_articles/well_women/05.2006domesticabuse.pdf

45 Simmons School of Social Work. Domestic Violence Training Program. Boston, MA. http://www.simmons.edu/ssw/dvtraining/training/01/06.html

46 Office for Victims of Crime. Family Violence: An Intervention Model for Dental Profession-als. 2004. http://www.ovc.gov/publications/bulletins/dentalproviders/pg3.html

47 http://www.counselcareconnection.org/SRone.asp . Accessed May 1, 2007.

48 Washington State Coalition Against Domestic Violence. Covering Domestic Violence: A Guide for Journalists and Media Professionals. Undated. http://www.wscadv.org/projects/FR/Media_Guide.pdf

49 http://www.stopvaw.org/sites/3f6d15f4-c12d-4515-8544-6b7a3a5a4e/uploads/MythsModule.PDF . Accessed May 1, 2007.

50 http://www.courts.state.ri.us/domesticnew/ . Accessed November 18, 2006.

51 Foster v. West Virginia Children's Justice Task Force. Complaint for Declaratory and Injunctive Relief and Damages. 2006.

52 National Domestic Violence Hotline. Abuse in America. http://www.ndvh.org/educate/abuse_in_america.html . Accessed April 30, 2007.

53 Communication with Stanley Green, April 30, 2007.

54 Gelles RJ. The politics of research: The use, abuse, and misuse of social science data—The cases of intimate partner violence. Family Court Review, Vol. 45, No. 1, January 2007.

http://www.blackwell-synergy.com/doi/pdf/10.1111/j.1744-1617.2007.00127.x?cookieSet=1

55 Cook P. Abused Men: The Hidden Side of Domestic Violence. Westport, CT: Praeger, 1997.

56 Straus MA. Women's violence toward men is a serious social problem. In Gelles RJ and Loseke DR (eds.): Current Controversies on Family Violence. Newbury Park, CA: Sage, 2004.

57 RADAR Services, Inc.. Has VAWA delivered on its promises to women? Rockville, MD: Respecting Accuracy in Domestic Abuse Reporting, 2008. http://www.radarsvcs.org/docs/RADARreport-VAWA-Has-It-Delivered-on-Its-Promisesto-Women.pdf

58 RADAR Services, Inc.. VAWA programs discriminate against male victims. Rockville, MD: 2008. http://www.radarsvcs.org/docs/RADARreport-VAWA-Discriminates-Against-Males.pdf

59 RADAR Services, Inc.. Without restraint: The use and abuse of domestic restraining orders. Rockville, MD: 2008. http://www.radarsvcs.org/docs/RADARreport-VAWARestraining-Orders.pdf

60 RADAR Services, Inc.. Justice denied: Arrest policies for domestic violence. Rockville, MD: 2008. http://www.radarsvcs.org/docs/RADARreport-Justice-Denied-DV-Arrest-Policies.pdf

61 RADAR Services, Inc.. Bias in the judiciary: The case of domestic violence. Rockville, MD: 2008. http://www.radarsvcs.org/docs/RADARreport-Bias-In-The-Judiciary.pdf

Chapter 13

1 Lassiter A. Marriage. Washington, DC: Independent Women's Forum, October 2005. http://www.iwf.org/pdf/civ_soc_marriage1.pdf

2 U.S. Bureau of the Census. Current Population Reports, Series P20-537. America's Families and Living Arrangements. March 2000 and earlier reports, and Current Population Surveys, March 2003, supplement, raw data.

3 Hamilton BE et al. Births: Preliminary data for 2004. Hyattsville, MD: National Center for Health Statistics. December 29, 2005. http://www.cdc.gov/nchs/data/nvsr/nvsr54/nvsr54_08.pdf

4 Horn WF and Sylvester T. Father Facts. Gaithersburg, MD: National Fatherhood Initiative. 2004.

5 RADAR Services, Inc. $1 billion for DV programs that misuse taxpayer money and place victims at risk. Rockville, MD. 2008. http://www.radarsvcs.org/docs/RADARreport-DVPrograms-Misuse-1-Billion-Tax-Dollars-Per-Year.pdf

6 Miller N. What does research and evaluation say about domestic violence laws? A compendium of justice system laws and related research assessments. Alexandria, VA: Institute for Law and Justice, 2005, footnote 28. http://www.ilj.org/publications/dv/DomesticViolenceLegislationEvaluation.pdf

7 Ibid.

8 Gelles RJ. The hidden side of domestic violence: Male victims. Women's Quarterly, 1999.

9 Williams S and Frieze I. Patterns of violent relationships, psychological distress, and marit-al satis-faction in a national sample of men and women. Sex Roles, Vol. 52, Nos. 11/12, pp. 771–785.

10 Archer J. Sex differences in aggression between heterosexual partners: A meta-analytic review. Psychological Bulletin, Vol. 126, No. 5, 2000. pp. 651–680.

11 RADAR Services, Inc: Expanding definitions of domestic violence, Vanishing rule of law. Rock-ville, MD: 2008.
http://www.radarsvcs.org/docs/RADARreport-Vanishing-Ruleof-Law.pdf

12 RADAR Services, Inc: Perverse incentives, false allegations, and forgotten children. Rockville, MD: 2008.
http://www.radarsvcs.org/docs/RADARreport-Perverse-Incentives.pdf

13 RADAR Services, Inc: Without restraint: The use and abuse of domestic restraining orders. Rock-ville, MD: 2008.
http://www.radarsvcs.org/docs/RADARreport-VAWA-Restraining-Orders.pdf

14 Miller N. Domestic violence: A review of state legislation defining police and prosecution duties and powers. Alexandria, VA: Institute for Law and Justice, 2004.
http://www.ilj.org/publications/DV_Legislation-3.pdf

15 American Bar Association. Custody decisions in cases with domestic violence allegations. 2004.
http://www.abanet.org/legalservices/probono/childcustody/domestic_violence_chart1.pdf

16 Kentucky Revised Statutes, Section 403.720: Definitions for KRS 403.715 to 403.785.
http://162.114.4.13/KRS/403-00/CHAPTER.HTM

17 Kentucky Revised Statutes, Section 403.320.

18 RADAR Services, Inc. Education for injustice. Rockville, MD. 2008.
http://www.radarsvcs.org/docs/RADARreport-Education-For-Injustice.pdf

19 RADAR Services, Inc: Bias in the judiciary: The case of domestic violence. Rockville, MD: 2008. http://www.radarsvcs.org/docs/RADARreport-Bias-In-The-Judiciary.pdf

20 Bleemer R. N.J. judges told to ignore rights in abuse TROs. New Jersey Law Journal, April 24, 1995. http://www.ancpr.org/amazing_nj_legal_journal_article.htm

21 http://www.courts.state.ri.us/domesticnew/ Accessed November 18, 2006.

22 Durose MR et al. Family Violence Statistics. Washington, DC: Department of Justice. NCJ 207846, 2005. http://www.ojp.usDepartmentOfJustice.gov/bjs/pub/pdf/fvs.pdf

23 Durose MR et al. Table 5.9.

24 Eng P. Safety and Justice for All. New York: Ms. Foundation for Women, 2003.
http://www.ms.foundation.org/user-assets/PDF/Program/safety_justice.pdf

25 Peterson R. Comparing the processing of domestic violence cases to non-domestic violence cases in New York City criminal courts. New York City Criminal Justice Agency, 2001. http://www.cjareports.org/reports/dv01.pdf

26 Criminal law comes home. Overlawyered.com. Posted December 12, 2006. http://www.overlawyered.com/2006/12/criminal_law_comes_home.html

27 Erickson charged with assault. ESPN.com, July 22, 2002. http://www.espn.go.com/mlb/news/2002/0722/1408560.html

28 Raskin-Zrihen R and Brown JM. Domestic abuse: Does money fuel false allegations? Times-Herald (CA). December 17, 2006. http://www.timesheraldonline.com/ci_4857258

29 Shalley J, Murray D. New York City domestic violence cases. No date. http://www.queensdefense.com/domestic_violence_cases.htm

30 Cook P. Abused Men: The Hidden Side of Domestic Violence. Westport, CT: Praeger, 1997.

31 Young C. Hitting below the belt. Salon.com, October 25, 1999. http://www.salon.com/mwt/feature/1999/10/25/restraining_orders/

32 McElroy W. Abuse of temporary restraining orders endangers real victims. Fox-News.com, December 27, 2005. http://www.ifeminists.net/introduction/editorials/2005/1228.html

33 Zorn E. A seminar in divorce, Down-and-dirty style. Chicago Tribune, November 4, 1988, p. 1.

34 Epstein E. Speaking the unspeakable, Massachusetts Bar Association Newsletter, 1993.

35 Leving JM and Sacks G. Some progress for California fathers, but still a long way to go. Ifeminists.net, July 5, 2006. http://www.ifeminists.net/introduction/editorials/2006/0705sacks.html

36 Heleniak DN. ibid.

37 RADAR Services, Inc: Without restraint: The use and abuse of domestic restraining orders. http://www.radarsvcs.org/docs/RADARreport-VAWA-Restraining-Orders.pdf

38 Catalano S. Intimate Partner Violence in the United States. Washington, DC: Department of Justice, 2006. http://www.ojp.usDepartmentOfJustice.gov/bjs/intimate/table/wommar.htm

39 Quoted in Cathy Young, Domestic violations. Reason, February 1998. http://www.ncjrs.org/pdffiles1/nij/188199.pdf

40 RADAR Services, Inc: Expanding definitions of domestic violence, Vanishing rule of law, http://www.radarsvcs.org/docs/RADARreport-Vanishing-Rule-of-Law.pdf

41 Anderson C. ibid.

42 Anderson C. Batterer Bias? San Francisco Daily Journal, April 4, 2003.

43 Laframboise D. One-stop divorce shops. National Post, November 21, 1998.
http://www.familyviolencetruth.org/pages/menu1/submenu4/..%5C..%5Cmenu1%5CSub-Menu4%5CLaframboise-OneStopDivorceShops.pdf

44 Sacks G. Domestic violence system manhandles woman, family. October 31, 2006.
http://www.glennsacks.com/enewsletters/enews_10_31_06.htm

45 Maiuro R et al. Are current state standards for domestic violence perpetrator treatment adequately informed by research? Journal of Aggression, Maltreatment, and Trauma. Vol. 5, 2001. pp. 21-44.

46 Quoted in Healey, Smith, and O'Sullivan. Controversial approaches in batterer intervention. In Healy KM: Batterer Intervention, U.S. Dept. of Justice, National Institute of Justice, 1998, p. 25.

47 Suk J. Criminal law comes home. Yale Law Journal, Vol. 116, No. 2, 2006.
http://www.yalelawjournal.org/pdf/116-1/Suk.pdf

48 Sanderson M. Domestic violence leader takes the low road with false information and scare tactics. North Dakota Shared Parenting Initiative. September 29, 2006.
http://ndspi.org/index.php/site/blog/domestic_violence_leader_takes_the_low_road_with_false_information_and_scar/

49 Fagan P. Why Congress Should Ignore Radical Feminist Opposition to Marriage. Washington, DC: Heritage Foundation, 2003. Backgrounder # 1662.
http://www.heritage.org/Research/Family/bg1662.cfm

50 Whitehead BD and Popenoe D. The marrying kind: Which men marry and why. Rutgers University, 2004.
http://marriage.rutgers.edu/Publications/SOOU/TEXTSOOU2004.htm

51 U.S. Census Bureau. Statistical Abstract of the United States, 1999. Tables 155, 159. Washington, DC: U.S. Government Printing Office, 2000.

52 Johnston J et al. Allegations and substantiations of abuse in custody-disputing families. Family Court Review, Vol. 43, No. 2, April 2005.

53 Posted December 19, 2006.
http://mensnewsdaily.com/2006/12/19/domestic-abusedoesmoney-fuel-false-allegations/#comment-25146

54 Raskin-Zrihen R and Brown JM. Domestic abuse: Does money fuel false allegations?
http://blog.moschettilaw.com/2006/12/domestic_abuse_does_money_fuel.html

55 Kposowa AJ. Marital status and suicide in the National Longitudinal Mortality Study. Journal of Epidemiology and Community Health, Vol. 54, 2000, pp. 254–261.

56 Horn WF and Sylvester T. Father Facts. pp. 103–105.

57 Administration for Children and Families: Child Maltreatment 2004. Figures 4-2 and 5-1. Washington, DC: U.S. Government Printing Office, 2006.

http://www.acf.DepartmentofHealthandHumanServices.gov/programs/cb/pubs/cm04/index.htm

58 Finkelhor D. Sexually abused children in a national survey of parents: Methodological issues. Child Abuse and Neglect, Vol. 21, 1997, pp. 1–9.

59 Sedlak AJ and Broadhurst DD. The Third National Incidence Study of Child Abuse and Neglect (NIS-3): Final Report, U.S. Department of Health and Human Services, National Center on Child Abuse and Neglect, Washington, DC, September 1996. http://www.healthieryou.com/cabuse.htm

60 Whelan R. Broken Homes and Battered Children. London: Family Education Trust, 1993.

61 Luster T and McAdoo HP. Factors related to the achievement and adjustment of young African-American children. Child Development, Vol. 65, 1994, pp. 1080–1094.

62 National Center for Health Statistics: Survey on Child Health. Washington, DC: Government Printing Office, 1993.

63 Nord DW and West J. Fathers' and Mothers' Involvement in their Children's Schools by Family Type and Resident Status. Washington, DC: National Center for Education Statistics, 2001. NCES 2001-032.

64 Flewelling RL and Bauman K. Family structure as a predictor of initial substance use and sexual intercourse in early adolescence. Journal of Marriage and the Family, Vol. 52, 1990, pp. 171–181.

65 Rubenstein JL et al. Suicidal behavior in adolescents: Stress and protection in different family contexts. American Journal of Orthopsychiatry, Vol. 68, 1998, pp. 274–284.

66 Dawson D. Family structure and children's health and well-being: Interview survey on child health. Journal of Marriage and the Family, Vol. 53, 1991, pp. 573–584.

67 Schwartz JE et al. Sociodemographic and psychosocial factors in childhood as predictors of adult mortality. American Journal of Public Health, Vol. 85, 1995, pp. 1237–1245.

68 Federal Interagency Forum on Child and Family Statistics. America's Children: Key National Indicators of Well-Being, 2001. Washington, DC. Table ECON 1.A. 2001.

69 Duncan WS. Economic impact of divorce on children's development: Current findings and policy implications. Journal of Clinical and Child Psychology, Vol. 23, 1994, pp. 444–457.

70 House Committee on Ways and Means. 2000 Green Book, Washington, DC: U.S. Government Printing Office, 2000.

71 Hill MA and O'Neill J. Underclass Behaviors in the United States: Measurement and Analysis of Determinants. New York: City University of New York, 1993.

72 Cubbin C, Pickle LW, and Fingerhut L. Social context and geographic patterns of homicide among US black and white males. American Journal of Public Health, Vol. 90, 2000, pp. 579–587.

73 Russert T. Wisdom of Our Fathers. New York: Random House, 2006. 245

Chapter 14

1 McDonald R. Estimating the number of children living in partner-violent families. Journal of Family Psychology, March 2006.
http://www.smu.edu/experts/study-documents/family-violencestudy-may2006.pdf

2 Archer J. Sex differences in aggression between heterosexual partners: A meta-analytic review. Psychological Bulletin, Vol. 126, No. 5, 2000, pp. 651–680.

3 Straus MA. Behind Closed Doors: Violence in the American Family, Anchor Books, 1980, pp. 36–37.

4 Gelles RJ. Intimate Violence in Families. Thousand Oaks, CA: Sage Publications, 1997.

5 Miller N. What does research and evaluation say about domestic violence laws? A compendium of justice system laws and related research assessments. Alexandria, VA: Institute for Law and Justice, 2005, footnote 28.
http://www.ilj.org/publications/dv/DomesticViolenceLegislationEvaluation.pdf

6 RADAR Services, Inc: Expanding definitions of domestic violence, vanishing rule of law. Rockville, MD: 2008. http://www.radarsvcs.org/docs/RADARreport-Vanishing-Rule-of-Law.pdf

7 Catalano S. Intimate Partner Violence in the United States. Washington, DC: US Department of Justice, 2006. http://www.ojp.usDepartmentOfJustice.gov/bjs/intimate/ipv.htm

8 Parmley A. Violence against women post VAWA. Violence Against Women Vol. 10, No. 12, 2004. p. 1424.

9 Dugan L, Nagin D, and Rosenfeld R. Exposure reduction or backlash? The effects of domestic violence resources on intimate partner homicide. NCJ Number 186194. 2001.
http://www.ncjrs.gov/app/Publications/Abstract.aspx?ID=186193

10 Hotaling GT and Buzawa ES. Forging criminal justice assistance. Document No. 195667, 2003.
http://www.ncjrs.gov/pdffiles1/nij/grants/195667.pdf
Has VAWA Delivered on its Promises to... 181

11 Rebovich D. Prosecution response to domestic violence: Results of a survey of large juris-dictions. In Buzawa E and Buzawa C (eds.): Do Arrests and Restraining Orders Work? Thousand Oaks, CA: Sage Publications, 1996.

12 Davis RC, Smith BE, and Davies HJ. The effects of no-drop prosecution of domestic violence upon conviction rates. Justice Research and Policy, Vol. 3, No. 2, 2001, pp. 1–13, (NCJ Number 193235).

13 RADAR Services, Inc: Without restraint: The use and abuse of domestic restraining orders. 2008. http://www.radarsvcs.org/docs/RADARreport-VAWA-Restraining-Orders.pdf

14 Epstein E. Speaking the unspeakable, Massachusetts Bar Association Newsletter, 1993.

15 McElroy W. Abuse of temporary restraining orders endangers real victims. Fox-News.com, December 27, 2005. http://www.ifeminists.net/introduction/editorials/2005/1228.html

16 Maxwell CD, Garner JH, and Fagan JA. The effects of arrest on intimate partner violence. Washington, DC: National Institute of Justice. Report No. NCJ 188199. 2001.

17 Hudson Z. Jury acquits Rucker Smith. Americus Times-Recorder, May 5, 2006. http://www.americustimesrecorder.com/siteSearch/apstorysection/local_story_125003348.html

18 Lininger T. Bearing the Cross. Fordham Law Review, Vol. 74, 2005. pp. 1353-1364.

19 Dugan L, Nagin D, and Rosenfeld R. ibid.

20 Personal communication from Harry Crouch, Director, San Diego Men's Center, February 20, 2006.

21 Anderson C. Batterer bias? San Francisco Daily Journal, April 4, 2003.

22 Mills LG. Insult to Injury: Rethinking our Responses to Intimate Abuse. Princeton, NJ: Princeton University Press, 2003, p. 50.

23 Dutton D. The Abusive Personality: Violence and Control in Intimate Relationships. New York: Guilford Publications, 1998.

24 Kruttschnitt C, McLaughlin BL, and Petrie CV (eds). Advancing the Federal Research Agenda on Violence against Women. Washington, DC: National Research Council, 2005, p. 6. http://www.nap.edu/catalog/10849.html

25 Ford DA and Regoli MJ. The preventive impacts of policies for prosecuting wife batterers. In Buzawa ES and Buzawa CG (eds.): Domestic Violence: The Criminal Justice Response. Thousand Oaks, CA: Sage Publications, 1996.

26 Grau J, Fagan J, and Wexler S. Restraining orders for battered women: Issues of access and efficacy. Women and Politics, Vol. 4, 1984, pp. 13–28.

27 Harrell A and Smith B. Effects of restraining orders on domestic violence victims. In Buza-wa C and Buzawa E (eds.): Do Arrests and Restraining Orders Work? Thousand Oaks, CA: Sage Publications, 1996, p. 229.

28 Independent Women's Forum. Domestic Violence: An In-Depth Analysis. Washington, DC, 2005.

29 RADAR Services, Inc: Expanding definitions of domestic violence, vanishing rule of law. 2008. http://www.radarsvcs.org/docs/RADARreport-Vanishing-Rule-of-Law.pdf

31 Miller N. Domestic violence: A review of state legislation defining police and prosecution duties and powers. Alexandria, VA: Institute for Law and Justice, 2004. http://www.ilj.org/publications/DV_Legislation-3.pdf

32 Smith L. Increasingly, abuse shows female side. Washington Post, November 18, 1997, p. B1.
33 RADAR Services, Inc: Justice denied: Arrest policies for domestic violence. 2008. http://www.radarsvcs.org/docs/RADARreport-Justice-Denied-DV-Arrest-Policies.pdf

34 Langeland T. Railroaded for domestic-violence defendants, El Paso County's fast track may not always lead to justice. Colorado Springs Independent, August 15–21, 2002. http://www.csindy.com/csindy/2002-08-15/cover.html

35 Straus MA. Women's violence toward men is a serious social problem. In Gelles RJ and Loseke DR (eds.): Current Controversies on Family Violence. Newbury Park, CA: Sage Publications, 2004.

36 Cook P. Abused Men: The Hidden Side of Domestic Violence. p. 110.

37 Kelly L. Disabusing the definition of domestic abuse: How women batter men and the role of the feminist state. Florida State University Law Review, Vol. 30, 2003, p. 847. http://www.law.fsu.edu/journals/lawreview/downloads/304/kelly.pdf

38 Dutton-Douglas MA and Dionne D. Counseling and shelter services for battered women. In Steinman M (ed.): Woman Battering: Policy Responses. Cincinnati, OH: Anderson Pub-lishing Co., 1991.

39 Epstein S, Russell G, and Silvern L. Structure and ideology of shelters for battered women. American Journal of Community Psychology, Vol. 16, 1988, pp. 345–367.

40 Taylor JS. No shelter from the storm. Liberty, July 1997. http://www.ejfi.org/DV/dv-34.htm#pgfId-1378699

41 Moore N. Inside a batterers program'for abused' women. Ifeminists.net, July 29, 2003. http://www.ifeminists.net/introduction/editorials/2003/0729moore.html

42 Winslow MV, Young C. Suspect in SafeSpace stabbing in Martin County claims selfdefense. TCPalm November 14, 2007. http://www.tcpalm.com/news/2007/nov/14/30suspect-in-safespacestabbing-claims-self/

43 Moore N. http://www.ifeminists.net/introduction/editorials/2003/0729moore.html

44 Sacks G. Domestic violence system manhandles woman, family. October 31, 2006. http://www.glennsacks.com/enewsletters/enews_10_31_06.htm

45 Catalano S. http://www.ojp.usDepartmentOfJustice.gov/bjs/intimate/table/wommar.htm

46 Suk J. Criminal law comes home. Yale Law Journal, Vol. 116, No. 2, 2006. http://www.yalelawjournal.org/pdf/116-1/Suk.pdf

47 An Abuse, Rape and Domestic Violence Aid and Resource Collection. http://www.aardvarc.org   Accessed December 6, 2006.

48 RADAR Services, Inc: A culture of false allegations: How VAWA harms families and child-ren. 2008. http://www.radarsvcs.org/docs/RADARreport-VAWA-A-Culture-of-False-Allegations.pdf

49 Horn WF and Sylvester T. Father Facts. Gaithersburg, MD: National Fatherhood Initiative. 2002.

50 Independent Women's Forum, 2005.

51 Schlaffly P. Time to defund the hate-men law. Eagle Forum, October 2005. http://www.eagleforum.org/psr/2005/oct05/psroct05.html

52 Ms. Foundation for Women. Safety and justice for all. New York, 2003. http://www.ms.foundation.org/user-assets/PDF/Program/safety_justice.pdf

53 RADAR Services, Inc: VAWA programs discriminate against male victims. 2008. http://www.radarsvcs.org/docs/RADARreport-VAWA-Discriminates-Against-males.pdf

54 RADAR Services, Inc: Bias in the judiciary: The case of domestic violence. 2008. http://www.radarsvcs.org/docs/RADARreport-Bias-In-The-Judiciary.pdf

55 RADAR Services, Inc: Without restraint: The use and abuse of domestic restraining orders. 2008. http://www.radarsvcs.org/docs/RADARreport-VAWA-Restraining-Orders.pdf

56 RADAR Services, Inc: Justice denied: Arrest policies for domestic violence. 2008. http://www.radarsvcs.org/docs/RADARreport-Justice-Denied-DV-Arrest-Policies.pdf

57 RADAR Services, Inc: An epidemic of civil rights abuses: Ranking of states' domestic violence laws. 2008. http://www.radarsvcs.org/docs/RADARreport-Ranking-of-States-DVLaws.pdf

Chapter 16

1 Dutton DG, Corvo K.. Transforming a flawed policy: A call to revive psychology and science in domestic violence research and practice. Aggression and Violent Behavior, Vol. 11, No. 5, pp. 457-483.

2 Gelles RJ. The politics of research: The use, abuse, and misuse of social science data The cases of intimate partner violence. Family Court Review, Vol. 45, No. 1, 2007.

3 Straus MA. Processes explaining the concealment and distortion of evidence on gender symmetry in partner violence. European Journal of Criminal Policy and Research Vol. 13, 2007. pp. 227-232. http://pubpages.unh.edu/~mas2/V74-gender-symmetry-withgramham-Kevan-Method%208-.pdf

4 Dobash RE, Dobash RP. Violence against Wives: A Case against the Patriarchy. New York: Free Press, 1979.

5 Walker L. Psychology and violence against women. American Psychologist Vol. 44, 1989. pp. 695-702.

6 Hamberger LK, Guse CE. Men's and women's use of intimate partner violence in clinical samples. Violence Against Women Vol. 8, No. 11, 2002. pp. 1301-1331.

7 Kantor K, Jasnski JL, Aldarondo E. Sociocultural status and incidence of marital violence in Hispanic families. Violence and Victims Vol. 9, 1994. pp. 207-222.

8 Graham-Kevan N. Power and control in relationship aggression. In Hamel J and Nicholls TL (eds.): Family Interventions in Domestic Violence. New York: Springer Publishing Co., 2007.

9 Sugarman DB, Frankel SL. Patriarchal ideology and wife-assault: A meta-analytic review. Journal of Family Violence Vol. 17, 1996. pp. 13-40.

10 Felson RB, Outlaw MC. The control motive and marital behavior. Violence and Victims, Vol. 22, No. 4, 2007. pp. 387 - 407.

11 Straus MA. Dominance and symmetry in partner violence by male and female university students in 32 nations. Children and Youth Services Review Vol. 30, 2008. pp. 252-275.

12 Dutton DG. Patriarchy and wife assault: The ecological fallacy. Violence and Victims Vol. 9, No. 2, 1994.

13 Lie G, Schilit R, Bush J, Montague M, Reyes L. Lesbians in currently aggressive relationships: How frequently do they report aggressive past relationships? Violence and Victims Vol. 6, 1991. pp. 121–135.

14 Fiebert MS. References examining assaults by women on their spouses or male partners: An annotated bibliography. Long Beach, CA: Department of Psychology, California State University, 2009. http://www.csulb.edu/~mfiebert/assault.htm

15 Whitaker DJ, Haileyesus T, Swahn M, Saltzman L. Differences in frequency of violence and reported injury between relationships with reciprocal and nonreciprocal intimate partner violence. American Journal of Public Health, Vol. 97, No. 5, 2007.

16 Gelles RJ. The politics of research: The use, abuse, and misuse of social science data The cases of intimate partner violence. Family Court Review Vol. 45, No. 1, 2007.

17 Straus MA. The controversy over domestic violence by women: A methodological, theoretical, and sociology of science analysis. In Arriaga XB and Oskamp S (eds.): Violence in Intimate Relationships. Sage Publishers, 1999. http://pubpages.unh.edu/~mas2/CTS21.pdf

18 Stets JE and Straus MA. Gender differences in reporting marital violence and its medical and psychological consequences. In Straus MA and Gelles RJ (eds): Physical Violence in American Families, New Brunswick, NJ: Transaction Publishers, 1990. Table 15.

19 Rosenthal M. Origin of claim that domestic violence kills as many women every 5 years as the number of U.S. soldiers killed in Viet Nam. 2005. http://www.breakingthescience.org/OriginOfComparisonBetweenDVDeathsAnd-VietNam.php

20 Stets J, Straus M. Gender differences in reporting marital violence. Physical Violence in American Families. New Brunswick, NJ: Transaction Publishers, 1992. pp. 151-166.

21 Follingstad D, Wright S, Lloyd S, and Sebastian J. Sex differences in motivations and effects in dating relationships. Family Relations, Vol. 40, 1991, pp. 51–57.

22 Carrado M, George MJ, Loxam E, et al. Aggression in British heterosexual relationships: A descriptive analysis. Aggressive Behavior, Vol. 22, 1996. pp. 401–415.

23 Stith S, Smith DB, Penn CE, et al. Intimate partner physical abuse perpetation and victimization risk factors: A meta-analytic review. Aggression and Violent Behavior Vol. 10, 2004. pp. 65-98.

24 Respecting Accuracy in Domestic Abuse Reporting: Analysis of HR 590. August 16, 2007. www.mediaradar.org/docs/RADARanalysis-HRES590.pdf

25 National Center on Family Homelessness. Violence in the Lives of Homeless Women. www.familyhomelessness.org/pdf/fact_violence.pdf

26 O'Leary K, Barling J, Aria I, et al. Prevalence and stability of physical aggression between spouses: A longitudinal analysis. Journal of Consulting and Clinical Psychology, Vol. 57, 1989. pp. 263–268.

27 Feld S, Straus M. Escalation and desistance of wife assault in marriage. Criminology, Vol. 1, 1989. pp. 141–161.

28 Department of Justice. Intimate partner violence and age of victim, 1993–99. Washington, DC: Bureau of Justice. NCJ 187635, October 2001, Figure 4. http://www.ojp.usDepartmentOfJustice.gov/bjs/abstract/ipva99.htm

29 National Center for Women and Policing: Police Family Violence Fact Sheet. No date. www.womenandpolicing.org/violenceFS.asp

30 Davis RL. Proactive domestic violence intervention for LE families. PoliceOne.com News February 13, 2006. www.policeone.com/writers/columnists/RichardDavis/articles/123264-Proactive-domestic-violence-intervention-for-LE-families/

31 Dutton D, Bodnarchuk M. Through a psychological lens: Personality disorder and spouse assault. In Loseke D, Gelles R, Cavanaugh M (eds.). Current Controversies on Family Violence, Thousand Oaks: Sage Publications 2005, p.14.

32 Carney MM, Buttell FP. A multidimensional evaluation of a treatment program for female batterers: A pilot study. Research on Social Work Practice Vol. 14, No. 4, 2004. pp. 249-258.

33 Henning K, Feder L. A comparison of men and women arrested for domestic violence: Who presents the greater risk? Journal of Family Violence, Vol. 19, No. 2, 2004.

34 Dutton DG. Patriarchy and wife assault: The ecological fallacy. Violence and Victims Vol. 9, No. 2, 1994.

35 Dobash RE, Dobash RP. Violence against Wives: A Case against the Patriarchy. New York: Free Press, 1979.

36 Simon TR, Anderson M, Thompson MP et al. Attitudinal acceptance of intimate partner violence among U.S. adults. Violence and Victims Vol. 16, No. 2, 2001. pp. 115-126.

37 Straus MA, Kaufman KG, Moore DW. Change in cultural norms approving marital violence: From 1968 to 1994. In Kantor KG and Jasinski JL (eds.): Out of the Darkness: Contemporary Perspectives on Family Violence. Thousand Oaks: Sage Publications. 1997.

38 Straus MA. Dominance and symmetry in partner violence by male and female university students in 32 nations. Children and Youth Services Review Vol. 30, 2008. pp. 252-275.

39 Graham-Kevan N. Power and control in relationship aggression. In Hamel J and Nicholls TL (eds.): Family Interventions in Domestic Violence. New York: Springer Publishing Co., 2007.

40 Medeiros RA, Straus MA. Risk factors for physical violence between dating partners. In Hamel J and Nicholls TL (eds.): Family Interventions in Domestic Violence. New York: Springer Publishing Co., 2007.

41 Dutton DG, Corvo K. Transforming a flawed policy: A call to revive psychology and science in domestic violence research and practice. Aggression and Violent Behavior, Vol. 11, No. 5, pp. 457-483.

42 Catalano S. Intimate partner violence in the United States: Victim characteristics. Washington, DC: Department of Justice. 2007.
http://www.ojp.usDepartmentOfJustice.gov/bjs/intimate/victims.htm

43 Medeiros RA, Straus MA. Risk factors for physical violence between dating partners. In Hamel J and Nicholls TL (eds.): Family Interventions in Domestic Violence. New York: Springer Publishing Co., 2007.

44 Department of Health and Human Services. Leading causes of injury among women aged 18 and old, by age, 2006.
http://mchb.hrsa.gov/whusa08/hstat/hi/pages/226i.html

45 Domestic violence victims in the Emergency Department. Journal of the American Medical Association, June 22-29, 1984.

46 Cook P. Abused Men: The Hidden Side of Domestic Violence. Westport, CT: Praeger, 2009. p. 129.

47 Gelles RJ. The politics of research: The use, abuse, and misuse of social science data the cases of intimate partner violence. Family Court Review Vol. 45, No. 1, 2007.

48 H.R. 539, Security and Financial Empowerment Act
www.govtrack.us/congress/billtext.xpd?bill=h111-739

49 National Center for Injury Prevention and Control. Costs of Intimate Partner Violence Against Women in the United States, Atlanta: Centers for Disease Control and Prevention, 2003.

50 Zorza J. Women battering: High costs and the state of the law, Clearinghouse Review, Vol. 28, No. 4, 1994.

51 Miller TR, Cohen MA, Wiersema B. Victim Costs and Consequences: A New Look. Washington, DC: National Institute of Justice, U.S. Department of Justice. 1996.
www.ncjrs.gov/pdffiles/costcrim.pdf

52 Foster BP. Analyzing the cost and effectiveness of governmental policies. Cost Management Vol. 22, No. 3, 2008.

53 Office of the Commissioner of Probation, Massachusetts Trial Court: The tragedies of domestic violence: A qualitative analysis of civil restraining orders. October 12, 1995.

54 www.fbi.gov/ucr/cius2007/offenses/violent_crime/forcible_rape.html

55 Sommers CH. Who Stole Feminism? New York: Simon and Schuster. 1994.

56 www.ojp.usDepartmentOfJustice.gov/bjs/glance/tables/viortrdtab.htm

57 www.hrw.org/legacy/reports/2001/prison/report7.html#_1_48

58 Ellis E, Atkeson B, Calhoun K, An assessment of the long term reaction to rape, Journal of Abnormal Psychology Vol. 50 No. 3, 1981.

59 Centers for Disease Control. Youth Risk Behavior Surveillance —- United States, 2003. Morbidity and Mortality Weekly Report, May 21, 2004. Table 10. www.cdc.gov/mmwr/preview/mmwrhtml/ss5302a1.htm

60 Sommers CH. Who Stole Feminism? New York: Simon and Schuster. 1994. pp. 203-204.

61 RADAR Services. Why have domestic violence programs failed to stop partner abuse? Rockville, MD. 2008. http://www.radarsvcs.org/docs/RADARreport-Why-DV-Programs-Fail-to-Stop-Abuse.pdf

62 Grau J, Fagan J, and Wexler S. Restraining orders for battered women: Issues of access and efficacy. Women and Politics, Vol. 4, 1984, pp. 13–28.

63 Harrell A and Smith B. Effects of restraining orders on domestic violence victims. In Buzawa C and Buzawa E (eds.): Do Arrests and Restraining Orders Work? Thousand Oaks, CA: Sage Publications, 1996. p. 229.

64 McFarlane J, Malecha A, Gist J et al. Protection orders and intimate partner violence: An 18-month study of 150 Black, Hispanic, and White women. American Journal of Public Health, Vol. 94, No. 4, pp. 613–618.

65 Dugan L, Nagin D, and Rosenfeld R. Exposure reduction or backlash? The effects of domestic violence resources on intimate partner homicide. NCJ Number 186194, 2001. http://www.ncjrs.gov/app/Publications/Abstract.aspx?ID=186193

66 Iyengar R. Does the certainty of arrest reduce domestic violence? Evidence from mandatory and recommended arrest laws. Cambridge, MA: National Bureau of Economic Research, June 2007.

67 Cited in Young C. Domestic violence: An in-depth analysis. Washington, DC: Independent Women's Forum, 2005, p. 3.

68 U.S. Department of Justice. Domestic violence: Violence between intimates. Washington, DC, 1994.

69 GAO: Domestic Violence Prevalence and Implications for Employment among Welfare Recipients. GAO/HEHS-99-12. November 1998. www.gao.gov/archive/1999/he99012.pdf

70 GAO: Domestic Violence Prevalence and Implications for Employment among Welfare Recipients. GAO/HEHS-99-12. November 1998. Appendix III.
www.gao.gov/archive/1999/he99012.pdf

71 National Center for Injury Prevention and Control. Costs of Intimate Partner Violence Against Women in the United States, Atlanta: Centers for Disease Control and Prevention, 2003.
www.cdc.gov/ncipc/pub-res/ipv_cost/ipv.htm

72 NIOSH: Violence in the Workplace:
http://www.cdc.gov/niosh/violhomi.html

73 American Psychological Association. Violence and the Family: Report of the American Psychological Association Presidential Task Force on Violence and the Family. Washington, DC. 1996.

74 Communication with Julia Silva, Director, APA Adults and Children Working Together Against Violence Office, January 31, 2008.

75 Trocme N, Bala N. False allegations of abuse and neglect when parents separate. Child Abuse and Neglect, Vol. 29, 2005. p. 1341.

76 Rosenthal, M., 71% of children killed by one parent are killed by their mothers; 60% of victims are boys. 2008.
http://www.breakingthescience.org/SimplifiedData-FromDEPARTMENTOFHEALTHANDHUMAN SERVICES .php

77 Abrams and Greaney, Gender Bias Study of the Supreme Judicial Court, Massachusetts Supreme Judicial Court, 1989.

78 Rosenthal M. Misrepresentation of gender bias in the 1989 Report of the Gender Bias Committee of the Massachusetts Supreme Judicial Court. November 23, 2005.
http://www.breakingthescience.org/SJC_GBC_analysis_intro.php#mbr_analysis

79 Morril A, Dai J, Dunn S, Sung I, Smith K. Child custody and visitation decisions when the father has perpetrated violence against the mother. Violence Against Women, Vol. 11, No. 8, 2005.

80 Garcia-Moreno C, Jansen HAFM, Ellsberg M, Heise L, Watts C. WHO Multi-Country Study on Women's Health and Domestic Violence Against Women. Geneva, Switzerland: World Health Organization, 2005.

81 Straus MA. Processes explaining the concealment and distortion of evidence on gender symmetry in partner violence. European Journal of Criminal Policy and Research Vol. 13, 2007. pp. 227-232.
http://pubpages.unh.edu/~mas2/V74-gender-symmetry-withgramham-Kevan-Method%208-.pdf

82 Schulman M. A survey of spousal violence against women in Kentucky. Washington, DC, US Government Printing Office, 1979.

83 Johnson MP and Leone JM. The differential effects of intimate terrorism and situational couple violence. Journal of Family Issues Vol. 26, No. 3, 2005. pp. 322-349.

84 Krug EG et al. World Report on Violence and Health. Geneva: World Health Organization, 2002.

The Future Goals of N.C.D.V.A.M

National Coalition on Domestic Violence against Men.
Founded By: John Hayes (Elmy) In 2004
In Brush, Colorado.

Emergency Domestic Violence Shelter For Up to 90 Days

Transitional Housing for Up to 36 Months for both Men / women and their children

Legal Advice and / or Representation for Low-Income Survivors

Advocacy / Accompaniment through Legal and Medical Processes

24-hour Crisis Hotline and Crisis Intervention Counseling

Response-Team Services with Law Enforcement, District Attorney, and Hospital Staff

Individual Counseling for Adults and Children

Weekly Support Groups for Survivors of Domestic Violence, Emotional Abuse, Financial Abuse and Sexual Assault

Child Abuse Prevention Education in Local Schools

52-week Batterers Intervention and Treatment Program for Men and Women

Anger Management Program for Teen Boys and Girls

52-Week Parenting Course

160-Hour Crisis Intervention Certification Course (Required for All Staff and Volunteers) will be covering domestic violence issues on both men and women and how to respond.

Emergency Clothing, Food and Transportation

Referrals to Other Social Service Providers and Local Government Agencies

Job retraining

www.ingramcontent.com/pod-product-compliance
Lightning Source LLC
Chambersburg PA
CBHW051954280526
45793CB00005B/716